Bioarchaeology

Bioarchaeology covers the history and general theory of the field plus the recovery and laboratory treatment of human remains.

Bioarchaeology is the study of human remains in context from an archaeological and anthropological perspective. The book explores, through numerous case studies, how the ways a society deals with their dead can reveal a great deal about that society, including its religious, political, economic, and social organizations. It details recovery methods and how, once recovered, human remains can be analyzed to reveal details about the funerary system of the subject society and inform on a variety of other issues, such as health, demography, disease, workloads, mobility, sex and gender, and migration. Finally, the book highlights how bioarchaeological techniques can be used in contemporary forensic settings and in investigations of genocide and war crimes.

In *Bioarchaeology*, theories, principles, and scientific techniques are laid out in a clear, understandable way, and students of archaeology at undergraduate and graduate levels will find this an excellent guide to the field.

Mark Q. Sutton received his Ph.D. in Anthropology from the University of California, Riverside in 1987. He taught at California State University, Bakersfield from 1987 to 2007 where he retired as Emeritus Professor of Anthropology. He now teaches at the University of San Diego. Dr. Sutton has worked with a variety of human remains in western North America and has published more than 240 books, monographs, articles, and reviews in archaeology.

Bioarchaeology

An Introduction to the Archaeology
and Anthropology of the Dead

Mark Q. Sutton

Routledge
Taylor & Francis Group

LONDON AND NEW YORK

First published 2021
by Routledge
2 Park Square, Milton Park, Abingdon, Oxon OX14 4RN

and by Routledge
52 Vanderbilt Avenue, New York, NY 10017

Routledge is an imprint of the Taylor & Francis Group, an informa business

British Library Cataloguing-in-Publication Data
A catalogue record for this book is available from the British Library

Library of Congress Cataloging-in-Publication Data
Names: Sutton, Mark Q., author.
Title: Bioarchaeology : an introduction to the archaeology and anthropology of the dead / Mark Q. Sutton.
Description: Abingdon, Oxon ; New York, NY : Routledge, 2020. | Includes bibliographical references and index.
Identifiers: LCCN 2020013361 (print) | LCCN 2020013362 (ebook) | ISBN 9781138481039 (hardback) | ISBN 9781138481060 (paperback) | ISBN 9781351061117 (ebook)
Subjects: LCSH: Human remains (Archaeology) | Human skeleton—Analysis.
Classification: LCC CC79.5.H85 S87 2020 (print) | LCC CC79.5.H85 (ebook) | DDC 930.1—dc23
LC record available at https://lccn.loc.gov/2020013361
LC ebook record available at https://lccn.loc.gov/2020013362

ISBN: 978-1-138-48103-9 (hbk)
ISBN: 978-1-138-48106-0 (pbk)
ISBN: 978-1-351-06111-7 (ebk)

Typeset in Bembo
by Apex CoVantage, LLC

Contents

Figures

Tables

Preface

Bioarchaeology is a diverse and fascinating field, and there is a considerable literature on the subject. There are several recent general treatments of bioarchaeology, including those of Mays (2010), Martin et al. (2013), and Larsen (2015), but these seem intended mostly for professionals. Much of the bioarchaeological literature is quite specialized, and there are many volumes on specific subjects, such as cremated remains (e.g., Kuijt et al. 2014; Schmidt and Symes 2015), paleopathology (e.g., Weiss 2015a), commingled and disarticulated remains (e.g., Osterholtz et al. 2014a; Osterholtz 2016a), trepanation (Verano 2016), violence (e.g., Martin et al. 2012a, 2012b; Tegtmeyer and Martin 2017a, 2017b), gender (e.g., Agarwal and Wesp 2017; Geller 2017a), forensics (e.g., Moran and Gold 2019), the impact of climate change on increasing violence (Schwitalla 2013; Harrod and Martin 2014a; also see Redfern 2017a:64–67), discussions of particularly interesting remains (e.g., Bahn 2012), and others. In addition, there are a number of journals specifically dedicated to bioarchaeological subjects, such as the *International Journal of Osteoarchaeology*, the *International Journal of Paleopathology*, and *Bioarchaeology International*.

This book is different. It is intended to be a general treatment of the field for students who take just one introductory class in bioarchaeology. Its coverage is intended to be broad but purposefully does not go into great detail so as to make the field digestible to the student. It includes chapter summaries, a glossary, and a fairly extensive bibliography so someone can pursue specific issues, perhaps as a stepping stone for a class term paper. The organization and content of the book was used when I taught Introduction to Bioarchaeology and so has been successfully "alpha tested."

Acknowledgments

I greatly appreciate the comments, suggestions, and assistance of Celeste Ely, Jill K. Gardner, Kevin Maxwell, Jennifer Parkinson, and Mike Sage on the text, and the comments of Eric J. Bartelink were particularly helpful. I further thank Eric J. Bartelink, Martin Brown, Henry Chapman, Jim Chatters, James Dickman, R. Paul Evans, Jane Hickman, Marni LaFleur, Stephanie Panzer, Jennifer Parkinson, Victor Mair, Simon Mays, Tim Sutherland, John Verano, Tony Waldron, and Elizabeth Weiss for kindly providing figures and photographs. Emily Miller helped with some of the photography. The assistance of Matthew Gibbons and Katie Wakelin with Taylor & Francis was critical to the completion of this project. Finally, I appreciate the patience of the students of the last two times I taught Bioarchaeology while working on this book.

Chapter 1

The discipline of bioarchaeology

Introduction: what is bioarchaeology?

Everybody dies, and each society deals with that fact in some manner. Those practices can vary widely in both contemporary and past societies (e.g., Parker Pearson 2003; Matsunami 2010; Tarlow and Stutz 2013). Some of the dead are buried, some are cremated, some are mummified, some are worshiped, some are hidden, and some are forgotten. Which of these and other approaches were practiced depended on the beliefs of the society of the deceased and sometimes those of their enemies.

What were the various belief systems regarding the dead? How did different groups treat their dead? Why did they use the methods they used? What is the meaning of those practices? How did things change through time? Why? What are the practical applications of understanding past practices?

These questions, and many others, are ultimately anthropological in nature. **Anthropology** is the study of humans, and anthropologists want to learn all they can about people and societies, including their social, political, religious systems, and much more. Within the domain of anthropology, **ethnography** is the study of a living society, while **ethnology** is the comparative study of culture and society. One of the strengths of ethnography and ethnology is the ability to directly observe human behavior and to ask questions of the participants.

Archaeology is the study of past societies. However, unlike ethnography, archaeologists cannot directly observe human behavior and must infer such behaviors from the context and patterns of material remains. Among the materials recovered in archaeological investigations are human remains (the past people themselves), and the "very presence of human remains affects archaeological interpretation" (Stutz 2018:324). Thus, human remains, if present, become central in an archaeological study. **Bioarchaeology** now forms the "interpretive framework" in the analysis of human remains in an effort to be able to address anthropological questions (Ortner 2006:xiv).

The initial step in bioarchaeology is to describe the remains themselves (typically bone) and identify any disease or trauma. Next, the cultural context of the remains must be considered, so the archaeological data regarding the remains and associated artifacts or facilities are crucial. In addition, bioarchaeology uses data obtained from a variety of other subdisciplines to add to the analysis, such as biological anthropology, forensics, ecology, and public health (Martin and Osterholtz 2016:39), among others. It is truly interdisciplinary.

With a few exceptions, early studies of human remains were made in isolation and not integrated with other archaeological data. Thus, paleoethnobotanists or botanists analyzed the plant remains; zooarchaeologists or zoologists examined the animal remains; others dated the sites; and bioarchaeologists, biologists, or human anatomists evaluated human skeletal remains and those data sets were not typically integrated into an overall understanding of a site or its anthropological context. As a result, many still see bioarchaeology as being descriptive, while anthropology is seen as humanistic, and it is difficult to envision an integration of those approaches. But the field does now integrate these aspects into a general biocultural approach that seeks to use bioarchaeological data to examine socioeconomic conditions experienced by human communities of the past.

Not all scholars share this definition. For example, in the United Kingdom (UK), the term "bioarchaeology" (first coined in 1972) is commonly used to refer to the biological constituents from a site, such as faunal and botanical remains (Buikstra 2006a:xvii), although it is now often linked to the field of human osteoarchaeology (see Roberts 2006, 2009). In the United States, the study of faunal and botanical remains in an archaeological site is generally called **archaeobiology** (Sobolik 2003).

In **forensics**, analysis of human remains is focused on medico-legal issues (Ubelaker 2019); that is, efforts to solve crimes or to identify the missing. In these situations, the social or religious system of a deceased individual is not germane to the question of who may have killed them (there are exceptions, such as a religiously motivated murder). Nevertheless, both bioarchaeologists and forensic investigators begin with the same basic data set: the human remains themselves.

What constitutes human remains?

Initially, the definition of **human remains** seems obvious: a deceased person, in whole or part. Following this, most legal definitions in the United States generally specify a "dead body." For example, the Nevada Revised Statute, Section 451.005, specifies human remains as "the body of a deceased person . . . the body in any state of decomposition and the cremated remains of a body," the general implication being a complete body of some sort (Joyce 2015:175). Certainly, most skeletal or mummified remains would fall into such a category and everyone would view them as human remains.

But what about fragmentary remains, such as parts lost in life through trauma? For example, are the bones of an amputated leg from a Civil War soldier who survived the wound considered human remains? What about the terminal phalanx from the finger of someone who had an accident with a power saw or a person who had a finger removed as part of a mourning ceremony?

What about human material lost in the normal course of life without trauma? Such material could include hair (humans typically lose 50 to 100 hairs a day), fingernail clippings, and sluffed skin cells. Are these human remains? Everyone loses their primary teeth (deciduous, or "baby," teeth) as they mature. Are such loose and isolated teeth considered human remains? What about remains such as blood, proteins, or DNA? What about paleofeces?

The determination of what constitutes human remains is generally made based on the nature and context of the remains, their age, and whether they were associated with a group whose belief systems might consider any human material "human remains." Certainly, the remains of an actual deceased person would qualify, while remains that could be lost in life are generally not considered "human remains." Nevertheless, there is considerable gray area with this issue.

The development of the discipline

A very brief history of the development of what we now call bioarchaeology is presented here (for more detailed histories, see Buikstra et al. [2011], Baker and Agarwal [2017], Larsen [2018]). The discipline initially arose out of early interest in classifying and quantifying morphological variation in modern human populations into racial groups. Other goals included an understanding of the position of modern humans in relationship to early fossil forms, such as *Homo erectus* and Neandertals, and to other primates (Armelagos et al. 1982). A great deal of effort was also expended in an attempt to discern and standardize morphological measurements that would be the most useful for the analysis of biological affinity in human populations. Much of this early work had strong elements of racism, sexism, and biological determinism.

A focus on measurement and classification

Much of the early osteological work was centered on the measurements of crania, most of which were retained in the considerable museum collections of human skeletal materials that were acquired in the late 1800s and early 1900s from archaeological sites in North America (Buikstra 2006b:7–20; also see Redman 2016; Stone 2018). The study of crania gave rise to the subfield of **craniometry**, which was frequently used in phrenology, a technique to determine character, personality traits, and criminality on the basis of the shape of the head (skull) in living people. The general approach of craniometric classification was criticized early on (Virchow 1896; Boas 1912), but such protests were ignored or attacked (Radosavljevich 1911; Shapiro 1959).

Johann Friedrich Blumenbach (1752–1840) was a physician who is often referred to as the father of physical anthropology. His primary work was on the variation in cranial morphology (shape) to determine various races of modern humans (Cook 2006). Blumenbach (1776) used measurements (although no accurate measuring devices had been invented yet) on a collection of crania to describe his earliest views on racial classification and human variation. Based on his analysis, Blumenbach (1776) developed a **classification** of five "races" of humans: (1) Caucasian or white; (2) Mongolian or yellow, including all East Asians and some Central Asians; (3) Malayan or brown, including Southeast Asian and Pacific Islanders; (4) Ethiopian or black, including sub-Saharan Africans; and (5) American or red, including American Indians.

Blumenbach believed in a "degenerative" model of race; that is, that Adam and Eve were Caucasian and all other races came about by degeneration from the original Caucasian. Interestingly, at the same time, he argued that the different races resulted from living in different environments, and that there were no fundamental differences between the "races."

Samuel George Morton (1799–1850), also a physician, conducted studies on cranial shape and capacity (e.g., size of the brain). Using skull metrics from Peru, Mexico, and the "Moundbuilders" of North America (see Willey and Sabloff 1993:22–28, 39–45), he demonstrated that they were all the same "race" (Morton 1839; also see Cook 2006:35, 41), a major finding of the time. Further, he argued that **cranial capacity** was the determining factor in intelligence and the capacity for culture. In his seminal work, *Crania Americana*, Morton (1839) measured the volume of a series of skulls of different races and determined that Caucasians had the largest brains, Native Americans the second largest, and Negros the smallest. At the time, these theories were popular, as they reinforced the prevailing opinion. Upon his death in 1851, the *Charleston Medical Journal* (in South Carolina) noted that "we of the South should consider him as our benefactor, for aiding most materially in giving to the negro his true position as an inferior race."

Morton was criticized by Stephen Jay Gould (1981) as having "mismeasured" the skulls to find his desired numbers to "prove" his thesis. Gould (1981) argued that (1) Morton selected and/or deleted skulls from his sample depending on whether they fit his theory; (2) seeds were used to measure cranial capacity, an unreliable and unreproducible method; (3) the normal variation in populations was not considered; and (4) rounding the numbers was done to support his theory. Others (e.g., Cook 2006; Lewis et al. 2011) believed that Morton did not intentionally mismeasure and that, despite not having proper tools, his measurements were fairly accurate. The small sample size and issues with skeletal variation remain problematic with Morton's work.

Pierre Paul Broca (1824–1880), another physician, measured cranial capacity and asserted that men had larger brains than women (implying men were more intelligent) and that "superior races" had larger brains than "inferior races." Modern scientists reject such "research" for using a priori expectations and scientific racism. In his analysis of prehistoric human skeletal material, Broca (1871, 1875) developed techniques of anthropometric craniometry still used today. Broca made other contributions to the field of neurology (see Schiller 1992).

Aleš Hrdlička (1869–1943) was one of the main originators of physical anthropology in America (Brace 1982; also see Cook 2006). Hrdlička founded the **American Association of Physical Anthropologists** in 1928 and created the *American Journal of Physical Anthropology* in 1918, which is still the foremost journal in the field. Hrdlička considered Broca to be the principal founder of physical anthropology and viewed France as the mother country of that science (Brace 1982; Buikstra and Beck 2006). Hrdlička was a proponent of standardizing anthropometric measurements (Stewart 1947), with particular emphasis on measurements of the crania to determine biological affinity. He developed measurement tools that are still used today. Hrdlička was also interested in the origins of Native Americans and in preserving the Smithsonian collections (Buikstra 2006b:21; also see Ubelaker 2006).

Earnest A. Hooton (1887–1954) was also one of the main pioneers of physical anthropology in America (Brace 1982; also see Cook 2006). Hooton was a professor and researcher at Harvard University for more than four decades and educated most of the physical anthropologists that were hired by universities and colleges in the middle part of the twentieth century. Hooton (1918) made many contributions, including data on the peopling of the Americas. He also analyzed the remains of 1,254 individuals excavated from Pecos Pueblo in the southwestern United States and argued that the Pecos Pueblo individuals could be racially typed and the racial history of the population understood through analysis of the individuals (Hooton 1930; also see Beck 2006). Interestingly, Hooton also did some work in ergonomics, using anthropometric data (buttocks measurements) in chair design.

Much of this early work was geared toward the definition of races using questionable methods, an approach called **scientific racism**. This approach has been completely discredited, as it is very clear that (1) all living (and recently living) people belong to the same species; (2) that variation was due to evolutionary adaptation to different environments; (3) that this adaptation resulted in different populations; (4) that such populations share physical characteristics; (5) that adaptation and variation are ongoing processes; (6) that mental capacities are not related; and (7) that culture accounts for social differences. Further, it has been argued that the term "ethnic group" be substituted for the term "race" (DiGangi and Moore 2012a:9).

By the mid-twentieth century, the classificatory approach was being replaced by a more holistic approach to skeletal morphological measurements. Researchers began looking at functional craniology in which it was believed that there were significant environmental and developmental processes that affect bone and cranial growth, processes other than those of racial identity or grouping (e.g., Carlson and Van Gerven 1979). This biocultural approach was used with increasing frequency by bioarchaeologists such as Angel (1969; also see Jacobsen and Cullen 1990) on morphological changes in populations from classical Greece, Buikstra (1977) on prehistoric populations in the lower Illinois River Valley, and Martin et al. (1991) on populations from Black Mesa in the North American Southwest.

Interest in paleopathology

At the same time as the focus on classification and craniology was taking place, other researchers were interested in **paleopathology**, the analysis of disease that can be detected in tissues, primarily bone (e.g., Martin and Osterholtz 2016). The earliest paleopathological reports were on the remains of extinct animals.

Significant research in human paleopathology did not begin until the late nineteenth century. One of the earliest studies was by Meigs (1857) on two Hindu crania, one exhibiting syphilitic ulcers and the other displaying fractures. Wyman (1868) observed periosteal lesions and dental anomalies on Polynesian skulls. The first treatment of prehistoric human disease was presented by Jones (1876) on archaeological human remains from the eastern United States. Interest in paleopathology increased with studies of the origins of diseases, such as syphilis (Langdon 1881; Putnam 1884; Whitney 1886), other medical "anomalies" (Hrdlička 1910, 1927, 1941), and paleopathology syntheses (Williams 1929; Moodie 1931).

A revival of mortuary analysis

Early work on **mortuary analysis**, the study of burial patterns (e.g., Hooton [1918, 1930], Hrdlička [1910, 1927, 1941]), was primarily confined to measurement, classification, and studies of ancestry. The use of such data for anthropological questions was discouraged. It was argued (Kroeber 1927:314) that mortuary behavior was a matter of style and so not socially informative, and this view continued to be held by many archaeologists as late as the 1960s (Buikstra 2006c:197).

Beginning in the early 1970s, there was a renewed interest in mortuary analysis from an anthropological and materialist perspective (e.g., Saxe 1970; Binford 1971; Brown 1971; Alekshin et al. 1983) in what would become known as the Saxe-Binford Research Program (Brown 1995; Carr 1995). This occurred at about the same time archaeology emerged from its "classificatory/historical" period (see Willey and Sabloff 1993) to take a scientific approach following the "New Archaeology" (e.g., Binford 1962, 1964). Physical anthropology shifted focus from its descriptive/classificatory emphasis at about the same time.

Changing perspectives: an integrated biocultural approach

The field of bioarchaeology was formally defined by Buikstra (1977; also see Blakely 1977a, 1977b; Buikstra 2006a:xviii; Powell et al. 2006) as having a **biocultural approach**; an interdisciplinary methodology that integrated the study of human remains with archaeology and anthropology and included mortuary practices (the funerary system), social organization, daily activities and division of labor, paleodemography, population movements and relatedness, and diet and health. This approach is not just descriptive but is problem oriented and defines the scope of the discipline followed herein. The field of physical anthropology is now typically referred to as biological anthropology to recognize the expansion of its breadth beyond physical aspects to include cultural ones (e.g., DiGangi and Moore 2012a:7; also see Zuckerman and Armelagos 2011). Larsen (2018:865) called this the transition "from classifications of the dead to conditions of the living."

Larsen (2006a) delineated three major research foci of bioarchaeology, investigating (1) quality of life (diet and nutrition, disease, growth and development); (2) behavior and lifestyle, including biomechanics; and (3) population history, including biological relationships and population movements. This approach appears to be driven more by evolutionary issues than biocultural or social ones and may best be viewed as a "skeletal biology of the past."

Martin et al. (2012b:2) identified four principal aspects of bioarchaeology (reordered here): (1) consideration of the body, including mortuary and funerary behaviors; (2) consideration of taphonomy; (3) the connection between past and living groups; and (4) the interdisciplinary nature of the field. The initial data set for bioarchaeology is the body itself (the study of which is called somatology), since it can "reveal tangible biological features of each individual human and because bodies are also influenced and shaped by cultural and environmental factors" (Martin and Osterholtz 2016:1). For the first aspect, the management of the body immediately following death is generally defined as mortuary treatment, while mourning and commemorative practices are often called funerary behavior.

The second aspect, taphonomy, is fundamentally about preservation and is central to the ability of obtaining data on both mortuary and funerary behavior. Without preservation at some level, the archaeologist would not recover anything and there would be nothing to study.

For the third aspect, the connection between past and present groups to help understand past practices is made using ethnographic analogy (Testart 1988:1; also see Headland and Reid 1989:49–51), ethnoarchaeology (e.g., O'Connell 1995), and experimental archaeology (e.g., Outram 2008), all of which are part of a general category of middle-range approaches (see Chapter 9). In addition, it is now common to seek the perspectives and concerns of descendant communities (e.g., Rose et al. 1996).

Finally, bioarchaeology is today a highly interdisciplinary empirical specialty integrated with social theory (Agarwal and Glencross 2011:3). Analyses include osteology (the study of bones), paleodemography (the study of past populations), biodistance (relatedness) studies, biogeochemistry (the study of the chemistry of bones), and taphonomy, all of which have become increasingly sophisticated (Knudson and Stojanowski 2008; Larsen 2018). Such developments permit the study of social identities, such as gender, age, disability, impairment, and life course, as well as ethnic and community identities (Knudson and Stojanowski 2008).

Ethics and politics in bioarchaeology

The disturbance of burials in modern graves or those in recognized and maintained cemeteries is illegal in almost every country. This has generally not been the case for the remains of subjugated peoples (Fourth World people, see Neely and Hume 2020) or the remains from unknown prehistoric societies (Fifth World people, see Sutton 2017a), although there are exceptions. However, in last few decades, there has been a considerable shift in the attitude of researchers working with human remains, and the **ethics** of excavating or disturbing burials have become an important issue (Watkins 2013; Sayer 2017). This change is in large part due to the efforts of indigenous peoples throughout the world who have gained more political power and have denounced the disturbance of their ancestors and the burial objects from their graves.

A spate of legislation in the United States and many other countries now requires that indigenous groups be consulted prior to conducting archaeological excavations, and the treatment of human burials is often negotiated prior to the commencement of fieldwork. If there are known burial areas, the first option is to avoid them.

Most archaeologists are now sensitive to the rights and wishes of indigenous peoples. Larsen and Walker (2005; also see Lambert and Walker 2019) suggested that conflict between archaeologists and descendant communities could be avoided or mitigated through increased communication with the viewpoint that (1) the remains be treated with dignity, (2) descendant communities should have control over their disposition, and (3) the remains should be preserved when possible due to their scientific value. In addition, the display of human remains in museum settings remains an issue.

It is not just the wishes of the living descendants that create an ethical issue. Scarre (2003, 2006, 2013; also see Joyce 2015; Kreissl Lonfat et al. 2015) argued that disturbing the dead could break a social contract made with the living (or then-living) regarding the disposition of their bodies after death. A violation of this contract, even by a person not party to it (such as an archaeologist), could cause harm to one or both parties, the party that agrees to deal with the dead and respect their wishes, and the dead (or future dead) themselves, who in life would worry about their future disposition if they knew that the first party did not keep their promises. It is an ethical challenge.

There is also an ethical issue in the destructive testing of human remains, such as radiocarbon dating and many other analytical techniques, including medical examinations. Kreissl Lonfat et al. (2015) proposed an ethical code of conduct for research projects that use human remains in scientific, educational, or professional areas of work. The code was not intended to be a strict set of rules, but as a mechanism to support and foster ethically desirable conduct for the research process as a whole, its involved participants, and possible stakeholders.

Repatriation: humanistic and scientific issues

Early on in the discipline, little thought was given to the ethics of the study of the remains of past people, most of which had been subjugated by western societies. Remains were collected, studied, placed in repositories, and displayed in museums – practices that are now seen as part of colonial repression (L. Smith 2012; also see Atalay et al. 2014). In recent years, there have been concerted efforts to locate and identify human remains and sacred items held in various institutions (e.g., museums and universities) and to return them to their appropriate descendant communities (generally for reburial), a process called **repatriation**. In the United States, this has resulted in the return of thousands of sets of human remains for reburial although coupled with the potential loss of information on unanalyzed remains (e.g., Buikstra 2006d; Colwell 2017).

Thus, there is tension between the humanistic and scientific value of remains. To bioarchaeologists, human remains and their associated materials are the core of the discipline, so they tend to view them as data sets. In some cases, very old or unique remains have been considered too important to science to just rebury without study (e.g., Thomas 2000) (see the Kennewick Man case study on page 10). In other instances, the study and repatriation of human remains not only adds to a scientific understanding of the past but positively engages a society and its cultural heritage; for example, to help the Yaqui understand the violence perpetrated on them by the Mexican government in the early twentieth century (Bauer-Clapp and Pérez 2014).

To most descendant communities, however, human remains are emotionally connected and not seen as scientific data sets. To many indigenous people, this is a very important issue, touching on religion (reclaiming their dead through repatriation; Redman [2016]), politics (the return of their heritage), and empowerment (ownership and interpretation of the past). Although most archaeologists understand and agree with these matters (Killion 2008), there can still be issues to resolve.

The interpretation of remains is also an issue. Contemporary archaeology is a western enterprise, and western archaeologists tend to view things with western logic and value systems and impose their own cultural experiences on the remains they study, a clear problem for interpretation. However, as observed by Atalay (2008:33), "the discipline of archaeology is not inherently good or bad; it is the application and practice of the discipline that has the potential to disenfranchise and be used as a colonizing force." It is now common to engage descendant communities to seek their views and interpretations of materials in question (e.g., Nicholas and Watkins 2014).

It is important to understand that descendant communities are made up of contemporary people with contemporary identities, not past people living in societies unchanged through time. As such, one could argue (see McGhee 2008) that indigenous archaeology could interpret the past through the political and social lenses of contemporary special interest groups, which ultimately would not be beneficial to such groups (e.g., perpetuating stereotypes) or to our understanding of the past. The **Vermillion Accord** on the treatment of human remains called for "mutual respect for the beliefs of indigenous peoples as well as the importance of science and education" (Day 1990:15), and is probably a good place to begin.

One final note: Who is reburying whom? Recall that there was an original social contract between the living and the dead regarding the disposition of one's body and that a violation of that contract, even by a person not party to it, could be unethical. If the contemporary person tasked to rebury the remains of someone turned out to be from a different group (and perhaps religion), would that break the social contract? For example, if a Muslim person was reburied in a Catholic ceremony, would that do harm to either party? Food for thought.

International laws on human remains

Most countries have laws and regulations regarding the treatment of archaeological human remains. A comprehensive guide to the legislation in some 60 countries was provided by Márquez-Grant and Fibiger (2011). For example, Israel contains remains from a large number of different societies, some as old as 1.5 million years, and human remains are commonly recovered from excavations (Nagar 2011). However, Israeli law does not consider human remains of any age to be antiquities, so when human remains are found they are turned over to the Ministry of Religious Affairs for reburial. In addition, Jewish Orthodox law generally opposes disturbance of the dead, except when they "disturb public activities" (e.g., construction). These rules have resulted in the necessity of conducting rapid (and so incomplete) analyses of human remains in the field (Nagar 2011:614).

In Australia, extensive excavations prior to 1984 brought about the collection of many Aboriginal remains. After that time, control of these human remains was given to the Aborigines (Donlon and Littleton 2011; Pardoe 2013). As a result, many such remains have been repatriated, and permission to study extant collections must be obtained from the Aborigines. Thus, when human remains are encountered by archaeologists, every effort is made to record the remains in place to prevent excavation (Donlon and Littleton 2011:635). This practice obviously limits the types of data that can be obtained. The specific laws regarding the treatment of human remains vary by state in Australia (Donlon and Littleton 2011:637), but federal laws may also apply, depending on the circumstances. For example, the excavation of Aboriginal human remains requires a permit from the Department of Environment, Conservation, Climate Change and Water, but such a permit is only granted if the remains are in danger of being damaged, such as by construction. The forensic identification of human remains as Aboriginal or not is another issue.

War graves

War graves contain people who died in active military service (although not necessarily in combat) but who are not interred in cemeteries. For example, sunken ships or submarines, downed aircraft, or other such vehicles that contain unrecovered human remains would be classified as war graves, are considered to be sacred places, and are protected under international law. If the remains are later recovered, the site is no longer considered a war grave.

A fairly large number of war graves have been designated. Perhaps the most famous is that of the USS *Arizona*, sunk in Pearl Harbor on December 7, 1941 (see Chapter 4). Most recently, a World War I German submarine was discovered with 23 bodies on board (Associated Press 2017).

When the remains of U.S. war dead are discovered and recovery is planned, forensic teams from the **Defense POW/MIA Accounting Agency (DPAA)** are tasked with their recovery, identification, and repatriation. The French, British, Australians, and Germans make similar efforts.

U.S. laws on human remains

A variety of federal and state laws apply to human remains (e.g., Buikstra 2006d; Ubelaker 2011; King 2012), and local agencies may have additional requirements. First, a permit must be obtained to conduct work if the land is owned by the government. If the land is privately owned, permission to work must be obtained from the owner. Some types of sites, including known cemeteries, cannot be excavated without a special permit. If an unknown cemetery or burial is found, special permission must be granted to continue the work. In most states, human burials are protected by law, whether on public or private lands. The federal **Native American Graves Protection and Repatriation Act (NAGPRA)** of 1990 reflects the concerns of indigenous peoples about the treatment of the dead by archaeologists, biological anthropologists, and museums. Other laws that affect archaeology as it relates to human remains are the Abandoned Shipwreck Act and the National Historic Preservation Act. In some cases, such as on certain military installations, there are specific agreements with local Native groups.

NAGPRA

The federal NAGPRA (25 United States Code (U.S.C.) 3001–3013), passed in 1990, requires federal agencies and institutions receiving federal funding or licensing to inventory their collections for any human remains, associated funerary objects, and other sacred objects, as well as to identify the tribal affiliation of those materials, to notify the identified tribes, and to repatriate the materials if so requested. Materials whose affiliations cannot be determined remain in the collections pending further review. It is further required that if human remains or sacred objects are accidentally unearthed, such as during construction, the appropriate Native American groups will be consulted, sometimes a difficult task (Goldstein 2013; also see Kakaliouras 2017). In most cases, the wishes of the group(s) determined to be ancestral are followed, often with little or no analysis. As noted by Ousley et al. (2006), however, federal law does not halt research on human remains; in fact, such research is required to determine cultural affiliation.

Case study: the battle for Kennewick

The Kennewick burial, known as the "Ancient One" by the Native Americans, was discovered in 1996 eroding from the bank of the Columbia River near Kennewick, Washington (Figure 1.1). Upon discovery, the police and coroner were contacted. Realizing that the remains were relatively old, the coroner contacted Dr. James Chatters, a local archaeologist who specializes in human osteology. Due to the general shape of the cranium, Chatters initially thought that the individual may have been a nineteenth-century white settler. This fit with the remains having been found near a known historical archaeological site and historical artifacts that were eroding into the river. Chatters visited the burial site and found additional skeletal material, ultimately recovering nearly 90% of the skeleton.

The remains were taken to Chatters's laboratory for further analysis. The individual was identified as a robust adult male, then thought to be between 45 and 55 years of age. The skull and femur appeared to have a generally European rather than Native American morphology. During the analysis, Chatters noticed a hard, dark object embedded in a partially healed wound in the ilium of the pelvis. To determine the nature of the object, the pelvis was given a computerized tomography (CT) scan, and the object was found to be a Cascade projectile

Figure 1.1 Location of the Kennewick site in Washington State
Source: Author

point, a type of point that generally dates to between 5,000 and 9,000 years ago. Chatters considered the possibility that the remains were Paleoindian and was granted permission to obtain a radiocarbon date. The initial results indicated an age of about 9,500 years old, but additional dating has shown that this individual is actually 8,600 years old.

The Kennewick site is located on federal land administered by the Army Corps of Engineers. Upon learning that the skeleton was Native American, the Army Corps reported the discovery to the local Native Americans, the Yakama, Umatilla, and Colville tribes, as required under NAGPRA. The Umatilla immediately demanded that no further analysis be undertaken and that the remains be instantly repatriated for reburial. The Army Corps then instructed the coroner to secure the remains from Chatters for transfer to the tribe. Given very little time (literally a few hours) to examine the skeleton before the transfer, Chatters was unable to complete most of the planned documentation and analysis.

There was no question that the remains are Native American in a strictly literal sense, but since the skeleton is so old, its ancestry was not at all clear. Furthermore, such rare remains offer a unique glimpse into the prehistory of all humanity. Concerned that information about the origins and life of this individual would be lost to science, a group of archaeologists and biological anthropologists sued the federal government for permission to conduct a complete analysis of the remains before they were reburied.

The suit alleged that the government had not adequately addressed the issue of the right of the Umatilla and several other tribes to claim the remains for reburial because the tribes had not clearly shown a direct affiliation with the remains (NAGPRA requires a "preponderance of evidence"). In response, repatriation was postponed and the government conducted a four-year independent investigation of the remains. Biological anthropological, archaeological, and ethnological studies were unable to show that the remains were affiliated with the tribes of the Northwest. Nevertheless, the government argued that they did, in fact, demonstrate affiliation with those groups.

In August 2002, the district court ruled that the Kennewick Man remains were not Native American (as technically defined under NAGPRA), set aside the determination made by the government, and allowed scientific study of the remains. The government appealed, but the Ninth Circuit Court of Appeals upheld the original ruling allowing the study. No further appeal was filed by the government, but the tribes still wanted a say in how the remains would be studied. The scientists filed a motion to keep the tribes from further participation in the lawsuit, but that motion was denied by the federal district court on August 17, 2004. On September 9, 2004, the tribes filed another motion that argued they have a right to intervene under statutes other than NAGPRA, including the Archaeological Resources Protection Act (ARPA) and the National Historic Preservation Act (NHPA). This legal challenge was rejected by the court, and Kennewick Man was turned over to the scientists for analysis. In 2005, a bill to amend NAGPRA to make it easier for tribes to claim unaffiliated remains was introduced in Congress but was not passed. However, in 2010, that same change was made to the federal regulations under NAGPRA. The issues leading up to the formal study of the Kennewick skeleton are well documented (e.g., Thomas 2000; Owsley and Jantz 2001, 2014; Watkins 2013).

In 2005 and 2006, Douglas Owsley of the Smithsonian Institution's National Museum of Natural History and others conducted a detailed examination of the remains. A copy of the skull and the projectile point were made with a 3-D printer and additional radiocarbon dates were obtained. Every possible study was conducted, and the findings were published in 2014 (Owsley and Jantz 2014).

The analyses indicated that Kennewick Man was an approximately 40-year-old male and was intentionally buried. He had lived a hard life; he had a number of healed fractures and some osteoarthritis, suggesting considerable mobility. His skeletal morphology suggested he was related to the Jōmon of prehistoric Japan. Isotopic studies indicated a diet primarily of salmon or marine mammals with little input from terrestrial foods, illustrating the likelihood that he had lived in a coastal context for much of his life. The presence of auditory exostoses (bone growth in the ear canal) was indicative of a life spent in and around cold water, and his worn teeth signified the consumption of foods with a high abrasive content, such as dried fish. Finally, analysis of his DNA showed that he was related to the same Native groups – the Yakama, Umatilla, and Colville – that had originally claimed him under NAGPRA. In February 2017, the skeleton was turned over to the tribes and reburied.

State laws

All 50 states that make up the United States have laws and regulations regarding the disposition and study of human remains on nonfederal lands. While these rules are highly variable, most states have some form of archaeological protection statutes, frequently related to the discovery of aboriginal burials (generally called "burial laws"), that protect burials and any associated grave goods. Most states require a halt to excavation work and that proper authorities and relevant ancestor groups be contacted and issues resolved (Ubelaker 2011:534). The laws and regulations related to the disposition of human remains and their availability for scientific study are also variable.

For example, in California, if human remains are discovered on private or state-owned lands, Section 7050.5(b) of the Health and Safety Code applies. First, the work that resulted in the discovery (such as an archaeological excavation) must cease and the county coroner must be notified within 24 hours. The coroner then must notify the state Native American Heritage Commission who, in turn, designates a "most likely descendant" to deal with the matter. This person (or persons) then instructs the archaeologist as to what is acceptable treatment (ranging from closing the excavation, to removal and immediate reburial, to removal and study prior to reburial). Failure to comply with this law constitutes a felony.

Regarding other cultural groups

Most of the laws in the United States dealing with archaeological human remains are focused on Native American remains; however, non–Native American remains must also be considered. For example, the new Pima County Joint Courts Complex in Tucson, Arizona, was planned at the location of a large historical cemetery in use between about 1860 and 1875. Prior to construction, more than 1,300 burials were located, excavated, studied, and reburied in another cemetery (another 500 to 800 burials were left in place). The burials represented many ethnicities, including Hispanics, U.S. soldiers, Euro-Americans, Native Americans, and a few African Americans (Heilen 2012). Research into the historical records was able to identify the descendant communities of some of the burial population, and each was consulted and involved in the work, as required by federal, Arizona, and Pima County laws and regulations.

The construction of another federal courthouse in New York City resulted in the discovery of a large cemetery containing the remains of many African slaves that had worked and died in the city in the late 1700s and early 1800s. This cemetery was found during the construction of the court house and is discussed in the following case study.

Case study: the New York African Burial Ground

In 1991, during the construction of a federal courthouse in lower Manhattan, a portion of an eighteenth-century cemetery was discovered (Hansen and McGowan 1998). The cemetery, shown as "Negroes Burying Ground" on eighteenth-century maps of New York City (Figure 1.2), was located on a small plot of land then outside the city limits that was used from the early 1700s to about 1790. It is estimated that between 15,000 and 20,000 people were buried there. The area was eventually built over and the cemetery was forgotten. After rediscovery of the site in 1991, construction was halted, and work to document and evaluate the site was undertaken.

Excavations in the footprint of the courthouse resulted in the recovery of the remains of some 419 individuals. Most of the interments were enslaved Africans, but other groups were also represented, including the poor and indigent, as well as prisoners held during the American Revolution. Analysis of the skeletons (Barrett and Blakey 2011) revealed information about general health conditions and mortality of the burial population. Nearly half of the bodies are those of

Figure 1.2 Location of the "Negro Burying Ground" in New York City, circa 1750
Source: Alamy Image ID: KEBP5G

children under age 12, and some of the adults showed the effects of being over-worked, which may have led to their deaths. Many of the bodies were buried in traditional African ways (as evidenced by the orientation of the body and the types of grave goods present), attesting to the persistence of African cultural practices. A great deal was also learned about the demographics (sex and age at death) of the African population. Of note was the realization that during the 1700s, slavery was as pervasive in the northern part of the country as in the South and that only South Carolina had more slaves than New York City.

After the excavations, the federal building was completed. The cemetery was designated a historical district by the City of New York, was named a National Historic Landmark in 1993, and in 2006 was designated the African Burial Ground National Monument, operated by the National Park Service (visit www.nps.gov/afbg). A memorial to those interred in the cemetery was built on the site and dedicated in 2007. Most of the human remains were transported outside of New York to Howard University near Washington, D.C., creating a bit of a political problem (Harrington 1993), and were reinterred in the cemetery in 2003.

Since the discovery of New York's African Burial Ground, other such cem-eteries have come to be recognized as important to the local African American communities. Examples of this new understanding include slave cemeteries in Philadelphia, Pennsylvania (McCarthy 2006), and Richmond, Virginia (Hong 2017).

Chapter summary

As part of anthropology, bioarchaeology is the interpretive framework by which human remains and associated artifacts and facilities are studied in their cultural context. Bioar-chaeology is interdisciplinary in nature, using data from a variety of other disciplines in analyses. In contrast, forensics is focused on the analysis of human remains in an effort to solve crimes or to identify the missing, not to answer anthropological questions. Still, both bioarchaeologists and forensic investigators begin with the same basic data set: the human remains themselves.

Human remains can be defined as complete or portions of a deceased person, such as most skeletal or mummified remains. Some human materials, such as "baby" teeth, are lost in life, and while they do not represent deceased persons, they are still generally con-sidered human remains. Other human materials, such as hair, blood, or even proteins, fall into a gray area. The determination of what constitutes human remains is made based on the nature and context of the remains, their age, and whether they were associated with a group whose belief systems might consider any human material "human remains."

Bioarchaeology evolved from the measurement and description of crania in an effort to develop classifications of race and, by association, intelligence. This "scientific racism" dominated the field until the mid-twentieth century when the analysis of mortuary patterns became common, eventually leading to the development of the biocultural approach that better incorporated anthropological questions into the analysis of mortuary patterns (treat-ment of the body) and funerary behaviors (bereavement, mourning, and commemoration).

There are ethical issues in the study of human remains both in breaking the contract between the dead and the living and in the western study of nonwestern remains, often seen by indigenous people as a continuation of colonialism. These issues have resulted in conflicting interests in human remains: one to study them and one to repatriate them. As a consequence, a number of laws exist around the world governing the study of human remains.

Key concepts and terms

American Association of Physical Anthropologists
archaeobiology
bioarchaeology
biocultural approach
Blumenbach, Johann Friedrich
Broca, Pierre Paul
classification
cranial capacity
craniometry
Defense POW/MIA Accounting Agency (DPAA)
ethics
forensics
Hooton, Earnest A.
Hrdlička, Aleš
human remains
Kennewick Man (the Ancient One)
Morton, Samuel George
mortuary analysis
Native American Graves Protection and Repatriation Act (NAGPRA)
paleopathology
repatriation
scientific racism
Vermillion Accord
war graves

Chapter 2

In the field

Discovery and recovery

Outside of formal burial areas, human remains are usually discovered by chance, either in an archaeological excavation or by accident. To be sure, some remains are searched for purposefully, such as mummies in a tomb complex, or a recently missing person, or in areas of known mass graves (e.g., a war zone). Once found, two major questions need be answered: (1) Are the remains human? and (2) if so, how old are they (e.g., more than 50 years since death)? If they are human, recent remains become a concern to law enforcement and would be recovered and investigated as such. If they are old, they are of archaeological interest and may or may not be excavated and analyzed.

Human? How old?

Once biological (e.g., bone) remains are discovered, the first step is to determine whether they are human (e.g., Byers 2017:64–76) or otherwise associated with human activity (e.g., a purposeful animal burial that was part of a funerary practice). If the remains do relate to humans, it is important to determine whether they are archaeological or contemporary. If they are archaeological, bioarchaeologists deal with the material and ask anthropological questions. If they are contemporary, forensic anthropologists deal with the material and ask (mostly) legal questions (see Chapter 11). In both cases, the material must be properly recovered, treated, described, and compared with existing databases to address issues of age, sex, ancestry, pathology, trauma, and the like.

Species identification is fairly straightforward. Humans have the same basic skeletal structure as most mammals, and many of the bones are similar. However, the morphology of the various mammals differs in detail, and it is relatively easy to visually recognize human bones if they are complete enough. Highly fragmented and/or burned remains can present problems in identification, and specialized efforts may be necessary to determine whether the specimens are human. Such techniques include the microscopic structure (histology; see Chapter 3) of the bone and the analysis of DNA (see Chapter 8).

A determination of whether the remains are archaeological is made in a variety of ways. First, and most commonly, if the remains are found within a known archaeological context or associated with artifacts known to be archaeological, they would usually be considered archaeological. In a few cases, dating of the material is necessary to establish its age and whether it is archaeological.

The archaeological record

Evidence of the past exists in the **archaeological record** – the material remains and patterns of past human activities and behaviors (even if not yet found). The archaeological record includes the physical remains of people and their tools, houses, foods, or any other materials lost, discarded, abandoned, or hidden by them, as well as the geographic localities where these materials are located. The record also includes the various relationships between these materials and the patterns of those materials formed by their relationships.

Contained within the archaeological record are human remains and associated sites and other materials. **Sites** are geographic locations that contain evidence of human activity and commonly contain artifacts, features, ecofacts, and other aspects of the archaeological record. Sites may range in size from very small (e.g., a single artifact) to huge (e.g., a city). Sites take many forms and reflect the full range of human behaviors.

Artifacts consist of portable tools, ornaments, or other objects manufactured or used by people to accomplish a specific task and come in a vast array of types and forms, from simple to very complex. Artifacts convey a wide range of information about a group, including human skill, knowledge, symbolism, and activities.

Features are nonportable objects used or constructed by people. Examples of features include graves, cremation pits, tombs, mausoleums, hearths, houses, and walls.

Ecofacts are the unmodified remains of biological materials used by or related to people and are common constituents of the archaeological record. Examples of ecofacts include food residues (animal bones or plant parts), pollen, and charcoal.

The nature of archaeological evidence

Archaeologists currently have no method of directly observing any actual human behavior in the past, so most archaeological data indirectly reflect such behavior, and the conclusions reached regarding that behavior are primarily inferential. As such, interpretations of behavior that produced a particular pattern of evidence are hypothetical and are tested based on a number of assumptions and theoretical approaches. In addition, it is usually difficult to identify the behavior of specific individuals, so archaeologists typically view the past at the population level.

On the other hand, human remains are different than most archaeological evidence in that they constitute a direct record of the living behavior of specific individuals, including aspects of diet, activity patterns, migration, and disease. Thus, the analysis of human remains can directly inform us about individuals, which in turn can be used to learn more about populations. Further, the analysis of a funerary system opens a door into the beliefs (and other) systems of a society, a difficult task using conventional archaeological data.

Taphonomy

Taphonomy is the study of what happens to biological materials from the time of death to their recovery (Schotsmans et al. 2017a:2); essentially, the transformation processes that affect preservation. Efremov (1940), a paleontologist, defined taphonomy as the study of the transition of animal remains from the biosphere (living) to the lithosphere (dead). Because the term was defined by a paleontologist, most taphonomic studies have focused on the recovery and analysis of bone remains, although the taphonomy of plant (and other) remains is just as important for archaeological interpretations. Since its inception, the definition of taphonomy has been altered to fit the needs of both paleontology and archaeology. The study of taphonomy has evolved to include the post-fossilization period (Lyman 1994), and its scope now encompasses the history of biological remains, including their collection and curation (see Sobolik 2003).

Major taphonomic issues include biological processes, environmental conditions, natural processes that result in decomposition and **diagenesis** (chemical changes in the material), and **bioturbation** (the disturbance of remains by plants or animals, such as roots, burrowing rodents, and even ants). In addition, human action on postmortem remains (e.g., **excarnation**, or defleshing the body before burial) will also affect their condition. A detailed and comprehensive treatment of the taphonomy of human remains was presented in Schotsmans et al. (2017b; also see Marden et al. 2012; Stodder 2019).

Understanding taphonomic processes is difficult. *Anthropologie de terrain* is a detailed analytical approach that uses the position of each skeletal element and artifact in a burial, or set of burials, precisely recorded in the field, to help understand the taphonomic processes that may have affected them. The goal is to understand the conditions and changes of a body and its associated materials (e.g., Castex and Blaizot 2017). Coupled with a geographic information system (GIS) analysis (Wilhelmson and Dell'Unto 2015; Stewart and Vercellotti 2017), this approach can offer a greater understanding of associated mortuary processes. Such an approach is particularly useful with mass graves (Cabo et al. 2012).

Preservation

Preservation is a complicated issue. For something to be considered preserved in the archaeological sense, an archaeologist has to recognize it and have the ability to recover data from it. This includes the physical remains themselves, as well as their associated cultural context. Thus, preservation of organic (and all other) materials, as well as their archaeological and cultural contexts, is really the intersection of recognition and recovery. Each of these factors is dependent on research design, field methods, training, laboratory analyses, and skill. If an archaeologist was unable to visually recognize something in the field, then it would not be recovered and so would not be "preserved" in an analytical sense.

In the laboratory, "preservation" of data is at least partly due to the analytical techniques used, the skill of the technician, and the quality of the records kept. Recognition, and so preservation, is dependent on four major factors: (1) cultural treatment, if any, of the material prior to it entering the archaeological record; (2) taphonomic processes; (3) methods of recovery (e.g., a backhoe or a paintbrush) used in an archaeological excavation; and (4) the training and experience of the archaeologist.

CULTURAL FACTORS IN PRESERVATION

Virtually all materials that enter the archaeological record are first modified to some extent by cultural activities. Items are broken, burned, scraped, cut, crushed, wrapped, dried, treated, embalmed, placed in containers, and so on. Each of these cultural impacts will influence the rate of natural decomposition of the subject materials once in the record. For example, burning (carbonization) converts the chemical constituents of an item largely to elemental carbon, a durable substance that is quite resistant to further decomposition. Thus, burned bone, such as from a cremation, can preserve very well and would generally be recognized by most archaeologists.

Human mortuary practices can also affect the preservation of remains. Most bodies are subjected to some sort of initial treatment and so may have been culturally transformed prior to their final treatment (e.g., burial). Initial treatment may simply involve washing, an action that would have little effect on decomposition, whereas others may be placed in containers (e.g., a coffin), or excarnated, or fragmented and dispersed. Most of these practices can greatly affect preservation. For example, intentional mummification can greatly enhance preservation, whereas cremation would largely destroy the body while enhancing the preservation of the resulting fragmentary bone.

In addition, remains in the archaeological record are commonly disturbed by subsequent human activities, such as the excavation of a new grave into an existing cemetery. Such an action could result in considerable damage to an existing burial, with the older remains being fragmented and commingled. Finally, archaeological excavation and laboratory analysis can also damage and degrade remains.

NATURAL FACTORS IN PRESERVATION

A number of biological factors can influence the preservation of organic remains from archaeological sites (e.g., Junkins and Carter 2017). The most important is the presence of **saprophytic organisms**, those plants and animals that subsist by consuming dead matter, in archaeological contexts. Saprophytic organisms can include bioturbators such as large scavengers and rodents, but the term refers mainly to small organisms such as earthworms, insects, fungi, bacteria, and microbes. These organisms consume organic materials, including biological materials, from archaeological sites.

Other important biological factors that determine whether organic remains preserve include their robustness, durability, and/or density. The more durable an item is, the longer it will survive degradation by saprophytic organisms and chemical decomposition. Thus, bone will usually preserve better and longer than less dense soft tissues. The larger and denser a particular skeletal element is, the more likely it will preserve; for example, femora will generally preserve better than ribs.

The environment in which remains are found greatly influences their rate of decomposition. Because saprophytic organisms are the main cause of decomposition, preservation is highly dependent on what types of depositional environments are conducive or inhibiting to these organisms. Carbone and Keel (1985) listed four environmental factors that influence preservation of biological assemblages: soil pH, temperature, moisture, and aeration.

Soil **pH** (a measure of acidity) is important to understand, since saprophytic organisms are intolerant of highly acidic soils and live almost exclusively in alkaline soils. Therefore, organic materials will preserve better in acidic soils, such as in peat bogs, whereas alkaline soils will tend to poorly preserve biological materials. However, bone will generally preserve better in alkaline soils. The organic components of bone will tend to be consumed by saprophytes in alkaline soils, leaving mineral bone components intact, meaning that the structural components of bone are preserved. Bone does not survive well in acidic conditions because acids dissolve the structural bases of minerals, leaving only organic traces of bone in the soil (Tjelldén et al. 2018).

Environments with extremes in temperature and moisture are conducive to organic preservation. Saprophytic organisms do not thrive in hot, dry conditions, and therefore preservation of organics in such areas tends to be good, particularly in protected places such as caves or tombs that are protected from the elements (such as wind and rain). Cold temperatures also inhibit the decomposition of organic remains because saprophytic organisms do not do well in such conditions. Thus, remains in very cold regions, such as the Arctic, can be as well preserved as those in hot, arid regions such as Egypt.

Anaerobic environments, those lacking oxygen, can also affect the preservation of organic materials. Saprophytic organisms cannot live without oxygen, so such environments are more favorable to preservation. These include peat bogs (also highly acidic), which are famous for the preservation of bog bodies (e.g., Lynnerup 2015a), and water-logged sites such as Windover in Florida, where a 8,200-year-old cemetery containing preserved bodies and perishable artifacts was discovered in a peat bog (e.g., Wentz 2012).

A few other environmental conditions influence preservation. These include potential damage from geological processes, such as volcanic eruptions, earthquakes, mudslides, and erosion from both water and wind. Alternating cycles of wet and dry and/or hot and cold can also degrade remains through the physical expansion and contraction of the remains and their resulting fragmentation.

Discovery of human remains

Human remains can be located almost anywhere. The funerary system of a society would largely dictate where the dead were placed in the landscape. In many cases, a formal cemetery or other specific locations (e.g., burial beneath a house) were used. In other cases, the dead were placed in convenient locations, a practice common in highly mobile societies. As a result, it can be difficult to determine if or where human remains might be discovered. Thus, human remains can be discovered during the course of archaeological investigations, modern development, or by accident.

Known sites and locations

In many cases, the location of human remains is known, such as cemeteries, formalized locations where the dead were placed. Some cemeteries are highly organized internally (as in contemporary cemeteries in the United States). Other cemeteries may have some sort of general organization, such as high-status people buried in a particular area, whereas others may have no real (or remembered) internal organization. A large cemetery associated with a city or large funerary complex (e.g., Sakkara in Egypt) is often called a **necropolis** ("city of the dead"). Other examples of a necropolis include the one at the Pyramids at Giza and in Bahrain, where there are some 170,000 tombs dating to ca. 4,000 BP (Figure 2.1) (BP means years ago). Other locations of known human remains include war graves and mass graves in war zones.

Many decades ago in the United States, the excavation of cemeteries was a major research goal in archaeology, and large numbers of skeletons were removed for study (although many were never actually studied). Today, cemeteries are avoided if at all possible, primarily due to humanistic and legal issues, although in some places (e.g., Europe or Egypt) these issues are less restrictive.

Figure 2.1 A view of the necropolis in Bahrain
Source: Alamy Image ID: EDCY0H

Accidental discoveries

As known cemeteries are typically avoided, most human remains are now discovered by accident, such as during the construction of a highway or building (recall the African Burial Ground in New York). Other examples include the discovery of a number of lost cemeteries containing the victims of bubonic plague (*Yersinia pestis*), sometimes called "plague pits," during construction projects in London and elsewhere in Europe (Antoine 2008; DeWitte 2014).

In other cases, human remains might be accidentally discovered during an archaeological investigation of a site not initially known to contain such materials. Finally, human remains might be encountered by nonprofessionals, such as hikers or hunters, and should be reported to law enforcement for evaluation as to their age and identity.

Recovery of human remains

Once human remains are discovered, a decision must be made regarding their recovery. If the possibility of the encounter had been anticipated, the previously agreed upon protocol for treatment, either recovery or avoidance, would be followed. If the discovery was unanticipated, the legal protocol for informing the authorities and possible descendants must be followed. Any decision regarding recovery would take into consideration the project (e.g., the importance of the project and the associated cost of recovery or avoidance), the scientific value of the remains, and the concerns of descendants. If it is decided that recovery is required, a research design must be developed to guide the work.

Excavation methods

If it is decided that recovery will occur, the remains must be carefully excavated, usually with small tools such as trowels, dental picks, and paintbrushes. The goal of such careful methods is to record as much information as possible, including the position of the body, any pathologies or trauma, the presence or absence of grave goods, and other associated materials, such as the remains of a fetus in the abdominal area of a female.

Excavation is normally conducted from the top down (as opposed to a side-on excavation, although that is sometimes necessary) to expose the remains without having to move them (Figure 2.2). In addition, the degree of preservation of the remains will influence how excavation will proceed. If the remains are in good condition, excavation might proceed fairly rapidly, but if not, it can be a slow process. Even greater care may be required in the excavation of children due to the small size and fragility of the remains (see Baker et al. 2005:13–24). In some cases, chemical preservatives might be used to stabilize fragile remains, although this practice could complicate dating and other analyses. Soil samples may also be taken from around the body to analyze for pollen and/or DNA, whereas other soil samples might be taken from the abdominal area of an inhumation to try to recover dietary information (e.g., Reinhard et al. 1992). In most cases, all of the remains and associated materials are left in place until they have been recorded.

Figure 2.2 Burials being excavated, Germany
Source: Alamy Image ID: BJDC7P

Recordation

Once the remains are exposed, they are recorded and documented. Feature and/or burial record forms (see Sprague 2005:34–36) are filled out, and detailed notes (measurements, where possible, and observations on any pathologies) are made on each of the bones. The remains are also mapped and photographed (if permitted). If it is not possible to remove the remains for additional analyses (e.g., **radiographs** and/or DNA), the field records would be the only information available, so they must be as complete as possible. A serious issue in this regard is whether the field crew had the necessary training and expertise to adequately record the remains and whether the excavation had the proper protocol to rapidly record human remains (e.g., Průchová et al. 2017). Having an osteologist on the field crew would help to mitigate those concerns.

Post-excavation handling

If the remains are to be left in place at the site, they must be carefully reburied to prevent disruption of their original context and orientation. If the remains are removed from the site and taken to a laboratory for further analysis, great care must be taken to protect them from damage during removal and transport. In all cases, the remains must be treated with dignity and respect. The remains are labeled, carefully removed from the soil, and placed in cushioned (e.g., with cotton) containers for transport. In some cases, a block of soil containing the remains might be encased in plaster and transported to the laboratory for careful further excavation and analysis.

Once at the laboratory, the remains are unpacked and cleaned gently to avoid damaging them or destroying any evidence of pathology or trauma. They are then measured and examined, with any important information recorded. Some of the remains might be radiographed, and some samples for DNA or isotopic studies might be removed.

Once analysis is complete, the remains must then be either repatriated or placed in storage so that additional research may be conducted at a later date. If repatriated, the remains should be placed in cushioned containers for transport. If stored, they should be carefully wrapped and stored in environmentally controlled spaces.

Chapter summary

Once remains identified as human are discovered, it must be determined whether they are recent or archaeological and treated accordingly. Archaeological evidence consists of sites, artifacts, features, and ecofacts, all of which indirectly inform us about the past. Human remains, however, allow a direct view of the lives of past people.

When materials enter the archaeological record, they are subject to taphonomic processes that will affect whether they are preserved in a form that can be recognized by archaeologists and so recovered. These processes include mortuary practices that affect the body, bioturbation, saprophytic organisms that feed on the remains, soil pH, and general environment.

Once discovered, some remains may be excavated and removed, whereas others will be left in place or repatriated. Excavation and recordation must be conducted carefully to be able to document as many data as possible and are always done with dignity and respect.

If the remains are taken to a laboratory, additional recordation may be conducted and some testing of samples may be allowed. Human remains are always considered fragile and must be treated accordingly.

Key concepts and terms

anaerobic environments
anthropology
anthropologie de terrain
archaeology
archaeological record
artifacts
bioturbation
diagenesis
ecofacts
ethnography
ethnology
excarnation
features
necropolis
pH
preservation
radiograph (X-rays)
saprophytic organisms
sites
taphonomy

Chapter 3

In the laboratory
Description and basic analysis
of human remains

As we have seen, human remains can consist of a variety of materials, from bone to proteins. However, the most common type of remains consists of hard tissues, typically bones and teeth. In some cases, however, soft tissues are preserved and can be very informative. Soft tissues are the fleshy parts of the body, such as the muscles, skin, connective tissues, and organs. Any soft tissue that is found preserved would likely be desiccated or frozen and so would be "hard," but if rehydrated or thawed, it would again become "soft and wet."

The general techniques utilized in the analysis of individual skeletons include metric measurements to determine gross morphology (which can provide indicators of age, sex, and stature), methods to measure bone development, and methods to determine and describe any pathologies (e.g., disease, trauma, deformation, and nutritional stress). The skeletons of subadults differ in morphology from those of adults and present their own analytical challenges (Scheuer and Black 2004; Baker et al. 2005; Schaefer et al. 2009; Cunningham et al. 2016).

Laboratory treatment

When handling human remains, analysts should remember that they represent actual people, and great care should be exercised to ensure they are treated with dignity and respect. Of equal importance, to avoid damaging or altering the bone, care should be taken to never mix elements of one group of bones with those of other groups or to misplace them. Even poorly preserved remains can contain important data and should be analyzed with the same care as well-preserved remains (Brickley and Buckberry 2015).

Some basic rules apply to laboratory treatment. These include (1) do not wash the bone, and only clean what is necessary to take measurements; (2) avoid, if possible, writing catalog numbers on the bone; (3) do not unnecessarily use preservatives; and (4) do not glue pieces together. Of course, there are always times when such treatment is required (e.g., Cassman et al. 2006). In some cases, casts (plaster or plastic) or 3-D scans can be made to serve as a proxy record of a bone if it were to be repatriated. If permitted, remains should be photographed for the record. In some cases, such as mummified remains, computerized tomography (CT) scanning could be employed to discover and record bone morphology that might not be apparent without destructive analyses. In some cases, such as mummified remains, specialized photography could be employed to discover and record tattoos or other body modifications (e.g., Samadelli et al. 2015).

The terminology used in the identification and classification of human remains is fairly extensive (see Buikstra and Ubelaker 1994:177–182; White and Folkens 2005; White et al. 2012; Schaefer et al. 2009; Mann 2017). For the skeleton, the basic terms consist of the name of the bone (**element**); the side of the body (left or right, although some bones, such as vertebrae, have no such orientation but may be referred to as axial); which part of the bone (**proximal** [the end nearest the center of the body], **distal** [the end most distant from the center of the body], or **shaft** [the midsection of limb bones]); the growing ends of many bones (**epiphyses**); and the joints (**articular surfaces**).

When pathologies or trauma are identified in either the skeleton or soft tissues, it is important to determine, if possible, when the event occurred. If it occurred prior to death, it is called **antemortem** (or premortem), such as a broken bone that shows evidence of healing or infection (which can only occur during life). If it is clear that the bone had been broken after death (e.g., a "dry" bone fracture), it is described as **postmortem**. If the trauma occurred approximately around the time of death (e.g., a blunt force trauma to the head that may have been the cause of death), it is classified as **perimortem**.

Skeletal remains

The most frequently recovered categories of human remains consist of bone and teeth, from isolated elements to complete skeletons. The bones of the skeleton have plasticity; that is, they change through time and reflect "a lifetime of interaction with the world, displaying physical responses to damage, mechanical stress, and disease" (Buzon 2012:60) and are both a "biological and cultural entity" (Agarwal 2016:130). The remains of adults are more commonly found, since their bones are typically more durable than those of subadults, whose remains tend to be more poorly preserved and fragmented such that they are sometimes not recognized in the field (e.g., Baker et al. 2005:11).

The identification and study of the skeleton is called **osteology**. The task of the osteologist is to identify which elements are present, their metric and nonmetric details, how many individuals they represent (the **minimum number of individuals [MNI]** in the collection), and if there is any evidence of pathology (disease) or trauma. These tasks are conducted using a variety of methods (e.g., DiGangi and Moore 2012b).

Bones of the skeleton

The adult human skeleton normally comprises 206 bones and 32 teeth (Figure 3.1). The skeleton is usually divided into two major closely associated groups of bones. The **axial skeleton** forms the core of the human skeletal system; it includes the cranium (skull), the vertebral column, the ribs, and the sternum. The **appendicular skeleton** includes the pectoral girdle (clavicles and scapulae); the pelvic girdle; and the bones of the arms, hands, legs, and feet. Detailed treatments of the morphology and description of the adult skeleton are provided in White and Folkens (2005), White et al. (2012), and Mann (2017). The skeletons of subadults are morphologically different and are described in Baker et al. (2005), Schaefer et al. (2009), and Cunningham et al. (2016). A brief overview of the general skeleton is presented here.

The skull (Figure 3.2) normally has 29 separate bones, many of which fuse together as an individual ages, along with 6 small bones (ossicles) of the inner ear. Some bones of the skull occur singly, such as the mandible (lower jaw); others occur in pairs, such as the maxilla (upper jaw) and zygomatics (cheekbones).

The vertebral column (spine) is composed of 24 movable vertebrae, of which there are 7 cervical (neck) vertebrae, 12 thoracic (upper back) vertebrae, and 5 lumbar (lower back) vertebrae. At the base of the vertebral column is the sacrum (4 or 5 fused sacral vertebrae)

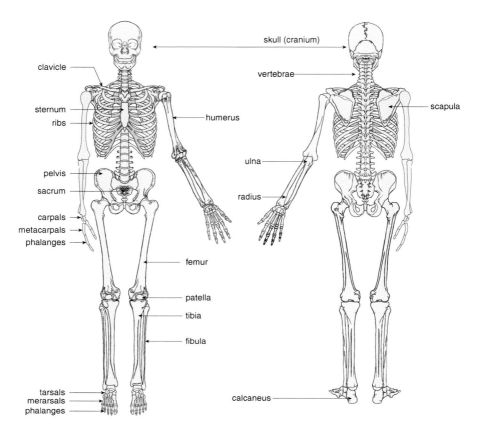

Figure 3.1 The major bones of the skeleton
Source: Author

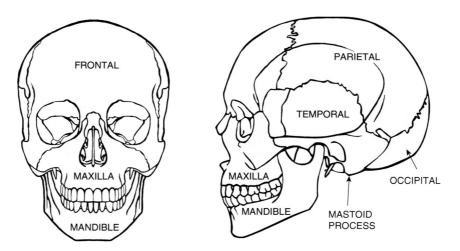

Figure 3.2 The major bones of the skull
Source: Author

and the coccyx (3 or 4 coccygeal vertebrae), a remnant of our remote tailed ancestors. Humans have 12 paired ribs (24 total), most of which are connected by cartilage to the sternum, forming a rib cage that protects the major organs.

The pectoral girdle consists of the scapula and clavicle that support the arms, each side having a humerus, ulna, radius, 8 carpals, 5 metacarpals, and 14 phalanges. The pelvic girdle consists of the pelvis (two sets of three fused bones: the ischium, the ilium, and the pubis) and supports the bones of the legs, each composed of a femur, tibia, fibula, patella, 7 tarsals (including the talus and calcaneus), 5 metatarsals, and 14 phalanges.

Bones are also divided into categories based on their shape. In humans (after Bass 1987:7), the **limb bones** (often called long bones) are tubular in cross-section and are relatively long (>20 cm). **Short bones** are small (<10 cm) tubular bones; these include the bones of the hands and feet, as well as the clavicles (collar bones). **Flat bones** include the pelvis, scapulae (shoulder blades), ribs, and sternum (breastbone). Such flat bones might be confused with cranial bones. **Irregular bones** (again, easy to confuse with some cranial bones) include the vertebrae, carpals (wrist bones), tarsals (ankle bones), and patellae (kneecaps).

Supernumerary bones

There may be a number of additional bones in a skeleton. In the skull, small cranial bones, called **wormian** (or sutural) bones (Figure 3.3), may occur along the margins of the **sutures** (junctions of bones), particularly at the occipital-parietal junctions. Other supernumerary bones could include extra vertebrae, ribs, hands, and feet (accessory ossicles).

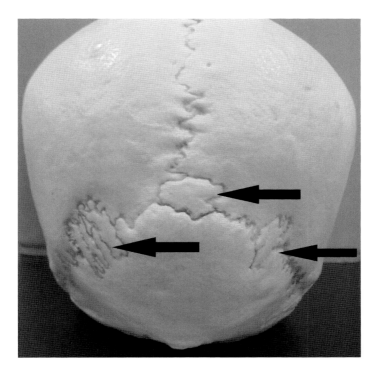

Figure 3.3 Extra bones (wormian or sutural bones) in a skull
Source: Author

Exostoses (e.g., bone spurs) may also be present. In many cases, these extra bones result from genetic issues, but in some cases, trauma is the cause.

Measuring and describing the skeleton

Each of the elements recovered is described and measured in some manner. For some purposes (e.g., stature estimations), the measurements of only complete specimens (perhaps reconstructed from fragments) can be used. In other cases, the measurements of fragmentary specimens can have analytical value. Nonmetric data (e.g., nonmeasurable aspects of anatomy, such as observations on preservation) are also recorded.

A number of basic tools are used to take skeletal measurements, always in the metric system (centimeters, millimeters). Both sliding (Figure 3.4a) and bow (or spreading) **calipers** are important basic tools. In addition, an **osteometric board** (Figure 3.4b) is used

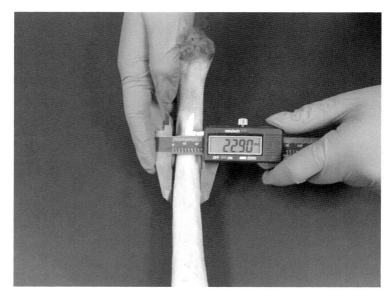

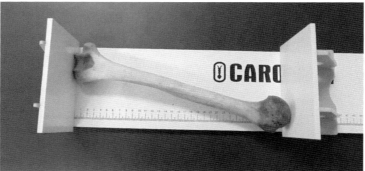

Figure 3.4 Some instruments used to measure bones: (a) sliding calipers, (b) an osteometric board

Source: Author

to measure tubular bones. Other osteometric tools used for more specialized purposes include a coordinate caliper and a head spanner (see Bass 1987:11). A new method of taking three-dimensional measurements (3-D geometric morphometrics) has now been developed and is useful for comparing overall shape differences between individuals, particularly in crania (e.g., Adams et al. 2013; Spradley and Jantz 2016; Errickson et al. 2017). Such measurements can be used to digitally "print" replicas of bones or other items (e.g., the projectile point in the pelvis of Kennewick Man), thus retaining metrically accurate models if the material is to be repatriated.

Metric traits

Metric (or quantitative) traits are those that can be empirically measured and given in numbers. The measurement of living people is called **anthropometry**, the measurement of skeletal remains is called **osteometry**, and the measurement of the skull is called craniometry. Most of the data derived from metric analyses are linear distances (e.g., length, width, thickness, and diameter) and angles defined by specific places on an element (as detailed by Bass [1987]). Simple metric measurements are useful for some purposes (e.g., estimations of stature), whereas indices (various combinations of absolute measurements) are used for other purposes. Pietrusewsky (2019) detailed techniques on the application of multivariate statistical procedures using traditional craniometric landmark data.

Nonmetric traits

Nonmetric traits are those that cannot be discovered by the metric measurements of the bones. These are variations in normal anatomy, such as variations in the number of bones (e.g., wormian bones in the skull), supernumerary (extra) teeth (e.g., extra molars), heterotopic ossification (unusual bone formation in soft tissue), crowding or impaction of teeth (which may result in a pathology), the natural variation in the shape of the bones (they are never exactly alike), variation in the number and placement of various foramina (nerve and blood vessel holes in the bone), degree of ossification (bone density), variation in the interior structure of the bone, and the like, as detailed in Mann et al. (2016).

Other nonmetric traits may be related to environmental influences or to circumstances relating to the life of the specific individual. An example of such a trait is the presence of **auditory exostoses**, the bony protuberances found in the ear canals of individuals who have spent a great deal of time in cold water (Özbek 2012; Kuzminsky et al. 2016) and can result in hearing loss.

Bone development and growth

Bone growth, and body growth in general, is most evident in the young, reaching terminal size by early adulthood (see Larsen 2015:9–10). Factors influencing growth include genetics and disease, but growth is most heavily influenced by diet and nutrition (Larsen 2015:9). Thus, children who are undernourished will experience slower growth rates.

Most bones begin their development and growth as cartilage. Mineralization (ossification) then proceeds from "ossification centers" to eventually form fully mineralized

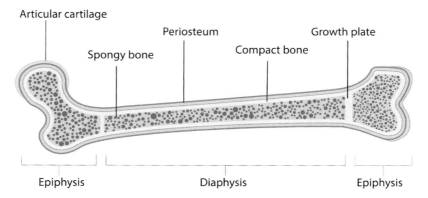

Figure 3.5 The general structure of a long bone
Source: Alamy Image ID: EG0XW9

mature bone. The cranial vault and clavicles are exceptions to this process, each developing from the ossification of membranes (Waldron 2009:12). Linear bones of the limbs,
hands, and feet (those with marrow cavities, such as the femur and humerus) begin with
three ossification centers, one at each end (**epiphysis**) and a third in the midsection (the
diaphysis) (Figure 3.5). The junction of the epiphyses and diaphysis is called the **metaphysis** where the growth plates are located. Once terminal growth has been reached at
approximately 20 years of age (Mielke et al. 2006:261), the diaphysis and epiphyses fuse
to form a single bone (although the fused epiphyseal suture will remain visible for years).
It is this sequence that permits age estimations of juvenile individuals.

Types of bone

Bone is living tissue composed of minerals (hydroxyapatite, calcium carbonate, and trace
elements) and organics (collagen, bone protein, fats, and lipids) in an approximately 2:1
ratio. Two general types of bone are recognized: cortical bone and cancellous bone (Waldron 2009:12).

   Cortical bone (also known as compact bone) is the dense layer of bone that forms the
exterior surface of the bone and protects its interior structure (see Figure 3.5). Cortical
bone provides the strength of a bone, and its thickness varies depending on the element.
For example, the cortical bone in a femur is very thick, whereas it is thin on ribs and
vertebrae. Cortical bone makes up some 80% of the bone mass of a skeleton.

   Cancellous bone (also known as spongy or trabecular bone; see Figure 3.5) makes
up the interior of a bone and forms a latticework of structural members (trabeculae) that
support the marrow. Cancellous bone is prominent in the ends of some limb bones (e.g.,
femur and humerus), in the center of flat bones (e.g., sternum and ribs), and constitutes
most of the pelvis and vertebrae.

   Marrow is contained within bones. Red marrow, found in flat bones and the ends of
the long bones, produces blood cells. Yellow marrow, found in the shafts of long bones,
is stored fat.

Remodeling

Bone **remodeling** (or bone metabolism) is the process by which old bone is replaced by new bone (see Waldron 2009:17–19). Old bone (excluding dental tissues) is broken down into its chemical constituents (e.g., calcium) and transferred to the blood, a process called **resorption**. In concert with resorption is the replacement of the "old" bone by new bone, a process called remodeling, or new bone replacement. This bone "maintenance" ensures that the bone remains healthy and strong. This is an ongoing process, and there is a complete replacement of bone about every 10 to 20 years, depending on the specific skeletal element.

As a result of remodeling, some pathological conditions apparent in bone will slowly fade, making identification increasingly difficult. In other cases, such as a healed broken bone that had been poorly set, the pathology (the fracture) will remain easily detectable. For chemical analyses, bone will only retain data from the ten years or so prior to death.

The resorption/remodeling process is also applicable to bone affected by disease or trauma. Traumatized bone is resorbed and initially replaced by woven bone, a weak and immature or pathologic bone (e.g., at a fracture repair) with disorganized collagen fibers. Woven bone is then remodeled into strong lamellar bone, mature and healthy bone with organized collagen fibers. A good example of the remodeling of traumatized bone is the loss of a tooth. Any remnant tooth root will be resorbed, and the space left by the tooth will eventually be filled in with new bone, although likely below the old gum line (Figure 3.6).

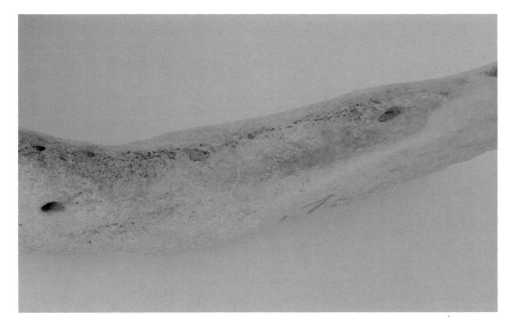

Figure 3.6 Remodeled tooth sockets in a mandible

Source: Author

Deossification

In the process of bone remodeling, calcium is resorbed back into the body to be used, in part, in new bone formation. Recycled calcium from remodeling and new calcium from diet assures a constant supply of calcium for metabolic purposes and is also used to form new bone. However, if resorption outpaces new bone formation (as it will after the age of 25 to 30), there will be a resultant loss of bone density (**deossification**) and the skeleton will begin to degenerate. Mild deossification is called osteopenia, and its more severe form is called osteoporosis, where bone loss compromises the integrity and strength of the bone. Bone can also be lost due to insufficient calcium in the diet (e.g., Huss-Ashmore et al. 1982) or vitamin deficiencies (see Brickley et al. 2005, 2006).

Bone histology

Histology is the microscopic study of tissues. In bioarchaeology, the majority of tissues studied is bone (Crowder and Stout 2012; also see Martin et al. 1985; Martin 1991; Trammel and Kroman 2012). Bone histology emphasizes histomorphology, the microscopic analysis of bone structure, to deduce a variety of conditions, including "skeletal growth, pathology, maintenance, and repair" (Martin 1991:55). Diagenesis, the alteration of chemical or structural components of bones and teeth based on time and environmental factors, is an important aspect affecting preservation of tissue structure.

The goals of bone histological analyses are to examine bone remodeling in populations and to identify patterns that might indicate differential health status (Martin 1991:55; Stout and Crowder 2012). Histological analyses may also provide information that helps to distinguish human from nonhuman bone (e.g., France 2017; Crowder et al. 2018a, 2018b), age at death (e.g., Streeter 2012; Gocha et al. 2019), biomechanical function (e.g., Gosman 2012; Maggiano 2012), and pathological conditions (e.g., De Boer et al. 2013). Histological analysis of bone should include "measure of *bone quantity* (cortical thickness, cortical area, and rate of remodeling) and *bone quality* (quantification of the size, distribution, and level of mineralization of discrete units of bone)" (Martin 1991:55, italics in original).

Another histological approach is the study of the skeletal intermediary organization (IO) of bone between the level of the cell (e.g., osteon, Figure 3.7) and the organ (the bone structure) (Stout 1989:41). The basic functions of the IO are "growth, modeling (changes in geometry of bones), remodeling [e.g., pathology], repair, and homeostasis" (Stout 1989:41). An understanding of the IO may permit the inference of a variety of factors, including disease, nutrition, and mechanical usage (e.g., Marchi et al. 2006). It may also be possible to use bone histology to identify the species of origin of bone (e.g., Martiniaková et al. 2006) and even to identify disease (e.g., von Hunnius et al. 2006).

Most archaeological bone specimens consist of "dry bone," so called since most of the organic constituents have been lost by the time they are recovered. As such, it is important to understand the taphonomy of the recovered specimens (Bell 2012). Examination of "dry bone" for evidence of paleopathology is conducted using microscopy. However, it appears that only a few conditions exhibit a specific histomorphology, including Paget's disease, osteoporosis, hyperparathyroidism, and possibly osteomalacia (De Boer et al. 2013). Otherwise, histology can only assist in the general diagnostic process, as many pathological conditions can affect bone histology in similar ways (De Boer et al. 2013).

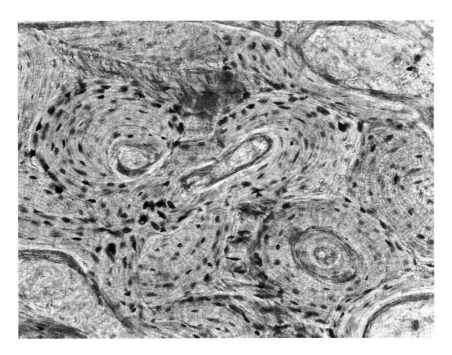

Figure 3.7 Osteons in human bone
Source: Alamy Image ID: AJBY3R

Dentition

Dentition refers to the teeth. Osteologists are interested in their formation, eruption, condition, wear, loss, preservation, and relationships to social conditions (e.g., Hillson 2005; Hammerl 2012; Irish and Scott 2016; Zinni and Crowley 2017a; Scott et al. 2018; Scott and Pilloud 2019). Here, we consider only human dentition, although dental anthropology in general also studies the teeth of other primates (e.g., Irish and Scott 2016:3). Several brief histories of dental anthropology are presented by Rose and Burke (2006) and Scott (2016).

Teeth are of great interest, as they are typically numerous and very dense, so they preserve extremely well. They preserve data on diet, health, nutrition, and even tool use. Dentition is influenced by genetics and so can contain information regarding ancestry, ethnicity, migrations, and evolution. Because teeth do not remodel, this information can be well preserved (Irish and Scott 2016:3). Teeth are also among the best places to recover preserved DNA.

Describing teeth

Teeth are divided into four separate types; incisors, canines, premolars, and molars. Each tooth has three major sections: the **crown** (the upper portion of the tooth with the **enamel**), the neck, and the root (Irish 2016a:88; Scott and Pilloud 2019). Teeth are aligned in the **mandible** and **maxilla** along a parabolic arch, a shape unique to humans. For analytical purposes, the jaws are divided into quadrants; the right and left sides of both the mandible and maxilla. The dental formula denotes the number and type of teeth in one quadrant. When added together and multiplied by four, the dental formula gives the total number of teeth. Each tooth type is designated by a letter: M = molars, P = premolars, C = canines, and I = incisors. In general, the left and right quadrants are symmetrical, although some asymmetry may be present, so it is important to describe each quadrant (Scott et al. 2016:257).

Humans have two sets of teeth, the **primary** dentition (deciduous, or "baby," teeth) (Figure 3.8) and the **secondary** dentition (permanent teeth). Normally, there are 20 primary teeth: 2 incisors, 1 canine, and 2 molars located in each quadrant, with a dental formula of 2–1–2 (5 teeth per quadrant, for a total of 20 teeth). The primary teeth are lost as a child matures; the crowns exfoliate (fall out), whereas the roots are resorbed (see Irish 2016a:90).

The buds of the secondary teeth form in the jaw below the primary dentition (some even prenatally) and erupt in a relatively well-known sequence (see Table 3.1). Normally, there are 32 secondary teeth: 2 incisors, 1 canine, 2 premolars, and 3 molars in each

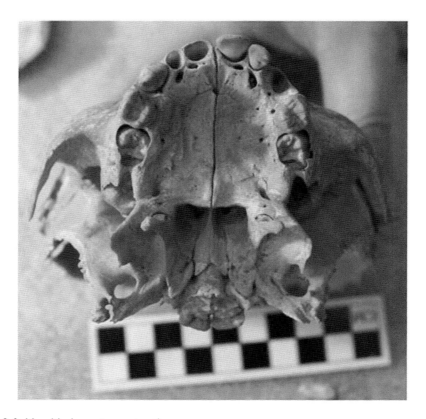

Figure 3.8 Mandibular primary teeth

Source: Marni LaFleur

quadrant, with a dental formula of 2–1–2–3 (8 teeth per quadrant, for a total of 32 teeth). If secondary teeth are somehow lost in life, there are no natural replacements.

Many methods are used to label teeth (Zinni and Crowley 2017b:115–116), with the simplest called the Universal Numbering System (UNS), where the primary teeth are labeled with letters (A to T) and the secondary teeth are assigned numbers from 1 to 32; for example, the third secondary mandibular molar on the right side would be numbered 32. A second commonly used system is that of the Fédération Dentaire Internationale (FDI). In the FDI method, each quadrant is numbered (1 to 4 for secondary teeth and 5 to 8 for primary teeth) and each tooth within the quadrant is numbered (1 to 8 for secondary teeth and 1 to 5 for primary teeth). Thus, the third secondary mandibular molar on the right side would be numbered 48 (quadrant 4, tooth 8). It is also common to label teeth based on their tooth type and position; for example, the third secondary mandibular molar on the right side would be designated M_3, the location of the number indicating lower right and the letter designating molar (lowercase letter for primary teeth and an uppercase letter for secondary teeth). This is the same tooth as the one numbered 32 in the UNS system and 48 in the FDI system. There are also other less frequently used systems.

Metric and nonmetric dental traits

A variety of dental traits can be recorded, and these traits can be used to infer population affinity (Scott et al. 2016, 2018; Scott and Pilloud 2019). Incisors have an incisal edge, but all other teeth have at least one cusp, the elevated portion of the crown (canines have one, premolars have two or more, maxillary molars have three or four, and mandibular molars have four or five) (Scott et al. 2016:248). The number of cusps on the molars is an important trait. For example, most people (ca. 99%) have four cusps on M^1, three major ones with the fourth (the hypocone) being a late evolutionary addition in mammals. However, there is considerable variation in the presence of a hypocone in M^2 and M^3, and the frequency of that trait in a population is important in comparing them with other geographically dispersed populations (Scott et al. 2016:247–248). The number of cusps on other teeth can also vary.

Other nonmetric traits are also important. For example, the presence of **shovel-shaped incisors** is a feature used to help identify Asian and American Indian populations (e.g., Irish 2016b). The number of roots in the different teeth also varies, with the presence of a third root on some molars being a Native American trait (Turner 1971). Tooth shape is determined using a specific mathematical formula of measurements (Bernal 2007), and tooth size also varies in populations (Hemphill 2016). Other nonmetric traits include supernumerary teeth and supernumerary cusps on molars; for example, some Australian Aborigines have six cusps (Townsend and Brown 1981). Finally, tooth wear can be measured to explore diet, pathologies, and age (e.g., Eshed et al. 2006).

Finally, nonmetric dental traits can be the result of the activities of an individual; that is, use wear (Stojanowski et al. 2016a). Such activities include using teeth to process fibers for basketry (e.g., Sutton 1988a), clenching a pipe in one's mouth, the toothpick grooves in Neandertal teeth (Estalrrich et al. 2017), and using the teeth to pressure-flake stone tools (Larsen 1985; Milner and Larsen 1991). Purposeful modification of teeth is a separate issue (e.g., Burnett and Irish 2017) and is discussed later.

Basic analysis of skeletal remains

The first step in the analysis of human remains is their basic description, including any observable variability in the bones (Nawrocki et al. 2018:5). Comparisons of the descriptive data to other data sets is used to generate estimations of age, sex, stature, and ancestry (Nawrocki et al. 2018:5) and to formulate a biocultural profile (see Chapter 9).

Most of these analyses require data obtained in a laboratory setting to assure proper measurements, sample selection, adequate data for MNI calculations, and the like. However, if researchers are not allowed the time and facilities for proper analysis, a field analysis must be conducted, often with inadequate resources. In such cases, only a minimal amount of information can be obtained. In addition, analyses are hindered by limited comparative materials and often small sizes of archaeological samples.

Determining the minimum number of individuals

The MNI is an estimation of the minimum number of individuals within an analytical unit. The analytical unit could be a site, a cemetery within a site, a mass grave, a small grave feature, an excavation unit, or even a level within an excavation unit. It is important to define the analytical unit prior to analysis, and it should relate to something of cultural meaning (e.g., a grave) rather than some arbitrary entity such as an excavation unit.

MNI estimations are determined by counting the most abundant element in the sample. When using this method, it is important to determine the age categories (and sex, if possible) of the individuals in the assemblage and to identify the side (left or right) of bilateral elements. For example, the presence of four complete adult left humeri would indicate an MNI of four, since you cannot get four left arms from two or three people. Although there may be more than four people in the assemblage, the *minimum* number is four. If there are four complete left humeri but five left femora from adults, the MNI is five – the minimum number of people needed to account for the five left femora. If you have five complete adult femora but do not know whether they are left or right, the MNI would be three; because each person has two femora, the elements must represent at least three people. The same procedure applies to each age (and sex) category.

The presence of fragmented, disarticulated, or commingled remains could complicate the assessment of MNI, depending on the analytical unit employed. If an MNI based on femora was three in one excavation unit and an MNI based on humeri were three from another unit, the total MNI could range from three to six. If the remains are fragmentary, it may be necessary to use proximal or distal ends as the basis for determining MNI. Care must be taken when estimating these numbers.

Estimating age at death

It is not (yet) possible to determine the precise age of a person at death strictly from skeletal remains due to the variation of indicators by sex and population. Thus, the ages at death of humans are commonly divided into age categories, here defined as (1) **infant** (up to 2 years), (2) **juvenile** (2 to 10 years), (3) **adolescent** (11 to 21 years) (all combined into a category of **subadult**), and (4) **adult** (21 and older).

Age at death is estimated using a variety of techniques (Uhl 2012; Langley et al. 2017; Schaefer et al. 2018), none of which should be used in isolation. For juveniles, dental development and eruption sequences and epiphyseal fusion are commonly used. For adults, the most common method is looking at the pubic symphysis and the auricular surfaces of the pelvis. Sternal rib ends are used sometimes but are not often preserved (but are common in forensic cases). In the absence of the pelvis, the closure of cranial sutures might be used to obtain a very general age estimate. A new method of aging older (50+) adults involves measurement of the pulp chambers of teeth (D'Ortenzio et al. 2018). Transition analysis, a statistical analysis of a number of traits, has become a popular aging method and works well for aging older individuals

Epiphyseal fusion (the fusing of the epiphyses with the diaphyses, typically in the bones of the leg) is a good indicator of general age. Completely unfused epiphyses indicate an infant or early juvenile, partly fused ends suggest an older subadult, and fully fused bones are likely those of adults (Figure 3.9) (Baker et al. 2005:Tables 10.1 to 10.5; also see Langley et al. 2017:Figure 10.2). Phalanx epiphyseal fusion can also be used to estimate age. Phalanges complete fusion between the ages of 13 and 15 in females and 15 and 16 in males (Scheuer and Black 2004). It is common that estimates of the degree of fusion

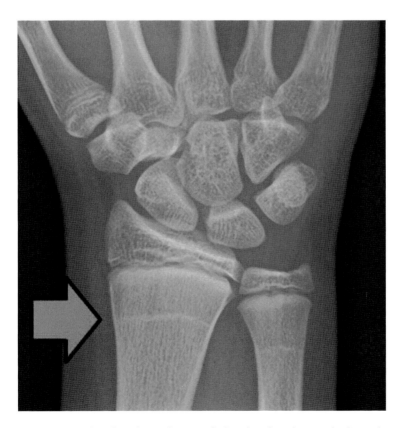

Figure 3.9 Radiograph of unfused epiphyses of the distal radius and ulna, also note the Harris line (arrow)

Source: Public domain

are based on visual examination, but much better techniques are the use of radiographs, magnetic resonance imaging (MRI), or CT scans (Schaefer et al. 2018).

Although no longer commonly used, the closure of cranial sutures (Figure 3.10), both endocranially (interior of the skull) and ectocranially (exterior of the skull), might be useful to estimate general age (e.g., White and Folkens 2005:369–372), particularly

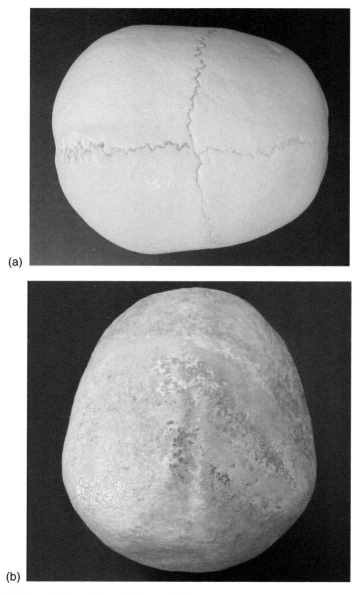

(a)

(b)

Figure 3.10 Unfused (a) and fused (b) cranial sutures

Source: Author

in the field. The cranial sutures of infants and juveniles are completely unfused and cranial bones may be only loosely connected. Subadults have loose sutures, with closure proceeding with age. The suture lines can remain visible throughout adulthood, but by the time an individual is about 60 years old, the sutures might be obliterated. However, suture closure and obliteration schedules seem to vary considerably with population and sex.

Dental attributes may also be employed to estimate age at death. The analysis of dental eruption is useful, as both the sequence and timing of tooth eruption and replacement are reasonably well known (Table 3.1) and can help (coupled with other indicators) estimate the age of subadults (see Liversidge 2016; Zinni and Crowley 2017a; Ubelaker 2018a). In the growth phase of teeth (in infants and subadults), enamel is deposited daily in a series of very thin incremental layers, called **cross-striations** (Antoine et al. 2019:230), that can be seen microscopically in thin section. It is possible to count these layers to obtain an age of death.

General tooth wear is also an indicator of age (e.g., Miles 2000; Oliveira et al. 2006), but diet is also a major factor. Tooth microstructure (Antoine et al. 2019) and the dimensions of the pulp chamber within teeth (e.g., Luna 2006) may also be used to estimate skeletal age.

Other methods of estimating age include analyses of the **pubic symphysis** (Suchey and Brooks 1986a, 1986b), the surface of the ilium where it joins the sacrum (Lovejoy et al. 1985a, 1985b; but see Storey 2006); the morphology of the basiocciput (where the occipital bone meets the foramen magnum at the base of the skull) (Tocheri and Molto 2002); and sternal rib end morphology (e.g., Yoder et al. 2001). Bone histology is also a useful technique for age determination, as osteon density increases with age (e.g., Crowder et al. 2016, 2018a, 2018b).

Table 3.1 General ages of primary and secondary tooth eruptions (from Irish 2016a:90 and Liversidge 2016:Figure 12.1)

	Primary	Secondary
Maxillary teeth		
First incisor	8–12 months	7–8 years
Second incisor	9–12 months	8–9 years
Canine	16–22 months	11–12 years
First premolar	N/A	10–12 years
Second premolar	N/A	10–12 years
First molar	13–18 months	6 years
Second molar	24–30 months	12 years
Third molar	N/A	18 years
Mandibular teeth		
First incisor	6–10 months	6–7 years
Second incisor	10–16 months	7–8 years
Canine	16–22 months	9–10 years
First premolar	N/A	10–12 years
Second premolar	N/A	10–12 years
First molar	14–18 months	6 years
Second molar	22–30 months	12 years
Third molar	N/A	18 years

On the other hand, some research has indicated that these methods of age at death estimates may not be suitable for all populations (Schmitt 2004; Buckberry 2015). It is also possible that these methods may be biased, reflecting the age structure of the reference sample (Bocquet-Appel and Masset 1982), one of the paradoxes noted by Wood et al. (1992). Nevertheless, there is promising work on a new technique called transition analysis (e.g., Boldsen et al. 2002) that has the potential to be more objective and accurate by attempting to resolve some of the problems associated with estimating adult age.

Estimating sex

The second basic analytical determination is the sex of the individual. One can distinguish between an assessment of sex and an estimation of sex (Spradley and Jantz 2011). An assessment of sex is done using subjective visual characteristics, such as those visible on the pelvis and skull. An estimation of sex is reliant on more objective metric data analyzed using statistical models such as discriminant analysis.

The vast majority of humans are either male or female, with a very small percentage (less than 1%) being **intersexual** (having variations in chromosomes, gonads, hormones, or genitals). General differences between the sexes are referred to as **sexual dimorphism**. Two broad categories of sexual characteristics can be identified: primary and secondary. **Primary sexual characteristics** are the soft tissue reproductive anatomy: either a vagina or penis. **Secondary sexual characteristics** develop after puberty and consist of morphological changes in the skeleton, such as a broadening of the pelvis (although this characteristic has issues, see Walrath [2017]), or size and robustness of skeletal elements. In addition, there are changes in the soft tissues, such as the development of facial and body hair (primarily in males) and the development of breasts (primarily in females).

For infants and juveniles, a determination of sex mostly relies on the presence of primary sexual characteristics, since secondary sexual characteristics were undeveloped at the time of death. However, as most archaeological specimens are osteological, it is difficult to determine sex in infants and juveniles using primary or secondary characteristics, although the older the child, the better the estimate (e.g., Baker et al. 2005). However, recent advances in the measurement and analysis of juvenile skeletal remains has made sex determination more reliable (Aris et al. 2018; Spradley and Stull 2018), and it is also possible to determine the sex of subadults using **ancient DNA (aDNA)** (e.g., Skoglund et al. 2013; Geller 2017b; Nieves-Colón and Stone 2019:529–530; see Chapter 8).

For adults, primary sexual characteristics would be used if present, as in mummified remains. However, most remains are osteological, and one must rely on the morphological traits of the skeleton. In adults, sexual dimorphism in the skeleton is not significant and there is no single skeletal indicator of sex. Whereas the skeletal elements of females tend to be smaller and less robust than those of males, there is significant overlap in metrics. Any single metric can offer a fair to reasonable probability of correct sex estimate, but concordance of multiple lines of evidence can greatly increase confidence.

The sex of adults can be assessed using several different methods of osteological analysis (Garvin 2012; Moore 2012; Rowbotham 2016), some of which can be applied in the field. Observations and measurements that can be made in the field include examining traits of the postpubescent pelvis (but see Walrath 2017), such as the size of the "passage" through the complete pelvis (Figure 3.11a), width of the **sciatic notch** in the ilium (wider in females) (Figure 3.11b), and **subpubic angle** (Figure 3.11c) (e.g., Phenice

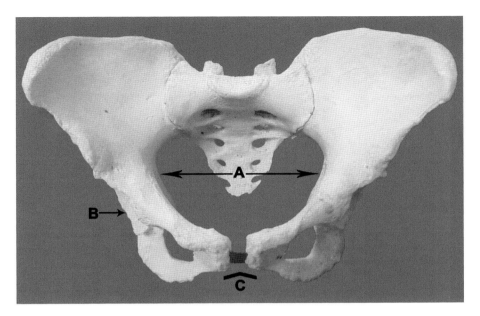

Figure 3.11 Several methods for estimating the sex of an adult: (a) the size of the "passage" through the complete pelvis; (b) the width of the sciatic notch; and (c) the subpubic angle

Source: Author

1969). Other methods include a discriminant analysis of the femur and humerus (Dittrick and Suchey 1986), the femoral neck diameter (e.g., Stojanowski and Seidemann 1999), the metrics of hand and foot bones (e.g., Wilbur 1998), and cranial shape (Nikita and Michopoulou 2018).

General skull morphology can also be used to estimate sex. Williams and Rogers (2006) suggested that the size and architecture of the skull, the size of the **mastoid process** and the **supraorbital ridge** (both typically larger in males), the size and shape of the nasal aperture, and perhaps the gonial angle of the mandible (but see Upadhyay et al. 2012) are traits to use in combination (Figure 3.12). Using these methods, bioarchaeologists assess the probability of the sex of an individual on an ordinal scale, normally 1 to 5 (Buikstra and Ubelaker 1994). In this method, definitively female is 1, probable female is 2, indeterminate is 3, probable male is 4, and definitively male is 5. Most recently, aDNA has been used to sex an individual (Geller 2017b; Nieves-Colón and Stone 2019:529–530).

In addition, statistical techniques have been developed for dealing with estimating the sex of fragmentary skeletal material (Kjellström 2004). An interactive computer program, Fordisc 3.0 (Ousley and Jantz 2012; Jantz and Ousley 2017), can be used for the classification of adults by ancestry and sex using any combination of standard metric measurements. For more detail on sexing techniques, refer to the discussions in Bass (1987:200–206), Buikstra and Ubelaker (1994:16–21), White and Folkens (2005:385–398), Garvin (2012), and Spradley and Stull (2018).

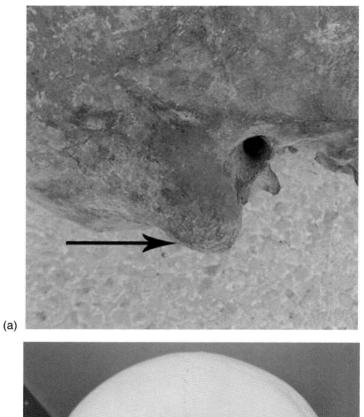

(a)

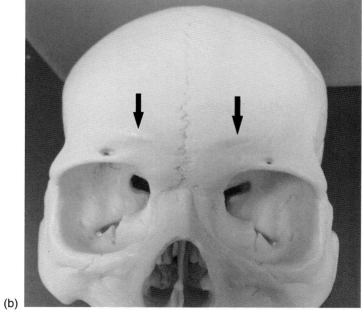

(b)

Figure 3.12 Several important sex markers on the skull: (a) the mastoid process and (b) the supraorbital ridge

Source: Author

Sex and gender

It is important to remember that sex and **gender** are different categories of analysis, even if commonly conflated. In anthropology and osteology, sex is generally a binary biological classification based on reproductive anatomy, that is, either male or female (or intersex). Gender, on the other hand, is a description of the culturally defined role an individual plays in their society – nonbinary categories that include heterosexuals, homosexuals, transvestites, eunuchs, transsexuals, and others. One of the issues involved in the study of past sex and gender is the common projection of a standard western binary classification onto past societies and people (Joyce 2008, 2017:1; also see Holliman 2011; Geller 2017a, 2019). Other societies may have been less binary than our own.

As gender is a cultural construct, its identification in human remains is difficult. The process begins with the identification of the sex of an individual, although this is not always straightforward (see earlier and Walrath 2017). Once sex is assigned, comparisons of associated artifacts and activity wear patterns on the skeleton could be used to model gender roles, although this approach has issues based on assumptions of a binary system (Wesp 2017). These subjects are considered further in Chapter 10.

Estimating stature

Adult stature, or the height of a person, reflects ancestry, nutrition, and age. Stature is influenced by a number of factors, including genetics, environmental stress, nutritional intake, disease rates, and psychological stress. Stature estimations can be made using two basic approaches: mathematical and anatomical. The mathematical approach "uses regression formulae based on the correlation of individual skeletal elements to living stature" (Raxter and Ruff 2018:105). Such determinations are made using the measurements of long bones, primarily the femur and tibia, and usually follow general formulae devised by Trotter and Gleser (1952; also see Fully 1956; Trotter 1970, also see Moore and Ross 2012; Ousley 2012; Willey 2016; Langley 2017; Konigsberg and Jantz 2018; Ruff et al. 2019). The anatomical method uses the measurements of various skeletal elements from head to toe "added up" to form an estimate (Raxter and Ruff 2018:105).

However, since populations vary widely, there is no universal, reliable measure. In addition, the comparative data from which mathematical estimates are made come from contemporary populations that may or may not relate to prehistoric ones. Thus, different prehistoric populations require different formulae. Stature tables for American whites (male and female), American blacks (male and female), and Mesoamericans (male and female) were provided by Bass (1987:22–29). Estimates of stature of various specific populations have been developed by Formicola and Franceschi (1996), Ruff et al. (2012), Sládek et al. (2015), and Mays (2016). Fordisc 3.0 can be used to estimate stature on modern forensic remains from bone measurements and also for nineteenth-century white and black individuals. It has custom-made reference equations for different ancestry groups and for males and females, as well as an "all" function for when sex or ancestry is known.

Estimations of ancestry

To estimate ancestry is to place remains into broad categories of human variation: populations that vary due to evolutionary adaptations. Based on current knowledge of the skeleton, ancestry can only be generally estimated, primarily from the skull and dentition (Bass

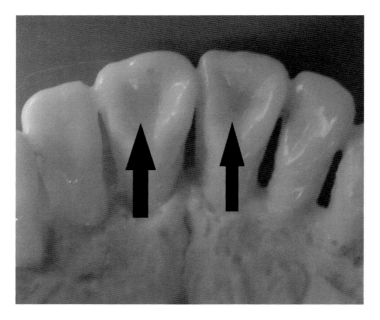

Figure 3.13 An example of shovel-shaped incisors

Source: Author

1987:83; DiGangi and Hefner 2012; Walsh-Henry and Boys 2015; Spradley and Weisensee 2017; Ousley et al. 2018). The skulls of Europeans, Africans, Asians, and Native Americans exhibit a number of distinguishable characteristics (see Bass 1987:83–92). One of the indicators of Asians and Native Americans is the presence of shovel-shaped incisors (Figure 3.13), a depression present in the lingual aspect of the maxillary incisors (Zinni and Crowley 2017a:371).

Other characteristics, such as forehead shape, mandible shape, **prognathism** (a measure of the jaw relative to the plane of the face), and dental traits may also be indicative of ancestry (e.g., Turner 1994). The development of metric standards in the measurement and analysis of certain landmarks on the skull and mandible are now being employed (Spradley and Jantz 2016), but the task remains difficult.

Fordisc 3.0 can also be used to estimate ancestry from both modern and archaeological samples (using William W. Howells Worldwide Craniometric Database). You can also import your own databases into Fordisc 3.0 and compare unknowns to knowns for group classification. Other methods use either nonmetric traits or morphoscopic traits to estimate ancestry or biological affinity.

Soft tissue and other remains

Soft tissues such as skin, muscle, organs, and even brains are occasionally recovered, although usually from mummies. In such cases, the tissues are examined from a medical perspective to determine the presence of any pathologies, such as cancers, tumors, or arterial or lung disease. Any evidence of trauma (e.g., wounds, surgery, autopsy) would also be recorded. In addition, any evidence of purposeful body modification in the soft tissues, such as tattoos or piercings, would be documented.

Among the most interesting instances of soft tissue recovery is the occasional discovery of preserved brain tissue. One of the best examples of this is the 8,200-year-old cemetery at Windover in Florida, where some 91 of the 168 burials contained preserved brain tissue (e.g., Wentz 2012). Other uncommon remains include hair and paleofeces, each of which can provide a variety of data on diet, pharmacology, and lifestyle.

Hair

Human hair is sometimes recovered in archaeological contexts. Hair is of interest for a number of reasons, including determination of color, style, and biological data (e.g., chemistry).

Hair consists of two analytical parts. The internal (endogenous) portion of the hair contains a diachronic (over time) record of the metabolism of an individual during the growth phase of the hair. Hair grows about 1.25 cm per month, so the longer the hair, the longer the record. The analysis of the endogenous component can provide data on a number of issues, including diet, pollution, and toxicology (e.g., Benfer et al. 1978). Sandford (1984:97–268) suggested that calcium, magnesium, iron, zinc, copper, and manganese are the six primary elements that are important to study in hair.

In contrast, the exterior (exogenous) component of hair consists of materials that accumulated at some point in time on the surface of the hair (e.g., Sandford 1984:58; Sandford and Kissling 1993). An analysis of the exogenous component of hair can reveal details regarding external environmental conditions.

Hair may be preserved in a variety of circumstances, including general site soils (e.g., Grupe and Dörner 1989) and attached to (or as part of) artifacts. Hair found associated with specific individuals (e.g., mummies) whose age, sex, and/or pathologies are known are of special interest. Hair can also be radiocarbon dated, the follicles can be analyzed for aDNA (e.g., Bonnichsen et al. 2001), and isotopic analysis can help reveal details about past diet (Knudson et al. 2007).

Sandford (1984) studied hair from 168 individuals from Medieval Christian Period cemeteries in Sudan, one from the early Christian Period (AD 550 to 750), and one from the late Christian Period (AD 750 to 1450). It was determined that there had been little change in the basic diet between the two periods, but iron deficiency was identified as an issue (Sandford et al. 1983). In another study, Bresciani et al. (1991:164) employed X-ray fluorescence to determine the quantities of trace elements in the hair from the mummies discovered at Qilakitsoq, Greenland, showing an increase in heavy metal pollutants over the last 500 years. Hair has also been used to identify other compounds, including drugs; for example, Balabanova et al. (1995) identified cocaine and nicotine in the hair of a Peruvian mummy. Isotopic analysis of hair from Nubian mummies (Schwarcz and White 2004) revealed a pattern in the use of stored foods. Studies of hair in Peruvian mummies have revealed patterns of cortisol concentrations indicative of stress (also see page 98).

Most recently, Mora et al. (2017) examined single hairs from a number of mummified individuals from the Andes region, using liquid chromatography–isotope ratio mass spectrometry (LC/IRMS). It was revealed that early coastal hunter-gatherers relied on aquatic resources and that the early farmers living on the coast also relied on aquatic resources. However, other nearby farmers apparently used terrestrial resources seasonally. The Inca appear to have had a broader diet of mixed terrestrial and aquatic foods.

Fingernails and toenails

Fingernails and toenails are also found in archaeological contexts, although rarely. Such nails are primarily of keratin, a hardened protein that is also in hair. One of the conditions that can be detected in nails is Beau's lines (Zaiac and Walker 2013), which are horizontal ridges and indentations that can be observed visually. These lines are thought to be the result of a pause in growth of the nail reflecting some sort of metabolic or nutritional stress within the growth period of the nail (ca. six months prior to death). This source of metabolic stress could be injury to the nail, disease, or malnutrition (Dickson et al. 2005).

Paleofeces

Preserved ancient human fecal matter, or **paleofeces**, is sometimes recovered from archaeological sites (Bryant and Reinhard and 2012; also see Sutton et al. 2010). Paleofecal specimens contain the residues of food and other materials ingested by an individual and so constitute direct evidence of what was consumed. Materials may have been ingested for food, as condiments (Trigg et al. 1994; Sutton and Reinhard 1995), as medicine, and/or as part of ritual activities (Sobolik and Gerick 1992; Trigg et al. 1994). Paleofeces can also be used to investigate general health and nutrition, food processing, and food preparation (Reinhard and Bryant 1992:270–272; Rylander 1994). In addition, paleofeces may contain body fluids, chemicals, cellular elements, and bacteria. Unfortunately, paleofeces are only rarely recovered from sites due to poor preservation, lack of recognition in the field, and a tendency for such materials to be located away from the habitation areas typically excavated by archaeologists.

Paleofeces take three forms: coprolites, gut (intestinal) contents, or cess (e.g., Holden 1994:65–66). Coprolites are specimens that are individually distinct and are found either singly or in concentrations that probably represent latrine features. They usually are not associated with particular human remains, so they contain less information than is available from the gut contents of specific people.

Gut contents are materials preserved and recovered from the intestinal tract of an intact human body, such as a mummy. They can be associated with specific people of known age, sex, general health, and sometimes even social status, allowing a correlation of these factors with diet (Reinhard and Bryant 1995). For example, an analysis of the gut contents of Lindow Man, the 1,500-year-old body of an executed (sacrificed?) man found preserved in a peat bog in England (Holden 1986), showed that his last meal consisted of a number of grains, suggesting that he had eaten bread just prior to his death. The lack of evidence of psychotropic drugs, as are present in some other bog bodies, suggests that Lindow Man was not drugged before his demise.

Cess is a deposit formed by a mixture of numerous feces, such as would be found in a cesspit or privy, and often includes other debris, such as discarded artifacts. Materials recovered from cess cannot be used to reconstruct individual diet but can be useful in reconstructing group diet and health.

Dating human remains

Some understanding of the chronological placement of the human remains, accompanying grave goods, associated mortuary or commemorative features, and the like is necessary to document change through time. A variety of dating methods can be used to determine the age of remains and associated materials.

The initial method of dating is by association; if a body is in a Roman crypt, it probably is Roman and dates to the Roman period. The style of the crypt and inscriptions on it may allow for a more precise estimate. Second, if there are grave goods of known age, they can be used to date the remains; for example, pottery types are commonly used for such purposes. However, one cannot blindly assume that the associations noted earlier are good indicators, since a body could have been buried in an existing facility (e.g., a post-Roman person placed in an "old" Roman crypt) and sometimes "old" grave goods are placed in later burials. These methods can provide a general estimate of age, and it is best to use multiple and concordant data sets.

If needed, a number of chronometric dating techniques could be employed. For example, dendrochronology (tree ring dating; Nash 2002) might be used to date a wooden coffin or other wooden items in a grave. Dating obsidian tools using the obsidian hydration method (e.g., Rogers and Duke 2011) may be useful in some cases.

Perhaps the most common method of dating human remains is **radiocarbon dating**, a technique that measures the radioactive decay of carbon-14 atoms within an organic sample, allowing for the determination of a date of the death of the sample material (Taylor and Bar-Yosef 2014). Thus, this direct dating of human bone provides the date of the death of the person and is not reliant on presumed associations with other materials. However, only materials younger than about 50,000 years can be dated by radiocarbon. In addition, radiocarbon is a destructive analytical technique, and permission to conduct such studies may be required.

Chapter summary

In the laboratory, human remains must always be treated with care and respect. The skeleton normally consists of 206 bones and 32 teeth, although there is variation. The skeleton is often divided into an axial component (skull, vertebral column, rib cage, and sternum) and an appendicular component (arms, legs, and their support structures). Two types of bone are present in the skeleton: cortical (the compact exterior) and cancellous (the spongy interior). Bone remodels throughout life to keep the structure strong. In this process, old bone is broken down (resorbed) and new bone is formed. If old bone is resorbed faster than new bone can be formed, deossification will occur, resulting in osteoporosis. The study of the microscopic structure of bone (histology) can inform about age, health, and deossification.

Human dentition includes molars, premolars, canines, and incisors. In infants, 20 primary ("baby") teeth erupt and are later replaced by 32 secondary (permanent) teeth in a well-known sequence. Teeth are described by their metric and nonmetric traits, such as size and number of cusps. Certain dental traits, such as shovel-shaped incisors, can be used in estimations of ancestry.

Basic analysis of the skeleton includes the identification of the elements, documenting their metric and nonmetric traits, determining how many individuals are represented, and describing any pathologies or traumas. Next, attempts are made to estimate the age of the individual at death, their sex (and gender if possible), stature, and ancestry. All of these data combined can provide considerable information on a particular person.

Soft tissues (e.g., skin, muscle, brain) are sometimes recovered, mainly from mummies. Such tissues are examined for any evidence of disease (pathologies), trauma, or modification. Preserved hair, fingernails, and toenails can be analyzed for information such as nutrition, drug use, and environmental conditions. If paleofeces are recovered, they may provide information regarding diet, health, and social status.

Understanding the age of remains is always an important task that allows the researcher to place the individual within a cultural context. Age may be determined through a variety of techniques, including artifact or feature association, or direct dating methods, such as radiocarbon dating.

Key concepts and terms

adolescent
adult
ancient DNA (aDNA)
antemortem
anthropometry
appendicular skeleton
articular surfaces
auditory exostoses
axial skeleton
Beau's lines
calipers
cross-striations
crown
dentition
deossification
diaphysis
distal
element
enamel
epiphyses
exostoses
gender
histology
infant
intersexual
juvenile
mandible
mastoid process
maxilla
metaphysis
minimum number of individuals (MNI)
os pubis

osteology
osteometric board
osteometry
paleofeces
perimortem
postmortem
primary sexual characteristics
primary teeth
prognathism
proximal
pubic symphysis
radiocarbon dating
remodeling
resorption
sciatic notch
secondary sexual characteristics
secondary teeth
sexual dimorphism
shaft
shovel-shaped incisors
subadult
subpubic angle
supraorbital ridge
suture
wormian bones

Chapter 4

Treating the dead
The funerary system

Each society, past and present, employs an overall **funerary system** to treat the dead. This treatment includes both their body and soul, with the details of the systems being dependent on the belief system of that society (Parker Pearson 2003:5). Thus, treatment of the dead involves a sequence of specific behaviors following the belief system that varies depending on the identity and status of the deceased. Each society views this process differently.

Concepts of the body

What is the body? People from western societies (and western archaeologists) typically view the body as a tangible object, an individualized and "self-contained unit" with clear boundaries between its inside and outside (Duncan and Schwarz 2014:149). This is the body that is also a historical entity, in that it changes through life and contains a record of those changes (Sofaer 2006).

A second way to perceive a body is that of a social construct, being permeable with porous boundaries that can gain and lose aspects of personhood during life (see Duncan and Schwarz 2014:149; Sofaer 2006; also see Boutin 2016; Voas 2018). A third view is of the body as a political entity, something that embodies power and control (Van Wolputte 2004:254; also see Gramsch 2013). Bodies are also partible, with different animating aspects found in different places. Finally, bodies can be defined in relation to other bodies or objects, definitions that can be fluid. Thus, in many societies, a body is not just a thing to "dispose of" but continues to be an integral part of the living community (Shimada et al. 2015). These views, which are of immense anthropological interest, are reflected in the archaeological record by the treatment of the body before, during, and after "burial." If these concepts seem foreign, consider the presence, maintenance, and visitation of cemeteries within western cities.

Cultural constructs of death

What happens when a person dies? Most societies have some concept of an afterlife into which the "soul," and in some cases even the body itself, would enter. In such a system, biological death may just be one of the steps in the journey from birth to ancestorship or even to reincarnation. The mortuary process could be seen as a transformation of social identities from the living to the dead (Fowler 2013).

One could conceptualize a funerary system as reflecting the societal view of the transition from life to death; that is, a rite of passage with preliminal, liminal, and postliminal stages (e.g., Hertz 1960; also see Metcalf and Huntington 1991). Prior to death, in the preliminal stage, "the body is composed of flesh and bone, the soul is in the world of the living, and the mourners are within their proper social roles" (Rakita and Buikstra 2005:98). Death, the liminal stage, could be viewed as the "transition from life" (Metcalf and Huntington 1991:38) in which the body, soul, and mourners assume different roles. The body begins to decompose, the soul leaves the body, and the mourners are "removed from [normal] society because of their bereavement and kinship obligations to the deceased" (Rakita and Buikstra 2005:98). The mourning and commemorative behaviors of the liminal stage continue until the conclusion of the mortuary process, the postliminal stage, at which time the remains of the body (in whatever form) are placed in a permanent facility, the soul enters the realm of the ancestors, and the mourners reenter normal society.

In some systems, such as in ancient Egypt, more than just the soul enters the afterlife. The body accompanies the soul, and so it is necessary for the body to be preserved so it can function after death. In addition, the material items needed by the deceased in the afterlife, such as tools, games, and food, accompany the body and soul.

Keep in mind that the dead come in all ages and conditions, from neonatal to geriatric and from relatively healthy to diseased or traumatized. It seems that most archaeological attention has been given to the adult dead, partly due to issues of preservation and opportunities for analysis (e.g., children are difficult to assess sex), but as children become more visible in the archaeological record, consideration of them has increased (Dawson-Hobbis 2017; Murphy and Le Roy 2017a, 2017b; also see Baxter 2008; Halcrow and Tayles 2011; Halcrow et al. 2012).

The funerary system

Every society maintains a funerary system, a prescribed and comprehensive process by which that society deals with the body and soul of its dead. Archaeologists have used a variety of terms to refer to such systems, including "burial patterns," "burial rites," "mortuary practice," "funerary ritual," or "disposal of the dead." This latter phrase has a long history of use (Sprague 2005:3) but is a misnomer, since in many societies the dead are never really gone, but are "always present and revered" (Sprague 2005:9).

Funerary systems are often regarded as reflecting social structure such as age, sex, gender, social position, and personal identity (e.g., Binford 1971). Although that is certainly the case in most systems, it is also thought that philosophical–religious belief systems hold an "essential place . . . in the study and interpretation of mortuary practices and remains" (Carr 1995:106). Such belief systems may have included "many categories of socially institutionalized 'folk' beliefs and world-view assumptions about disease, dying, death, the soul, the afterlife, and the cosmos" (Carr 1995:107). They are complex systems.

In some instances, the dead may be from a different society (such as an enemy), so would be subjected to a different and perhaps less complex funerary system, one that may not include any commemorative behaviors. Some individuals, such as unrecovered war dead, received little to no mortuary treatment but were likely commemorated.

Here, a funerary system is defined as having three aspects: (I) pretreatment of the living, (II) mortuary treatment, and (III) commemorative behaviors (Figure 4.1), all of which can span through time (Figure 4.2). These aspects might correspond to the three stages of a transition, preliminal, liminal, and postliminal (see Metcalf and Huntington 1991:29–33). However, this suggested correspondence should be seen as only a very broad association.

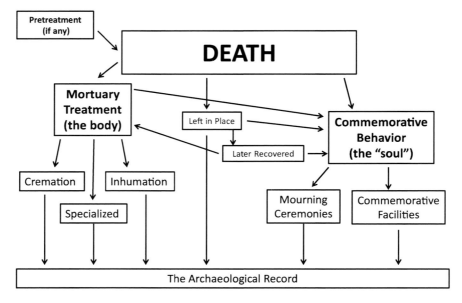

Figure 4.1 A general schematic of a funerary system
Source: Author

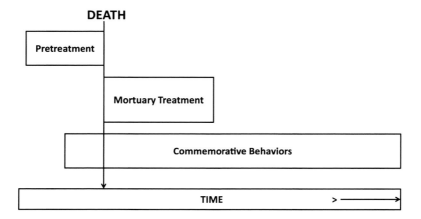

Figure 4.2 A timeline model of a funerary system
Source: Author

The funerary system I: pretreatment of the living

The first aspect of a funerary system is **pretreatment**, activities undertaken in preparation of a person for their death, the entry to the next stage of existence. This might include a variety of behaviors, such as caring for and preparing the person for death. The beginning of the mourning process would be a part of this aspect. Unless a death is unexpected, most past societies had some sort of pretreatment for the deceased.

Any number of events or rituals could be included, and the timing of pretreatment would depend on the society and the people responsible for the process. Such activities prior to death could include anticipatory grief, prayer vigils, ritual meals, placing someone in hospice, living with the dying, caring and preparing the person for death, the pre-death dispersal of property, and/or the gathering of relatives.

Simple pretreatments may be afforded to persons embarking on dangerous or suicidal missions, such as the ceremonial drinking of sake prior to kamikaze flights. There are also examples of pretreatments of people being prepared for sacrifice. The Moche of Peru sacrificed enemy warriors in elaborate ceremonies where the captives were transported to Sipán, stripped naked and bound, their throats slit, and then were decapitated and dismembered (Verano 2005; Verano and Phillips 2016). The Mexica (aka Aztec) and the Maya had similar ceremonies and associated pretreatments.

In some cases, people were selected and prepared for sacrifice in a fairly extensive and elaborate pretreatment process. For example, the Inca selected girls of about the age of four, who were then raised by priestesses and treated and fed very well. At about age 14, they became one of the "chosen women" (*aclla*) to be offered as human sacrifices during Inca *capacocha* ceremonies (Wilson et al. 2007, 2013). The ceremony was intended both to maintain political unity among the Inca and to appease the gods. La Doncella (see the Case Study on page 62) is an example of such a girl.

The funerary system II: the mortuary process

The second aspect of a funerary system is the **mortuary process**, or the various practices, behaviors, and facilities that are involved in directly dealing with the physical body of the deceased. In general, each body goes through an **initial mortuary treatment** followed by a **final mortuary treatment**. As the body ages in life, it changes, and its initial and final treatments may vary accordingly (Scott 1999). Unless a person died in isolation and was never recovered (such as in a sunken ship), some sort of mortuary process would have been afforded to each member of a society.

Initial mortuary treatment

Once a death occurred, the body was subjected to initial treatment, and some ceremonies may also have been conducted. Such treatment might include washing and dressing the body for immediate disposition. In other cases, techniques to delay the decomposition of the body, such as embalming, evisceration, or excarnation (defleshing), might have been used for a number of reasons, such as to provide time to transport the body to a distant burial place (Weiss-Krejci 2005). In other cases, excarnation was actually the pretreatment of the body, since it was the bones that were formally buried. A body might also be adorned and displayed to reflect social identity. There is little evidence of autopsies having been done in prehistory (Aufderheide 2013), but they are fairly common now.

Some societies sought to permanently preserve a body prior to burial. Techniques to accomplish that task include embalming, drying (heat and salts), smoking, or intentional mummification.

Final mortuary treatment

Once the initial treatment of the body was completed, a funeral of some sort would be held during which the body would receive its final treatment. Although there are a number of techniques for final treatment, most bodies were either cremated or inhumated (buried), both of which are considered here to fall under the general term **interment**. Either way, the place of the final treatment (grave or cremation pyre) must be prepared. Such a process could be fairly simple, such as digging a grave, or fantastically complex, such as the construction of a pyramid. The body then would be transported to the place of interment. During interment, and immediately after, it is likely that some commemorative behaviors would have been undertaken, such as a graveside service or post-funeral gathering of relatives.

CREMATION

Cremation is the destruction of the body by burning. It is a form of interment, sometimes called a "cremation burial" or a "burnt burial." Cremation can be seen as both a method to treat the dead and as a social process for the living, including pretreatment, mortuary treatment, and commemorative practices (Quinn et al. 2014a:5–6; also see Oestigaard 2013) involving bodies, goods, and places (Quinn et al. 2014b:28–31). Cremation creates a rapid and observable transformation of the body from one form to another (Quinn et al. 2014a:3), an alteration that immediately puts the body in a different state. In some cases, cremations are purposefully incomplete, perhaps just a "symbolic" burning effort (Barber 1990:383), resulting in "partial cremations." Barber (1990:382) suggested that in some societies, a major purpose of cremation was to render the body inert to make it uninhabitable, such as by vampires.

Cremation is expensive in both time and effort (Barber 1990:380). It involves the gathering of firewood (or other fuel) and tending the pyre until the task is complete. In cases where large numbers of bodies were involved, such as the dead from epidemics or battles, cremation could be very inefficient. In many cases, the remaining materials – bone, burned grave goods, charcoal, and/or ash – were collected from the primary cremation pit and reburied in a secondary location, sometimes in a container such as a pottery vessel.

Most prehistoric cremations were accomplished with simple firewood, producing temperatures between 800 and 1,000°C, not hot enough to completely consume the skeleton. The surviving remains are called **cremains** and are considerably altered from the heat (Figure 4.3). Bone and teeth will be distorted, warped, and fragmented; will have shrunk in size and mass; and will have taken on various colors depending on the temperature of the fire (McKinley 2015; Schmidt 2015; Schurr et al. 2015; Schmidt et al. 2017; Thompson and Ulguim 2016; Thompson et al. 2017). Nevertheless, some elements will probably survive in identifiable form. Modern cremations are conducted using a much higher temperature, with the bones reduced to ash.

Cremains have received relatively little study compared to inhumated remains (Kuijt et al. 2014:vii; also see Wells 1960; Davies and Mates 2005; Mays 2010:319–320; Schmidt 2015; Williams 2015; Devlin and Herrmann 2017), as they are more difficult to identify and study (McKinley 2013, 2015). Nevertheless, it is sometimes possible to estimate sex, age, and even detect pathologies (McKinley 2013). Also, despite temperature-induced diagenesis, it appears that stable isotope data can still be obtained from cremains and used

Figure 4.3 Examples of cremated bone from the Stonehenge site in England, note the distortions and fragmentation

Source: Alamy Image ID: R19HBJ

to model diet (Schurr et al. 2015). In addition, strontium is highly resistant to thermal alteration and can be used to determine the geographic origin of cremated remains (e.g., Graham and Bethard 2019), as discussed later.

Cremations could reflect different management by sex, gender, or status; that is, biological and social constructs that reflect the structure of the society. For example, a study of Bronze Age cremations from Britain (Brück 2014:132–133, Table 6.3) showed that in some cases, only part of the cremated individual was present in the secondary location, constituting a "token" burial (McKinley 1997:142). Brück (2014:126–127) suggested the possibility of incomplete collection of the remains, or purposeful partitioning (and dispersal?) of the remains, possibly reflecting status or some other phenomenon.

In another study of the distribution of remains in secondary (not in their original location) cremation features, Pankowská et al. (2017) discovered a pattern in the arrangement, with bones from the peripheral parts of the body being at the bottom while cranial elements were usually concentrated in the upper portion of the cremation feature. This pattern suggested the careful collection of certain elements and a complex postmortem manipulation.

INHUMATION

Inhumation involves the actual burial of an uncremated body. The body is often placed in the soil, but other types of inhumations include placement under a rock cairn, in a rock crevasse, in the back of a cave, or in a tomb or mausoleum. Inhumation is generally preceded by some sort of initial treatment of the body, from simple wrapping to formal mummification. Depending on conditions, some inhumated bodies might become naturally mummified.

If the body is buried in a place intended to be permanent and not intentionally moved after burial, it is called a **primary inhumation**, meaning that a single treatment was used, as with a simple burial (Sprague 2005:28). Primary inhumations reflect single burial events, either with a single individual or multiple individuals within a grave, and are discrete units of archaeological analysis.

In some cases, a burial was temporary, later to be purposefully exhumed after the soft tissues had decomposed. In these cases, the bones would have been collected and possibly cleaned and then reburied in a different location. This second burial event results in a **secondary inhumation** (or secondary burial), one not in its original location, sometimes called a compound burial (Sprague 2005:28). A secondary inhumation would require two mortuary treatments over an extended time and likely a separate set of commemorative behaviors.

The process of exhumation, subsequent cleaning of the bones, and reinterment of the bones in a new location would result in the disarticulation of the skeleton, perhaps some defleshing marks on the bone, and even the accidental loss of some of the smaller bones, such as phalanges. Given their disarticulated state, secondary burials are generally easy to identify as such. Secondary burials could be placed in a new grave, placed within a new container, or placed in a facility designed for the storage of such remains, such as an **ossuary** (also known as a charnel house) or an underground **catacomb** (Figure 4.4). Even if not actually reburied in the ground, such remains are still typically referred to as secondary burials. In Europe today, secondary burial in ossuaries is a common practice

Figure 4.4 The bones of uncounted persons in the catacombs of Paris
Source: Alamy Image ID: F05BC9

due to a lack of cemetery space. In many cases, a second set of commemorative behaviors would have been conducted at the reburial or placement in an ossuary.

A third type of inhumation is an **exposed burial**. This involves the body being placed in the open to facilitate decomposition, either by exposure to the elements and/or to scavengers. Some researchers have called these "non-burials," since the body was not deposited in some type of grave (see Weiss-Krejci 2013), but exposed burials still involve a complete funerary process with mortuary treatment.

Examples of exposed burials include the scaffold burials on the North American Plains, the Sky burials of Tibet, and canoe burials in the South Pacific. The Kajemby, fisher people of Madagascar, place their dead on the beach so they can be claimed by the ocean as offerings (Radimilahy 1994:88).

MUMMIES

Mummies are bodies in which soft tissues, such as muscles, skin, organs, or connective tissues, are preserved by means of complex processes, either intentional or not (Piombino-Mascali et al. 2017; also see Chamberlin and Parker Pearson 2001; Aufderheide 2003, 2011; Giles 2013). Mummies have both fascinated the public and contributed a great deal toward an understanding of the dead (Nystrom 2019). The term "mummy" derives from a Persian word (múmiyá) meaning bitumen (Piombino-Mascali et al. 2017:101), a substance widely used by the Ancient Egyptians in their mummification process. Mummification can result in differential preservation of soft tissues, with some organs, particularly the digestive tract, being more susceptible to decomposition (Piombino-Mascali et al. 2017:101). There are, in essence, two basic ways mummies are formed: either by natural processes or intentionally by humans.

Natural mummies   **Natural mummies** derive (usually) from a primary inhumation in which the soft tissues were unintentionally preserved due to natural processes. Such processes include a lack of available moisture, resulting in the body being desiccated either from hot or freezing temperatures. In other cases, natural chemical processes, such as those that occur in anaerobic or acidic environments, will arrest decay and result in mummification (Piombino-Mascali et al. 2017:103). In rare cases, persons that died away from society and received no mortuary treatment are found preserved (e.g., Dickson 2011).

Bodies that are naturally desiccated are usually found in arid environments, such as coastal Peru, Egypt (see the Case Study on page 60), the Great Basin of North America, or other hot desert areas. In the arid Tarim Basin of western China, numerous naturally mummified bodies dating between 2,000 BC and AD 500 have been found, often with their clothing and other perishable items in excellent condition (Figure 4.5) (Mair 1995; Barber 1999). Of interest is that these bodies have a "European" appearance, suggesting linkage between western Europe and western China at an early date (Kuzmina 1998; Mallory and Mair 2000). Analysis of ancient DNA (aDNA) from the mummies supported the idea of a European-related population (Cavalli-Sforza 2000). Subsequent genetic work suggested a relationship to Near Eastern people (Hemphill and Mallory 2004). It seems that the Tarim mummies appear to be descendants of immigrants from the west rather than the northwest and may have had close ties with farmers of ancient Persia.

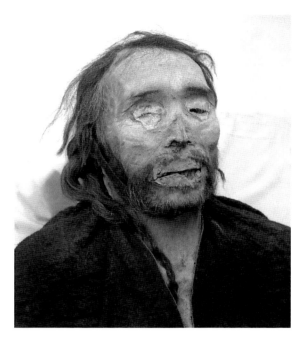

Figure 4.5 A well-preserved mummy from the Tarim Basin, western China
Source: Almay ID: 2B017KX

Case study: Fag el-Gamous: the "million mummy" cemetery, Egypt

The Fag el-Gamous cemetery is located in the Faiyum Basin southwest of Cairo (Figure 4.6) and covers an estimated 310 acres. It was found in 1980 by archaeologists from Brigham Young University and dates to the Graeco-Roman Period, ca. AD 100 to 800 (Griggs 1988; Evans et al. 2015). The size of the cemetery and the density of the burials resulted in an estimate of "a million" mummies. However, all of the mummies found were naturally mummified, and most of the individuals recovered are skeletons, making it more of a "million burial" cemetery. Nevertheless, the preservation of the remains is very good.

As of 2019, some 1,700 burials have been excavated (Figure 4.7) and appear to represent commoners. The burials had been placed in rectangular shafts, often with multiple burials in each shaft. Earlier (deeper) burials were placed with their heads facing east, whereas later ones were placed with their heads facing west. Christian icons (e.g., crosses) appear as early as AD 545 (Evans et al. 2015).

Of great interest is the large percentage (54%) of blondes and redheads in the mummified remains (Griggs 1988). Further, it appears that these burials are clustered by hair color, with redheads in a separate area from blondes. In some cases, portraits of the dead were placed on their sarcophagi (e.g., Muhlestein and Jensen 2013).

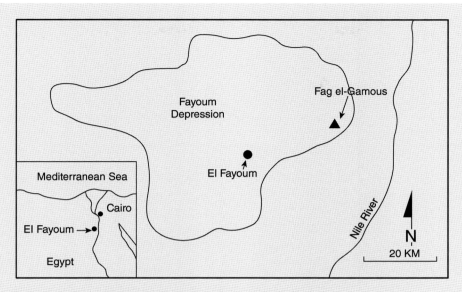

Figure 4.6 Location of the Fag el-Gamous site in Egypt
Source: Author

Figure 4.7 Burials from the Fag el-Gamous cemetery in the process of being excavated
Source: R. Paul Evans

Other bodies became naturally mummified by freezing. After the tissue freezes, the resulting ice crystals can sublimate, phase directly into water vapor, and evaporate – essentially "freeze drying" the body. Freezing may also lock up the water, making it unusable by decomposing organisms, and the low temperature will slow the metabolic processes of any decomposing organisms.

The earliest known frozen mummies are four individuals thought to date between 8,000 and 10,000 years ago, from a site in the high-altitude mountains of Peru (Wann et al. 2015). A number of other frozen bodies have been found. For example, the mummies of eight Inuit women and children were discovered at Qilakitsoq, Greenland (Bresciani et al. 1991) and six more were discovered at Nuuk, Greenland (Lynnerup 2015b). Ötzi, the "iceman" found in the Italian Alps (see Case Study in Chapter 9) was likely killed and accidentally preserved in a glacier. Among the best-known frozen bodies are the Children of Llullaillaco, sacrificial victims of the Inca (see the following Case Study).

Case study: La Doncella (the maiden), a child of Llullaillaco, Argentina

In 1999, while looking for Inca sacrifice sites, Dr. Johan Reinhard and his crew discovered three naturally mummified bodies on the upper slopes of Mount Llullaillaco, located in Argentina near the border with Chile (Reinhard and Ceruti 2010; Ceruti, 2015). The three bodies, two girls and one boy, were found placed within a small stone platform on the top of the mountain and were dated to about 500 years ago. These children were believed to have been ritually killed, part of the Inca *capacocha* sacrificial ritual at sacred places, such as the volcano at Mount Llullaillaco, to ensure good health, harvests, and weather. An example of a similar mummy is shown in Figure 4.8.

Figure 4.8 A pre-Inca mummy

Source: Alamy Image ID: EKJWBD

Each of the children was fully clothed and adorned with metal headbands, feathered headdresses, necklaces, and bracelets. Other associated artifacts included small anthropomorphic and camelid figurines in gold, silver, and marine shell, as well as textiles, feather items, ceramics, wooden vessels, and slings (Wilson et al. 2007:16457). The boy was about seven years old and was bound with a rope into a fetal position. The younger of the two girls was about six years old and placed in a sitting position. She had burn marks on her face and shoulders, the apparent result of having been struck by lightning after her death.

The eldest of the girls was about 15 years old and was called "La Doncella," or "The Maiden." She wore a dress, and her hair was braided. Using chemical data obtained from her hair, it was determined that her diet changed significantly for the better part of one year prior to her death, suggesting preparation (pretreatment) for sacrifice (Wilson et al. 2007). It was determined that La Doncella had been drugged with coca leaves, some of which were still in her mouth, and likely died soon afterward (Wilson et al. 2007, 2013).

It appears that La Doncella was an *aclla*, one of the "chosen women," "Virgins of the Sun," or "Virgins of the Inca," who were selected at the age of four, raised by priestesses, and at about 14 years of age were eligible to be offered as a human sacrifice during a state *capacocha* ceremony (e.g., Ceruti 2015). The mummies of the three girls are on display at the Museum of High Altitude Archaeology in Argentina.

Another example of a frozen mummy is that of the "Ice Princess," a burial in a log tomb (kurgan) discovered in the Ukok Plateau of southeastern Russia in 1993. In this case, the kurgan contained the well-preserved remains of a woman about 30 years of age (Polosmak and O'Rear 1994). She was clothed in felt, silk, and leather and preserved for more than 2,500 years by a combination of freezing and embalming. Elaborate images of animals and flowers tattooed on various parts of her body were still visible, and her three-foot-long felt headdress, her silk blouse, and her soft leather riding boots were intact. Wooden ornaments depicting fanciful beasts and snow leopards and covered in gold leaf adorned her remains. Also found were two other people, perhaps sacrificial victims, and six horses complete with saddles and harnesses. She and other individuals found in other kurgans of the same time period had been embalmed; their organs were removed, and their body cavities were stuffed with tannin-rich peat.

Little is known about the people represented by the mummies from these Russian tombs. They are believed to belong to a group known as the Pazyryks, a pastoral people who dominated the steppes of that region for hundreds of years until their disappearance sometime around 400 BC. Fortunately, some historical information about these people exists. Herodotus, the fifth-century BC Greek historian, described their "fierce nature" and "war-like tendencies" in some detail.

Bodies can also naturally preserve in anaerobic environments, in which there is no oxygen present so decomposing organisms cannot survive. Such environments exist in

Figure 4.9 Tollund Man; note the noose and beard hair
Source: Henry Chapman, Museum Silkeborg

a number of places in the world, including the lowest depths of the Black Sea (where wooden shipwrecks are preserved) or in thick mud. For the preservation of human remains, these environments may include peat bogs, places that are wet but cold, highly acidic, and contain tannin. Peat is organic material that, because of the conditions of the bog, has not decomposed and piles up on itself.

A number of bodies have been found in peat bogs across Europe. These "bog bodies" (Lynnerup 2015a; also see Aldhouse-Green 2015) have often been discovered accidentally during the removal of peat for use as fuel. There is generally good preservation of soft tissues but often poor preservation of bone (due to the peat being acidic), with the result that the bodies tend to be "flattened" by the weight of the peat and the near absence of the skeleton (Piombino-Mascali et al. 2017:109). One of the more famous of the European bog bodies is that of Tollund Man (Figure 4.9), found in Denmark in 1950 (Nielsen et al. 2018). Bodies have been found in other bog environments as well, such as at the Windover site in Florida (Wentz 2012).

Purposeful mummies

In a number of places and at various times, concerted attempts were made to preserve the body of the deceased by some artificial process. Such purposeful mummification processes are a type of mortuary treatment, with the bodies usually being inhumated afterwards. The reasons for purposeful mummification are varied, from preservation of royal power, to maintenance of the body for use in the afterlife, to regulation of the deceased, or as war trophies (e.g., shrunken heads) (Aufderheide 2003).

A variety of techniques has been employed to preserve bodies, the most famous being that of the ancient Egyptians (Ikram and Dodson 1998). The purpose of the ancient Egyptian practice was to ensure the survival of the body for use in the afterlife. However, proper mummification was very expensive, so was only affordable by the rich. The entire process took about 70 days, 40 for drying and 30 for wrapping and entombment (Ikram and Dodson 1998:104). The drying process involved the removal of certain organs (to be preserved in canopic jars), the removal and disposal of the brain (usually through the nose), and the packing of the body with natron (salt) and linens to remove the moisture. After drying, the body would be treated with a variety of oils and resins and wrapped in strips of linen, with offerings placed in the wrappings (see Ikram and Dodson [1998:106] for a list of required materials for mummification) (Figure 4.10). Bodies of persons of

Figure 4.10 An Egyptian mummy

Source: Alamy Image ID: ACXR4J

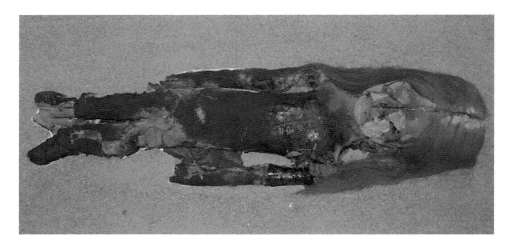

Figure 4.11 A Chinchorro mummy
Source: Karl Reinhard

lesser means would have been treated in a less comprehensive manner, with the poor simply inhumated and perhaps becoming "mummified" naturally (common in Egypt's environment).

Another method of mummification was practiced by the Chinchorro people of coastal Peru and Chile, as early as 8,000 BP (Guillén 2005). Upon death, the bodies were skinned and excarnated (defleshed) and the bones were cleaned and wrapped in fiber. The skin was then placed back over the wrapped bones, covered in clay, and painted. These "artificial bodies" (Figure 4.11) may have been displayed and would have continued to play a role in the lives of the living prior to their ultimate placement in a cemetery (Guillén 2005).

Preservation might also occur if the bodies had been placed in hermetically sealed containers so that decomposing microbes could not get to the body, such as was the occasional practice in ancient China (e.g., Bonn-Muller 2009). In more recent times, some Melanesian groups preserved bodies by placing them over a fire so that the heat and smoke would desiccate and preserve them (Figure 4.12). They would then be displayed and continue to be involved in the daily lives of the living. Some Buddhist monks would self-mummify by starving themselves to the point of having very little body fat and would dehydrate themselves by refusing fluids. At the point of death, they would be encased in some form of container. In the case of the 1,000–year–old Liuquan Mummy (Yuen 2018), the body was within a Buddha statue. Purposeful mummification was also apparently practiced in Bronze Age Europe (Booth et al. 2015), although such remains are not well preserved. In contemporary western society, embalming has been used to preserve the bodies of some famous icons, idols, villains, religious figures, or eccentrics (Quigley 1998).

Figure 4.12 A "smoked" mummy from New Guinea
Source: Alamy

Preserved body parts

In some cases, specific body parts were taken as trophies and preserved, generally by desiccation rather than by any elaborate process. Many such trophies were obtained in war, serving to demonstrate prowess, as a warning to others, and/or to exert dominance over the enemy. Trophy heads and scalps were taken in many parts of the world, including South America (e.g., Rubenstein 2007), North America (Seeman 1988; Chacon and Dye 2007; Schmidt and Osterholt 2014; Schwitalla et al. 2014; Sundstrom 2015; Hodge 2018), Mesoamerica (Storey 2014), and Melanesia (Zegwaard 1959).

Another important trophy was the penis, the taking of which was long considered proof of bravery by numerous groups in the Old World. For example, following the battle of Khesef-Tamahu (in present-day Syria), Egyptian soldiers took many thousands of penises and presented them to the Pharaoh Ramses III (Massey 2011:102). The taking of body parts as war trophies was outlawed by the 1929 Geneva Convention, but the practice still continues.

Mortuary facilities

At least two classes of **mortuary facilities** can be defined: those in which bodies undergo initial treatment and facilities (or features) of final treatment. In both cases, their formal characteristics would be based on social and/or political criteria such as sex, class, and/or status.

Upon death, bodies were transported to a facility for initial treatment. In small societies, such a facility could be as simple as a bed where the dead were washed and/or dressed and prepared for interment. In large societies, the dead may be transported to specialized mortuary facilities where more elaborate initial preparations were accomplished, such as embalming or mummification. For example, the ancient Egyptians had full-time specialists to treat (mummify) the dead, with highly specialized buildings, tools, and supplies.

Once the initial treatment was completed, the bodies were interred, either by cremation or inhumation. If cremated, a simple cremation pit or an elaborate crematorium might be employed for the task. The resulting cremains would usually be collected and often placed in a container (e.g., an urn or pottery vessel) for (secondary) burial. If inhumated, the body would likely be placed in a container of some sort (from a linen shroud, to a wooden coffin, to a stone sarcophagus) and then placed in its grave. Inhumations in pottery vessels (a pot burial) were commonly seen as a low-status treatment, but Power and Tristant (2016:1474) suggested that "the ceramic containers may have reflected symbolic associations between pots, wombs and eggs, facilitating rebirth and transition into the afterlife."

A **grave** is "any location at which human remains are located; a grave can be above-ground, below-ground, indoors, outdoors, aquatic, or within any other possible natural or anthropogenic habitat" (Junkins and Carter 2017:145). Some graves are simple holes in the ground, whereas others are much more elaborate, such as complex tombs (e.g., a pyramid), barrows, or even ships (as sometimes used by the Norse [Harris et al. 2017]). A function of a grave is to protect and/or contain the remains. Although isolated primary interments may be located anywhere, it is more common that bodies are placed in a **cemetery**, locations that separate the living from the dead.

Cemeteries used over time are called **collective cemeteries**. In such facilities, new graves were commonly excavated into existing (and so earlier) burials, thus disturbing them and disarticulating, fragmenting, and commingling those remains. In addition, any grave goods originally associated with such disturbed burials would be mixed. As such, only the most recent of the burials would be undisturbed and fully articulated (Lull et al. 2013). A further complication in the analysis of collective cemeteries, even if the remains are not commingled, is the lack of temporal control of individual burials, making it difficult to analyze change through time.

In some instances, however, existing burials were not disturbed by later ones, allowing the analysis of changing funerary patterns. For example, Salanova et al. (2017) analyzed the contents of a Late Neolithic chambered tomb at Bury in northern France, dating from the fourth and third millennia BC. They found that funerary practices changed significantly over time but that the population using the tomb did not change. They interpreted this as signifying a shift toward more selective inclusion into the tomb, perhaps reflecting broader changes in that society.

Body management

People were not buried in a random manner, although some (such as unrecovered war dead) might appear to be. The dead were usually interred following culturally specific procedures that involve individuality, articulation, position, and orientation (Sprague 2005). Individuality involves how many individuals, or parts of individuals, are interred in a single facility (e.g., a grave). For example, a grave might contain one, two, or more than two individuals; in complete or fragmentary condition; and interred at the same or different times. Depending on the number of individuals within a grave, it may be considered to be a **mass grave**, defined here as one in which the individuals received little funerary treatment due to disease, war, or genocide (Cabo et al. 2012).

Articulation refers to the degree that the body is in anatomical position. If it is complete and in anatomical position, it would be considered fully articulated. If the skeleton is disturbed to some extent (e.g., by bioturbation), it is considered partly or semi-articulated. If the body is completely out of anatomical position (e.g., a secondary burial), it is considered to be disarticulated. The degree of articulation can inform us about taphonomic processes and/or cultural practices.

The **position** of a body when it is interred is determined by cultural preferences. The most common positions (Figure 4.13) are flexed (arms and legs brought close in to the torso), semi-flexed (arms and legs loosely bent toward the torso), extended and lying face up (supine), and extended and lying face down (prone). Less common positions include standing or sitting. In addition to the general position of the body, it is important to note on which side (left or right) the body is lying and a description of which parts are where, such as the position of the head and the placement of the arms (e.g., on the side or crossed on the chest).

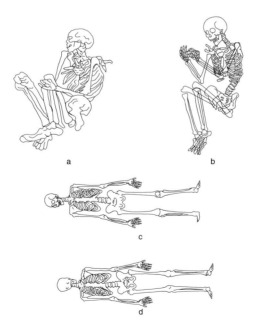

Figure 4.13 Common inhumation positions: (a) flexed, (b) semi-flexed, (c) extended (supine), and (d) extended (prone)

Source: Author

The **orientation** of a body refers to its horizontal alignment, measured in degrees relative to north (e.g., due west at 270 degrees), although its incline may also be measured. Orientation is figured from the direction the head is pointed, but this can sometimes be difficult to determine. Orientation is recorded to determine if there are patterns between different sexes, ages, or statuses, or if celestial features (such as orientation to the North Star or to a solstice) were factors. These latter possibilities are the subject of the field of archaeoastronomy (e.g., Magli 2015).

Disarticulated, fragmented, and commingled remains

If remains are disarticulated, it could be the result of natural processes, such as bioturbation or erosion. It could also be the result of human activity in prehistory, such as the excavation of new graves into older ones or purposeful dismemberment as part of a mortuary treatment. It may also be related to modern disturbance, such as from a backhoe or bulldozer or even vandalism (Figure 4.14). In addition to disarticulation, disturbances could result in the breakage and fragmentation of remains, even extreme fragmentation. If a disturbed interment was one in a multiple burial or was within a collective cemetery, the disarticulated and fragmented remains could be **commingled** with other burials.

It is also possible that the disarticulation, fragmentation, and commingling of remains were part of an intentional mortuary treatment. Purposefully disarticulated remains are the hallmark of secondary burials whose bones are then placed in an ossuary or catacomb (Koudounaris 2011) (see Figure 4.4). Due to space limitations, contemporary practice in some places in Europe (e.g., Crete, Germany, Paris, and Rome) permits a body to stay in

Figure 4.14 A vandalized cemetery in Peru; note the disarticulated, fragmented, and commingled remains, including fragments of mummies

Source: Alamy Image ID: G36C3T

a grave for about 20 years. The bones must then be removed and stored elsewhere to make room for a new burial. In some cases, the bones of the dead were used in construction. For example, the Sedlec Ossuary is a small Roman Catholic chapel located in Sedlec, in the Czech Republic. Within the chapel are chandeliers, skull-lined arches, and other constructs made of human bone taken from an estimated 40,000 to 70,000 skeletons.

One should always remember that dismemberment, disarticulation, and excarnation could result from purposeful mortuary treatment. Examples include the charnel fields in Tibet (see the Case Study beginning on page 73) and possibly (probably) in the ancient American Southwest (see the Case Study beginning on page 133). In addition, specific body parts (e.g., limbs) are sometimes buried together, disarticulated from the missing remainder of the body, and commingled with parts from others (e.g., Chenal et al. 2015).

However they originated, remains that are disarticulated, fragmented, and/or commingled are difficult to analyze (Kendell and Willey 2014; Osterholtz et al. 2014b; Tung 2016). First, the numbers and types of elements would be identified and assessed for their age, sex, and pathologies. This information would then be compiled to determine the minimum number of individuals (MNI) represented in the collection. Any information on associated artifacts, ecofacts, grave type, orientation, and the like would also be recorded to create as complete a picture as possible. In addition, aDNA could be used to distinguish and separate commingled remains (e.g., Verdugo et al. 2017). These issues make the analysis of collective cemeteries difficult.

Commingled remains are common in poorly curated museum collections (e.g., Zejdlik 2014), and some remains, such as subadults, were even discarded. In both archaeological studies and contemporary forensic cases, it is necessary to separate the commingled remains and to identify individuals using detailed analyses of age, sex, condition, and preservation (e.g., Barker et al. 2017).

Specialized mortuary treatments

A variety of "specialized" mortuary treatments is known. Such practices may be afforded to high-status people, such as the excarnation treatments in Tibet (see the Case Study beginning on page 73) or excarnation facilities in Bolivia (Smith 2016:125–126). In large-scale death events, such as from disease, war, or genocide, individuals might be placed in mass graves with relatively little formal mortuary treatment (see Cabo et al. 2012). Specialized treatments may be afforded to some famous or important people, such as the publicly displayed bodies of Vladimir Lenin; the preserved Saints (the Incorruptibles; Pringle 2001) (Figure 4.15); bodies exhibited in venues such as Las Vegas hotels (Linke 2018); or part of the ongoing public display of the dead in museums (e.g., the Mütter Museum in Philadelphia), film, and art, all influenced by contemporary attitudes (H. Williams et al. 2019). Other specialized treatments include keeping ashes of cremated relatives in the home or preserved parts as relics, supernatural objects, or war trophies.

Mortuary treatments that are considered atypical in a society are often called **deviant**. The term "deviant" is commonly applied to unusual interments of people who are presumed to be undesirable, such as criminals, enemies, unwanted infants, or people thought to have been witches or vampires. Some of these individuals may have been treated atypically as a postmortem punishment (Shay 1985; Walker 1998; Weiss-Krejci 2013) or an attempt to keep them from rising from the dead. By denying enemies and criminals their own burial rites, power can be exerted over them in death (Duncan 2005:211–212).

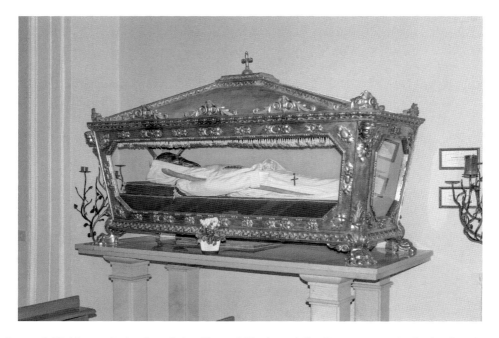

Figure 4.15 Mummified relic of the Blessed Ugolino delle Caminate in the little church in San Donato in Belvedere Fogliense, Italy

Source: Alamy Image ID: ER6FFF

In some cases, unwanted infants were unceremoniously killed (infanticide). In Late Roman period contexts at the site of Ashkelon in Israel, a large collection (ca. 100) of neonatal infants of both sexes (identified using aDNA) were found in a sewer directly below what is believed to have been a brothel (Smith and Kahila 1992; Faerman et al. 1998). This suggests that the children were unwanted and were simply thrown into the sewer without any real funerary treatment.

In another example of specialized mortuary treatments, a number of bog bodies have been found in Europe (e.g., Lynnerup 2015a), often the victims of violent deaths from beatings, stabbings, strangling, or throat slitting. The bodies were then placed in bogs, an unusual treatment in European societies. One interpretation is that they were executed criminals. However, further analysis suggests that many of the victims were tall (as seen in the ruling classes) but had physical abnormalities, such as scoliosis (curved spines), abnormally short limbs, spina bifida (exposed spinal cords), and nonsymmetrical limb lengths. Thus, it seems possible that these were "special" people, selected and cared for (pretreatment) until they were ritually sacrificed (Parker Pearson 2003:71). Indeed, it seems that some of the victims had been given psychotropic drugs prior to death (see Hillman 1986:103).

One of the more interesting examples of deviant burials is from northern Europe, particularly in medieval Poland. Archaeologists have found a number of individuals inhumated in an unusual extended prone position, sometimes with stakes driven through the body, the deceased covered with rocks, or a large brick-sized rock placed in the mouth of the corpse. What explains this pattern? Local folklore had it that vampires existed and would victimize the population at night. Legend held that people suspected of being vampires would be afforded specialized, or deviant, mortuary treatments so they could not rise from the dead to resume their vampire activities; this belief is seen as a possible explanation for the unusual nature of these burials (e.g., Gardela and Kajkowski 2013; but see Barrowclough 2014). A similar "vampire" burial was found in Italy, placed within the mass burial of plague victims (Nuzzolese and Borrini 2010). Another idea is that the deviant burials were those of outsiders, but Gregoricka et al. (2017) showed that the deviant burials from at least one site in Poland had the isotopic signatures of locals.

Case study: mortuary practices in Tibet

In Tibet, five different types of burials are practiced, each based on one of the five inner elements of the body: fire, air, water, earth, and space (Malville 2005). The choice of mortuary treatment is determined by a number of factors, including the status of the individual, whether the ground is rocky or frozen, and the like.

The noblest burial is the stupa, a disposition reserved for very high-status people, such as a lama. A stupa burial involves embalming the body with salt and mummifying the corpse (sometimes self-mummification) and placing it in a monument called a stupa.

Sky burial, typically reserved for high-status people, involves complete destruction of the body so that the soul is freed from it. In one form, both flesh and bones are cut up and fed to vultures (Figure 4.16), which then transport the

Figure 4.16 An excarnated body undergoing Sky burial in Tibet
Source: Public domain

remains to the sky. In another form, the bodies are taken to charnel grounds and left out in the open to be consumed by wild animals. These charnel grounds are visited by mourners who leave offerings.

Water burials are for low-status people, where the body is wrapped with white cloth and submerged in a river. Earth burial is considered an inferior type of interment. Only those who died from infectious disease or were murdered are buried in the ground. Earth burials may offer two meanings: either to halt the spread of contagion or to castigate the dead by lowering the corpse toward hell. Tree burial is for children; the dead child is entombed in a wooden case and hung on a tree in a secluded forest.

Remains left in place

There are various reasons that the dead would be left in the place where they died. For example, the war dead are left in places that are inaccessible, such as sunken ships located in deep water. Other locations are designated as memorials, such as the USS *Arizona* (see page 80) or the World War I battlefield of Verdun where the remains of an estimated 80,000 French and German soldiers still lie within a restricted area considered sacred by the French (Kornei 2018).

People killed in natural disasters, such as volcanic eruptions or tsunamis, may also not be recovered. Probably the most famous of these disasters is that of Pompeii, a city buried in ash during an eruption of Mount Vesuvius in AD 79. The nearby town of Herculaneum was also buried. Many had fled the eruption, but many others were encased in ash. Once the bodies decayed to the point of obliteration, they left "hollows" in the hardened ash that could be filled with plaster, allowed to dry, and excavated to discover the shape of the body, foods, or other objects within the ash.

So far, about two-thirds of Pompeii have been excavated, and the architecture, art, and artifacts found there offer an in-depth view of Roman life (Zanker 1998). Wealthy Romans typically cremated their dead, so skeletal remains are relatively rare in Roman sites and, when found, they provide insight into the health and diet of the upper-class Romans themselves. The remains of some 2,000 people (and some animals) have so far been found.

In some cases, bodies were temporarily buried in one location, later to be disinterred and reburied. The first burial would have received an expedient mortuary treatment, whereas the subsequent burial would have been more formal. In some instances, however, the locations of temporary graves were forgotten. This was the case with hundreds of U.S. Marines killed in the Battle of Tarawa in 1943, only to be rediscovered decades later. Hundreds of sailors killed on the USS *Oklahoma* (in the Pearl Harbor attack) could not be identified at the time and were buried together in mass graves. With the advances in DNA analysis, some of these remains are being disinterred and can now be identified.

Case study: World War I trenches in France

Since about 1990, serious research began on the archaeology of battlefields from conflicts in the twentieth century, a field now called battlefield or conflict archaeology (Saunders 2017). The goal is to investigate the technologies involved, to understand and correct historical accounts, and to fill in gaps in the often-spotty records. However, the interpretation of these materials and remains is tied to nationalism, emotion, and veneration, and is sometimes misinterpreted or deliberately ignored (Munsch 2019).

Formal archaeological work on World War I (the "Great War") battlefields was only undertaken after about 2000, although relic collecting had begun even before the war had ended in 1918 (Saunders 2007). Ironically, the excavation of tens of thousands of kilometers of trenches in France during the war resulted in the accidental discovery of uncounted ancient archaeological sites and artifacts, most of which were subsequently destroyed or lost (Saunders 2007:4).

Contemporary archaeological projects in the World War I battlefields of northern France have attempted to discover and recover human remains and to map the trenches and fortifications, to both understand the systems used and to determine their defensive merit (e.g., Stichelbaut and Chielens 2016; Stichelbaut et al. 2017). In addition, material culture is sought to investigate the multiethnic Allied armies and to assist in the development of tourism. During such studies, unexploded ordnance (which still kills people every year) is flagged for safe disposal.

To this day, it is common for human remains from the war to be accidentally found, generally isolated bones or individuals, but sometimes mass graves are found. Although there are extensive records regarding the casualties during the World War I, there is very little information on the osteological record of these soldiers (Loe et al. 2014:575). One well-known case is that of Private Alan J. Mather, killed in 1917 and whose body was discovered in 2008 (Figure 4.17) and reburied with full military honors. One can read about him at http://oa.anu.edu.au/obituary/mather-alan-james-16818.

In 2009, eight mass graves of Allied soldiers killed in the Battle of Fromelles in 1916 were excavated and the remains of 250 soldiers were recovered. The skeletal remains were studied for trauma (Loe et al. 2014) and reburied in a formal cemetery. Four major forms of trauma were identified: blast, projectile, blunt force, and sharp force, each with subcategories reflecting different types of injuries. Skeletal trauma was detected on 231 (92.4%) of the individuals, a third of which showed multiple traumas.

Figure 4.17 Excavating the remains of Private Alan J. Mather, killed in World War I
Source: Martin Brown

Funerary system III: commemorative behavior

The final aspect of a funerary system is **commemorative behavior**, the various belief systems, practices, and facilities that are involved primarily with the afterlife; the remembrance of a person; and the management of their soul. Such behaviors could include bereavement, mourning, offerings, ceremonies, events, and continuing rituals, perhaps carried out in specialized facilities constructed and maintained to accommodate or venerate a particular person or group of persons. Even if a body was never recovered and so never received any mortuary treatment, some sort of mourning and commemorative behaviors would certainly have occurred.

Commemorative behaviors can span the entire funerary system, from pretreatment to time immemorial (see Figure 4.2). **Primary commemorative behaviors**, those proximate to death, include grief or bereavement (Danely 2018; also see Cannon and Cook 2015), remembrance (Hallam and Hockey 2001), and commemoration. This can begin prior to death and continue throughout both the initial and final mortuary treatments. Examples of such behaviors include ceremonies at the funeral, erecting a grave marker, and making offerings or sacrifices.

Secondary commemorative behaviors, those occurring after the mortuary treatments ended, can occur over a considerable period of time (see Figure 4.2) and could be integrated into larger mourning ceremonies. Examples of such behaviors may consist of subsequent ceremonies, display of the bodies, remembering the dead in daily life, and continued offerings. In many cases, simple secondary behaviors, such as a visit by a relative to a grave site or a mourning ceremony that involved saying prayers for the dead, are quite difficult to detect archaeologically. On the other end of the secondary spectrum would be the massive funerary complexes of the ancient Egyptians or the spectacular temples and mausoleums of some other societies.

Mourning ceremonies

Many societies hold post-funeral **mourning ceremonies**, commonly conducted some period of time (e.g., one year) after the interment. Such ceremonies may have been conducted at a grave, a cemetery, or elsewhere. A good example of such a ceremony is the Mexican Day of the Dead, a multiday event conducted at the same time each year to commemorate all who died that year and to aid in their journey to the afterlife.

Sacrificial offerings

It is quite common for the dead to be interred with an assortment of materials, such as artifacts, foods, flowers, animals, and even other people. Materials placed in a grave, sometimes called votive offerings, could include a variety of foods or artifacts such as pottery, weapons, or ornaments. In some cases, objects were ritually "sacrificed," such as the "killing" (breakage) of tools. Such materials fall into the general category of grave goods.

Animals were sometimes killed as part of the mortuary treatment of an individual. Such animals may have been killed for food at the funeral and/or as a ritual for the animal to accompany the dead (Pluskowski 2012; Ekroth 2014). A variety of animals have been identified in such interments, such as deer, seals, horses, dogs, birds, and llamas (e.g., Szpak et al. 2016). In ancient Egypt, baboons, cats, crocodiles, dogs, ibises, and other animals were killed and mummified. The Apis bulls (Jones 1990) are among the most spectacular of such animals due to their large size and dedicated temple. Sapir-Hen et al. (2017; also see Yeshurun et al. 2013) argued that the intentional burial of animals with humans had religious, social, and political meanings and that food animals may have had both economic and social value.

The burials of high-status individuals may include other people sacrificed to accompany a person into the afterlife. Such sacrificed people may have been servants, guards, and/or concubines, each of which would have had their own mortuary treatments and would also have been part of the larger funerary system. Such sacrificial victims may fit within a specific demographic (e.g., military-aged males or young women), may have been buried in "unconventional" positions, and/or may have been placed alongside the primary interment.

Commemorative facilities

Most people are commemorated in some material way after death. This could manifest as a grave marker, continued offerings, or the construction and maintenance of some type of commemorative facility. Such facilities are varied, ranging from a formal cemetery (perhaps containing small mausoleums and/or religious structures), a standalone mausoleum or tomb (e.g., the Taj Mahal), or a large funerary complex. Such a complex would consist of mortuary facilities; the actual grave/tomb of a person or people; and commemorative facilities and features associated with memorials, venerations, or the afterlife. Examples of such funerary complexes include the pyramids and necropolis at Giza in Egypt, the tomb of the First Emperor of China, and the USS *Arizona*.

THE EGYPTIAN FUNERARY COMPLEX AT GIZA

The Egyptian funerary complex at Giza, just outside Cairo (Figure 4.18), is dominated by three major pyramids, built by the pharaohs Khufu (Cheops), Khafre (Chephren), and Menkaure (Mykerinos) during the Old Kingdom (Lehner 1997). The complex also includes the pyramid tombs of several queens and other high officials, a number of smaller pyramids, the Sphinx, temples, workshops, workers' living quarters, causeways, quarries, and a harbor. There is also a necropolis, consisting of a large number of mastabas (small underground tombs with above-ground chambers) and other cemeteries (containing

Figure 4.18 The Egyptian funerary complex at Giza
Source: Alamy

skeletons showing trauma likely due to construction accidents). Also buried there are a number of boats, including the famous 4,500-year-old intact boat found in a pit located next to the Pyramid of Khufu (Altenmüller 2002).

The alignment of the facilities may even be of supernatural importance. Nell and Ruggles (2014) proposed that many of the structures at Giza were purposefully aligned to the cardinal directions, paying particular attention to the position of the sun. In addition, it is possible that the placement of the three main pyramids match the relative positions of the three major stars in the constellation called Orion's Belt, and the heights of the pyramids match the relative luminosity of those same stars (Orofino and Bernardini 2016).

Of interest at Giza is the intermingling of Old Kingdom mortuary and commemorative facilities in the same location. In contrast, New Kingdom funerary facilities at Thebes (Luxor) and Karnak are located separate from the mortuary facilities in the Valley of the Kings and Queens located in the hills to the west.

THE TOMB OF THE FIRST EMPEROR OF CHINA

In 221 BC, Qin Shi Huangdi united the warring states of China into one nation, became its first emperor, and ruled until his death in 210 BC (Li 1975). His funerary complex (also referred to as a necropolis) is one of the largest and most elaborate known (Man 2009). The huge earthen pyramid of the tomb (also referred to as a mausoleum) itself is some 350 meters on a side and 76 meters in height (Figure 4.19). The huge complex of associated tombs, cemeteries for workers, mass burials of sacrificial victims, structures, and other features cover an area of about 28 square miles, attesting to the enormous power wielded by the state and the emperor and to the huge force of skilled artisans, architects, engineers, soldiers, and laborers who built it.

Figure 4.19 The pyramid containing the tomb of the First Emperor of China
Source: Public domain

Figure 4.20 The life-size Terra Cotta Army buried near the tomb of the First Emperor of China
Source: Alamy Image ID: ECYK48

The emperor's tomb structure, lying under the pyramid, is said to be huge and to contain a representation of the empire, complete with flowing rivers of mercury. It has never been excavated, partly due to the possible presence of mercury (which is very dangerous), so its actual contents and condition are unknown.

Perhaps the best-known feature of Qin Shi Huangdi's funerary complex is its associated Terra Cotta Army (Figure 4.20), discovered in 1974. It consists of some 7,000 figures of soldiers with weapons and 100 chariots with horses, all life-sized and ready for battle (Portal 2007). The figures represent a complete military force – infantry, archers, cavalry, and chariots. The army is thought to have been manufactured and placed to accompany the emperor to the afterlife.

THE USS *ARIZONA*

The USS *Arizona* is a battleship that sunk in place during the Japanese attack on Pearl Harbor on December 7, 1941. In that attack, a single bomb penetrated the forward magazine of the ship, resulting in a cataclysmic explosion that sunk the ship and killed most of her crew. After the attack, the damage was so extensive that the ship was left in place, although several of the main gun batteries were recovered and its superstructure was removed. The remains of some 1,177 of her crew remain entombed in the hull of the ship. In 1962, a memorial was built over the sunken hull (Figure 4.21), engraved with the names of the dead. The memorial is operated by the National Park Service, is a National

Figure 4.21 The memorial at the USS *Arizona*, Pearl Harbor, Hawai'i
Source: Alamy Image ID: B4M13W

Historic Landmark, and is a major tourist attraction. Commemorative ceremonies continue to be conducted at the memorial, and many of the crew that survived the attack were later interred there to be with their shipmates.

Chapter summary

A deceased body can have a number of cultural meanings, from a simple vessel in life, to a historical or political entity, to a continuing member of the community. Most societies see biological death as just one of the aspects of the journey of life. In some societies, the preservation of the corporeal body is necessary for use in the afterlife.

All societies have a funerary system, defined herein as having three major aspects: (I) pretreatment, (II) mortuary treatment, and (III) commemorative behaviors. Pretreatment of the living in preparation for death could include hospice care or perhaps brief or extended specialized management in preparation for the sacrifice of a person.

Mortuary treatment involves the actual management of the body after death, including the initial preparation of the body and its final interment. Final disposition generally involves cremation or inhumation, either primary or secondary, although there are other forms of interment. In some cases, the body is preserved, either by natural means (e.g., hot or cold environments) or purposefully, such as in ancient Egypt. Mortuary facilities include mortuaries, graves, tombs, and cemeteries.

Commemorative behaviors, which can begin during pretreatment and last long after mortuary treatment, include bereavement, mourning, and patterns of ritual. Memorial facilities such as mausoleums or temples may be constructed.

Archaeologically, human remains may be found as cremations or inhumations, the latter of which would be in some state of articulation and have some burial position and orientation. Remains might be disarticulated, fragmented, and/or commingled with other individuals, creating issues in analysis.

Specialized mortuary treatments might be afforded to people of unusual status, such as those who were very important. Deviant burial treatments, those outside the normal practices within a society, could reflect undesirable people such as criminals, enemies, or those thought to have been malevolent, such as "vampires." Other remains, as in the example of unrecovered war dead, may be left in place and have little to no mortuary treatment, although they would be commemorated.

Key concepts and terms

articulation
catacomb
cemetery
collective cemeteries
commemorative behaviors
commingled
cremains
cremation
deviant burials
exposed burial
final mortuary treatment
funerary system
grave
inhumation
initial mortuary treatment
interment
mass grave
mortuary facilities
mourning ceremonies
natural mummies
orientation
ossuary
position
pretreatment
primary commemorative behaviors
primary inhumation
purposeful mummies
secondary commemorative behaviors
secondary inhumation
Sky burial (Tibet)

Chapter 5

Paleopathology I
Metabolic, nutritional, and occupational stress

Paleopathology

Paleopathology is broadly defined as the analysis of changes that manifest on human tissues during the life of a past individual (e.g., Ortner 2003, 2011; Waldron 2009; Mann and Hunt 2012; M. Smith 2012; Weiss 2015a). Such change is generally observed on bone and can be due to a variety of factors, including stress of various kinds, disease, and trauma. In this chapter, the various stressors that affect the body – metabolic, nutritional, and occupational – are considered.

Paleopathology is a major focus in bioarchaeology (Martin and Osterholtz 2016:41). Histories of American paleopathology were provided by Cook and Powell (2006) and Grauer (2018). Biographies of many of the pioneers in paleopathology were included in Buikstra and Roberts (2012). The paleopathology of disease is discussed in Chapter 6 and of trauma in Chapter 7.

Mays (2018) noted that the major epistemological framework that guides most diagnoses in paleopathology is based on a comparative approach. Unknown lesions are compared to reference samples with known lesion origins, and diagnoses are proposed. Although this system is fruitful, it also has weaknesses, partly due to an overdependence on skeletal collections from museums, on medical imaging data, and a poor understanding of the biology of bone lesions. This approach continues to be the primary one used, but Mays (2018) argued that it should be expanded to include a greater understanding of the pathophysiology of bony responses to disease.

In any assessment of a pathological condition, it is important to determine whether the pathology was antemortem, perimortem, or the result of postmortem alterations. For example, if a broken bone shows signs of healing, it was broken antemortem. In many cases, it is difficult to tell if something happened before death or was a contributing factor in the death. Further, paleopathologies in subadults often derive from issues in the early development of the skeleton and can be different from those in adults (Lewis 2018).

Some pathologies in bone are obvious and fairly easy to see by even untrained eyes, but some are very subtle. However, even in obvious pathologies, it is often difficult to assess their cause. In general, the more of the skeleton that is present and the better its preservation, the better the diagnosis (Waldron 2009:21). It is also important to understand that some alterations in bone are postmortem taphonomic changes – those due to chemical action, bioturbation, excavation damage, and the like – and can appear pathological. Such "pseudo-pathologies" must not be confused with real ones (Waldron 2009:22–23). In describing the cause of a pathology, one of three categories is used: (1) **pathognomic** (certainty of diagnosis), (2) **diagnostic** (high level of confidence of diagnosis), or (3)

consistent with (nonspecific diagnosis, since the pathology may occur in many diseases or traumas) (M. Smith 2012:190). A fourth category could be "unknown."

Stress

Stress is a general term that means an unusual pressure, strain, or disruption on some system, object, or person; that is, a deviation from a homeostasis of environment, culture, and/or host (Temple and Goodman 2014:188). Here, four basic types of stress are defined: (1) metabolic, (2) nutritional, (3) occupational (mechanical), and (4) psychological, all of which are interrelated. This follows the **paleoepidemiological stress model** (or biocultural stress model) (Goodman et al. 1984) that considers environment, culture, and biology as relevant factors.

Stress had a significant impact on the health and well-being of individuals in the past and is central to studies of **mortality** (rates of death) and **morbidity** (rates of disease). A period of stress might be very short-lived, recurring or episodic, or chronic. Each form can leave some signature in the surviving tissues of an individual, but chronic stress is more likely to result in some pathological condition that can be seen in the skeleton. Given that the majority of human remains recovered from archaeological contexts are skeletal, most assessments of stress are made using skeletal remains and so reflect chronic conditions. Finally, it is important to understand that in determining levels of stress in skeletal remains, the **etiology** (cause) of the conditions are poorly understood, prehistoric populations are compared to modern standards (which may not be analogous), and terminology is often not standardized (Lewis and Roberts 1997; also see Steckel and Rose 2005; Steckel and Kjellström 2019).

Stress is also associated with concepts of health in past populations, and the terms "stress" and "health" are sometimes used interchangeably (Temple and Goodman 2014). However, the notion of health is subjective to some degree, since it is defined by bioarchaeologists rather than by the society to which the past person belonged and that we are only saying something about the "health of the skeleton." As such, Temple and Goodman (2014; also see Buzon 2012) emphasized a biocultural approach integrating human biology, primatology, and social epidemiology. Wood et al. (1992) cautioned that skeletal indicators of stress may not simply relate to health and that survivorship may be a better measure than prevalence (also see Temple and Goodman 2014:189).

Stress in early childhood is also a critical factor in the future health of an individual. If a person was subjected to nutritional, metabolic, and/or general stress during the fetal or postnatal period, it will adversely affect developmental trajectories and increase the impact of morbidity and mortality of those who survived into adulthood (e.g., Barker 2012:186; also see Beaumont et al. 2015; Hoy and Nicol 2019). Further, there is growing evidence that the effects of early stress might result in epigenic changes (through such individuals having lower fertility) that can be transmitted across generations and "demonstrates that health cannot be understood in terms of immediate environmental circumstances alone" (Gowland 2015:530).

Metabolic stress

Metabolic stress results from the disruption of some biological function of the body. Such a disruption may originate through a genetic defect, disease, nutritional deficiency, and even psychological stress. At issue is the difficulty in discriminating these conditions, since a metabolic disruption is generally nonspecific. In many cases, metabolic stress is presumed to be related to a nutritional deficiency.

The metabolic disruption pathologies most commonly associated with nutritional deficiencies involve growth interruptions, such as porotic hyperostosis and cribra orbitalia on the skull, Harris lines on long bones, and developmental defects of enamel. Each category is discussed next.

Porotic hyperostosis and cribra orbitalia

The best-studied manifestation of a metabolic (presumed nutritional) deficiency is **porotic hyperostosis** (a term coined by Angel 1966a), believed to be a skeletal manifestation of iron-deficiency anemia, an abnormally low number of red blood cells. Anemia can be caused by blood loss, genetic (e.g., sickle cell, thalassemia) disease, and nutritional (e.g., iron-deficiency) issues, the latter being most commonly proposed (e.g., Roberts and Manchester 2007:225–232; Larsen 2015:31–41; Papathanasiou et al. 2019). However, the iron-deficiency model has been questioned (Walker et al. 2009), and there seems to be a shift in thinking that vitamin B$_{12}$ and B$_9$ deficiency may be the issue, although there remains considerable disagreement (Larsen 2015; Mcilvaine 2015; Rivera and Lahr 2017). Brickley (2018) argued that evidence of marrow expansion was necessary to diagnose anemia as a cause.

Anemia acts on the kidneys to release erythropoietin, which will stimulate an increase in production of red blood cells, and if the condition persists, it may ultimately result in enlargement of the diploë space (the cancellous layer in between the inner and outer layers of the bones of the skull) with lesions and pitting developing on the surface of the frontal, parietal, and occipital bones of the cranium (Figure 5.1).

Figure 5.1 An example of porotic hyperostosis in cranial bones
Source: Simon Mays

Hooton (1930:316) first identified porotic hyperostosis from observations he made on crania from Pecos Pueblo, calling them "symmetrical osteoporosis" and a "mysterious disease."

Although anemia can occur at any time in life, severe porotic hyperostosis tends to be found more frequently in infants and children because their bones are thinner and not fully mineralized, whereas adult bone is more resistant. In addition, by six months of age, children have depleted the accumulated iron stores obtained from their mother in utero and are trying to triple their blood supply (hematopoietic activity), so they need more iron. The increased need for iron may be complicated by malnutrition, and the lack of iron in their diet will likely produce severe iron-deficiency anemia. If a child with porotic hyperostosis survives into adulthood, the lesions and pitting can remain with that individual for a long time, eventually becoming healed and remodeled and less evident on the bone (e.g., Lewis 2018:194–197).

Porotic hyperostosis also appears to be related to stress, perhaps due to nutritional deficiencies, disease, or other factors such as childbearing, quality of life, or status (recognizing that these are not independent variables). In addition, the adoption of maize agriculture may have had a negative impact on dietary nutrition, leading to an increase in the condition (El-Najjar et al. 1976; also see Larsen 2015).

A second condition commonly associated with anemia is **cribra orbitalia**, lesions that involve the upper interior (roof) of the eye orbits (Figure 5.2). The etiology of cribra orbitalia is commonly believed to be the same as porotic hyperostosis (Lallo et al. 1977; but see Rivera and Lahr 2017). Nevertheless, there is now evidence that cribra orbitalia may also be the result of inflammation of the orbit bones, perhaps due to vitamin deficiencies, such as vitamin C, or trauma-related bruising (Larsen 2015:39).

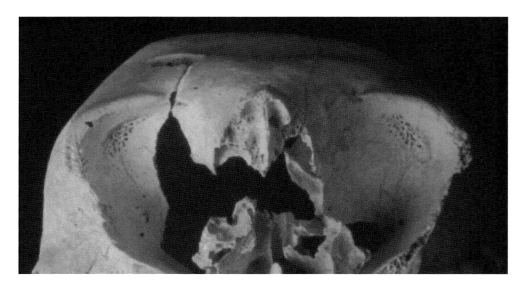

Figure 5.2 An example of cribra orbitalia

Source: Simon Mays

Harris lines

During times of stress, such as metabolic or nutritional stress, normal bone growth of infants and adolescents may be interrupted, resulting in the formation of **Harris lines**, lattice-like plates of bone that form in the metaphyses of long bones after growth resumes, resulting in alternatively thinner and denser bone mineralization seen as lines in the bone (Figure 5.3; also see Figure 3.9). There is some debate about the origin of Harris lines. Papageorgopoulou et al. (2011; also see Alfonso-Durruty 2011) suggested that Harris lines could also occur in healthy persons; the result of normal growth and growth spurts, rather than being strictly related to nutritional or pathological stress.

Harris lines are usually deposited transverse to the length of the bone (Larsen 2015:42–44) and are a common aspect of examination in skeletal analysis. Harris lines may be visible

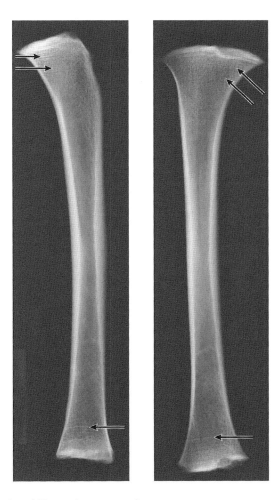

Figure 5.3 An example of Harris lines in a tibia

Source: Author

either by radiograph or in cross-section. Due to bone remodeling during the adult years, evidence of Harris lines fades with age and typically disappears by the time a person is about 30 years old (Vyhnanek and Stoukal 1991).

Harris lines appear most frequently in long bones, and the tibia (particularly the distal tibia), femur, and radius are the best elements to examine (Martin et al. 1985:259). The location of the lines relative to the epiphyseal plates may be used to estimate the age at which the individual was stressed, although this is a difficult process (Martin et al. 1985:261–263) due to problems in accurately dating the events relative to the age of the individual. Hughes et al. (1996) cautioned that Harris lines from one bone or type of long bone is not sufficient to determine the overall health of an individual.

Developmental defects of enamel

Dental health and condition can be correlated with metabolic disruptions within populations, typically seen as reflecting diet and stress (Hillson 2005, 2019; Larsen 2015:44–57; Bereczki et al. 2019). The enamel on teeth contain a partial record of metabolic disruptions (nutrition and morbidity) during their development (even prenatally), so can provide a record of stress from before birth to about 7 years of age in primary teeth and from about 7 to 18 years of age in secondary teeth. As enamel is not living tissue (it is crystalized hydroxyapatite), it does not resorb and so it retains a permanent record (Hillson 2005:158).

There are general associations between developmental defects of enamel (DDE) and a variety of clinical conditions, diseases, and malnutrition, but it is not currently linked to any specific disorder (see Bereczki et al. 2019:175–176). Thus, caution must always be exercised in the diagnosis of these types of conditions. DDE might also be produced as the result of other stressors, such as warfare, population pressures, or contact with Europeans (e.g., crowd diseases) (Wright 1990; Hutchinson and Larsen 2001). In addition, DDE may be used to measure developmental stress on some domestic animals (e.g., pigs, [Dobney and Ervynck 2000]), providing information on resources employed in raising them or on hunted animals, with implications regarding subsistence (e.g., Niven et al. 2004).

DDE can manifest in several conditions, such as **Wilson bands** and/or **linear enamel hypoplasia**. The ordeal experienced by a newborn during the birth process results in the formation of a **neonatal line** in their teeth that is easily recognized under magnification. Because enamel bands form on a daily basis, counting the bands from the neonatal line forward could provide a precise age at death (Smith and Avishai 2005), or at least the age when the primary tooth stopped growing.

WILSON BANDS

During normal crown formation, enamel is deposited daily in a series of very thin incremental layers called cross-striations (Antoine et al. 2019:230). However, metabolic stress of just a few days may cause short-term disruption of enamel growth, which may result in slight alteration of the matrix of the enamel. These irregular episodes may be visible under magnification as discolored lines and are commonly called Wilson bands (Antoine et al. 2019:236). As the normal tooth growth sequence is well known, the location of Wilson bands in the enamel matrix can be used to deduce the age of the individual at the time of the metabolic disruption.

LINEAR ENAMEL HYPOPLASIA

More profound disruptions (weeks to months) may affect the overall development of the enamel and may be manifested in variation of its thickness. Once the disruptive stress recedes, the enamel will resume its normal development, leaving an area of thin enamel that can be seen as transverse variations in enamel thickness, called linear enamel hypoplasia (LEH) (Bereczki et al. 2019). An episode of some nonmetabolic trauma could affect only a few teeth, whereas a hypoplasia caused by metabolic disruption should show up as a simultaneous event in many teeth relative to the development of the teeth. LEH lines can be seen with the naked eye (Figure 5.4), and the distance between the hypoplasia and the gum line can be used to estimate the age of the disruption (Goodman and Song 1999).

HYPOCALCIFICATION

Hypocalcifications are discolored patches of enamel that can form during mild disruptions of the mineralization process. Such patches of enamel are softer than normal enamel. The relationship of hypocalcification to diet is unclear.

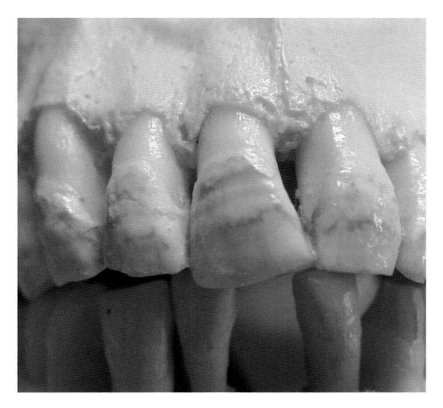

Figure 5.4 An example of linear enamel hypoplasia

Source: Author

Nutritional stress

Nutritional stress is the result of a lack of proper nutrition, which in turn could cause metabolic disruptions (as discussed earlier). Thus, in many cases, it is difficult to distinguish metabolic from nutritional stresses, as they both can cause the same types of disorders. For example, the current "go-to" explanation for porotic hyperostosis is a metabolic disruption due to anemia, but the underlying cause might actually be a more generalized nutritional stress. Protein-energy deficiencies will manifest themselves in nonspecific ways (so are difficult to diagnose), whereas some vitamin-related deficiencies may be more specific. Martin et al. (1985:234) noted that, in general, "the skeletal response to nutritional stress is an increase in [bone] resorption and a decrease in [bone] formation resulting in a net loss of bone." Another indicator of developmental stress is asymmetric growth (e.g., DeLeon 2006).

Paleonutrition

Paleonutrition is the study of prehistoric human diet in relation to health, nutrition, morbidity, and mortality for both individuals and populations (Sutton et al. 2010). Paleonutrition is not confined only to the study of foods and other consumed materials, but to the methods, technology, and organizations used by prehistoric peoples to obtain, process, and ingest such materials. It also includes the study of food choice (no society eats all of the possible foods present in their habitat); the natural, social, and political influences on diet (e.g., drought or war-related famine); and how these factors influence human adaptations through time.

Currently, studies related to paleonutrition are overwhelmingly concerned with diet and how diet affects health. To understand how diet and health are related, however, it is necessary to understand the entire subsistence system. Diet can be seen as what is eaten; nutrition as how the diet provides the necessary materials to maintain the body; and subsistence as the entire system (strategies, tactics, settlement, and technology) of procurement, processing, and consumption of foodstuffs. Health reflects nutrition as well as other stress experiences. These components are intertwined, and an understanding of all the components is necessary for an understanding of both individuals and populations.

Although "diet" is typically regarded as the foods that were consumed, it also includes any other materials ingested into the body, such as condiments, medicines, ritual substances, recreational substances, and things swallowed accidentally. Thus, when diet is analyzed, some or all of the other nonfood materials that are consumed may be present in the data and require analytical consideration. Even the diet of certain domesticated animals may be of interest in that they may mirror human diet (e.g., dogs) or relate to other cultural practices (e.g., growing certain crops as animal feed).

PALEONUTRITION DATA SETS

Paleonutrition data are derived from many different sources, including plant and animal remains, skeletal materials, procurement and processing technology, and even settlement patterns. These data sources can be characterized as either direct or indirect (Sutton 1994). Direct data are those where no inference is necessary; the remains are directly linked to human paleonutrition (such as constituents in paleofeces). Indirect data require an inference to link them to human paleonutrition and constitute the vast majority of paleonutritional information from archaeological sites. Data related to prehistoric diet, nutrition, and health are present in the archaeological record in five basic types: bioarchaeological, biomolecular, paleobotanical, zooarchaeological (faunal), and paleofecal. Bioarchaeological data are discussed throughout this volume, and biomolecular data are discussed in Chapter 8. The following considers the paleobotanical, zooarchaeological (faunal), and paleofecal data sets.

Paleobotanical remains include macro seeds, nuts, fruits, fiber, wood, and charcoal, as well as micro pollen, phytoliths, and fibers. Such remains reflect the plants used by societies in their diets and manufacturing processes. In most cases, plant remains would need to be carbonized to be preserved in the archaeological record, although some plant remains might be preserved on mummified remains. In any archaeological investigation of a site, all paleobotanical remains found in direct association with human remains should be compared, if possible, to those found in the general site deposit.

Like plant remains, animal remains (zooarchaeological or faunal) can include a variety of materials, primarily bone but also shell, chitin (e.g., insect exoskeletons), soft tissues (e.g., skin, muscle, hair, feathers), blood, proteins, and ancient DNA (aDNA). Most terrestrial animals, including humans, share a similar skeleton architecture, but a few (such as turtles and tortoises) have bony shells that, if fragmented, may appear to be parts of a skull. Fish and birds have unique skeletal structures. Invertebrates consist of insects, mollusks (e.g., shellfish), crabs, lobsters, shrimp, spiders, scorpions, and worms. As with plant remains, most faunal remains are interpreted as food residues, or as food offerings if found in association with human remains. There are major exceptions, such as animals (e.g., horses or dogs) that are sacrificed and buried with their presumptive owners. Such occurrences can shed a great deal of light on funerary systems and social standing.

Paleofeces (desiccated human fecal matter) are a unique resource for analyzing health and paleonutrition because they offer direct insight into prehistoric diet. The constituents of paleofeces are mostly the remains of intentionally consumed items. Endoparasites found in paleofeces reflect the parasitic load of the individual, and potentially the load of the population, therefore providing direct data on health. Proteins and aDNA have also been identified from paleofeces (Sutton et al. 1996; Gilbert et al. 2008), providing information regarding a variety of questions of interest to bioarchaeologists.

GENERAL NUTRITIONAL DEFICIENCIES

Typically, nutritional deficiencies indicate a lack of calories and/or protein, depending on climate, diet, and age. Calories are units of energy obtained from food. Some 70% of calories consumed by humans are utilized to maintain body temperature and the rest for fuel, with excess calories being stored as fat. Proteins are complex combinations of amino acids. As protein is consumed, it is broken down into its amino acids, which are then used to build new proteins in the consumer or converted into fuel. If the body does not take in sufficient calories or proteins, it will begin to "digest" itself to maintain its metabolic functions, beginning with fats, then muscles, and eventually organs, ultimately resulting in death. Nutritional deficiencies will result in an increase in frailty (e.g., Marklein et al. 2016; Yaussy et al. 2016), morbidity (through a declining immune system), and ultimately mortality.

Severe nutritional deficiency is often referred to as starvation in individuals and famine in populations. Four categories of famine were defined by Horocholyn and Brickley (2017): (1) an ecological disaster, (2) an event of mass starvation, (3) sustained periods of nutritional stress, and (4) and population-wide food shortage. Food shortages might be due to ecological factors, such as drought, but may also be due to social factors such as warfare.

VITAMIN DEFICIENCIES

Vitamins are organic compounds needed to maintain certain body functions. Most vitamins cannot be manufactured in the body, so they must be obtained in the diet. The body requires a variety of vitamins, some in fairly large quantities and some in very small amounts. Some vitamins are fat-soluble and can be stored in the body for long periods. Others are water-soluble and are easily lost in the process of cooking and by the body during urination.

A number of vitamin-related nutritional deficiencies (see Huss-Ashmore et al. 1982; Brickley et al. 2005, 2006) may be reflected in the skeleton, often resulting in osteopenia (bone loss). For example, scurvy (vitamin C deficiency; see Crandall and Klaus 2014) results in bone thinning and pathological fractures and lesions in fast-growing portions of bones. It is most notable in children and has been identified in infant skeletons (Brickley and Ives 2005; Snoddy et al. 2018).

A deficiency in vitamin D prevents the proper mineralization of bone proteins. The resulting condition (called **rickets** in subadults and **osteomalacia** in adults) may cause bent and distorted bones (often limbs; Figure 5.5) and a number of other issues, such as immunoregulation disorders, complications with blood pressure homeostasis, and cell division diseases (Snoddy et al. 2016). Both rickets (e.g., Roberts and Manchester 2007; Waters-Rista and Hoogland 2018) and osteomalacia (Brickley et al. 2005, 2006; Ives and Brickley 2014; Brickley and Buckberry 2015) have been identified in skeletal populations by radiological, bone density, and histological studies (D'Ortenzio et al. 2016; Alonso-Llamazares et al. 2018; Mays and Brickley 2018). Rickets is often seen among agricultural

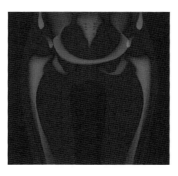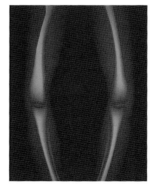

Figure 5.5 An example of rickets in the leg bones of a subadult

Source: Alamy Image ID: R93JA5

groups dependent on grain crops due to a lack of calcium absorption caused by the grain chemistry (e.g., Ivanhoe 1985).

Occupational and activity stress

Activity of any kind will put mechanical stress on the structure of the body in bone, muscle, and connective tissues. Such stress will produce changes in the various structures, depending on the intensity, repetition, and permanence of the activity, following the tenets of biomechanics. If overworked, structures will eventually degenerate and fail. In each case, the signatures of these activities will manifest on the skeleton (see Pearson and Buikstra 2006).

Biomechanics

Biomechanics is the study of the mechanical laws relating to the movement or structure of living organisms, in our case, humans (e.g., Özkaya et al. 2017). Biomechanics is a measure of work load and stresses and is also a factor in the response of the skeleton to trauma, such as a bone fracture.

Bone is affected by degrees of physical activity through remodeling and new bone formation. Under mechanical stress, bone tends to be become thicker and stronger and can be measured by its cross-sectional geometry. An understanding of the biomechanics of bone permits estimates of work load, even by age and sex (e.g., Skedros 2012).

Factors such as nutritional deficiencies and disease must be considered in an analysis of biomechanics in bone, since such maladies can result in the overall loss of bone (even under mechanical stress) and a weakening of the structure. An understanding of bone histology and dynamics of remodeling can mitigate these issues (see Pearson and Buikstra 2006:211–215).

Occupational patterns in bone

Many occupations require long periods of repeated motion or heavy workloads on body structures. In stress-bearing bones, such as the arms and legs, cortical bone will increase in thickness, and the overall geometry of the bone will change to adjust to the stress. These changes in geometry and robustness can be measured in the skeleton.

For example, Holt and Whittey (2019) reported that habitual travel over rough terrain resulted in the alteration of the diaphyseal structures of the lower limb bones in response to mechanical stress. In a related study, Ruff (2019) reported that the leg bones of agriculturalists showed a weakening of the leg bones from their hunter-gatherer ancestors, likely due to a decrease in mobility and less stress on the legs. The humeri of Native American women in eastern North America showed increased robustness, suggested to be the result of processing deer hides (Cameron et al. 2018). Other examples include "atlatl elbow," the wear on the elbow joint from the consistent use of a spear thrower (Angel 1966b; Bridges 1990), and changes in the shape of the pelvis in habitual horse riders (Berthon et al. 2019).

The locations where muscles are attached to the bone (called entheses) may also be indicative of activity stressors (called **entheseal changes** or musculoskeletal stress markers) (Pearson and Buikstra 2006:220–224). Entheseal changes (Figure 5.6) have been widely used in the study of activity patterns, although there is no single protocol for the

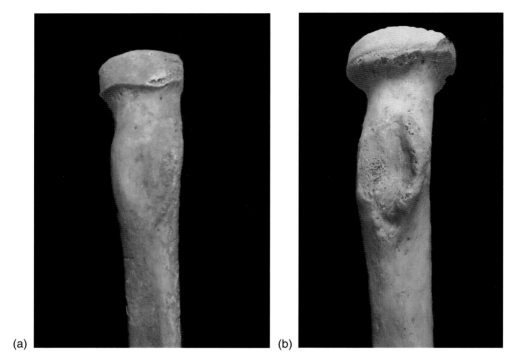

(a)   (b)

Figure 5.6 An example of entheseal change in a proximal radius: (a) a typical muscle attach-
        ment and (b) an enlarged muscle attachment
Source: Elizabeth Weiss

measurement and evaluation of such changes (Michopoulou et al. 2015, 2016; Weiss 2015b; Henderson et al. 2017). It is now apparent that other factors, such as age and sex, are also significant components (Milella et al. 2012; Henderson and Nikita 2016). Examples of such entheseal changes can be seen in the robust muscle attachments in the arm bones of English archers (Stirland 2012) and in the lower limbs of horse riders (Djukic et al. 2018).

Worn out: osteoarthritis

Osteoarthritis (OA), sometimes referred to as degenerative joint disease, is a condition caused by the cumulative effects of wear and tear on the joints through activity. OA takes many forms (e.g., erosive arthritis, rheumatoid arthritis, psoriatic arthritis) and is a disease caused by a malfunction of the autoimmune system (see Chapter 6 for details). OA is the second most common condition found in the skeleton, second only to dental disease (Waldron 2009:26). It can develop in any joint but is primarily seen in mobile joints such as those of the vertebrae and the appendicular skeleton. A related problem, osteoarthrosis, involves degeneration of the vertebrae and is also considered to be OA (Larsen and Ruff 2011:294).

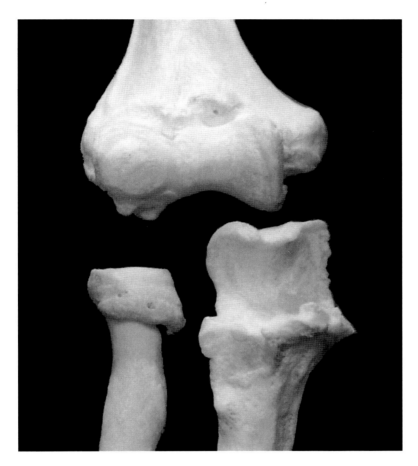

Figure 5.7 Eburnation (bone-on-bone wear) in an elbow
Source: Eric Bartelink

The development of OA involves the breakdown of cartilage, subsequent inflammation, and eventually the development of new bone in an attempt to "repair" the damage (Waldron 2009:27). Although there is disagreement regarding the etiology of the condition, it is clear that a "mechanical loading environment due to activity routinely figures most prominently" (K. Williams et al. 2019:253). Age and body mass are contributing factors (Weiss 2006). The visible manifestations of OA include (1) polished surfaces of articulating bones, called **eburnation**, from direct bone-on-bone wear (Figure 5.7); (2) the formation of bone lipping, called **osteophytes**, along the edges of the joint (Figure 5.8); (3) exostoses (bone spurs) in and around the joint, the latter commonly visible in vertebrae; and/or (4) the porosity of the joint surface.

As noted, OA is a common malady, found in most populations. For example, Fritsch et al. (2015) conducted computerized tomography (CT) scans on 52 ancient Egyptian mummies, examining all of the large joints. They found osteoarthritic changes in the

Figure 5.8 Osteophytes (lipping) in an osteoarthritic vertebra

Source: Marni LaFleur

spines of 25 individuals, 15 cases of other joint involvement, and 6 cases of scoliosis (curved spines). They concluded that the ancient Egyptians suffered from a variety of painful orthopedic conditions.

OA can be used as a measure of workload. In a study of 7,540 individuals from 103 sites in Europe dating from the pre-medieval period (ca. AD 500) through the Industrial/ Modern period (ca. AD 1900), K. Williams et al. (2019:297) showed an increase in OA workload between about AD 500 and 900, then a decrease in OA workload until about AD 1300, when it increased again. K. Williams et al. (2019:297) suggested that increasing urbanization led to poor health and quality of life.

Case study: mobility and pathology in the prehistoric Great Basin of North America

The Stillwater Marsh lies within the Carson Sink in western Nevada (Figure 5.9). Today, the Stillwater Marsh covers some 10,000 acres, but several thousand years ago was more than twice as large. In prehistory, the Carson Sink was occupied by populations of hunter-gatherers, although the nature of that occupation is poorly understood.

Major flooding in the Carson Sink between 1983 and 1986 exposed a large number of previously unknown prehistoric sites, including major residential locations and hundreds (ca. 400) of inhumations (Raymond and Parks 1990). The sites dated between 3,000 and 500 BP. Although none of the sites appeared to be permanent year-round occupations, it seems that the Stillwater Marsh was a "hub of residential activity" between about 2,000 and 600 BP (Kelly 2001:290).

Following these discoveries, a debate began regarding the role of marsh resources in the settlement and subsistence systems of hunter-gatherers. Two models (Bettinger 1993:45–47) were proposed: a "limogood" ("limo" referring

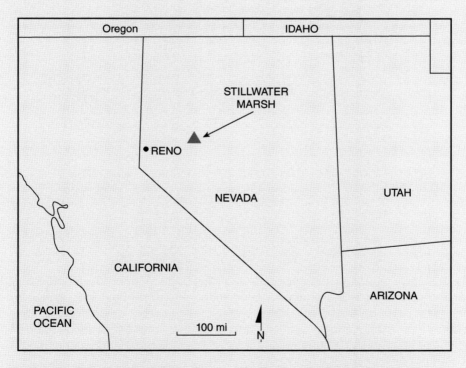

Figure 5.9 Location of the Carson Sink and Stillwater Marsh in western Nevada
Source: Author

to lakeshores) model stating that wetlands were oases supporting low-mobility, sedentary populations using a relatively small number of highly productive resources, and a "limobad" model stating that wetlands provided a large number of resources with low productivity used by highly mobile groups who did not have permanent villages.

To address these issues (and others), the Stillwater burial population (all ages and sexes) was examined for evidence of mobility patterns and subsistence practices (see Larsen and Kelly 1995; Larsen et al. 1995; Hemphill and Larsen 1999). It was found that, in general, the people were healthy but that both males and females had high rates of OA, indicative of heavy workloads (Larsen and Hutchinson 1999:201). Hemphill (1999; also see Larsen and Hutchinson 1999:196) found that females tended to have greater OA issues with their hands and knees, suggesting that females knelt and used their hands in a repetitive motion more than males did. Males tended to have more OA issues in their shoulders and arms, indicating that males used their upper bodies more than females did. In addition, males had more problems with their legs and hips, likely due to long-distance travel on rough terrain (hunting trips?). Together, this suggested that the people led a fairly semi-sedentary lifestyle (Hemphill 1999). Isotopic and pathological data demonstrated a generalized subsistence strategy and periodic food shortages (Schoeninger 1999:165). There was little skeletal evidence of violence (Kelly 1997:27).

In sum, the people living around the Stillwater Marsh seem to have been "limo-neutral." The population was relatively healthy, peaceful, had a diet with many resources, a clear sexual division of labor, and a fair amount of mobility.

Detecting general stress

Stress is a general term that describes a variety of conditions. When stress is seen in the bioarchaeological record, it is commonly categorized as either metabolic or nutritional. Although it seems likely that the immediate causes of stress would fall into one of these categories, it is also possible that in some cases other underlying issues, such as psychological stress, could have been the original problem. Diagnosing such general stress can be quite difficult. Stress can also depress the immune system, leading to an increase in the susceptibility to disease.

One possible indicator of general stress is cortisol, a steroid hormone produced in the adrenal gland. Cortisol has a variety of functions and effects, including an increase in blood sugar, suppression of the immune system, and as an aid in metabolism. An effect of too much cortisol is a decrease in bone formation. Contemporary medical studies have shown that general stress can be assessed using systemic cortisol levels that are known to fluctuate in response to stress (Webb et al. 2010).

In a study on the cortisol levels in the hair samples of 10 individuals from five archaeological sites in Peru, Webb et al. (2010) reported fluctuating patterns of cortisol production, suggesting that the stress of those individuals could be measured for the time represented by the samples. Thus, this technique can supplement other bioarchaeological studies of health and stress.

In a follow-up study, Webb et al. (2015) measured cortisol (and stable isotope) levels in the hair of five mummified juveniles from the Nasca region in Peru. Nitrogen was used to investigate dietary change, and cortisol levels were measured to infer exposure to stress. They found that the children shifted diet from nursing to a weaning diet and then to a diet more similar to that of adults. Of interest was the high level of cortisol in the children, suggestive of high stress that may be related to a lack of nutrition or abuse. In addition, high or low levels of cortisol in children can lead to cognitive impairment.

Chapter summary

Paleopathology is the study of stress, disease, and trauma in human remains and is a major focus in bioarchaeology. To adequately assess the impact of pathologies, a determination of when it occurred (antemortem, perimortem, or postmortem) is important, as are taphonomic considerations. In many cases, the cause of a pathology is difficult to determine.

Pathologies are often viewed in the framework of stress: metabolic, nutritional, or occupational. In each case, stress can result in a number of pathologies, including increased morbidity, interruptions in growth, skeletal damage, and ultimately mortality. Unfortunately, it is very difficult to determine the specific stressor associated with any particular pathology. Common pathologies reflecting either metabolic or nutritional stress include lesions and pitting in bone (porotic hyperostosis and cribra orbitalia), interruptions in bone growth (Harris lines), and interruptions in the growth of teeth (Wilson bands and LEH).

The study of diet, called paleonutrition, can also provide information applicable to determinations of nutritional stress. Direct evidence of diet is present in paleofeces, whereas indirect evidence is present in botanical and faunal remains. Some nutritional deficiencies can result in specific pathologies, such as rickets as the result of a vitamin D deficiency.

Mechanical stress from activity will cause alterations in bone, including an increase in thickness, changes in shape, and the development of more robust muscle attachments. Continued activity, perhaps coupled with age and morbidity, will result in OA, a common pathology. Severe OA can result in bone-on-bone wear (eburnation) and the development of bone formation (lipping and spurs) in and around the joint.

Key concepts and terms

biomechanics
consistent with
cribra orbitalia
developmental defects of enamel (DDE)
diagnostic
eburnation
entheseal change
etiology
Harris lines
hypocalcifications

linear enamel hypoplasia (LEH)
metabolic stress
morbidity
mortality
neonatal line
nutritional stress
osteoarthritis (OA)
osteomalacia
osteophytes
paleoepidemiological stress model
paleonutrition
pathognomic
porotic hyperostosis
rickets
Wilson bands

Chapter 6

Paleopathology II
Disease and abnormalities

Disease

Disease is an abnormal condition or disorder of a body structure or function. Some diseases, such as certain metabolic syndromes (discussed in Chapter 5), cancer, or autoimmune conditions, originate from some internal condition or defect. Others, such as bacterial or viral infections, primarily originate outside the body and can spread from person to person (contagious diseases). Disease is viewed as a medical condition associated with specific indications, and the study of disease is called pathology.

Pathology of disease addresses four components: (1) etiology (cause), (2) pathogenesis (mechanisms of development), (3) morphologic change (structural alterations of cells), and (4) clinical manifestations (the consequences of changes). Paleopathology of disease involves scientific research to increase accuracy in diagnosis in ancient human remains and to place disease within a biocultural context (e.g., Waldron 2009). The effects of disease on morbidity and mortality are poorly known (except in some cases such as the bubonic plague in Europe). For example, nonvenereal syphilis diseases often leave skeletal markers in their late stages but are not commonly fatal, whereas tuberculosis is rarely seen in skeletal remains but has a high risk of death, perhaps leading to an underestimation of the impact of tuberculosis on mortality (Cook and Powell 2006:311).

Epidemiology is the study and analysis of the patterns, causes, and effects of health and disease conditions in defined modern populations. **Paleoepidemiology** focuses on the same issues in past populations and is an integral part of understanding the impact of disease on those populations (e.g., Milner and Boldsen 2017).

Skeletal pathology of disease

The majority of skeletal pathologies result from infectious, degenerative, and nutritional deficiency diseases, with pathology related to degenerative disease the most common (White and Folkens 2005:312). Trauma, although not technically a pathology, is also often evident on skeletal remains and is considered in Chapter 7. Comprehensive reviews of human skeletal pathologies are present in White and Folkens (2005), Roberts and Manchester (2007), Waldron (2009), Mann and Hunt (2012), Larsen (2015), and Buikstra (2019). Dental pathology is discussed separately later.

Most diseases are too short-lived to form distinct lesions on the skeleton, although such evidence is sometimes present (e.g., Roberts and Manchester 2007; Waldron 2009)

(Table 6.1). However, some chronic conditions can result in the formation of lesions on the surface of the bone, but such lesions are usually nonspecific (Rothschild and Rothschild 1997) and poorly understood (Lewis 2004). A few diseases will produce diagnostic bone lesions that can be identified in individuals and populations. A relatively new approach to the identification of disease in bone is the detection of specific pathogens using ancient DNA (aDNA) (e.g., Rasmussen et al. 2015; Nieves-Colón and Stone 2019:530–533).

Table 6.1 Some diseases and corresponding general pathologies

Disease	Skeletal		Soft tissue	
	General locations	*Pathology*	*Tissue type*	*Pathology*
Cancer				
Carcinoma	anywhere	tumor	Soft	skin or soft tissue involvement
Osteosarcoma	mostly long bones	tumor	–	–
Infectious disease				
Pinta	N/A	N/A	Skin	sores and lesions
Bejel	legs and face	bone erosion	Skin	sores and lesions
Yaws	face and joints	bone erosion	Skin	lesions and nodules
Venereal Syphilis	primary: none secondary: none tertiary: skull and face, among others	bone erosion	Various	primary: skin chancre secondary: rash and sores tertiary: central nervous system, organs
Tuberculosis	skeletal involvement rare but could manifest in the vertebral column, cranium, ribs, hip, knee, or wrist	abscesses and loss of bone, especially in the vertebral column	Lungs	tubercles
Leprosy	hands, feet, and face	osteomyelitis, disfigurement	skin and respiratory tract	skin lesions, secondary infections
Polio	spine and limb bones	**subadults**: disrupted growth, possible osteoporosis, differential limb bone length **adults**: no differential limb bone lengths but affected elements would tend to be more gracile due to atrophy	Various	atrophied muscles

Disease	Skeletal		Soft tissue	
	General locations	Pathology	Tissue type	Pathology
Smallpox	rare skeletal involvement	new bone formation in the elbows	Skin	pox lesions
Dog Tapeworm	various	calcified cystic lesions in the bone with possible pathologic fractures	Various	calcified cystic lesions
Crowd Diseases	rare skeletal involvement	none visible on the skeleton	Various	infections, skin lesions
Degenerative conditions and diseases				
Osteoarthritis	most joints, vertebrae	eburnation, formation of bone along the edges of the joint, bone spurs in and around the joint, commonly visible in vertebrae	N/A	N/A
Rheumatoid Arthritis	joints, especially hands and feet	erosion of the bone, ultimately resulting in disfiguration	hands and feet	visible disfigurement
Marfan Syndrome	long bones and vertebral column	long bones of unusual length, scoliosis	heart, aorta, lungs, eyes	increased risk of systems failure
Other				
Sinusitis	sinus, orbits	development of new bone on the floor of the sinus	Sinus	inflammation of the sinuses
Periostosis	periosteum	development of new bone at site of infection	N/A	N/A
Paget's disease	pelvis, skull, spine, and legs	fragile and misshapen bone	N/A	N/A
Nonspecific Infections	anywhere	nonspecific	Anywhere	nonspecific
Fungal Infections	any bone, most commonly skull and vertebrae	small ovoid depression lesions	lungs and skin	nodules in lungs, ulcers and lesions on skin

Infections of the bone can occur on the surface or interior of the bone. If the **periosteum** – the tissue on the surface of the bone – becomes infected, it results in a **periosteal reaction** (or **periostosis**), frequently forming a lesion (Waldron 2009:84) (Figure 6.1). Periostosis is often the result of a trauma or other stimuli of the periosteum (see Waldron [2009:Table 6.7] for a list of some possibilities), typically results in the formation of new bone, and is most often identified on radiographs. New bone formation would indicate an infection or trauma but may not reveal a specific cause, and in subadults "should be regarded as physiological until proved otherwise" (Waldron 2009:116). Periosteal reactions on the interior surfaces of the ribs can be an indicator of lower respiratory tract disease (Davies-Barrett et al. 2019).

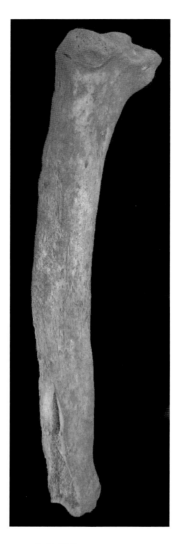

Figure 6.1 A periosteal lesion on a left tibia

Source: Eric Bartelink

If the interior of the bone becomes infected, it is called **osteomyelitis**. Such an infection could be the result of a penetrating injury (such as an animal bite or compound fracture), the direct spread of an infection from an adjacent (e.g., periosteal) area, or the indirect spread of an infection from another area via the bloodstream (Waldron 2009:84). Osteomyelitis infections result in the formation of a great deal of pus within the bone, causing internal pressure that may alter the shape of the bone and/or result in the formation of cloacae (drainage channels that appear to be foramina [openings in the bone for nerves or blood vessels]). In addition, new bone can form over the infected area in an attempt to "repair" the damage. Ear infections can involve the mastoid process, called mastoiditis, and can cause deafness (Flohr and Schultz 2009).

Cancers and tumors

Cancer is a "neoplastic" disease resulting in new and abnormal growth of tissue in some part of the body. Three major types of cancer can be defined: (1) carcinomas (those on the surface of tissues), (2) sarcomas (those within bone [**osteosarcoma**] or soft tissues), and (3) hematologic (those of the blood). The formation of malignant tumors (Waldron 2009:Table 9.4; also see Mann and Hunt 2012) that metastasize (spread) throughout the body is common (Waldron 2009:184–185), ultimately resulting in the death of the host. Cancer is a major cause of death worldwide today.

The study of cancers in the past, or paleo-oncology, is a newly developing field and includes the study of carcinomas and sarcomas in ancient human populations and their hominid precursors (Halperin 2004:1; Kirkpatrick et al. 2018). Of importance is the necessity to develop more accurate diagnostic methods and to deal with the problem of pseudopathology; that is, whether a pathologic lesion is antemortem (and so related to disease) or is not really a lesion but the result of postmortem taphonomic processes.

Many researchers believe that the prevalence of cancer was relatively low in the past and increased dramatically in recent times: a product of modern living, increased longevity, and pollution (e.g., Molnár et al. 2009). On the other hand, this view is tempered by the relative scarcity of data concerning the antiquity of cancer. Recently, a number of studies have suggested that cancer was a common disease through time; a database on ancient cancers, known as the Cancer Research in Ancient Bodies (CRAB) Database, is now available online. Other research is being conducted on molecular paleopathology with respect to data on carcinogenic factors (Nerlich 2018).

Skeletal or soft tissue evidence of cancer in the archaeological record (summarized by Hunt et al. [2018]) has been documented as early as 1.8 million years ago (Odes et al. 2016). The majority of reported examples are osteosarcomas (e.g., Molnár et al. 2009; Prates et al. 2011) (Figure 6.2), followed by myeloma (a blood cancer resulting from tumors in bone marrow). Other examples include metastatic carcinoma (Binder et al. 2014), metastasized prostate cancer (Klaus 2018), melanoma (Mark 2017), and leukemia (Rothschild et al. 1997).

Noncancerous (benign) tumors can also develop and are fairly common in bone and soft tissue (Waldron 2009:Table 9.2). In rare cases, a teratoma (exotic tissues typically in the gonad area) will develop. Such tumors might (among other possibilities) be the remains of an ectopic (outside the uterus) pregnancy or a parasitic twin. A parasitic twin could include amorphous fragments of bone and even teeth, as noted by Armentano et al. (2012) and Klaus and Ericksen (2013).

Benign tumors on the pituitary gland can cause acromegaly, an endocrine disorder that is a consequence of too much growth hormone in the body after childhood. Acromegaly is characterized by the enlargement of bone and soft tissue resulting from increases in the secretion of growth hormone. Onset typically occurs after epiphyseal fusion, a characteristic that distinguishes it from gigantism and can be identified in skeletal remains (Bartelink et al. 2014).

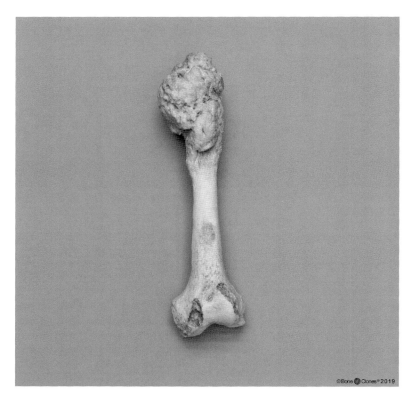

Figure 6.2 Example of an osteosarcoma on a femur (cast)
Source: Bone Clones

Infectious disease

Infectious diseases are those that can be transmitted from one individual to another through shared air, water, insect bites, or personal contact (see Table 6.1). Such diseases are usually caused either by viruses or protozoa (one-celled organisms such as bacteria, which are technically parasites). Disease is more prevalent in populations that are malnourished or otherwise immunocompromised. Some infectious diseases began as crossovers from diseases in domestic animals (**zoonosis**) that were in close contact with people, with some current examples being bird flu, swine flu, and COVID-19. Dutour (2013) presented a short history of the investigation of infectious diseases.

Most infectious diseases kill too quickly to leave any diagnostic traces on bone. Thus, they are difficult to recognize in skeletal remains. Mass burials could indicate disease as a cause of death, and the context and dating of such features could point toward a specific disease (e.g., plague cemeteries). The analysis of aDNA from the victims can also be used to identify the disease. However, treponemal diseases, tuberculosis, and leprosy often leave diagnostic traces in the skeleton.

Crowd diseases

Crowd diseases are those that are easily transmitted from person to person in crowded conditions, such as in large villages or cities. Such diseases include cholera, diphtheria, flu, leprosy, measles, smallpox, tuberculosis, typhus fever, and whooping cough, and are generally transmitted through personal contact, air, or water. A few other crowd diseases, such as bubonic plague, are spread after being bitten by infected fleas.

These diseases can be devastating and often pandemic. In the fourteenth century, bubonic plague (the "Black Death") killed millions of people (see DeWitte 2019), many of which were buried en masse in the "plague pits" now commonly found in European cities. Between about AD 1500 and 1900, European crowd diseases killed as much as 90% of the population of native North America (e.g., Cook 1998). A flu pandemic in the winter of 1918–1919 killed an estimated 20 to 50 million people, more than died in World War I. This type of disease remains a threat, as can be seen by outbreaks of Ebola and Covid-19.

TUBERCULOSIS

Tuberculosis (TB) is an infectious disease caused by the bacterium *Mycobacterium tuberculosis* (Waldron 2009:90; Roberts 2011), commonly associated with crowded conditions (Lewis 2018:155). Tuberculosis generally affects the lungs, and granulomas (or tubercles) can develop and interfere with breathing. The disease can also affect other parts of the body, even the skeleton, but in most cases are not detectable. The body mounts an effective immune response, and many people with TB are asymptomatic, although at one time the death rate in infants was relatively high (Lewis 2018:155). However, if a person is malnourished or otherwise compromised (e.g., with a different disease), the body is unable to contain the infection and the person will likely die.

Involvement of the skeleton is rare with TB (ca. 2% of cases; Waldron 2009:91), so even if a small number of individuals exhibit skeletal indications of the disease, it is likely that a much larger percentage of the population was infected. When skeletal indications are present, they are most often seen in the spine (Waldron 2009:93) but may also be found on the cranium, ribs, hip, knee, and wrist, among other places (see Lewis 2018:156–164). A TB infection in bone can cause considerable damage, including abscesses and loss of bone in the vertebral column.

Tuberculosis has been identified in the skeletal remains of individuals around the world based on evidence on the bones (e.g., Mariotti et al. 2015) and through molecular analyses (e.g., Mays and Taylor 2003; Zink et al. 2004). For example, a young child with probable signs of TB dating from the late medieval period (AD 1150–1539) in England was identified by Dawson and Brown (2012) based on a variety of lesions on the cranium, ribs, cervical vertebrae, and femora. Other research (e.g., Sparacello et al. 2016) has focused on skeletal traits that could result from a long-lasting TB infection, including body proportions, postcranial mechanical strength of bones, postcranial gracility, and disruption of development.

LEPROSY

Leprosy, also known as Hansen's disease, is a long-term infection caused by the bacteria *Mycobacterium leprae* or *M. lepromatosis* (Waldron 2009:98; Roberts 2011). It was a major disease during the Middle Ages and can be passed from mother to fetus (Lewis

2018:165). It is now easily treated with antibiotics; however, if left untreated, it can become a serious problem, causing disfigurement and disability. Leprosy typically manifests as nerve damage in the soft tissues of the skin (lesions) and respiratory tract and can lead to secondary infections (e.g., osteomyelitis) that may result in periosteal lesions in the bones of the face, hands, and feet (Roberts and Manchester 2007; Waldron 2009; Lewis 2018:167–170).

It is possible to diagnose leprosy in skeletal samples (Boldsen 2001; Roberts 2013). For example, Baker and Bolhofner (2014) identified the burial of a young woman dating from the medieval period on Cyprus. The skeleton showed multiple indications of leprosy, including pathologies of the face, teeth, hand phalanges, and metatarsals of both feet. In addition, periosteal reactions on the fibulae and distal tibiae demonstrated inflammation from the feet to the lower legs, suggesting disfigurement and debilitation. Nevertheless, the woman was buried within a high-status area of a basilica, suggesting that she was not ostracized in death. Skeletal evidence of leprosy has also been noted from burials in England (Roffey et al. 2017), Scotland (Taylor et al. 2000), and the Czech Republic (Likovsky et al. 2006).

Roberts (2013) reviewed the bioarchaeology of leprosy, outlined how it was treated in the past, and discussed its social dimensions. Of note was the common use of "leper colonies" to separate victims from the general population, a practice still used in some areas, such as India.

Treponemal diseases

Four infectious **treponemal diseases** are caused by different subspecies of the bacterium *Treponema pallidum*: pinta, bejel (endemic syphilis), yaws, and syphilis (venereal syphilis) (Waldron 2009:Table 6.4). Pinta is the least severe of the four, generally infects the skin, and does not leave a skeletal signature. Bejel begins as a skin infection but can affect the bones of the face and legs. Yaws is also a skin infection that results in lesions and nodules and can ultimately affect the bones of the face and joints. Venereal syphilis is the most serious of the treponemal diseases. It is sexually transmitted and passes through four stages: primary, secondary, latent, and tertiary. In primary syphilis, a skin chancre forms and heals. Later, secondary symptoms include rash and some sores that soon heal. The disease can then lie dormant (latent) for 3 to 15 years (or longer) before it enters its tertiary stage (about 30% of victims progress to tertiary syphilis). At that time, the disease will affect the central nervous system, organs, and bone, usually destructively (Figure 6.3). Venereal syphilis can be transmitted from a mother to her fetus (Lewis 2018:176).

There has been considerable debate regarding the geographic origin of syphilis: Was it in the Old World or the New World? Did Columbus's men introduce the dreaded disease to Europe after 1492, or did his men spread it to the native people of the New World? The debate over the origin of syphilis is not settled, but the current view is that at least some form of the disease initially developed in the New World and was transmitted to Europe by Columbus and others (Harper et al. 2008; Weiss 2015a). This view is supported by the discovery that treponemal infections of some type appeared as early as 5,000 years ago in fairly dense populations living along the coast of Santa Barbara, California (Walker et al. 2005).

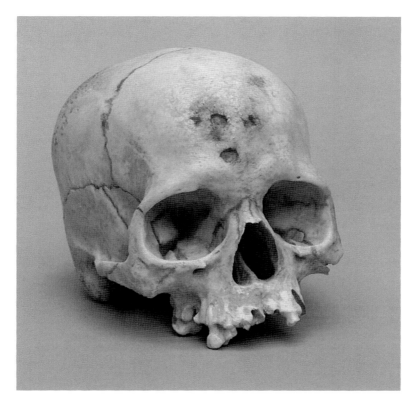

Figure 6.3 A human skull with syphilitic lesions (cast)
Source: Public domain

Polio

Poliomyelitis (**polio**; see Waldron 2009:109) is caused by a virus and has been present for at least several thousand years. A polio infection will usually cause little harm and will not leave visible traces in the body, but might be detected chemically. In about 1% of cases, though, the virus will attack the central nervous system and can cause paralysis of the associated muscles, sometimes leading to death. If this occurs in childhood, the affected skeletal elements will exhibit disrupted growth, possible osteoporosis, and limb bones that show asymmetric differences in length. If it is contracted in adulthood, limb bones will be the same length (having already completed growth) but the affected elements will tend to be less robust due to atrophy (Waldron 2009:109).

Malaria

Malaria is a mosquito-borne parasitic (*Plasmodium falciparum malaria*) disease. Once infected, the victim develops an infection in the blood and will have fever, chills, and flu–like illness, and may die if left untreated. Although it is possible to detect malaria from a visible pathological signature on the skeleton (Smith-Guzmán 2015), it can also be detected through aDNA (e.g., Soren 2003) or immunochemistry (e.g., AL-Khafif et al. 2018).

Another possible way to detect diseases is through the identification of unusual cemetery organization, such as mass plague cemeteries in London and elsewhere. In Italy, Soren (2003) discovered an unusual cemetery containing 47 infants dating from the Roman period. Included in the cemetery were a number of offerings associated with magical practices and an ancient epidemic, identified as malaria by aDNA. Soren (2003:193) proposed a protocol for the identification of abnormal cemeteries that included

> stratigraphy, the positioning of the mass burials, the nature of the material culture deposited with and around the burials, the palynological [pollen] evidence, various aspects of the skeletons themselves including the frequency of neonates and aborted foetuses, the tomb types and their hierarchical arrangement, evidence for ritual practices at the tomb site, the history of the area and parallels with other sites.

Degenerative disorders

Perhaps the most common affliction (though technically not a disease) reflected in the skeleton is bone loss (deossification), called **osteopenia** in its mild form or **osteoporosis** in its more severe form. Overall, skeletal (bone) mass increases until about the age of 40, then there is a net loss of bone that accelerates with age (Waldron 2009:118; Larsen 2015:57). Bone loss affects both men and women, but generally affects women more acutely (see Agarwal 2012) and can become severe after menopause, since the decline in estrogen accelerates bone loss. Most of the loss is in the cancellous bone, and as bone density decreases, the risk of fracture increases.

Bone loss is common (universal?) with age but can also be caused by a number of disorders, including dietary (Huss-Ashmore et al. 1982:423–432) and metabolic factors (Waldron 2009). This will result in a variety of problems, with fractures being the most common, particularly rib fractures (e.g., Brickley 2005). Bone density may also reflect stress in juveniles (see McEwan et al. 2005).

Erosive arthritis

Erosive arthritis, one type of degenerative disease, encompasses a number of joint diseases that are generally precipitated by inflammation (see Waldron 2009:46–71; Burt et al. 2013; Weiss 2015a:87–105). It is manifested as either degenerative joint disease (DJD) or degenerative disc disease (DDD). Of the DJD diseases, rheumatoid arthritis (RA) and gout are the most common. **Rheumatoid arthritis** is an autoimmune condition in which the body attacks the joints, causing inflammation that results in the irreversible erosion (damage) of the bone in the joints and ultimately in disfiguration (Waldron 2009:46–49). It is most common in the wrists and hands and is seen most frequently in women but is sometimes found in juveniles (Buikstra et al. 1990; Lewis 2018).

Gout is a form of inflammatory arthritis characterized by periodic and painful inflammation of a joint due to elevated levels of uric acid in the blood. Gout primarily involves the joints of the feet (especially the big toe), ankle, knee, or wrist (Waldron 2009:68). Left untreated, tophaceous gout can result, a condition where crystals erupt through the skin.

Figure 6.4 An example of eroded and deformed bones of an elbow as the result of rheumatoid arthritis

Source: Marni LaFleur

As both RA and gout cause erosion of bone, both conditions can be diagnosed in skeletal materials (Waldron 2009:69). Skeletal evidence of RA and gout includes erosion of the articular surfaces of the bones of the hands and feet, sometimes resulting in deformation of the bones (Figure 6.4).

A major DDD condition is vertebral osteophytosis (VOP) of the spine (see Chapter 5), likely resulting from wear and tear and/or age (osteoporosis). It is manifested by thinning, herniation (rupture), or dissolution of the discs and the formation of lipping, bone spurs, and perhaps bony fusion. Coupled with this condition may be spinal stenosis, an abnormal narrowing of the spinal canal or neural foramen that can affect the spinal cord, or ankylosing spondylitis, a condition that can result in vertebral fusion.

Other degenerative diseases

Several other degenerative diseases can be detected in human remains. **Sinusitis** is an infection of the nasal sinuses, and a severe infection can involve teeth and the eye orbits (Waldron 2009:113–115). As a result, teeth may develop abscesses and the thin bones of the sinuses and orbits can erode or fracture. If so, new bone will develop and can be detected archaeologically. In soft tissues (e.g., in mummies), the inflammation of the sinuses can be detected with an endoscope.

Paget's disease of bone (there are other kinds of Paget's disease) is a metabolic condition that interferes with bone resorption and new bone formation, and most commonly occurs in the pelvis, skull, spine, and legs. The bone can weaken; eventually become fragile; and result in fractures, misshapen bones, and arthritis in the joints near the affected bones. This condition can be diagnosed histologically.

Dental pathologies

There are several major types of dental pathologies, including linear enamel hypoplasia (LEH, discussed in Chapter 5), tooth wear, periodontal disease, and **caries** (cavities) (see Buikstra and Ubelaker 1994:47–68; Hillson 1996, 2001, 2005, 2019; Hammerl 2012; Legge and Hardin 2016; Nelson 2016; Temple 2016). Dental pathologies may reflect a number of issues, such as general health, some aspects of diet, techniques of food preparation, using teeth as tools, purposeful modification of teeth, and even geochemistry (e.g., fluoride in groundwater [Hildebolt et al. 1988; Yoshimura et al. 2006]). Whether due to dietary factors or inadequate maintenance, poor oral hygiene may result in gum disease, caries, abscesses, tooth loss, and general infection (spread through the bloodstream). In addition, dental problems can alter the normal diet and lead to nutritional problems that might appear unrelated to dental pathology. As a result, "population morbidity and mortality levels are directly affected to some degree by the prevalence of dental health, which is in turn influenced both directly and indirectly by dietary factors" (Powell 1985:308).

Dentition may be used as a partial measure of the subsistence economy and pathologies related to nutritional stress (Temple 2016). For example, changes in tooth wear and pathology could be used to infer shifts in diet among hunter-gatherers (e.g., Walker and Erlandson 1986), to detect the transition from hunting and gathering to agriculture (e.g., Larsen et al. 1991; Lukacs 1996; Eshed et al. 2006), and to delineate differences in the diet of agriculturalists due to relative status (e.g., Valentin et al. 2006; Michael et al. 2018).

Wear of the enamel crown occurs throughout life through a combination of factors, including abrasion (wear between teeth and other materials), attrition (tooth-on-tooth contact), and erosion (chemical dissolution of enamel) (Shellis and Addy 2014). Some degree of tooth wear is normal and not pathological, whereas excessive wear can result in a number of problems. Staining of the enamel may also be an issue (Burnett 2016).

Abrasion is common, and the amount and type of abrasion depend on a variety of factors (e.g., Krueger 2016). These factors include the types of food consumed (e.g., plants containing a significant amount of silica [phytoliths] may cause excessive wear [Reinhard and Danielson 2005; but see Sanson et al. 2007]), the technology involved in food preparation (e.g., presence of grit; Wolfe and Sutton 2006), and other uses to which teeth are subjected.

Attrition is normal wear on the enamel and is associated with age. Excessive attrition may result in pathological conditions that could be caused by abnormal occlusion or bruxism (grinding of teeth), which is a response to psychological stress. In modern populations, bruxism is also prevalent among populations in high-stress occupations such as the police and military (Xhonga 1977).

Erosion (chemical dissolution) of the enamel is caused by exposure to nonbacterial acids (e.g., citric acid) that may be in various foods, including wine (Shellis et al. 2014). Severe erosion can become pathological and can influence rates of caries (Powell 1985:320).

Abrasion and attrition may be distinguished by wear patterns observed microscopically (e.g., Teaford et al. 2001; Larsen 2015:277; Burnett 2016) to determine broad dietary patterns in humans (Fiorenza et al. 2018; Schmidt et al. 2019). For example, differences

Table 6.2 Some materials preserved in dental calculus

Category	Description	Tells us about
food particles	various, such as muscle fibers	foods eaten
pollen	from plants	plants ingested, general environment
phytoliths	silica bodies in plant cells	plants ingested
starch grains	from plants	plants ingested
grit	from food processing	processing technology
tephra	volcanic ash	general environment, dating
aDNA	DNA	general identification of materials
stable isotopes	various isotopes	general identification of materials and evidence of residence and migration

noted in dental wear between Neandertal and later Upper Paleolithic infants indicated that Upper Paleolithic infants received supplemental foods earlier than their Neandertal counterparts, suggesting that this dietary difference may have influenced a population increase in the Upper Paleolithic (Skinner 1996, 1997).

Another dental pathology that can be detected in ancient teeth is periodontal disease (e.g., Delgado-Darias et al. 2006), a bacterial infection of the tissues surrounding a tooth. Untreated infections can result in the erosion of gum tissue, abscesses, tooth loss, and bone remodeling.

Caries (cavities) result from the demineralization of the enamel by acids produced by oral bacteria (see Temple 2016; Hillson 2019:307–314). Plaque, a combination of bacteria and proteins from the saliva, forms on the surface of teeth, and the acid is the waste product of the sugar-consuming bacteria. If the pH of the plaque is low enough, tooth enamel begins to decalcify, producing a caries. If the pH level remains high enough, the plaque will instead mineralize to form **calculus** (tartar), a layer of calcified minerals and organic materials next to the tooth, with a layer of plaque on top of the calculus. This calculus can actually serve to protect the tooth, lowering the frequency of caries. Interestingly, the plaque and calculus preserved on ancient dentition is not commonly studied, but can contain a number of important data sets (Table 6.2), including evidence of foods and medicines consumed, technologies used for processing, general environment, aDNA (Black et al. 2011; Radini et al. 2017; Eerkens et al. 2018), and stable isotopes (Eerkens et al. 2016b).

If left untreated, caries may result in the formation of abscesses, resulting in tooth loss, bone loss, general infection, and even death. Many caries and abscesses are easily visible in ancient dentition (Figure 6.5), and evidence of bone remodeling may be present. The link between caries and diet is clear (Temple 2016), but there are a number of other factors to consider, such as enamel disruptions that may increase susceptibility to caries (Duray 1990). Efforts to treat dental issues (e.g., caries) are known as early as the Upper Paleolithic (ca. 45,000 to 12,000 BP) in Europe (Oxilia et al. 2017).

The degree of tooth wear has been utilized as a method of determining the age of an individual at death (e.g., Oliveira et al. 2006). Age is only one of the variables in tooth wear, however, and although it is fair to suggest that a significantly worn tooth belongs to an adult, the aging of skeletons based solely on tooth wear is not advisable. On the other

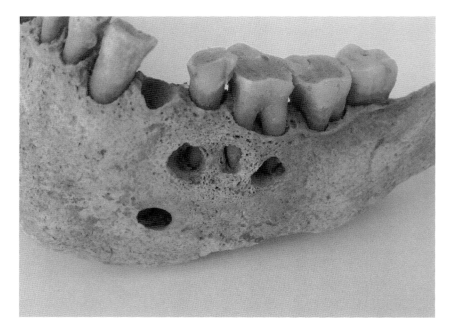

Figure 6.5 Abscesses in a mandible
Source: Marni LaFleur

hand, a recent study of crown height on molars on a skeletal population of nineteenth-century Dutch of known age at death (Mays 2002) revealed a linear relationship between crown wear and age at death, suggesting that molar wear might be a good indicator of age within a homogeneous population. Nevertheless, it currently seems imprudent to rely solely on dental wear as indicators of age at death.

Soft tissue pathology

Most of the human body is composed of soft tissue, such as organs, muscles, and hair, and most disease pathologies manifest themselves only in soft tissues (see Martin et al. 1985). In most cases, soft tissues are not sufficiently preserved to detect pathologies. The discovery and analysis of preserved soft tissues (e.g., in mummies) offers an opportunity to recognize conditions not normally found in skeletal remains alone, although taphonomic processes are an issue in tissue preservation (Aufderheide 2011). The study of soft tissues is a fairly recent practice (since the Renaissance), with the autopsy or dissection of humans conducted to gain medical knowledge. It was soon recognized that the examination of ancient remains, mostly mummies, could provide additional information about soft tissue. A history of the study of soft tissues was presented by Aufderheide (2013).

Methods employed to examine preserved human soft tissue remains (see Aufderheide 2003) include visual endoscopic examination (e.g., Beckett 2015), radiographs (Theodorakou and Farquharson 2008), computerized tomography (CT) scans (Hughes 2011), and magnetic resonance imaging (MRI) (which produces a more detailed image of soft tissues than a CT scan) (e.g., Rühli 2015). Both CT and MRI scans are used in virtual autopsies.

A few soft tissue diseases can be seen in skeletal remains, including some cardiovascular diseases that can leave impressions of abnormal blood vessels and tumors on bone (Waldron 2009:221–235). In addition, renal and bladder stone diseases are implied by the presence of stones (e.g., Steinbock 1985). The latter two conditions appear to be related, at least in part, to diet; thus, the presence of such stones in burial populations could be a source of both paleopathological and dietary information. Other soft tissue calcifications, such as pleural plaques, leiomyomas of the uterus, and lymph nodules, may also assist in determining disease and other anomalies in prehistoric populations (Baud and Kramar 1991).

Heart and other vascular issues may be possible to diagnose, such as the presence of plaque and calcifications. For example, Wells (1964:67–70) noted arteriosclerosis in mummies from Egypt and Peru, suggesting a variety of ailments, including stroke and diseases of the heart and lung. Zimmerman et al. (1981) examined a mummy from the Aleutian Islands in Alaska and discovered that the person suffered from atherosclerosis, degenerative joint disease, pulmonary issues from the use of indoor fires, ear infections, and lice infestation. Cheng (2012) reported that a 50-year-old Chinese noblewoman, known as Lady Dai, had a severely occluded left anterior descending coronary artery. Her condition was diagnosed as the cause of an anterior myocardial infarction (heart attack), resulting in her sudden death more than 2,200 years ago.

The ossification of connective tissues, often along the spine, may be observed as well. This condition is called diffuse idiopathic skeletal hyperostosis (DISH) and may be the result of repeated trauma (Waldron 2009:72–77). DISH may be diagnosed in skeletal material by the presence of extra bone, such as bone spurs, in the affected areas. On the spine, the extra bone may look like "melted candle wax down the front of the vertebrae" (Waldron 2009:73).

Infectious disease in soft tissues

Most of the virulent infectious diseases, such as smallpox, typhus fever, cholera, diphtheria, bubonic plague, pneumonic plague, and flu, generally kill the host too quickly to leave a visible record in human remains. However, it is possible to detect such diseases by chemical means, such as serology or aDNA. If sufficient soft tissue is preserved, visible indicators of disease may be present (see Table 6.1).

Parasitic infection

A fairly large number of parasitic diseases are known, but few leave indicators on bone (Waldron 2009). The field of paleoparasitology seeks to explore such diseases, but must be based in rigorous analysis linked to traditional archaeological analyses (Dittmar 2009; Reinhard 2017). Parasites within the body, typically in the intestinal tract, are called **endoparasites**, whereas those living on the exterior of the body are called **ectoparasites**. Understanding the origins of human parasites is an important aspect of not only interpreting the health of past populations (Mitchell 2013; also see Mitchell 2016) but also of human evolution and climate change (Dittmar 2009).

Endoparasites

Endoparasites are those living within the body (e.g., Reinhard 2017; also see Waldron 2009:Table 6.6). Such parasites are divided into two major groups: **protozoa** (e.g., bacteria that cause disease) and **helminths** (worms, including roundworms and flatworms). The infectious diseases caused by protozoa were discussed earlier.

In paleoparasitology, the focus is on helminths, with protozoa being the focus in the study of infectious disease. Roundworm helminths are generally found in the intestinal tract and include pinworms (*Enterobius* spp.), hookworms (e.g., *Ancylostoma duodenale* and *Necator americanus*), tapeworms (subclass Eucestoda), and whipworms (*Trichuris trichiura*). Flatworms (or flukes; class Trematoda) infect tissues, such as the lungs (e.g., *Paragonimus westermani*) or liver (various genera), with some that infect the blood (e.g., *Schistosoma* spp.). Endoparasitic infestation can deprive the body of vital nutrients and may block the absorption of iron, possibly causing iron–deficiency anemia.

Most endoparasites identified archaeologically are roundworms (Figure 6.6) found in the analysis of paleofeces or mummified intestinal contents, although preserved worm eggs can also be detected in site soils (Bathurst 2005; Seo et al. 2016). Chagas disease, a helminth transmitted by insects, was present in Peru as early as 9,000 BP (Aufderheide et al. 2004; also see Rothhammer et al. 1985). Panzer et al. (2014) reported a case of Chagas in a 500-year-old mummy of a young Inca adult female who had apparently been killed by a massive blunt force blow to the face, perhaps part of a ritual sacrifice.

A parasitic disease that is spread through dog feces is dog tapeworm, and a severe infection may cause the development of cystic lesions, some of which might calcify in soft tissues and in bone, the latter of which can lead to pathologic fractures (Waldron 2009:112–113).

The study of endoparasites can provide information on a variety of issues, including health, sanitation, foods, and culture contact. Studies on the health of populations

Figure 6.6 An example of a roundworm helminth

Source: Alamy

based on parasitic infection include those in the prehistoric Southwest of North America (Paseka et al. 2018) and in China from the Neolithic Period to the Qing Dynasty (Yeh and Mitchell 2016).

Mitchell (2017) discussed the evidence for parasites in the Roman era, finding that despite a variety of sanitation efforts, intestinal parasites were widespread. Fish tapeworm was also widespread, likely due to the common consumption of fermented, uncooked fish sauce (called garum). The identification of a nonindigenous species of whipworm in a mummy from southern Siberia suggested contact between southern Iron Age Siberian nomads and agricultural societies such as those in China (Slavinsky et al. 2018).

Finally, the presence of certain parasites in humans can provide evidence of people eating animals that those parasites inhabit, called false parasitism (Reinhard 1992:234). For example, fish tapeworm eggs recovered from coprolites in Peru suggested the consumption of raw fish, some eggs in Egyptian specimens were derived from the consumption of beef and pork, and the presence of other parasite species in Great Basin of North America specimens suggested the consumption of insects and/or rodents (Reinhard and Bryant 1992:253).

Ectoparasites

Ectoparasites are those that inhabit the outside of the body and include head and body lice, fleas, and ticks. Such parasites may be found on or in preserved human remains or in preserved clothing and may be useful in the inference of general health conditions and to understand vectors of disease. For example, fleas carry typhus, malaria, and other maladies, and were the prime transmitters of bubonic plague in Europe during the Middle Ages (Dean et al. 2018).

Gill and Owsley (1985) conducted an analysis of head lice found on a historic adult male mummy from Wyoming and discovered an extensive infestation. They suggested that the level of infestation was the result of a decrease in normal grooming activities, perhaps as a consequence of social stress related to Euro-American expansion (e.g., starvation and warfare).

Mummy II/7 from Qilakitsoq, Greenland (Bresciani et al. 1991:162), was heavily infested with head lice, suggesting "an extremely low hygienic standard, and perhaps, to some extent also, low resistance to the attack of lice." Lice were also discovered in the feces of the individual, indicating the probable consumption of lice, as has been observed ethnographically (Bresciani et al. 1991:162; also see Sutton 1988b, 1995).

Congenital abnormalities

The category of **congenital abnormalities** encompasses a "wide range of anatomical variations and defects that occur during embryonic and fetal development and that are present at or shortly after birth" (Lewis 2018:17). They are often referred to as birth defects, although some can manifest later in life. Many such defects are genetic in origin, but specific origins are unknown in most instances. However, environmental factors (Moore et al. 2015) are major causal factors and include drugs (e.g., thalidomide), chemicals (e.g., alcohol and nicotine), infections, and radiation. Exposure to lead and other toxins in prenatal and neonatal infants can be detected in their unerupted primary teeth (Arora 2005).

Most of the congenital abnormalities detected in the archaeological record are related to structural skeletal development in subadults (Waldron 2009:208–209; Lewis 2018) and include clubfoot, cleft palate, and supernumerary ribs. Involvement of the skull is common, such as **microcephaly**, an abnormally small head due to a number of causes (such as the recent outbreak of the Zika virus) and **macrocephaly**, an abnormally large head often caused by cranial expansion due to raised intercranial pressure, most often manifested as **hydrocephalus**. Other skeletal defects include **spina bifida** in children, where a portion of the spinal cord is exposed due to malformation of the spine. It can cause paralysis of the legs and can result in "severe neurological consequences" (Waldron 2009:219).

Other abnormalities include spinal deformation such as lordosis (an unnatural concave curving of a section of the vertebral column), kyphosis (an unnatural convex curving of a section of the vertebral column), and **scoliosis** (an unnatural lateral curvature of the spine), with the latter being the most common form recognizable in skeletal remains with well-preserved spinal columns (Waldron 2009:216–217) (Figure 6.7).

Thalassemia (a term coined by Angel 1966a) is a congenital blood disorder that results in anemia and is difficult to diagnose from skeletal remains but may be detected in aDNA. However, skeletal evidence of thalassemia was reported from the Atlit-Yam site in Israel (Hershkovitz and Edelson 1991), perhaps associated with early farmers being exposed to malarial parasites. Other examples from that same region have also been identified (Tomczyk et al. 2016). At the 8,200-year-old Windover site in Florida, a 20-year-old female exhibited skeletal indicators consistent with a diagnosis of thalassemia (Thomas 2016).

Figure 6.7 Scoliosis in a vertebral column from an inhumation

Source: Tony Waldron

Congenital syndromes

A syndrome is a group of conditions that consistently occur together (as opposed to a solitary birth defect), and a number of congenital syndromes can be detected in the archaeological record. Several syndromes detectable in skeletal remains, such as dwarfism, gigantism, elephantiasis, Down syndrome, and Marfan syndrome, are discussed next.

Dwarfism, a syndrome resulting in arrested growth and short stature, can be caused by a number of conditions, including a chromosomal deficiency resulting in abnormal bone growth, a lack of growth hormone (or pituitary dwarfism), and subadult malnutrition. Pituitary dwarfism is relatively easy to diagnose in adults, since the skeletal elements would have normal proportions but of a small size (Waldron 2009:196). The earliest known (ca. 11,000 BP) case of dwarfism is in the Romito 2 skeleton from Italy (Frayer et al. 1987).

Gigantism is a condition characterized by excessive growth and height significantly above average. In humans, this condition is caused by overproduction of growth hormone in childhood. Elephantiasis can have a variety of causes, one of which is a congenital disorder (Proteus syndrome or Wiedemann syndrome) that results in skeletal malformation, such as the case of Joseph Merrick (the Elephant Man) (Huntley et al. 2015).

Down syndrome is a congenital disorder due to a defect in chromosome 21 and is also called trisomy 21. It results in intellectual impairment and morphological features, including heart defects, short stature, almond-shaped eyes, and a broad face (e.g., Roizen and Patterson 2003). Only a few cases of Down syndrome are known from past populations. An example of great interest is a 5- to 7-year-old child from northeastern France, dated to the fifth or sixth century AD (Rivollat et al. 2015). Analysis of the skull using morphology, metrics, and CT scans revealed a number of pathological features, including brachycrany (a broad, short head), metopism (unfused suture of the frontal bones), hypodontia (missing teeth), periodontitis, a flattened occiput, vault thinness, and an open cranial base angle, all indicative of Down syndrome. Of interest socially is that this individual was given a normal burial and was not stigmatized, suggestive of acceptance and continuing care in life.

Marfan syndrome is a genetic disorder that affects the connective tissues. People with this condition tend to be tall and thin, with long arms, legs, fingers, and toes. They also typically have flexible joints and scoliosis. It has been speculated that the Egyptian Pharaoh Akhenaten (Figure 6.8) had Marfan syndrome (e.g., Burridge 1996) or some other genetic disorder that was also manifested in other family members (e.g., Braverman et al. 2009; Eshraghian and Loeys 2012).

Chapter summary

Disease is an abnormal condition of the body systems as a result of either internal (e.g., metabolic malfunction) or external (e.g., virus or bacteria) factors. Paleopathologists want to know the etiology, pathogenesis, morphologic change, and clinical manifestations of a disease and its impact on morbidity and mortality to place it within a biocultural context.

Most skeletal pathologies result from infectious disease, degenerative disease or affliction, or metabolic/nutritional deficiencies. Although few diseases leave distinctive signatures on bone or soft tissues, they can now be identified using chemical analyses, such as aDNA. Infection of the surface of the bone is called a periosteal reaction, and infection in the bone interior is called osteomyelitis.

Figure 6.8 A sculpture of Akhenaten showing his Marfan-like features
Source: Alamy Image ID: DGDC90

Cancers, primarily osteosarcomas, have been found in skeletal remains as old as 1.8 million years. Benign tumors indicative of a variety of conditions are also present in the record.

Infectious diseases, those that can be transmitted from person to person, generally have a short life cycle and kill their host before any telltale signature of the disease can be seen in the tissues. Some such diseases crossed over from animals to humans. Major infectious diseases that do result in tissue pathology include tuberculosis, leprosy, treponemal diseases (e.g., syphilis), polio, and malaria. Degenerative disorders (or afflictions) include deossification and erosive arthritis (e.g., rheumatoid arthritis and gout).

Dental pathologies are also common in skeletal remains. These include LEH, tooth wear, periodontal disease, and caries. Tooth wear can occur due to abrasion, attrition, or chemical erosion. Caries are the result of the chemical dissolution of the enamel by bacteria, and if untreated can result in abscesses, loss of the tooth, infection, and even death. Plaque will form on the surface of the teeth and may calcify to form calculus, a substance that can contain a variety of information.

Soft tissues are not commonly preserved, so pathologies in soft tissues are not often found. Extant soft tissues (and bone) can be examined visually or by scanning technologies (e.g., radiographs or CT scans), and it is possible to detect a number of conditions, such as heart disease. Chemical analysis can also detect the presence of pathogens.

Parasitic infections can also be detected in soft tissues. Endoparasites are found within the body, often in the intestinal tract, and can provide considerable information regarding diet, health, and sanitary practices. Ectoparasites are found on the exterior of the body and are useful in determining general health conditions and disease vectors.

A number of congenital abnormalities (cf. birth defects) and syndromes may also be detected. These include spina bifida, scoliosis, dwarfism, Down syndrome, and Marfan syndrome.

Key concepts and terms

abrasion
attrition
calculus
caries
congenital abnormalities
disease
Down syndrome
ectoparasites
endoparasites
erosion
gout
helminths
hydrocephalus
infectious disease
leprosy
macrocephaly
malaria
Marfan syndrome
microcephaly
osteomyelitis
osteopenia
osteoporosis
osteosarcoma
Paget's disease
paleoepidemiology
periosteal reaction
periosteum

periostosis
polio
protozoa
rheumatoid arthritis
scoliosis
sinusitis
spina bifida
treponemal diseases
tuberculosis
zoonosis

Chapter 7

Trauma

Trauma

Trauma is the "injury to living tissue that is caused by a force or mechanism extrinsic to the body, whether incidental or intentional" (Lovell and Grauer 2019:335). Trauma is usually included in paleopathology but is here considered separately. Trauma and injury usually reflect some sort of violence (e.g., Redfern 2017a), although some are the result of accidents. Trauma is often regarded as a physical injury, but psychological trauma (or stress, see Chapter 5) can also affect both past individuals and societies (Redfern 2017a:4–6). In this chapter, we will deal primarily with physical trauma to the skeleton and soft tissues, both **sublethal** (not causing death) and **lethal** (causing death).

Types of physical trauma

Trauma is most often observed in the skeleton, although it certainly is accompanied by some collateral soft tissue trauma. Due to preservation issues, however, the identification of trauma in soft tissues is rare. For the skeleton, Ortner (2003:120) identified the primary traumas as fractures, dislocations, disruption of nerve or blood supplies, and artificial deformation. Trauma is categorized as **blunt** (nonpenetrating), **ballistic** (bullets or other projectiles), or **sharp** (knives or other piercing instruments) force and as either **acute** (near or at time of death) or **chronic** (repeated and prolonged) (Kroman and Symes 2012:219, 226–229). In the analysis of trauma, it is important to distinguish whether it occurred perimortem or postmortem, as it could be related to the manner and cause of abuse or death (Passalacqua and Rainwater 2015; Cattaneo and Cappella 2017).

The following considers fractures of bone, incidental deformation of bone, and soft tissue traumas. Blunt, ballistic, or sharp force traumas are typically the result of violence and are discussed here, as are intentional modifications.

Fractures

Fractures in bone are the most frequent trauma identified in skeletal remains (Waldron 2009:138) and are often classified as blunt force trauma (e.g., Galloway et al. 2014). There are several types of fractures (Figure 7.1), broadly grouped into **transverse** (broken at a right angle), **oblique** (broken at a less than 90-degree angle, displaced or nondisplaced), and **comminuted** (broken into multiple fragments). They can also be classified as **spiral** or twisted fractures, **compression fractures** of the vertebrae, **depression fractures**,

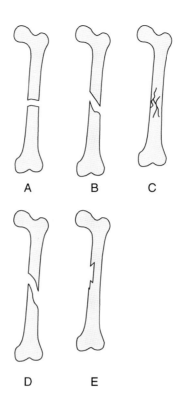

Figure 7.1 General types of fractures: (a) transverse, (b) oblique, (c) comminuted, (d) spiral, and (e) greenstick

Source: Author

and bone bruises (microfractures accompanied by bleeding). **Green bone (or green-stick) fractures** (incomplete, broken on one side but bent on the other, often seen in children who have softer bones) are fractures that are assumed to have occurred during life when the bone contained all of its water and organic material, whereas "dry" bone fractures are often presumed to have occurred postmortem after much of the moisture in the bone had disappeared. Waldron (2009:Tables 8.2 and 8.3) provided a classification of fractures (also see Galloway et al. 2014) and Waldron (2009:Table 8.7) presented fracture sites by activity. Teeth can also fracture.

The location, type, and timing of fractures are commonly analyzed in skeletal remains. For example, partially healed fractures indicate that the victim did not live long enough for the bone to completely heal, whereas healed fractures indicate that the person survived at least long enough for the bone to mend. The location of a fracture could indicate accidents or violence of some sort, including warfare. Multiple healed fractures would indicate a pattern of activity with a prevalence of injury. For example, a computerized tomography (CT) scan of the humerus belonging to Lucy (*Australopithecus afarensis*), an extinct hominin (early human) who lived approximately 3 million years ago in Africa, indicated the presence of a perimortem fracture, possibly related to her death (Kappelman et al. 2016).

Soft tissue trauma

Trauma to bone will typically result in some collateral trauma to soft tissues. Thus, any trauma to bone can be assumed to have also resulted in trauma to soft tissues. Types of observable trauma in soft tissue are generally the same as in bone, such as ballistic (e.g., bullet holes) or sharp (e.g., knife or sword) wounds (e.g., Milner et al. 1991).

An obvious issue in the analysis of soft tissue trauma is that such tissues are not commonly preserved. If someone is killed from a sword thrust into the abdomen, the skeleton of that victim might not exhibit any trauma, perhaps leading to a misinterpretation of the cause of death. In some cases, however, artifacts in association with a skeleton may provide clues. For example, if an arrowhead is found in the chest area of a burial, it could be reasonably surmised that the person died from an arrow wound.

Violence

The presence of traumatic injuries in skeletal remains immediately leads to a suspicion of violence (Martin et al. 2012a; Martin and Anderson 2014a; also see Martin and Frayer 1997; Waldron 2009; Knüsel and Smith 2014; Wedel and Galloway 2014), although some violent trauma could be due to animal predation, as seen in some hominin remains (e.g., Njau and Blumenschine 2012). As noted by Walker (2001), archaeological evidence of violence is unencumbered by revisionist interpretations of historical records and ethnographic reports, providing an unbiased view of past violence.

The two basic types of violence are **interpersonal** and **warfare**. Interpersonal violence occurs within one's community or family, and is usually small scale, intentional, and sublethal. Warfare is violence between members of two polities or factions, commonly leading to fatalities. In some cases, violence is not considered aberrant, but a normal part of life and even honorable (e.g., as in warfare) (Pérez 2012:14). Violence that is integrated into ritual is also common. Other aspects of violence, such as constant fear or oppression (e.g., stress), would undoubtedly have occurred but are difficult to detect in the archaeological record.

Interpersonal violence

Interpersonal violence, acts of violence perpetrated by one individual against another, is an unfortunate but common occurrence. Such violence, especially among men, was widespread through space and time and includes assaults, homicides, and mass killings (as in genocide) (Walker 2001; Redfern 2017a).

Interpersonal violence can take a variety of forms, from the intrafamily abuse of children, women, and the elderly, to the systematic abuse of classes of people such as captives or slaves (Walker et al. 1997; Ross and Abel 2011; Redfern 2017a; Love and Soto Martinez 2018). Such violence could be occasional or chronic. If it is occasional, the resulting trauma might be difficult to differentiate from accidents. If it is chronic, a distinct pattern could emerge from the remains of the victims (Judd 2004). In general, such violence is intended to be sublethal, but death might be the ultimate result.

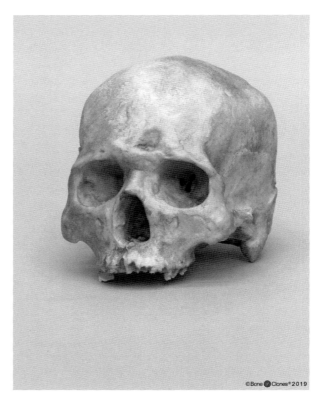

©Bone Clones®2019

Figure 7.2 An example of a healed cranial depression fracture (cast)
Source: Bone Clones

Trauma related to **domestic violence** of children (e.g., Marks et al. 2009; Love 2014; Lewis 2014, 2018), women, or the elderly would manifest itself in a number of ways, but primarily by the presence of healed cranial (Figure 7.2), facial, dental, and throat fractures (see Galloway and Wedel 2014; Velasco-Vázquez et al. 2018); defensive (parrying) fractures of the ulnae and radii; healed rib fractures (Walker 1997; Zephro and Galloway 2014); and fractures of the epiphyses (Verlinden and Lewis 2015). In children, broken ribs (particularly the first rib, which requires a great deal of force to fracture) are common markers of abuse, although some rib fractures might be the result of a difficult birth (Merbs 2012). Abuse might manifest itself in a combination of healed skeletal trauma and metabolic disturbances in children, such as that found in a child from the Roman period in Egypt (Wheeler et al. 2013). A review of domestic violence in the archaeological record was presented by Redfern (2017b).

Baustian et al. (2012) studied skeletal remains from Grasshopper Pueblo in Arizona and found that fully one-third of adults (of both sexes) had healed cranial depression fractures and that females had a higher prevalence of sublethal trauma than males. They concluded that interpersonal violence was ubiquitous within the pueblo (Baustian et al. 2012).

A study of 144 skeletons from the Chinchorro society (a maritime hunter-gatherer group in Chile), dating to ca. 4,000 years BP, was analyzed for traumatic injuries to determine whether the injuries were the result of interpersonal violence or work-related accidents (Standen and Arriaza 2000). They found that trauma in subadults was rare, whereas adult trauma was much more common, with most injuries being on the skull and upper extremities. The skull traumas were mostly nonlethal (healed) and seem to have been caused by impacts from stones. Males were the primary recipients of such trauma, with that frequency suggesting that interpersonal violence rather than accidents was the cause.

Another form of interpersonal violence is structural: the normalization of everyday violence within a society. For example, Torres-Rouff and King (2014) examined patterns of sublethal nasocranial fractures, primarily among males, in pre-Columbian Chile and suggested that the trauma patterns reflected culturally approved violence (e.g., fist fighting) for conflict resolution. A similar pattern was observed in prehistoric California (Walker 1997).

Other "normalized" violence could be chronic and directed against categories of people, such as women, slaves, and prisoners, to keep them subjugated for political or economic purposes. In some cases of hierarchical coercive control, the victim class could be dehumanized through propaganda to "justify" the subjugation. Such trauma could manifest itself through a variety of healed sublethal fractures, skeletal indicators of heavy workloads (see Chapter 5), or evidence of disease and poor nutrition (Klaus 2012).

In a study of commingled remains from a site in the American Southwest, Osterholtz (2012) found evidence of hobbling and torture, exhibited by trauma to the calcaneus and the plantar surfaces of other foot bones. Osterholtz (2012) suggested that this form of violence might have been the basis for social control of victims and witnesses by their aggressors.

Individuals taken captive, such as women and children seized in a raid, might also show signs of chronic abuse. In another study of human remains from a site in the American Southwest, Harrod and Martin (2014b; also see Kuckelman 2017) found patterns of healed fractures, infections, and nutritional deficiencies that suggested the women had been captured (with the males presumably killed), held captive, and beaten (see Tung [2012] for a similar example from Peru). In other cases, male warriors may have been captured for ritual sacrifice.

Warfare

Warfare is organized conflict between polities and nearly always results in trauma to individuals engaged in combat. Warfare can be broadly classified as either small scale with limited casualties or large scale with mass casualties. An interpretation of any specific trauma, or patterns of trauma, as being the result of warfare would depend on a variety of circumstances, such as cause and severity of the trauma(s) to an individual and the number of individuals involved (Table 7.1). Some of these same traumas indicative of warfare might also be present in persons other than combatants, such as sacrificial victims or executed prisoners.

Trauma resulting from warfare would typically consist of blunt, sharp, or ballistic force injuries to the skeleton (and to soft tissues). Other archaeological signatures of warfare would include defensive architecture, weapons, and iconography (Vencl 1984). Until recently, research into the biological impact of warfare was commonly limited to the bioarchaeology of male combatants, likely resulting in an underestimation of the impact on women and children (Tegtmeyer and Martin 2017b:2, 2017c).

Table 7.1 Some indications of warfare in human remains

Warfare type	Trauma	Burial context	Grave goods	Other factors
large scale, mass casualty	skeletal	mass grave	few, possibly some specialized personal military items	typically young males, possibly women and children at massacre sites
	soft tissue	mass grave	a projectile (e.g., arrowhead or bullet) within the body area	
		an individual with no skeletal trauma in a mass grave containing other individuals with skeletal trauma	few, possibly some specialized personal military items	
small scale, limited casualty	skeletal	generally individual	nonspecialized weapons	typically males
	soft tissue	generally individual	a projectile (e.g., arrowhead or bullet) within the body area	
unknown	skeletal	generally individual	nonspecialized weapons or warfare-oriented	typically males
	soft tissue	generally individual	nonspecialized weapons or warfare-oriented	
	unknown	disarticulated remains found at a battlefield	None	variable
	repeated, skeletal, sublethal, healed	probably individual	nonspecialized weapons or warfare-oriented	older(?) males

SMALL-SCALE WARFARE

Small-scale societies, such as hunter–gatherers, did engage in limited warfare (e.g., Keeley 1996; Arkush and Allen 2006; Allen and Jones 2014). This type of warfare would have resulted in relatively few causalities, making it challenging to detect in the few such skeletal remains currently known. The weapons used in warfare by such groups were probably not specialized, but were probably the same as those used in hunting, making identification of weapons used in war difficult. Further, small societies would lack formal militaries or the logistical capabilities to support them.

The difficulty in detecting small-scale warfare is illustrated at the 10,000-year-old Nataruk site in Kenya. There, Lahr et al. (2016) reported the discovery of a group of 27 skeletons (men, women, and children) that had seemingly died at the same time from apparent weapons trauma, a situation suggestive of warfare. Alternatively, Stojanowski et al. (2016b) argued that the deaths were not synchronic and that there was no firm evidence of weapons trauma, suggesting that warfare was not indicated.

LARGE-SCALE WARFARE

In larger societies (e.g., some agriculturalists), warfare can be easier to detect. There would likely be specialized equipment used by the militaries of these societies, artifacts that would likely be found in association with battle dead. Some architecture would be defensive in nature, and there would be evidence of military logistical support systems. Finally, large-scale warfare would usually produce mass causalities.

An excellent example of a mass grave resulting from a large-scale battle was discovered in England, near the site of the Battle of Towton (Fiorato et al. 2007; Goodwin 2012). In 1996, workers constructing a private garage at Towton Hall accidentally discovered the remains of 36 soldiers who had died on March 29, 1461 (Palm Sunday), during one of the bloodiest battles of the War of the Roses. According to historical records, the Battle of Towton resulted in the deaths of an estimated 28,000 men. The rectangular grave (Figure 7.3) was packed with bodies arranged in "sardine can" fashion. Most were placed in

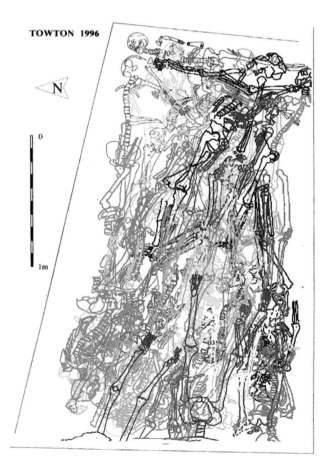

Figure 7.3 A view of a mass grave at Towton, England

Source: Tim Sutherland

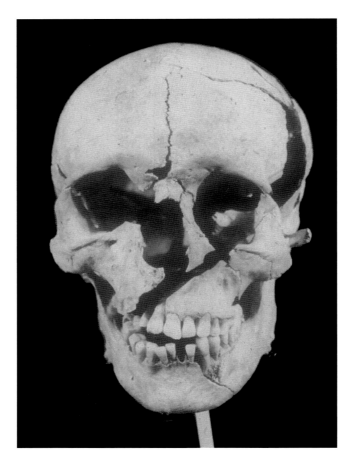

Figure 7.4 An example of trauma (battle axe?) to the skull of a soldier (Towton 25) from
the battle of Towton

Source: Jo Buckberry

a west–east orientation, the traditional burial custom in fifteenth-century Christendom.
The skeletons found within the tightly packed grave all bore lethal traumas to the skull
(Figure 7.4), indicative of brutal hand-to-hand combat using swords and axes.

Other mass graves can hold some surprises. Flohr et al. (2014) conducted a study of
commingled remains (minimum number of individuals [MNI] = 36) from a 1,200-year-
old site in northwestern Germany, suspected to be the mass grave from a battle. The
analysis of femoral cross-sections identified the remains as mostly young to middle-aged
males, consistent with what one would expect from a battle. However, some females were
apparently also represented, suggesting variation in gender roles.

Some known large battles have not produced remains, at least not yet. For example, in
the late summer of 480 BC, the Persians invaded Greece with an army variously estimated
to be between 100,000 and 2 million men (the actual number most likely is closer to the

lower end of the range; Barkworth 1993). While the Greeks organized themselves for the onslaught, several thousand Greeks, including the famous 300 Spartans, occupied the pass at Thermopylae and waited for the Persians to arrive. In the ensuing battle, all of the 300 Spartans, along with other Greeks and many thousands of Persians, were killed. Yet none of the human remains from this battle have been found (Kraft et al. 1987).

A similar example is the Battle of Cannae in Italy. On August 2, 216 BC, Hannibal defeated a Roman army, killing some 70,000 Romans (O'Connell 2010). The remains were likely cremated at or near the battle site, so large cremation pits probably exist. To date, however, none have been found.

Cannibalism

Cannibalism, defined here as humans eating other humans, is an emotional issue (e.g., Arens 1979; Askenasy 1994). In a cultural context, eating people from within one's social group (**endocannibalism**) is almost always prohibited, whereas eating people from other social groups (**exocannibalism**), such as strangers and enemies, is more common, and in some cases even expected (Turner and Turner 1999:1). There is evidence that some form of cannibalism may have been practiced by prehistoric groups in a number of places, including the Arctic (e.g., Melbye and Fairgrieve 1994), Europe (e.g., Santana et al. 2019), Mesoamerica (e.g., Harner 1977), and the American Southwest (see the Case Study, page 133).

Five categories of cannibalism can be defined: ritual, emergency, culinary, criminal, and sociopolitical. **Ritual (or funerary) cannibalism**, the eating of small portions of the dead to honor or gain power from them, is relatively common but would probably involve minimal trauma to the skeleton (except perhaps the skull) and can sometimes result in the transmission of disease, such as kuru in New Guinea (e.g., Alpers 2007).

Emergency cannibalism is the type most commonly known to westerners. People who are stranded or lost will sometimes resort to eating their dead in order to stay alive until they can be rescued or find other food. Famous examples include the Donner Party (Hardesty 1997; Dixon et al. 2010) and the soccer team whose airplane crashed in the Andes in 1973 (Read 1974). In 1993, a feature film titled *Alive* was made about the latter incident.

Culinary cannibalism is the eating of other humans as a normal, even if infrequent, part of the diet. A possible case is the Mexica (Aztec) processing and consumption of their sacrificial victims (Harner 1977; Ortiz De Montellano 1978; Winkelman 1998; Turner and Turner 1999:415–421). Nevertheless, there is considerable disagreement as to whether any societies actually practiced this form of cannibalism.

Criminal cannibalism, eating a person as part of a criminal act, is also known. In the United States, perhaps the most infamous case is that of Jeffrey Dahmer, a serial killer from the 1980s who murdered and ate his victims (Davis 1991). The fictional character of Hannibal Lecter from the movie *The Silence of the Lambs* is probably the most famous. In such cases, forensic law enforcement investigators, rather than archaeologists, become involved.

Sociopolitical cannibalism involves the eating of certain people from a society or segment of a society for the purpose of controlling, punishing, or intimidating that segment of society. Evidence of aggressive cannibalism has been identified in the American Southwest (see the Case Study, page 133). It seems more likely, however, that this evidence may actually reflect the execution of undesirables or the intimidation and control of certain populations. If cannibalism was actually practiced, it is possible that it was ritual and not culinary or emergency.

Archaeological expectations of cannibalism

If humans were being eaten by other humans, there would be a series of expectations in the archaeological data, including signs of certain types of trauma in the remains, taphonomic changes in the remains, and other archaeological signatures. First, the people would be killed in some manner, although determining a cause of death in cases where there is likely to be considerable damage to the body from the initial assault is difficult at best. It seems likely that the body would then be initially processed and disarticulated in a manner that is typically referred to as "butchering." The resulting parts would then be further processed, with soft tissues cut up and the bones likely broken and fragmented (e.g., for marrow). Some or all of these parts may then have been cooked in some manner, such as being boiled or roasted. Then, the leftover parts (primarily bone) would be discarded. Finally, it would be expected that residues of the consumed, such as proteins or ancient DNA (aDNA), would be present in the feces of the consumer. Hurlbut (2000) proposed that if cannibalism was present, the perimortem evidence on the skeleton should include a series of traits, summarized in Table 7.2.

Table 7.2 Some archaeological signatures of possible cannibalism (after Hurlbut 2000)

Trauma or trait	Elements involved	Comments
facial damage	skull	general indicator of interpersonal violence
disarticulation	all	from having been "butchered"
cut marks	at any location, but particularly at attachment sites of major muscles	from having been "butchered"
intentional fragmentation	any to all	to expose cancellous bone for nutrient extraction
green bone fractures	mostly thicker long bones	broken to obtain marrow
marrow extraction	long bones	associated with fragmentation and green bone fractures
hammerstone or chopper marks	most	more visible on thicker bone
absence of certain elements	e.g., vertebrae	fragile elements destroyed during processing
charring	any to all	evidence of exposure to fire (e.g., cooking)
"pot polish"	any to all	evidence of having been stirred in a pottery vessel, presumably during cooking
remains mixed in with other discarded "food" bone	all surviving fragments of bone	treatment of remains as just another food
all ages and sexes	all	suggesting the involvement of entire social groups

There are alternative interpretations of the apparent signatures of cannibalism. Pickering (1989) suggested that the patterns might actually reflect uncommon mortuary practices rather than cannibalism. This could be a reasonable interpretation, particularly considering the dismemberment, excarnation, and fragmentation of remains in the Tibetan Sky burial practice (e.g., Malville 2005) or the mortuary treatment afforded the Chinchorro of Peru and Chile (Aufderheide et al. 1993). Further, Bello et al. (2016) argued that a distinction between cannibalism and funerary defleshing could be made based on frequency, distribution, and micromorphometric characteristics of cut marks.

Case study: violence in the ancient American Southwest

Beginning in the early 1900s, archaeologists working at some Ancestral Puebloan (formerly called the Anasazi) sites in the American Southwest (Figure 7.5) noticed the presence of cut and burned human bone, suggesting that portions of those individuals had apparently been defleshed, cooked, and perhaps even

Figure 7.5 General location of the Ancestral Puebloans (and other groups) in the American Southwest

Source: Author

eaten. The evidence pointed toward cannibalism, but that was too terrible to contemplate and too sensitive to research. Beginning in the 1970s, however, studies on human bone (e.g., Turner and Morris 1970; Turner 1983; White 1992; Turner and Turner 1999) from the Southwest suggested that cannibalism had indeed occurred. At least 286 individuals from 38 Ancestral Puebloan sites dating between AD 900 and 1200 were documented as possible cannibalism victims (Turner and Turner 1999).

The human remains included men, women, and children (Osterholtz and Martin 2017) and were characterized by significant disarticulation, fragmentation, cut marks, percussion fractures, burning, and end polishing of bone fragments, all seen as evidence of the individuals having been defleshed and cooked. The bones were mostly found mixed in with other food bones in trash deposits but had sometimes been found lying unburied on the floors of kivas (ceremonial structures) or habitation rooms and were rarely encountered in formal cemeteries.

The taphonomic signature of cannibalism identified from these deposits may be comparable to other forms of cultural alteration of human bone. As noted earlier, the modification of human remains associated with mortuary practices, warfare, mutilation, human sacrifice, and execution can result in similar patterns. On the other hand, distinct combinations of taphonomic patterns appear to differentiate between cannibalism, violence, and other cultural practices. The numbers of individuals involved, the age and sex composition, and the burial contexts also differ. Intentional and extensive fragmentation, scattering of disarticulated elements, loss of vertebrae, and pot polish are taphonomic characteristics that combine to set human bone deposits in Ancestral Puebloan sites apart from documented cases of warfare or interpersonal violence. Finally, the case for cannibalism was strengthened when muscle protein (myoglobin) from one human individual was discovered in the fecal material of another human individual at the Cowboy Wash site in Utah (Marlar et al. 2000; also see Dongoske et al. 2000).

Critics of the cannibalism model have argued that defleshing and cooking did not demonstrate actual consumption and suggested that other activities may explain the patterns. Warfare is known to have been fairly common, but although a number of sites had defensive architecture (LeBlanc 1999), there is little bioarchaeological evidence of warfare (Martin 2016). Other possible explanations include the execution of witches (Darling 1998; Ogilvie and Hilton 2000), violent competition between rival priesthoods (Miller 2001:507), or intracommunity violence, with some individuals being seen as "nonpersons" and not worthy of human treatment (e.g., Palkovich 2012:114–115; Kuckelman 2017; also see Rautman and Fenton 2005). It also seems possible that the patterns seen in the remains were the result of mortuary practices (e.g., Reinhard 2006:241).

Another possibility is that this violence was a performance designed to intimidate groups, cement alliances with other groups, and possibly gain status

(Osterholtz 2016b). Finally, it may be that the bones had simply been damaged by carnivores, disturbed and broken by the digging of subsequent graves, and inadvertently burned in hearths and ovens, all of which could have left a pattern interpreted as cannibalism (Martin et al. 2014). Martin (2016:1) argued that the remains could be explained by a pattern of persistent forms of violence that may have included witch killings, massacres, executions, body annihilations, and raiding – efforts at social control integrated into ritual and ceremonial activities (also see Ogilvie and Hilton 2000; Harrod 2017).

Evidence from an Ancestral Puebloan village in Colorado is informative. Sometime about AD 1280, the village was attacked and all of the 41 people that were in the village at the time were killed (Kuckelman et al. 2002). Their bodies were dismembered, defleshed, smashed, burned, and otherwise desecrated, perhaps as an attempt to "erase" them from the landscape. Survivors returned to the village and "ritually closed" the abandoned village (Martin 2015:157), suggesting a culturally motivated "end-game" for the dead.

So, was cannibalism actually practiced in the Southwest? Whatever the pattern represents, it appears to have first appeared in the Southwest about AD 1000 (White 1992; Turner and Turner 1999; Billman et al. 2000), perhaps related to influences from Mesoamerica (Turner and Turner 1999:483–484). A sharp increase in the number of victims was noted about AD 1150, roughly the same time as a major drought (Billman et al. 2000:173), and this increase is thought to be related to warfare and raiding (Lambert et al. 2000; also see Hurlbut 2000; Kuckelman et al. 2002; but see Harrod and Martin 2014b).

It seems apparent that there was a widespread pattern of the violent treatment of some segments of the Ancestral Puebloan population, and there is a variety of possible explanations for that pattern, such as being part of a ritual or religious system or an effort to intimidate enemies. If actual cannibalism was practiced in the Southwest, it was likely never common and was probably ritual in nature. It has been argued that even the suggestion that some Ancestral Puebloan peoples practiced cannibalism "condemns" them all as cannibals and is insulting to contemporary Native peoples. However, ritual cannibalism is actually fairly common around the world (e.g., Askenasy 1994; but see Arens 1979) and forms one aspect of the diversity of human behavior.

Of comparative interest is the apparent massacre of the inhabitants of the Hopi town of Awatovi (or Awatobi) in about AD 1700. The remains of at least 30 individuals of both sexes and various ages were discovered in a primary mass grave (Turner and Morris 1970). They had been killed, excarnated, mutilated, burned, and perhaps cannibalized. The town appears to have been attacked by traditional Hopis, since the inhabitants of the town had recently converted to Christianity. Thus, this action may have resulted from the exercise of social or political control over those who had broken religious rules or norms and could be seen as a model to explain the earlier Ancestral Puebloan examples.

Human sacrifice

Human sacrifice (and other sacrifices, see Chapter 4) has been practiced by many groups through time and is one of the "most common manifestations of human religious thought and behavior" (Schwartz 2017:223; also see Murray 2016). Sacrificial victims would have participated in a specialized funerary system with a prescribed preparation (pretreatment), killed in a specific manner, and afforded a particular mortuary treatment. There would likely be little, if any, postmortem commemorative treatment other than as it related to the purpose of their sacrifice, although commemorative behaviors may have been undertaken in their original social unit. Schwartz (2017) identified a series of archaeological signatures and expectations for the identification of human sacrifice in the archaeological record (Table 7.3).

Upon sacrifice, the individual is removed from the human world and moved into the spiritual world (Toyne 2015a), then presumably accepted by the target deity. Using evidence from analysis of a skeleton, a bioarchaeological approach can help illuminate sacrifice rituals and practices. In addition, by using ethnographic analogy, the symbolic meaning behind body manipulation and burial practices can be modeled. Toyne (2015a:137) argued that "the treatment of the body reflects specific symbolic gestures as part of the ritual process and that the death of the individual is only part of a more complex process." In Peru, human sacrifice was part of the ritual context "in which sacrificial death was an important socially and symbolically controlled action experienced on a regular basis" (Toyne 2015b:173).

Table 7.3 Some archaeological expectations for the identification of human sacrifice (compiled from Schwartz 2017)

General trait	Corollaries	Examples
evidence of lifestyle change	special treatment prior to death, e.g., improved diet and health care	Inca *capacocha*, Neolithic European bog bodies
architecture	specialized facilities	various
	placed within a building during its construction	Maya
paraphernalia	altars, regalia, specialized tools (e.g., knives)	Greek, Moche
manner of death	specific trauma, drugs, exposure	various
postmortem treatment	associated with another burial	China, many others
	dismemberment and dispersal of parts	Mexica skull racks
geographic origin of victims	local or nonlocal (biodistance)	various
iconography	wall art or scenes on pottery	Maya, Moche
other	healed battle traumas indicating enemy warriors	Moche
	age and sex profiles	Mexica preference for young males
	infant sacrifice	Romans, Phoenicians, and Moche

Children were not exempt from sacrifice, as it was practiced in a number of societies, from the Phoenicians (e.g., Lee 1996) to the Moche (Verano 2000, 2005; Sutter and Cortez 2005) and others. Goepfert et al. (2018) reported the discovery of the remains of 140 Chimú children and adolescents and 206 juvenile camelids sacrificed on the northern coast of Peru from about 600 BP. The camelids were all young with mostly brown coats, indicating preferential selection of the animals by age and color.

Trauma on sacrificial victims would depend on the prescribed manner of death. In some cases, very little trauma would be present, such as with the Inca *capacocha*, who were apparently drugged and left to freeze to death (see Case Study, page 62). In other cases, trauma could consist of depression fractures in skulls from being hit with a club, cut marks on the ventral sides of cervical vertebrae from having one's throat slit, severing of the cervical vertebrae from decapitation, or damage to the interior side of ribs and sternum from having the heart cut out.

Execution

Execution of a person did not necessarily involve them being used as an offering, but served as a punishment of some sort, either legal or extralegal. Legal executions fall within the judicial system of that society, whereas extralegal killings lie outside of the system. Persons subjected to legal execution include enemies captured in war (e.g., Otterbein 2000), although such killings are now illegal, and criminals (as defined by the society performing the executions).

Methods of execution varied and included decapitation, shooting (with guns or arrows), crucifixion, and hanging. Decapitation was apparently a common punishment in Roman Britain, wherein the victims were inhumated with their heads buried next to them (Figure 7.6) (Montgomery et al. 2011), and both males and females are represented (Tucker 2014). Using this method, one would expect to see cutting damage to cervical vertebrae (and perhaps other upper body elements), possibly initiated from the back of the neck.

People executed by ballistic means may or may not have some obvious skeletal trauma, although the projectiles themselves (bullets or arrowheads) are sometimes found associated with the body. Another common method of execution by the Romans (and others) was crucifixion. In such cases, there would be obvious trauma in the feet and wrists from being nailed to a cross (Byard 2016). Hanging may be deduced from fractured cervical vertebrae or hyoid bone (Spence et al. 1999).

Medical trauma

A variety of trauma on both bone and soft tissues from medical procedures may be encountered. Premortem trauma would include that from general surgeries (mostly in soft tissues, but see discussion on trepanation later), accidents, combat wounds of various kinds, the loss of body parts (e.g., fingers) in mourning ceremonies, and the loss of body parts (e.g., hands) as punishment for crimes (see Redfern 2017a:46–47).

Until the late nineteenth century, the treatment of wounds often involved amputation of the damaged body part, particularly limbs. Such treatment would have resulted in severe trauma, both to soft tissue and bone, but also to the body as a whole through shock.

Postmortem damage to the body (technically not trauma but generally included in that category) include **autopsy** and **dissection**. During the late Middle Ages and the

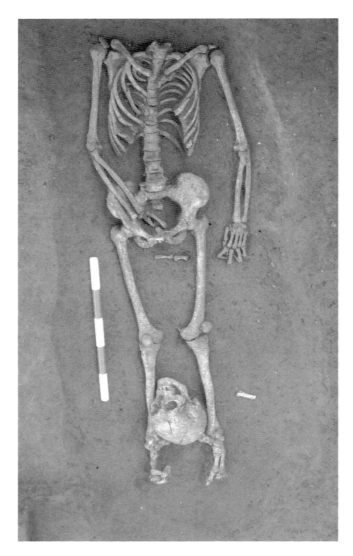

Figure 7.6 A decapitated burial from Roman Britain
Source: Simon Mays

Renaissance, autopsies began to be practiced for medico–legal purposes in order to investigate the causes of death (Giuffra et al. 2016; also see Nystrom 2011, 2017a; Bugaj et al. 2013) and to gain medical knowledge (Aufderheide 2013). Such procedures were more often conducted on the poor due to a disregard for the sanctity of their bodies (Nystrom 2011; Muller et al. 2017). Dissection was (and still is) used to gain medical knowledge but was sometimes used as a postmortem punishment in eighteenth-century England (Redfern 2017a:44).

Trepanation

Trepanation (or trephination) is the surgical cutting of holes into the cranial vault (Figure 7.7) (see discussions in Ortner and Putschar [1981:95–100] and Buikstra and Ubelaker [1994:159–160]). Trepanation is probably most common in Peru (Kurin 2013; Verano 2016) but has also been reported from other areas, including China (Hobert and Binello 2017), southern Russia (Gresky et al. 2016), Siberia (Slepchenko et al. 2017), and Europe (where it dates back at least 4,500 years; Lorkiewicz et al. 2018; Nicklisch et al. 2018). Trepanation has not been documented in North America. The purpose of such a procedure is varied and includes magical rituals (e.g., Faria 2015), medical treatment of wounds (Moghaddam et al. 2015; Verano 2016:267) or chronic headaches (Verano 2016:288),

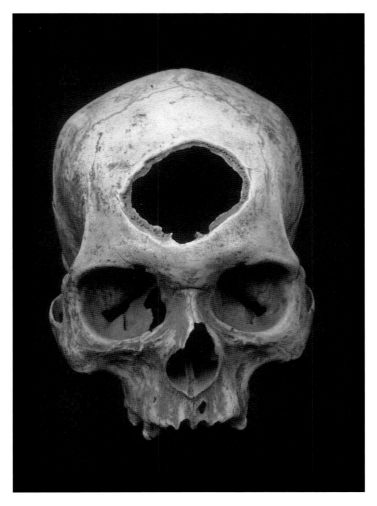

Figure 7.7 An example of a trepanned skull from Peru

Source: John Verano

and prestige. Methods used to produce the holes consisted of scraping, circular grooving, drilling or boring, and linear cutting. Survivors of the procedure would exhibit healing around the wound, perhaps even complete closure of the hole. It is important to remember, however, that other mechanisms can cause "holes" in the skull, such as antemortem defects, disease, or postmortem damage (Verano 2016:21).

Tissue modification

Tissue modification involves an alteration of the natural shape or integrity of a specific tissue. **Deformation** of bone, meaning a change in its natural shape, can be incidental or purposeful. Incidental deformation is not common but has been observed in a number of instances. For example, many societies placed swaddled infants in cradleboards. This often resulted in flattening of the occiput (Figure 7.8), a permanent trait that can be seen in skeletal remains.

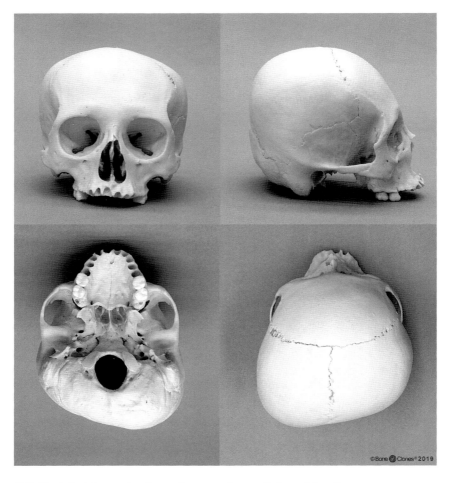

Figure 7.8 Occipital flattening from the use of a cradleboard (cast)

Source: Bone Clones

Although this practice apparently did not affect the development of the brain, the pressure and friction placed on the occiput may, in some cases, have resulted in infections that could cause the death of an infant (Holliday 1993:283). Other incidental skeletal modifications can result from chronic violence or control, particularly on women. The skeletal indicators of such practices might be seen in bone deformation due to foot binding (see page 142), neck rings, and tightlacing of the torso (Stone 2012; Berger et al. 2019).

Intentional modifications

People in many societies, past and present, have purposefully modified portions of their bodies for a variety of reasons, such as distinguishing social status (Sharapova and Razhev 2011:202) or ethnicity (e.g., Geller 2011; Lozada 2011), or for aesthetic purposes. Intentional modifications observable in skeletal remains include cranial deformation, dental modification, foot binding, and some types of piercings. Other modifications, such as tattooing and some piercings, are observable only in preserved soft tissues. It should be kept in mind that there is natural variation in the shapes of bones and that not all "unusual" traits are modifications.

Cranial deformation was widely practiced and is known as early as 45,000 BP in Eurasia (Sharapova and Razhev 2011). Among the Maya of Mesoamerica, head shape was an element of the overall ideology (concepts of tradition, identity, gender, and beauty) of the people (Tiesler 2014). To achieve the desired shape, the occipital and frontal bones of an infant would be bound in childhood so that the skull would grow in an elongated shape (Figure 7.9) that would transmit information regarding the identity and status of

Figure 7.9 An artificially elongated skull from the Maya area, Mexico

Source: Public domain

the person. In the early Neolithic Near East (ca. 10,000 BP), cranial deformation (head shaping) was noted on five males from the Tepe Abdul Hosein site in Iran (Lorentz 2017). Despite the small samples, it is possible that these examples represent an elaboration of status differentiation or group affinity and may reflect the elaboration of bodily difference and identity.

Intentional dental modification can be therapeutic or nontherapeutic (e.g., Burnett and Irish 2017). Therapeutic modifications focus on the treatment of dental pathologies, such as caries and abscesses. This treatment involved the **ablation** (removal) of teeth (e.g., Bolhofner 2017), fillings for caries (e.g., Oxilia et al. 2017), and the use of dental appliances such as false teeth (Crubzy et al. 1998). Nontherapeutic intentional dental modifications were intended to display some aspect of identity, status, or aesthetics. Such modifications could also include ablation, as well as filing, notching, and inlays (Figure 7.10), and carry the risk of developing a pathology (Rufino et al. 2017).

Foot binding, as formerly practiced in China, involved the tight wrapping of the feet so that the bones could not grow to their normal sizes (Stone 2012; Berger et al. 2019). In some cases, the bones would be purposefully broken to reduce their size. The purpose of this practice was apparently to demonstrate the high status of a woman who had servants to do her bidding and so did not need to walk. It may also be a method to control women. This practice leaves obvious traces in the bones of the feet.

A variety of soft tissue modifications is also known. The piercing of the bottom lip for a **labret** (lip plug) was fairly widespread. In addition to the artifacts themselves, biophysical

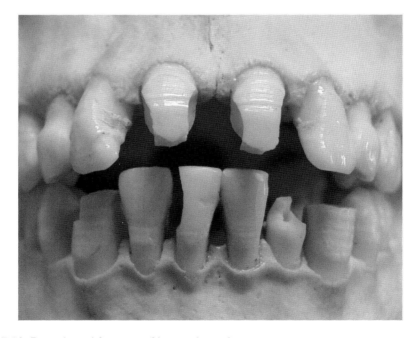

Figure 7.10 Dental modifications: filing and notching

Source: Author

evidence of a labret would manifest on the mandibular front teeth and the mandible itself in the form of grooves or other "wear." Severe wear could result in tooth loss and bone remodeling. In parts of ancient Chile, labrets were symbols of status and masculinity (Torres-Rouff 2011). Along the Northwest Coast of North America, the use of labrets may have been a signaling strategy for ascribed status (Rorabaugh and Shantry 2017). Other soft tissue piercings, such as those on earlobes or nasal septums, would be difficult to detect except on preserved remains.

Tattoos are commonly found around the world and have been documented on any number of preserved bodies, including those in central Asia (Argent 2013), Africa (Friedman et al. 2018), and the Arctic (e.g., Hansen et al. 1991). The oldest tattoos currently known were found on Ötzi (Deter-Wolf et al. 2016), the "Tyrolean Iceman" from northern Italy (see Case Study, page 169), for which soot was used as the "ink" (Pabst et al. 2009).

Postmortem modifications

Animal bone was used by most past societies to make artifacts, such as awls and needles. Some societies also used human bone for a variety of purposes (e.g., Hargrave et al. 2015), such as making tools, decorations, trophies, holy relics, and ritual items (e.g., the skull racks of the Mexica). The use of such materials for manufacture may have served to maintain the connections between the living and the dead (Schermer et al. 2015:1). For example, human femora and skulls were modified for use in Tibetan commemorative rituals (Malville 2005). Human long bones were used on Guam to make fishing harpoons (McNeill 2005:306). In North America, the use of human bone for tools and implements was common during the Woodland period in eastern North America (Hargrave et al. 2015) and during the Early Horizon in California (Ragir 1972; Eerkens et al. 2016a).

Chapter summary

Trauma is damage to living human tissue. Trauma can be blunt, ballistic, or sharp force and can be acute or chronic. One of the most common types of trauma in the archaeological record is bone fractures, of which there are a number of types. Soft tissue traumas are difficult to observe due to the paucity of such remains.

Much of the trauma present in skeletal remains resulted from violence of some kind, either interpersonal violence or warfare, although some violence may be integrated into ritual behaviors. Interpersonal violence was primarily intended to be sublethal and was most commonly directed at women, children, the elderly, and captives, and can be normalized within a society. Warfare, either small or large scale, often involved lethal trauma and is more commonly observed in males. Other signatures of warfare include the nature and context of the treatment of the dead (e.g., presence of mass graves), defensive architecture, types of weapons, and iconography.

Cannibalism is actually a rather common practice, but is generally ritual in nature. Other forms include emergency, criminal, sociopolitical, and culinary. Culinary cannibalism, eating other humans as a normal part of a diet, remains undemonstrated, although there are several suspected cases in the past. Archaeological expectations of cannibalism would include the excarnation (or "butchering") of victims, dismemberment, fragmentation, cooking, and certain patterns of disposal. Alternatively, these same basic patterns may reflect either specialized mortuary treatment or attempts to intimidate or control a population.

Human sacrifice was common in prehistory, and some societies believed the practice to be a critical issue in their survival. Victims would have been subjected to a specialized and ritualized funerary process. Persons of both sexes and various ages were sacrificed, depending on the specific society. Trauma on the victims would depend on the way in which they were killed.

Execution, the killing of certain people in either a legal or extralegal context, was widely practiced. As with sacrificial victims, trauma on executed persons would be dependent on the method of execution employed.

Medical trauma may also be present. In the skeleton, healed repairs of broken or otherwise damaged bone may be evident as would evidence of amputation. In addition, postmortem damage to the body through medical autopsy and/or dissection could be present. Some societies practiced trepanation, the surgical cutting of holes in the skull, and the evidence of such trauma would be quite evident.

Tissue modification was common in both bone and soft tissues. The deformation of bone may have resulted incidentally, such as from cradleboarding, or intentionally, such as from purposeful shaping of the skull of subadults or the binding of feet. In soft tissues, modifications include piercings and tattoos. Postmortem modifications include the manufacture of tools or other items from bone or preserved soft tissues.

Key concepts and terms

ablation
acute trauma
autopsy
ballistic trauma
blunt trauma
cannibalism
chronic trauma
comminuted fractures
compression fractures
cranial deformation
criminal cannibalism
culinary cannibalism
deformation
depression fractures
dissection
domestic violence
emergency cannibalism
endocannibalism
exocannibalism
green bone (or greenstick) fractures
human sacrifice
interpersonal violence
labret

lethal
oblique fractures
ritual (or funerary) cannibalism
sharp force trauma
sociopolitical cannibalism
spiral fractures
sublethal
tattoos
Towton
transverse fractures
trauma
trepanation
warfare

Chapter 8

Specialized studies

An array of specialized techniques is available to analyze and evaluate human remains, including the identification of organic residues, ancient DNA (aDNA), isotopes, biodistance studies, radiography, and scanning. Each is discussed next.

Biomolecular studies

The analysis of biomolecular materials is increasingly important in the analysis of archaeological materials and includes a number of specialized methods (Brown and Brown 2011; Katzenberg and Waters-Rist 2019). Such analyses are interdisciplinary and include chemists, biologists, geneticists, physicians, geologists, biological anthropologists, and archaeologists. The major avenues of study include organic materials such as blood, lipids, proteins, and aDNA, although inorganic materials, primarily isotopes, are also included. Data are collected from individuals, which, when combined, can be used to model populations.

The study of **biomolecules** in archaeology is applicable to a variety of research questions. Data derived directly from human remains can be used to address a variety of issues, such as human evolution; the paleobiology, paleogeography, and paleodemography of humans; and human diet, food webs, and subsistence systems. In addition, pharmacological substances can be identified and can contribute to an understanding of ethnopharmacology, religion, forensics, trade, and perhaps even recreation. For example, psychotropic drugs perhaps used for ritual purposes have been discovered in pre-Columbian New World mummies (Balabanova et al. 1995) and European bog bodies (see Hillman 1986:103). In a controversial finding, Parsche et al. (1993) identified the hallucinogenic drugs cocaine and nicotine in ancient Egyptian mummies. Because these compounds are thought to be New World in origin, their presence in Old World mummies cannot be explained at this time, but may involve problems in sampling, contamination, and/or laboratory procedures.

Studies can also be conducted on other materials. These include artifacts, animal bone, or mollusk shells, and can be used to address questions about artifact use (e.g., protein residue analysis, see page 147), adhesives and resins (e.g., Stacey et al. 1998), site formation processes, and environmental reconstruction (Brown and Brown 2011).

Organic residues: blood, lipids, and proteins

Organic residues, including blood, lipids, and proteins, may be present on or associated with human remains. Such residues can reveal the technological aspects of the treatment of the dead, as well as their mortuary and commemorative contexts. The application of appropriate techniques can isolate and identify such residues. Once identified, the biomolecular components of residues can be ascertained and the structure and isotopic composition of a particular residue can be identified (Evershed 2008; Brown and Brown 2011).

Blood may be detected using visual and/or specific chemical methods. For example, blood may be present in mummified remains, and individual blood cells can be observed microscopically (Zimmerman 1973). Several methods are used to detect blood residues, including Hemastix (Matheson and Veall 2014) and immunological techniques, although aDNA testing is now the preferred method of species identification.

The study of blood cell antigen groupings is useful in studying population genetics and population movements (see Brown and Brown 2011:39). Most of these studies have been conducted on soft tissues, and a number of analytical problems are known, including poor preservation and misidentification of remains. Albumin appears to be the most useful blood protein for genetic investigation (Smith et al. 1995:68). Several studies have identified blood groups on mummies, such as those from the Arctic (Zimmerman 1980:130, 1998:149), Egypt (Flaherty and Haigh 1986), and Lindow Man (Connolly et al. 1986:74).

All human tissues possess a human leukocyte antigen (HLA) system, which is important in modern medicine for matching transplant donors and recipients. The tissue types of family members tend to be similar. In one study, in an attempt to determine relatedness among the eight mummified individuals from Qilakitsoq, Greenland, Ammitzbøll et al. (1991:89–94) analyzed their tissue types and suggested that many of them were related.

Lipids include a wide variety of compounds, although most archaeological studies have concentrated on fatty acids, such as steroids and cholesterols (e.g., Evershed 1993:75–76; Fankhauser 1994:228). Evershed (2008; also see Brown and Brown 2011:54–67) reviewed the general application of lipid analysis to archaeological investigations. The recovery and analysis of lipids from human tissues can reveal important information about organic preservation and hormone levels, among other topics of interest (see Sobolik et al. 1996). Lipids have been discovered in the tissues of bog bodies (Connolly et al. 1986:73; Evershed 1990; Evershed and Connolly 1994) and mummies (Gülaçar et al. 1990). Lipid analysis is also used in the identification of foods (Lucejko et al. 2018) and as a biomarker for the location of inhumations (Ismail et al. 2016).

Proteins are present in all living tissues and can preserve in very small quantities on archaeological materials such as stone and ceramics. Proteins can be recovered and identified, sometimes to the genus level (Bernard et al. 2007; Pavelka et al. 2016; Barker et al. 2018). Identified proteins include those from food, resins, manufacturing materials, and even pathogens (Child and Pollard 1992). Several techniques can be used to identify proteins (Cattaneo et al. 1993:Table 2), including cross-over immunoelectrophoresis (CIEP) and the relatively new proteomic method (Brown and Brown 2011:50–51). Although some researchers remain skeptical about the identification of proteins in archaeological contexts, the issue may ultimately become moot with the continued development of aDNA analysis.

Ancient DNA

Deoxyribonucleic acid (**DNA**) is the material that carries the genetic information of an individual and is present in virtually all organic materials, including bone (e.g., Matisoo-Smith and Horsburgh 2012; Bramanti 2013; Baker 2016; Nieves-Colón and

Stone 2019). The DNA from archaeological samples is commonly called ancient DNA (aDNA). **Nuclear DNA (nDNA)** is the DNA that makes up the chromosomes in the cell nucleus and is a combination of the nDNA from both parents. **Mitochondrial DNA (mtDNA)** is present in the mitochondria outside the cell nucleus and originates only from the mother (Figure 8.1). The **Y chromosome** within the nucleus tends not to recombine and is used to study the male line (Nieves-Colón and Stone 2019:518).

The analysis of DNA only became practical after the development, in 1985, of a technique to produce readable copies of aDNA, called **polymerase chain reaction (PCR)**. Most recently, the development of **next-generation sequencing** (NGS; Goodwin et al. 2016) has expanded the analysis of aDNA, as it has made it fast and inexpensive.

The two major issues in aDNA analysis are preservation and contamination (see Bramanti 2013; Baker 2016; Nieves-Colón and Stone 2019). Although it is clear that some aDNA survives over time, even over millions of years, it is not clear in what form such molecules survive, whether they have been altered through diagenesis, and if they can be correctly identified. Even if well preserved, aDNA samples can be easily contaminated by

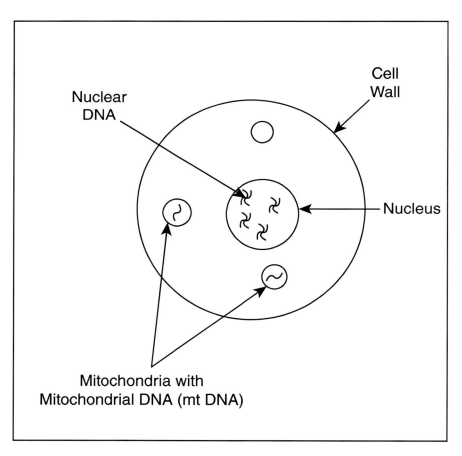

Figure 8.1 The location of nuclear and mitochondrial DNA in a cell

Source: Author

a variety of organisms, especially bacteria and fungi. Another issue is possible contamination by the researcher's DNA (Bramanti 2013; Nieves-Colón and Stone 2019).

There are different concentrations of aDNA in different tissues, so different sampling methods are required. The best-preserved aDNA appears to be located in the petrous bone (part of the temporal bone) of the skull (Hansen et al. 2017) and in dental calculus (Black et al. 2011). The calcified layer (called cementum) covering the roots of teeth may also contain high-quality aDNA, especially mtDNA (Adler et al. 2010). Under certain conditions, aDNA can even be recovered from the soils of archaeological sites (Slon et al. 2017).

Numerous anthropological questions can be addressed using aDNA. These include ethnicity and lineage (e.g., Scheib et al. 2018; but see Jobling et al. 2016), population migrations (Kaestle and Smith 2001; Konigsberg 2006), and the sex of human remains (Sutton et al. 1996; Skoglund et al. 2013; Geller 2017b; Nieves-Colón and Stone 2019). DNA analysis is also used for forensic applications such as the identification of war dead (Holland et al. 1993), including those from the American Civil War (Fisher et al. 1993), as well as murder victims.

Case study: discovering the origins of the First Americans

The origins and migrations of the earliest Americans continue to be the subject of spirited debate. A relatively new avenue of investigation into the origins of New World populations is the study of DNA, primarily mtDNA. In this approach, groups of specific mutations (haplogroups or haplotypes) in living peoples are identified and tracked back to their place of geographic origin, and estimates of the time of their divergence are made. Six haplogroups have been identified (A, B, C, D, M, and X), suggesting that the genetic diversity among colonizing Paleoindians was considerable and derived from either two or three waves of people coming from Asia.

Geneticists generally agree that the earliest (first) migration event probably began as early as 17,000 years ago in Asia, with people moving east across Beringia (the Bering Strait Land Bridge that connected Alaska with Siberia during the Pleistocene) and then south along the recently deglaciated west coast of North America (Figure 8.2) (Achilli et al. 2013; Raff and Bolnick 2014; Raghavan et al. 2015; Schurr 2015; Llamas et al. 2016; also see Moreno-Mayar et al. 2018; Pinotti et al. 2019). This matches much, but not all, of the archaeological evidence of early peoples (Dillehay 1997; Gilbert et al. 2008; Sutton 2017b; also see Adovasio et al. 1999).

A second migration across Beringia and through the midcontinental ice-free corridor as early as 13,500 years ago has been proposed by some geneticists (Achilli et al. 2013; Raff and Bolnick 2014) but more recently has been rejected by others as unnecessary to explain Native American genetics as currently understood (Raghavan et al. 2015; also see Fiedel 2017). On the other hand, all

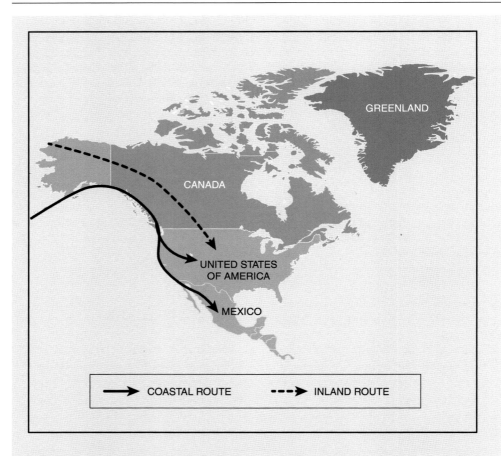

Figure 8.2 General migration routes of the First Americans from northeastern Asia and across Beringia

Source: Alamy image WE9N4N

modern genetic analyses support a more recent, final migration of Neo-Eskimo ancestors into the high Arctic by 1,000 years ago (Achilli et al. 2013; Raff and Bolnick 2014; Raghavan et al. 2015).

Genetic evidence gathered directly from Paleoindian skeletal material is controversial, both within Native American groups and within the archaeological discipline (Alonzi 2016). Virtually all of the Paleoindian remains from which aDNA has been successfully extracted belong to traditional Native American haplotype groups. However, Oppenheimer et al. (2014) suggested that the mtDNA X2a genetic marker was consistent with an entry from Europe (e.g., Bradley and Stanford 2004; Stanford and Bradley 2012), an assertion disputed by Walker and Clinnick (2014).

The extremely small sample size makes it problematic to discuss direction of movement or Paleoindian population characteristics on the basis of genetics. Nevertheless, haplogroup D4 has been found primarily in Pacific Coast populations scattered from British Columbia down to South America and has been put forward as a founding mtDNA lineage for the coastal migration theory (Kemp et al. 2007). Recent analysis of skeletons spanning a period of approximately 10,300 years on the Northwest Coast suggests genetic continuity from the early Holocene to the historical period, while suggesting that other early remains in northwestern North America (the Anzick-1 burial and Kennewick Man) may come from a different ancestral line (Lindo et al. 2017). Fiedel (2017) viewed the mtDNA haplotype (D4h3a) found in the Anzick-1 burial as evidence that Clovis people founded this DNA lineage in North America. The work by Lindo et al. (2017), however, specifically addressed the relatedness of the Anzick site remains to the Northwest Coast samples and found that although they share a haplotype, the sequence of the Anzick remains appears to be ancestral to a more southern lineage and the Northwest Coast samples appear to belong to a separate branch. Scheib et al. (2018) argued that Paleoindians arrived following a coastal route and once south of the ice sheets likely split into two distinct groups that eventually recombined to found the Native population in the Americas.

A less controversial proxy for Native American migration may be found in the ancient DNA of dogs that traveled to the Americas with colonizing groups (Witt et al. 2015). Although the oldest identified dog remains in the Americas are dated between 9,430 and 9,090 years ago (Tito et al. 2011), older specimens are likely to be found eventually. Recent studies of the genetics of modern purebred dogs of the Americas have shown that 30% or less of female dog lineages have mixed European ancestry, and comparisons to aDNA suggest genetic continuity of some dog breeds from pre-Columbian to modern times in Mexico and possibly Alaska (van Asch et al. 2013). Larger samples from both modern and precontact dog specimens, as well as more complete sequencing of these specimens (Witt et al. 2015), could provide a wealth of information about human migration and interaction in the Americas.

Pathogens in human remains can now be detected in aDNA (e.g., Krause-Kyora et al. 2018). The use of NGS technology has increased the speed and precision of aDNA analysis, thus making it less expensive. The voucher samples for identification are contemporary species, however, meaning that ancient ones may remain undetected.

Ancient bacterial pathogens detected using aDNA now include tuberculosis (*Mycobacterium tuberculosis* and *M. leprae*), bubonic plague (*Yersinia pestis*), typhus (*Rickettsia prowazeckii*), trench fever (*Bartonella quintana*) (Dutour 2013), meningococcal disease (*Neisseria meningitides*) (Eerkens et al. 2018), and hepatitis B, with the latter being at least 7,000 years old (Krause-Kyora et al. 2018; also see Ross et al. 2018). In addition, aDNA analysis of soils in a 2,000-year-old site in Denmark identified helminth eggs from both human and livestock hosts (cow, pig, horse, sheep, and dog) (Wegener Tams et al. 2018).

Isotopic analysis

An isotope is any of two or more forms of an element with the same number of protons but having different numbers of neutrons in its nucleus. They can be either stable or unstable, with the latter being radioactive. Whereas **radioactive isotopes** decay (emit a particle) over time (this is the basis of radiometric dating), **stable isotopes** do not decay, making them ideal for measurement. Isotopes are measured using isotope ratio mass spectrometry (IRMS) (Eriksson 2013; Katzenberg and Waters-Rist 2019).

Stable isotopic analysis (SIA), broadly based on the concept of "you are what you eat," has revolutionized the study of past diets and their relationship to other aspects of behavior (Bogaard and Outram 2013:333) and is increasingly being incorporated into archaeological analyses (Brown and Brown 2011; Katzenberg and Waters-Rist 2019; also see Pollard 2011). Isotopic analysis can be used to model the interaction between diet, nutrition, and disease. It can be useful for ascertaining place of residence (within the last ten years or so), migration patterns, paleoenvironments, evolutionary inferences (Cappellini et al. 2018), and the role of lipids (fats) (Evershed 2008). Isotopes of **carbon, nitrogen, oxygen**, and **strontium** appear to be the most informative (Katzenberg and Waters-Rist 2019) (Table 8.1), although hydrogen, sulfur, copper, and zinc also have potential (Nehlich 2015; Jaouen et al. 2017).

Isotopes are initially taken up by plants (e.g., Bethard 2012; Katzenberg and Waters-Rist 2019), which will have a particular isotopic signature that is dependent on the local soil chemistry and carbon pathways. In general, isotopic values will increase with trophic level. Thus, herbivores will have elevated values over the plants they eat, and carnivores eating the herbivores will have a further enriched signature. Omnivores, such as humans, will express the combined isotopic signature of the plants and animals they eat.

Table 8.1 Some isotopes studied in bioarchaeology

Element	Isotope/process	Used to
carbon	ratios of $^{13}C/^{12}C$	identify photosynthetic pathways (C_3, C_4, or CAM) to deduce categories of plants consumed
nitrogen	ratios of $^{15}N/^{14}N$	to deduce (1) the relative contribution of plant and animal proteins in the diet, (2) trophic levels, (3) breastfeeding patterns, and (4) past climates
oxygen	ratio of ^{18}O to ^{16}O	to deduce (1) breastfeeding and weaning, (2) mobility and residential history, (3) fish sources, (4) seasonality of shellfish, and (5) paleoenvironment (water temperature)
strontium	ratio of ^{85}Sr, ^{86}Sr, ^{87}Sr, and ^{88}Sr	to deduce (1) residence, mobility, and migration and (2) the geographic source of materials such as wood, shell, and textiles

The majority of stable isotope work has been conducted on bone (e.g., Katzenberg and Waters-Rist 2019), primarily **collagen** (the organic portion that can degrade), which is used to deduce dietary protein, but also **apatite** (the inorganic portion that is more stable), which is used to deduce the total diet. Collagen is probably more likely to be used in analysis, whereas apatite is more likely to show evidence of diagenesis.

As bone remodels, however, its isotopic signature becomes generalized, reflecting only the last 10 years (perhaps as much as 20) (Katzenberg and Waters-Rist 2019:483). On the other hand, tooth enamel, which does not remodel, can contain a permanent childhood isotopic record (e.g., Humphrey 2016). Isotopic analysis has also been conducted on fossilized hominin bone (Drucker and Bocherens 2004; Lee-Thorp and Sponheimer 2006), suggesting that isotopic signatures can preserve for a considerable time. Obtaining isotopic data from cremains is more difficult but still possible (Schurr et al. 2015). Hair and nails contain specific short-term records and are probably the best soft tissue materials to test (Katzenberg and Waters-Rist 2019:474).

Isotopes in dietary reconstruction

Studies of isotopes can reveal important information about diet, with carbon and nitrogen isotopes being the most commonly examined. The data gleaned from these studies include the types of foods eaten (e.g., Tafuri et al. 2018; Kusaka 2019), the ratios of terrestrial to marine foods (e.g., Schulting et al. 2008), the ratios of plant to animal foods (e.g., Lillie and Jacobs 2006), the relationship between diet and health (e.g., Reitsema and Holder 2018), and general stress (Garland et al. 2018). Moreover, dietary data can be used to infer social and economic status (e.g., Honch et al. 2006), quality of life (Gheggi et al. 2018), and resource intensification among hunter-gatherers (Bartelink 2006; Beasley et al. 2013). Most recently, it is becoming apparent that "a relationship exists between human (patho) physiology and stable isotope biochemistry" (Carroll et al. 2018:117) and that disease (e.g., anemia and changes in metabolic rate) and behaviors (e.g., anorexia) will influence isotopic ratios. This research avenue holds great promise.

Plants incorporate carbon into their tissues using one of three known pathways (Katzenberg and Waters-Rist 2019:481–483), each of which results in a distinct ratio of stable carbon isotopes ($^{13}C/^{12}C$). The three pathways are (1) the Calvin (or "C_3") pathway, (2) the Hatch-Slack (or "C_4") pathway, and (3) the crassulacean acid metabolism (CAM) pathway. Examples of C_3 plants (some 95% of all plants) include beans, squash, manioc, trees, shrubs, and cool-season grasses, whereas C_4 plants (some 5% of plants, almost all being cultigens) include amaranth, maize, and warm-season grasses. The role of maize in the diet is a major research focus of carbon pathway research. Further, marine resources (e.g., sea mammals, anadromous fish [salmonids], and shellfish) have elevated carbon isotope values that overlap with C_4 values.

Nitrogen isotopes derive mostly from protein in the diet, and the ratios of $^{15}N/^{14}N$ can be used to deduce the relative contribution of plant and animal proteins in the diet, trophic level (Katzenberg and Waters-Rist 2019), and breastfeeding and weaning patterns (Tsutaya 2017; King et al. 2018; Schurr 2018). Nitrogen ratios in bone may also be useful in inferring past climates (Heaton et al. 1986; but see Ambrose and DeNiro 1987). The application of a ratio of carbon and nitrogen values permits the modeling of the relative contributions of plant, terrestrial animal, and marine animal foods in human diets (e.g., Froehle et al. 2012). A study of osteometric and nitrogen isotope data in burials from a medieval (fourteenth to fifteenth centuries AD) church in Luxembourg demonstrated socioeconomic differences between two groups of burials (Trautmann et al. 2017).

Oxygen isotopes are also useful for exploring diet based on the relationship between the ratios of oxygen isotopes in tissues and of water ingested during life. Oxygen isotopes have been studied in an attempt to detect breastfeeding and weaning based on the premise of isotopic enrichment in mother's milk (e.g., Britton et al. 2015), to determine the source of fish (e.g., Dufour et al. 2007), to ascertain the seasonality of shellfish (e.g., Andrus and Crowe 2000), and to study mobility. They are also used in studies of paleoenvironment (Schoeninger et al. 2003; Leng and Lewis 2016), as well as some aspects of pollution (e.g., Bresciani et al. 1991:164–167).

Several examples illustrate the usefulness of isotopic analysis to explore a variety of questions. Applying nitrogen isotopic values, Greenwald et al. (2016) examined a number of skeletons from central California and found a decrease in the age of weaning over time, suggesting that foraging intensified in the Late Period (ca. 800 to 250 BP) and that the reliance on women's labor to obtain foodstuffs increased, resulting in a reduction of time devoted to child rearing.

A series of preserved burials from the pastoralist Tashtyk society of Siberia dating from the third to fourth centuries AD were studied by Shishlina et al. (2016). The carbon and nitrogen isotopes in the hair contained a record of diet over the last few months of their lives, and seasonal variations in diet were documented, indicating seasonal mobility among different areas.

Thirty-one individuals from two Late Neolithic–Copper Age (3,500–2,000 BC) burial sites in Portugal were investigated by Waterman et al. (2014). Two geographically and temporally close burial populations were studied: one from a cave and one from a stone tomb (or tholos). The isotopes of carbon, nitrogen, and oxygen were measured to determine if there had been a difference in diet associated with the differences in mortuary treatment. The results suggest that the diets of both populations consisted primarily of C_3 plants and terrestrial animals, with the addition of some marine resources. Thus, the diet of the two burial populations was essentially the same, and the reason for the differences in mortuary treatment was not related to social differentiation reflected in diet.

Examining carbon and nitrogen isotopic data on human bone from two separate Mesolithic cemeteries in coastal Brittany (France), Schulting and Richards (2001) detected differences in the consumption of marine foods between the two populations. Interestingly, they concluded that young women had consumed fewer marine foods and suggested that they had come to the coast later in life, possibly reflecting an exogamous, patrilocal marriage pattern. Another possible explanation may be differential access to certain foods based on sex or status.

Finally, Beasley et al. (2013) studied the Late Holocene record of the Ellis Landing site in the San Francisco Bay Area in California. Faunal data from the site suggested a pattern of increasing intensity of resource use and a decline in foraging efficiency through time. On the other hand, the isotopic data from human burials at the site showed a high level of dietary variability and did not support the idea of intensification late in time.

Isotopes in paleomobility studies

The mobility and migration of people can also be detected using isotopic analyses. Most of these studies have been conducted with strontium, although oxygen isotopes have been used in the study of mobility and residential history (e.g., Toyne et al. 2014) and (coupled with nitrogen) migration patterns (Hughes et al. 2014; Bonilla et al. 2018).

Strontium (Sr) has four natural isotopes (^{85}Sr, ^{86}Sr, ^{87}Sr, and ^{88}Sr) that become incorporated into bone and teeth through the consumption of food and water and can even be measured in cremains (Snoeck et al. 2016). Strontium isotopes are present in varying ratios in different geographic areas, and plants from those areas have the same isotopic strontium ratio as their soils. This ratio is passed up the food chain unaltered, and its measurement in bone can indicate the geographic origin of the foods and water consumed. As such, the measurement of strontium isotopes can be used to investigate paleomobility, including residential location (e.g., Bentley 2006; Chesson et al. 2018), migration and mobility (e.g., Montgomery 2010; Price et al. 2014; Eerkens et al. 2016c; Guo et al. 2018; Burton and Katzenberg 2019), population variation (Katzenberg 1993), and the transition to agriculture (Papathanasiou 2003; Hu et al. 2006). Further, strontium isotopes can be used to determine the geographic source of other archaeological materials, such as wood (e.g., Reynolds et al. 2005), shell (e.g., Henderson et al. 2005), and textiles (e.g., Benson et al. 2006).

For example, strontium isotopic ratios were measured on a burial lot from an Early Period (ca. 4,500–2,500 BP) site in central California (Harold et al. 2016). It was proposed that the inhabitants of the site practiced a patrilocal post-marital residence pattern and most of the adult females had been raised in other areas. The study further posited that males from the village had been born there, had moved elsewhere during adolescence, and had returned with a bride to their village of birth, suggesting an extended period of bride service (Harold et al. 2016:44). At another Early Period site in central California, some individuals were found buried with extra skulls. Strontium analysis at that site showed that the skulls were from the same area and were probably not enemy trophy skulls, a pattern suggestive of ancestor veneration (Eerkens et al. 2016a; also see Andrushko et al. 2005).

One of the issues in early Anglo-Saxon history is the biological origin of the populations, indigenous people acculturated either by the English or Germanic migrants. To test the competing models, Hughes et al. (2014) analyzed strontium and oxygen isotopic ratios from tooth enamel in a sample of 19 individuals from an early Anglo-Saxon cemetery. The isotopic data indicated a generally homogeneous sample, with only one individual being a probable immigrant from mainland Europe, supporting the acculturation model.

Slater et al. (2014) investigated the population history of the major Mississippian polity of Cahokia where the material archaeological evidence suggests a considerable ethnic and social diversity. Strontium isotope analysis of tooth enamel on individuals from diverse mortuary contexts at the site was undertaken to identify the general origin of the people and whether they were local or nonlocal. It was found that about a third of the individuals analyzed were identified as nonlocal and from a variety of places. Thus, the role of migration into the city and the formation of the polity is now better understood.

Biodistance studies

Biodistance is the study of how closely people (and populations) are related based on metric and nonmetric aspects of their skeletal and dental morphology. Biodistance studies are "based on the assumption that cranial, dental, and (less commonly) postcranial size, shape, and morphology are genetically conditioned" (Stojanowski 2013:71). Although the technique is limited by small sample sizes and fragmentation of remains, statistical techniques can be used to compensate (Byers and Saunders 2018). Analysis of aDNA, if available, could also measure biodistance, although Stojanowski (2019) argued that aDNA results should always be viewed with caution.

For example, it has typically been believed that victims of Moche sacrifice included local Moche warriors captured in ritual battles. However, a biodistance analysis of the remains of sacrificial victims at the Moche site of La Huaca de la Luna concluded that the victims originated from nonlocal competing Moche polities (Sutter and Cortez 2005). This finding altered our understanding of the Moche at La Huaca de la Luna and their relationships with other Moche groups.

In another biodistance study, Weiss (2018) conducted an analysis of skeletal traits on individuals from a site in central California that had been assumed to reflect cultural and biological continuity through time. The results indicated that at least two separate biological populations were represented, indicating a population replacement at some point, contradicting the assumed continuity and highlighting the need for such biodistance studies.

Imaging

Photography is an important technique for documenting human remains, but it produces only a two-dimensional (2-D) image of the surface of the remains. To view the inside of a bone or body, medical-grade imaging is needed. These techniques include radiography (X-rays; also 2-D) and a number of 3-D imaging methods, such as computerized tomography (**CT**) scans and magnetic resonance imaging (**MRI**). Positron emission tomography (PET) scans are not used in archaeology, since it requires a radioactive tracer that has to circulate in living tissue.

Radiography

The simplest and least expensive imaging technique in skeletal analysis is radiography. Radiographs can show features not visible to the naked eye, including healed traumas such as fractures (Figure 8.3), bone density (e.g., osteopenia or osteoporosis), unerupted

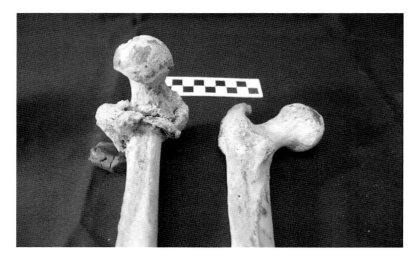

Figure 8.3 Example (obviously not a radiograph) of a very poorly healed fracture of the proximal femur next to an unbroken proximal femur

Source: Marni LaFleur

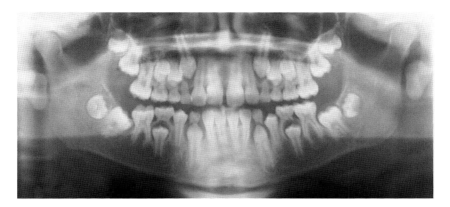

Figure 8.4 Radiograph of unerupted teeth
Source: Alamy Image ID: AMM408

teeth (Figure 8.4), and many other aspects of the skeleton. Because bone is in no danger of overexposure, multiple radiographs may be taken.

Scanning

Scanning imaging techniques produce a noninvasive 3-D image of the subject remains of different resolutions, depending on the method used. Common 3-D scanning techniques include CT scans and MRIs. In addition, several other types of scans are used for different purposes, such as photon absorptiometry to measure the density of a material (especially bone) and gravimetric techniques to measure mass. The potential of these technologies in bioarchaeology is considerable (Cox 2015; Panzer et al. 2019).

A CT scan (Hughes 2011) produces an image from a series of many hundreds of radiographic images processed and combined by computer to produce a 3-D image. As it is the fastest and cheapest of the scanning techniques, it is the one most commonly used in medicine, but it emits radiation, an issue for the technicians. An MRI uses a magnetic field and radio waves to produce a more detailed image of soft tissues than a CT scan. It is more expensive but there are no radiation risks (Rühli 2015). Many of the scanning studies have so far been on mummies, often to conduct "virtual" autopsies (see page 158).

A CT scan of the humerus of Lucy (*Australopithecus afarensis*; discussed previously) indicated a perimortem break, possibly due to a fall from a tree and perhaps related to her death (Kappelman et al. 2016). A recent study on the cremains of the two unidentified individuals from Tomb II at Aegae (Aigai), Greece, was conducted with CT scans and X-ray fluorescence scanning (XRF) (Antikas and Wynn-Antikas 2016). The results indicated that one of the individuals was Philip II of Macedon and father of Alexander the Great. The second individual was identified as the daughter of King Ateas of Scythia.

Several additional examples of soft tissue analysis of paleopathologies are illustrative. Bourke (1986) undertook a number of medical examinations on Lindow Man, including radiography, MRI, xeroradiography (also see Connolly 1986), and CT scans (also see Reznek et al. 1986), and discovered a number of pathologies. Later, Brothwell et al.

(1990) took radiographs and CT scans on the Huldremose Woman bog body (found in Denmark) to identify the intestinal tract for sampling purposes. Finally, Ammitzbøll et al. (1991) conducted detailed radiographic analyses of eight mummies discovered at Qilakit-soq, Greenland, and identified a variety of pathologies and disease (discussed previously). Radiographic, CT, and MRI scans, coupled with scanning electron microscopy (SEM) observations, were conducted on 8,200-year-old preserved human brain matter from the Windover site in Florida (Hauswirth et al. 1991, 1994).

Virtual autopsies

Mummies, often complete bodies, can contain the full range of bioarchaeological data of a particular population, and numerous studies can be conducted to retrieve those data. To that end, various procedures on their remains have been carried out, including invasive autopsies, **endoscopic** exams, and scans.

Many of the scanning studies that have been conducted on preserved bodies constitute **virtual autopsies** (Figure 8.5), intended to reveal highly detailed information regarding pathologies and cause of death. One of the famous applications of scanning was the virtual autopsy of Tutankhamun (Rühli and Ikram 2014). However, Wadea et al. (2019) cautioned that any diagnosis of conditions should not rely solely on scan data, but should have an interdisciplinary consensus. Scanning data on mummies have been compiled in a database (the Internet Mummy Picture Archiving and Communication

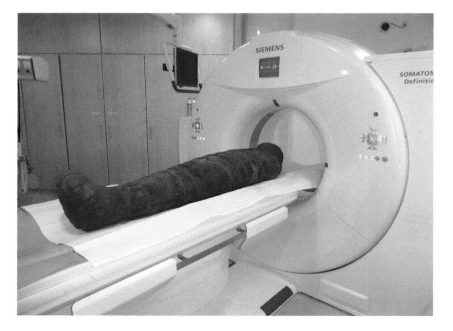

Figure 8.5 A CT scan of an Egyptian mummy in progress

Source: Stephanie Panzer

Technology, or IMPACT) to make such data available to other researchers (e.g., Nelson and Wade 2015).

Chapter summary

A number of techniques are available to analyze and interpret human remains, including the analysis of organic residues such as blood, lipids, proteins, and aDNA, as well as inorganic materials such as isotopes, along with biodistance, radiographic, and scanning data. These data sets can be employed to investigate a variety of issues, including human evolution; the paleobiology, paleogeography, and paleodemography of humans; and human diet, food webs, and subsistence systems.

The study of aDNA is a major focus of biomolecular research in bioarchaeology. Studies of mtDNA have the ability to trace relatedness through the female line, and the Y chromosome data can trace the male line. Issues that may be addressed with aDNA data include ethnicity and lineage, population migrations (such as the origins of the First Americans; see the Case Study, page 149), the sex of human remains, and pathogens associated with human remains. In forensic settings, DNA is used to identify war dead and murder victims.

Analyses of isotopes (particularly those of carbon and nitrogen) explore diet, including the types of plants consumed, the ratios of plants to animals eaten, and the origin (marine or terrestrial) of animal foods. Oxygen isotopes are also useful for dietary analyses as well as studies of past environments. Strontium isotopes are analyzed to determine the geographic origin of people (and other issues) and are central to studies of mobility.

Biodistance is the analysis of the relatedness of populations using the morphological (metric and nonmetric) characteristics of human remains. Studies of morphology can augment and test aDNA data to gain a better perspective on relatedness. Biodistance data can also assist in determining the diversity within a population.

A variety of techniques may be used to obtain imaging data to determine the presence or absence of pathologies and traumas. These methods include conventional photography and radiography (X-rays) and 3-D methods such as CT and MRI scans. Both CT and MRI scans can be utilized to conduct "virtual" autopsies of mummies and other preserved bodies.

Key concepts and terms

apatite
biodistance
biomolecules
carbon isotopes
computerized tomography (CT) scans
collagen
deoxyribonucleic acid (DNA)
lipids
magnetic resonance imaging (MRI)
mitochondrial DNA (mtDNA)
next-generation sequencing (NGS)
nitrogen isotopes

nuclear DNA (nDNA)
oxygen isotopes
polymerase chain reaction (PCR)
proteins
radioactive isotopes
radiographs (X–rays)
stable isotopes
stable isotopic analysis (SIA)
strontium isotopes
virtual autopsy
Y chromosome

Chapter 9

Interpretive theory and data integration

Theoretical approaches in interpretation

Any attempt at an explanation of archaeological data requires some sort of a theoretical framework. Explanation is a function of theory – the way something is interpreted is dependent on how it is viewed (e.g., Praetzellis 2015; Johnson 2019). There are two major "levels" of theory: general paradigms and middle range.

Most archaeologists operate within a scientific paradigm (a distinct way of looking at something) in which the past is seen as empirical, objective, and knowable – an approach commonly called **processualism** (or "New Archaeology") in the United States. Within that general paradigm is a number of more specific approaches to understanding the past, including **materialism** (solving practical problems), **evolutionary theory** (change through time), structuralism (how a society was organized), **systems theory** (interaction between cultural components), and **Marxism** (power in a society). Added to this is the statistical analysis of data.

A second general paradigm is **postprocessualism**, the idea that the past is largely subjective and thus unknowable. However, postprocessualism appears to actually be a number of new perspectives that augment processual archaeology (e.g., VanPool and VanPool 1999), what Hegmon (2003:213) called "processual-plus." These new approaches (see Chapter 10) include **feminist theory** (an emphasis on females, particularly the nature of gender inequality), **queer theory** (exploring diverse sexualities), and **agency** (an emphasis on the power of the individual).

All of these approaches share the **normative approach**, the idea that a past society would have been fundamentally similar to current ones. As such, past societies would have had the "normative" traits of culture, such as a population, a subsistence system, a settlement pattern, a religion, and most importantly here, a funerary system. Furthermore, it is believed that the behaviors associated with these traits would have generated a material record that can be discovered, recovered, and interpreted. This general approach forms the basis for much of the archaeological interpretation available today (e.g., Taylor 1948:110; Binford 1965; Lyman and O'Brien 2004; Johnson 2019).

Following the normative view, archaeologists attempt to describe a past society by creating a model – a hypothetical **archaeological culture** – to use as an analytical unit. Such a model makes it possible to organize archaeological data in space and time. To begin, traits are plotted and combinations of traits are noted. When some sort of inclusive pattern is detected, the entity reflected by that pattern may be called an archaeological culture. These archaeological cultures are essentially models that may or may not represent actual societies (although that is the goal), and like any model, they are subject to testing, rejection, or revision.

Middle-range theory

The past was dynamic, but its resultant material remains are not. The past cannot be directly viewed, and it is only possible to gain an "indirect" understanding through the formulation of hypotheses and models to be tested against archaeological data. For example, you cannot actually witness a past mourning ceremony – you can only find its patterned remains. How would we be able to infer that the materials found in the archaeological record reflect a mourning ceremony? To make such an inference, it is necessary to link the material from the archaeological record to a mourning ceremony through the application of logic, analogy, and theory, collectively called **middle-range theory** (Tschauner 1996; Schiffer 2010; Johnson 2019).

The central element of middle-range theory is the use of **analogy**, an argument that if two things are similar in some aspects, they will be similar in others. A great deal of the reasoning employed in archaeology is based on analogy. Nevertheless, conclusions reached through the use of analogy are themselves hypotheses and require testing. Thus, hypotheses and models generated by analogy must be continually tested and refined.

Because the past is not directly observable in the present, archaeologists seek to generate or observe contemporary situations that they can study and link to the past. This work involves learning how the archaeological record formed and trying to understand how past human behavior created a material record. Much of middle-range theory has been developed through the use of ethnographic analogy, ethnoarchaeology, and experimental archaeology.

Ethnographic analogy

Ethnographers have amassed considerable information about the funerary systems of many societies all over the world. An understanding of the various practices of these living people can provide a basis for understanding their practices in prehistory due to the development of testable hypotheses to explain past behaviors. As such, **ethnographic analogy** can link the present to the past.

It is important to remember, however, that living groups are not directly synonymous with past groups; they are different, living in different circumstances, with different people and histories (Testart 1988:1; also see Headland and Reid 1989:49–51). The behaviors and practices of contemporary societies can be used only to propose hypotheses about the past, hypotheses that must be tested. If archaeologists keep this point in mind, ethnographic analogy can be a useful tool.

Ethnoarchaeology

Ethnoarchaeology is the archaeological analysis of living peoples to gain insight into peoples of the past (e.g., O'Connell 1995). In this approach, an archaeologist (rather than an ethnographer) lives with a contemporary group and directly observes their behavior and the resulting material record of that behavior. For example, an archaeologist might observe a mourning ceremony and afterward record the material record of that event. If similar patterns of material remains are found in a prehistoric site, the archaeologist could develop a working hypothesis that similar behaviors may have been practiced. As noted earlier, however, it is important to remember that contemporary traditional peoples are not past peoples unchanged through time and that the insights gained through ethnoarchaeology are only beginning points for research.

Experimental archaeology

Experimental archaeology attempts to understand past cultural processes through the controlled and directed replication of artifacts, features, or processes (Outram 2008). It is natural to ask, "How did they do that?" One way to approach the problem is through experimentation, working with the material until the same result or form is achieved. Although experimental archaeology can provide clues to the past, it only demonstrates that something *could* have been done in a particular way, not that it *was* done that way, since there may be other ways to achieve the same result.

For example, experimental mummification of people was conducted to help understand the ancient Egyptian methods (Papageorgopoulou et al. 2015; Wade 2015). In another study, fresh bone was broken experimentally to help to understand if ancient bone had been broken while still green (e.g., Cattaneo and Cappella 2017). Finally, by gaining an understanding of carnivore gnawing patterns on modern bone, it is possible to ascertain whether ancient animal remains were processed by humans or were just damaged by scavengers (e.g., Young 2017).

Research design

One of the central aspects of contemporary archaeology is the nearly universal requirement for an explicit, written **research design** prior to conducting any work. As all archaeologists operate under a general theoretical framework, they all have some idea of what questions they want to ask when they conduct archaeological investigations. Until about the late 1960s, many research plans, goals, and justifications of methods were either poorly developed or nonexistent. Today, an explicit research design is an integral part of archaeology and of archaeologists' use of the scientific method.

A research design begins with the specific hypotheses, questions, or problems to be addressed, the theoretical approach to be used in the investigation, the biases of the investigators, the kinds of data needed to address the questions, the methods to be used to obtain the needed data, and the expected results. The development of a clear research design forces archaeologists to focus on what they are going to do, what they are looking for (you usually will not find what you are not looking for), and the best way to recover the necessary data. A written research design also allows other archaeologists or interested parties to review the plan and to provide ideas and suggestions. Of course, in some instances, such as an accidental discovery, there is no time to develop a complex research design, so the researcher must make the best of it and be flexible.

Cemetery organization

Cemeteries, places where a number of people were intentionally interred, contain significant information about funerary systems and a variety of other issues. All formal cemeteries were purposefully located at specific places in the landscape, and their locations can give clues to territorial organization (Saxe 1970; Goldstein 1980; Morris 2008) or as aspects of larger sacred landscapes (e.g., Carmichael et al. 1994; Hubert 1994). Formal cemeteries also demarcate boundaries between the living and the dead, or from the sacred and the profane. For example, the privilege of being buried in a church cemetery in medieval Europe was reserved for higher-status people, with lower-status individuals being buried outside the formal borders of the cemetery (Trautmann et al. 2017).

Once placed in the landscape, formal cemeteries have some internal structure in which space and placement of burials (i.e., concepts of social geography) are important considerations. The internal organization of a cemetery reflects the existence and power of social standing, such as status or kinship, within a society. Thus, analyses of the placement of interments within a cemetery can provide valuable information regarding a variety of subjects (e.g., Charles and Buikstra 1983:119–120; Morris 1992).

For example, Prevedorou and Stojanowski (2017) studied the development of formal cemetery organization at the early Bronze Age site of Tsepi at Marathon, Greece. Data on 292 individuals were analyzed, and it was found that the cemetery was organized along biological lineages, particularly for females. Biological kinship appears to have been the primary factor in tomb location, and a pattern of male exogamy and likely matrilocal residence was hypothesized.

Grave goods and status

Grave goods are generally those purposefully placed with a body at the time of its final treatment (Parker Pearson 2003:9) and reflect the "socio-political status or role of the deceased in a very direct way" (Ekengren 2013:174). Grave goods may be included to prepare the dead for the other world, to assist in their passage, to reaffirm their status (often for the living), to assert their identity (e.g., Effros 2006), or even to prevent their return to the living.

There is a distinction between what is put *in* a grave and what is left *on* a grave (Sprague 2005:116), with the latter being directly related to post-burial rituals (e.g., mourning behavior). Examples include flowers laid on a headstone or small stones placed on Jewish graves (see Halporn 2002). Further, grave goods associated with cremations could be mixed, so they can include those placed on the body and those placed on the pyre (Williams 2015:263).

Grave goods may consist of a variety of items: ships; chariots; weapons; everyday tools; personal possessions; clothing; jewelry; large or small items used in daily life; offerings related to commemorative or ritual behaviors; and sacrifices of humans, animals, and/or artifacts. Most grave goods were placed in some sequential order, with spatial arrangement, fragmentation (e.g., the breaking or "killing" of tools), and differences in purpose (for commemoration or for use in the afterlife).

People were often buried in their best clothing and jewelry, symbols of power and prestige to embellish them for entry into the next world. Many examples of this behavior include the Egyptian pharaohs, the Chinese emperor, and the Moche lords (see Case Study, page 181). Excavations at the Royal Cemetery at Ur, Iraq, revealed burials with elaborate dress and jewelry that had "clear social linkages – economic, technological, political, and so forth – to fashions embodied in multiple contexts" (Baadsgaard 2011:199).

Items of supernatural power, such as charms, amulets, or other objects thought to contain occult power, may also be grave goods. Gilchrist (2008) found many such items in an English medieval cemetery, suggesting that folk magic was employed to help the dead through the journey to the afterlife.

The Romans placed coins (called Charon's obol) of various denominations in the mouths of the deceased so they could pay the toll to the ferryman who conveyed souls across the river that divided the world of the living from the world of the dead (Stevens 1991). In other burials, inscribed metal-leaf tablets, or exonumia, took the place of coins, and gold-foil crosses were used in the early Christian era. The presence of coins or a coin hoard in Germanic ship burials suggests an analogous concept.

The specific grave goods found in any particular interment could reflect a number of social positions, including status, profession, societal role (e.g., gender), or any combination thereof. The type and quantity of grave goods are commonly used to hypothesize the status of the deceased (e.g., Binford 1971), as it is assumed that higher-status people will have greater quantities of better materials than lower-status people. The profession or labor focus of a person is also speculated based on grave goods; burials with weapons are typically attributed to males, and those with household items are attributed to females. As we shall see, this is a problematic assumption.

Integration of data sets

Among the early efforts to integrate biological data from burials was that of Krogman (1935), whose publication of "Life Histories Recorded in Skeletons" looked at age at death, growth, health, and the physical history of the individual to gain a better understanding of their lives. As the sophistication of osteological analyses increased, the term **osteobiography** was adopted to reflect the dominance of skeletal data (Saul 1972).

Now although skeletal analysis is still of central importance, the data sets are more diverse and can include various historical or ethnographic records and imagery, oral histories, mortuary and commemorative contexts, artifacts, bone chemistry, aDNA, skeletal pathologies, activity patterns, dietary patterns, pharmacology, and more (Stodder and Palkovich 2012; Walsh-Henry and Boys 2015). As a result, the term **life history** is now commonly used to describe the events of a life as deduced from the mortal remains and cultural context of an individual (e.g., Martin and Osterholtz 2016:34). Such "life history events" include "birth, weaning, puberty, sickness, marriages, and death . . . that find expression through ritual and other cultural behaviors in virtually all societies" (Martin and Osterholtz 2016:34).

Despite its current popularity, the use of the term "life history" seems limiting in that it reflects more of a record of events of an individual (like an osteobiography) and is less inclusive of an explanatory or social context that had affected that individual and the society the individual was from. The term **biocultural profile** (following Beatrice and Soler 2016) is proposed here as a more nuanced expression of a cultural context that better reflects the myriad of data sets used to form an understanding of the life and social context of an ancient individual.

Examples of biocultural profiles include a high-status person from Mesoamerica (Mayes and Barber 2008), a young Roman soldier at a site in Azerbaijan (Nugent 2013), a Roman-era wrestler from Ephesus (Nováček et al. 2017), and profiles of the Kennewick Man and Ötzi (see page 169). For animal remains associated with human behaviors within mortuary contexts, such as pets or sacrificial victims, the creation of a biocultural profile for these animals could also be informative to better understand the ritual aspects of the mortuary practices and even the geographic origin of the animals (e.g., Szpak et al. 2016).

Constructing a biocultural profile

To construct a biocultural profile, all of the available data on an individual, both biological and cultural, would be compiled and organized (see Table 9.1 for an example). First, all of the biological data are listed, much like a traditional osteobiography. Such data should

Table 9.1 A biocultural profile form

Category	Data sets	Significant traits
Biological aspects		
Age	pubic symphysis	
	auricular surfaces	
	dental eruption	
	epiphyseal fusion	
	tooth wear	
	skull suture closure	
	transition analysis	
Sex	soft tissue	primary sexual traits
	pelvis	
	skull morphology	
	long bones	
	aDNA	
Stature	long bone measurements	
Ancestry	skull morphology	
	dental traits	shovel-shaped incisors
	aDNA	
Activity Stressors	wear and tear	osteoarthritis
	indications of profession	entheseal change
Pathologies	skeletal indicators of metabolic stress	porotic hyperstosis
		cribra orbitalia
		Harris lines
		vitamin deficiencies
	dental indicators of metabolic stress	Wilson bands
		linear enamel hypoplasia
	disease	
	trauma	
Congenital Abnormalities		
Dietary Data	isotopic data	carbon, nitrogen, strontium
	intestinal contents	
	associated archaeological data	faunal data from site
		botanical data from site
		artifactual data from site
Season of Death		pollen data
Place of Residence	isotopic data	e.g., strontium
Other Analyses	exoparasites and endoparasites	intestinal worms, head and body lice

Category	Data sets	Significant traits
Manner and Cause of Death	disease obvious trauma	
Cultural aspects Pretreatment		
Mortuary Treatment	initial treatment final treatment	
Commemorative Behaviors		
Associated Artifacts		
Trade		
Medical Treatment		
Other		
Status/Profession	location in cemetery burial container grave goods	
Social Structure		
Kinship		
Political Structure		
Religion		

include age, sex, stature, pathologies, trauma, and the like, and would provide a comprehensive picture of the person and his or her life history. Next, any available data on funerary context would be listed, including any information on pretreatment, mortuary treatment, and commemorative behaviors. The funerary data, coupled with the biological data, would then be used to model the sociopolitical context of the person, including their profession, status, and origin.

Thoroughly done, this process can be expensive and time consuming. For example, analysis of the Kennewick Man took many years and culminated in a published volume with 32 chapters and 1,194 pages (Owsley and Jantz 2014). Most biocultural profiles are much less exhaustive. Also, if no laboratory analysis of a new find is permitted, it must be analyzed in the field and so only a brief analysis of the remains may be possible, with a resultant meager biocultural profile.

Case study: a biocultural profile of Kennewick Man

Background

The Kennewick skeleton was discovered in 1996 eroding from the bank of the Columbia River near Kennewick, Washington (see the Case Study, page 10). The individual was disarticulated in secondary context, and about 90% of the skeleton was recovered (Figure 9.1). The individual was dated to about 8,600 years old. In February 2017, the skeleton was repatriated to the tribes and reburied.

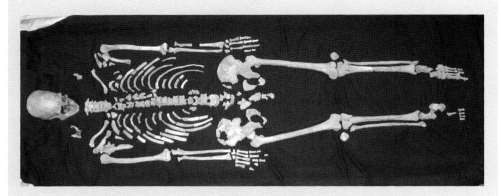

Figure 9.1 The mostly complete skeleton of Kennewick Man (the Ancient One)
Source: Jim Chatters

The data on the biocultural profile presented here are synthesized from the various studies in Owsley and Jantz (2014).

Biological aspects

Age: ~ 40.

Sex: Male.

Stature: ~160 cm in height (deduced from long bone measurements), wide-bodied, perhaps a weight of 160 lbs.

Ancestry: Morphologically similar to the Ainu and perhaps the Jōmon.

aDNA: Has mtDNA X2, related to the Yakama, the Umatilla, and the Colville, local Native American groups.

Activity Stressors: Robust entheses in right shoulder and arm (suggestive of some repetitive motion), wear in right shoulder and elbow and a stronger left leg (again suggestive of some repetitive motion), some osteoarthritis (suggestive of mobility), and auditory exostoses (suggestive of a life spent in and around cold water).

Pathologies

Metabolic Stress: None noted.

Disease: None detected.

Trauma: Two depression fractures in the skull, shoulder damage from repeated motion (spear throwing?), elbow injury, six improperly healed broken ribs from blunt force trauma, small lesions in cervical vertebrae, osteochondritis of both knees, healed projectile point wound in pelvis, dental abrasion, evidence of the use of teeth in holding cordage.

Congenital Abnormalities: None noted.

Dietary Data

Isotopic Data: Indicated a diet primarily of salmon or marine mammals (both salmon and marine mammals have similar isotopic signatures), suggesting that he had lived in a cold coastal context for much of his life, with little input from terrestrial foods; worn teeth suggestive of eating foods with high abrasive content, such as dried fish.

Season of Death: Unknown

Place of Residence: Oxygen isotopic data suggest he lived along the Pacific Coast before moving up the Columbia River some years before his death.

Other Analyses: Radiocarbon dating.

Manner and Cause of Death: Unknown.

Cultural aspects

Pretreatment: Unknown.

Mortuary Treatment: Purposeful inhumation.

Initial Treatment: Unknown.

Final Treatment: Extended supine inhumation with head toward the east, later in secondary position due to natural processes.

Commemorative Behaviors: Unknown but likely.

Associated Artifacts: No known grave goods, Cascade projectile point embedded in hip.

Trade: Unknown.

Medical Treatment: Some likely due to various healed injuries, but no known specifics.

Discussion and Conclusions: Little known, member of a hunter-gatherer group, engaged in some violence, possibly warfare.

Status/Profession: Probably a fisherman, but possibly a marine mammal hunter.

Social Structure: Unknown, apparently an isolated interment.

Kinship: Unknown.

Political Structure: Likely band level.

Religion: Unknown.

Case study: a biocultural profile of Ötzi

Background

Ötzi, the "Tyrolean Iceman," was discovered in 1991 by hikers in the Alps between Austria and Italy (Dickson et al. 2005; Dickson 2011). The body (Figure 9.2) was so well preserved that it was initially believed to be a recent death. The police

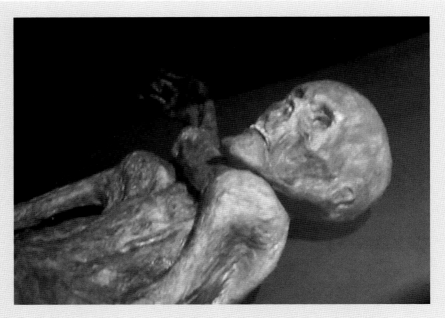

Figure 9.2 The frozen mummy of Ötzi, the "Tyrolean Iceman"
Source: Alamy Image ID: B2Y9P3

were called, and they roughly freed the body from the ice, discovered associated archaeological materials, and transported the body and artifacts to the medical examiner's office. Archaeologists examined the materials in that office and returned to the site to study it and recover additional material. The site was initially thought to be in Austria, and the University of Innsbruck was given permission to investigate it (see Piombino-Mascali and Zink 2011:225–226). The body was placed in a freezer at the Institute for Anatomy at the University of Zurich in Switzerland. Ötzi was radiocarbon dated to about 5,300 years old, and his copper axe head is the oldest artifact of its kind currently known. The copper came from a source many hundreds of miles to the south (Artioli et al. 2017).

The discovery became a sensation, and both Austria and Italy wanted the honor of claiming the site to be within their borders. A survey was done, and the site was found to be 92 meters within Italy. So, in 1998, Ötzi was transferred to the Museo Archeologico dell'Alto Adige in Bolzano, Italy, and was placed in a specially constructed facility that was controlled for temperature (−6°C) and humidity (98%) (see Piombino-Mascali and Zink 2011:226).

Both invasive and virtual autopsies were performed and numerous specialized studies were conducted (and are ongoing). The body was so well preserved because it was "freeze-dried," a process where the frozen water sublimates and converts directly to its gaseous state and disperses into the air.

Biological aspects

Age: ~ 46 (based on bone histology).

Sex: Male.

Stature: 160 cm, measured directly from the preserved body.

Ancestry: aDNA suggests genetic association with north-central Europe.

Activity Stressors: Worn teeth, little radiographic evidence of arthritis.

Pathologies

Metabolic Stress: None noted.

Disease: Beau's lines suggest three major illnesses in the last six months of life (the last illness being the most serious), many carious dental lesions, and discovery of a rare strain of intestinal bacteria (*Helicobacter pylori*) suggesting chronic gastritis.

Trauma: Fifth to ninth ribs broken and healed; deep wound on the hand; perimortem bruises and cuts to hands, wrists, and chest; and cerebral trauma (blow to the head?); arrowhead lodged in chest, entry through the scapula, lodged near the lung.

Congenital Abnormalities: Missing twelfth ribs, lactose intolerant.

Dietary data

Isotopic Data: Nitrogen data indicate a diet of about 30% meat and 70% plants, no seafood is indicated, diet similar to contemporary hunter-gatherers.

Intestinal Contents: Last meal (in stomach) consisted of ibex (wild goat) meat and wheat, two previous meals were found in the intestines, one of chamois (wild goat–antelope) meat, bread, roots, and fruits and the other of red deer, bread, roots, and fruits.

Associated Archaeological Data: Foods found near the body included grains of einkorn and barley, seeds of flax and poppy, kernels of sloes (fruit of the blackthorn tree), and various wild berry seeds. Pollen of wheat, legumes, and hop-hornbeam was also found.

Season of Death: Estimated to be in late spring or early summer (based on pollen from the intestines).

Place of Residence: Isotopic data from tooth enamel, bones, and intestines suggest he was raised in the Eisack Valley north of Bolzano, Italy, and later lived in the nearby Etsch and Schnals valleys.

Other Analyses: Traces of copper and arsenic found in hair analysis, suggesting involvement in smelting copper, but the presence of copper moss (*Mielichhoferia elongata*) near the body suggests contamination, presence of whipworm with unknown consequences; fleas in clothing, intact red blood cells found in body, blood from four other humans found on his weapons.

Manner and Cause of Death: Homicide; blood loss from arrow wound in his back that probably severed a major artery.

Cultural aspects

Pretreatment: None known.

Mortuary Treatment

Initial Treatment: Likely none.

Final Treatment: Likely none, body in secondary position due to natural processes.

Commemorative Behaviors: Unknown, but probably some by family when he did not return.

Associated Artifacts: Clothing (hat, cape, coat, loincloth, belt, leggings, and shoes) and equipment (copper axe, knife, bow and arrows, bark containers, backpack, pouches, ornaments, net, small tools).

Trade: Copper in axe originated in southern Tuscany several hundred miles to the south, suggesting some trade connections; gut flora suggests contact with people to the east.

Medical Treatment: Sixty-one tattoos on body parts that appear to have caused him pain (such as the lower back and joints) and may have either been actual treatments for those ailments or to mark locations for other treatments, such as acupuncture.

Other: Tattoos, but likely for medical purposes.

Discussion and Conclusions: Ötzi was a member of a farming community, one that also hunted wild animals and used wild plants. The presence of the blood of four other people and his apparently violent death suggest considerable violence in his community.

Status/Profession: Unclear, perhaps a herder or hunter, possibly a farmer.

Social Structure: Unknown.

Kinship: Unknown.

Political Structure: Unclear but agricultural, so likely at least tribe level.

Religion: Unknown.

Constructing a bioethnography

Given a large enough data set (i.e., multiple biocultural profiles from the same population), it is possible to examine the role of diet, health, morbidity, mortality, and funerary systems of a particular society as a whole. Using such data, a **bioethnography** of a subject group could be compiled and contribute to a greater understanding of that society. Examples of such work include studies on the impacts of the adoption of agriculture (e.g., Cohen and Armelagos 1984, 2013), the biological responses to conquest (Larsen and Milner 1993), the bioarchaeology of Spanish Florida (Larsen 2001), and three Nubian communities along the Nile River (Armelagos and Van Gerven 2017; also see Van Gerven et al. 1990). This type of research is one of the ultimate goals in bioarchaeology and is the focus of Chapter 10.

Issues in analysis

In addition to the ethical issues discussed in Chapter 1, there are other important analytical issues to recognize when analyzing bioarchaeological data. In all cases, we are dealing with specific individuals that were members of a larger society. We tend to extend the findings of a particular individual to others in that same society; this is accomplished in the form of hypotheses to be tested, but so often the additional testing required is not conducted, yet the conclusions somehow become "fact." The problem is sample size. If a past society had 500 members and we have bioarchaeological data on 1 or 2 of them, what do we really know about that society? We need larger samples, but all studies begin with the first specimen.

Another issue is dating. The death of each individual occurred at a specific time, but determining that time can be difficult. If a person is buried in a collective cemetery, there is little reason to believe that another person in that same cemetery dates to exactly the same time. Thus, it is almost certain that the other individuals from that cemetery died at different times. Nevertheless, it is common to "lump" cemetery populations together for analysis, even if burials date hundreds of years apart. As such, although such analysis can be used to form a general model of society, it is most likely wrong (Chapman 2005). We need better dating to resolve these problems. This is not an issue with mass graves, where it is obvious that everyone died at the same time.

Further, there are few standards in the recordation of data. There are published standards (e.g., Buikstra and Ubelaker 1994), but they are infrequently consulted, and if remains are analyzed in the field, the standards are difficult to follow. In addition, repatriation of remains before they can be studied results in a loss of data.

There is also the issue of contemporary researchers trying to understand past cultural systems. First, none of us is (are) members of that past society, so we have an **etic** (outsider's) perspective of it, making it difficult to fully understand that past society. Second, all people are **ethnocentric** (a bias toward one's own group) and tend to "look down" on other societies, although this is recognized by anthropologists and is hopefully mitigated. Until recently, most archaeologists were male, limiting research into past females. The issue is the same with children, and because no anthropologist is a child, understanding children becomes more difficult.

Finally, there are issues in the classification of archaeological materials. Most archaeological materials are classified based on descriptive categories, such as morphology. Such a system is needed so that archaeologists can communicate with each other using shared terms. However, past societies likely had different classificatory systems that are unknown to us, more or less forcing us to impose our system on their remains. For example, if it is determined that a person died at age 17, a bioarchaeologist would classify that person as a subadult, a classification that would include our assumptions of the role of persons of that age within their society. Yet not all societies had that same age distinction between subadult and adult; it may be that in a particular society, a 16-year-old may have been considered an adult and treated as such (Halcrow and Tayles 2011:348). We need to exercise caution with such assumptions.

Chapter summary

As in all sciences, the interpretation of bioarchaeological data is dependent on theory. In simple terms, two levels of theory can be defined: general paradigms and middle range. Most archaeologists operate within a scientific paradigm in which the past is seen as empirical, objective, and knowable, although some believe that the past is more subjective. Within the scientific paradigm are innumerable bodies of theory for specific issues or questions, including materialism, evolutionary theory, systems theory, Marxism, feminist theory, queer theory, and agency. All of these (and others) operate under the idea (or paradigm) that past societies were similar to contemporary ones, called the normative approach. In essence, this approach says that contemporary groups have formal funerary systems, so it is reasonable to expect that past societies did as well. As such, we construct a model of a past society, an archaeological culture, and test that model against new data.

Because archaeologists can only observe the past as patterns of remains in the present, middle-range theory connects the past to the present by analogy. We observe behaviors in ethnographic societies that result in a pattern of remains and use those observations to project those same behaviors into the past, an approach called ethnographic analogy. We also use experiments to try to determine how a past society may have done things, an approach called experimental archaeology. Although this approach can help us understand how tasks could have been accomplished, it is not necessarily evidence that they were carried out in that same way.

The location of a cemetery and its internal organization can provide considerable information on a variety of subjects, including territoriality, status, and kinship. Grave goods found with an interment can inform about status, profession, gender, ritual, religion, and commemorative behaviors.

To consider questions about the past, it is necessary to have a research design. In a research design, the investigator has to define one or more questions, build on past research on those questions, understand and be explicit about the kinds of data needed to answer the questions, define the methods to obtain and analyze those data, and then arrive at conclusions supported by the data, whether they conform to the original questions or not.

The integration of data sets begins with compiling all of the available data, both on the biology and the cultural context of the remains. Early attempts at this were generally limited to the information from the human remains themselves, a data set commonly called a life history or osteobiography. In combining the cultural context with the biology of the remains, the term biocultural profile has been proposed to reflect the integration of the two major data sets (biological and cultural) and is followed herein. Ultimately, a large enough sample of biocultural profiles for a particular society could be combined to propose an overall biocultural understanding of an entire group, that is, a bioethnography.

Several issues in the analysis of bioarchaeological data are known. One of the major problems is sample size; we have a very small sample of the dead, so generalizing about their past societies is challenging. Further, we only generally control the dating of the dead (with some notable exceptions), making it difficult to understand change through time. Next, there is the issue of bias. Because all researchers are human and all humans are biased in some way, it can affect our interpretations; we must compensate. Finally, we impose classifications on people and objects in the past, often without knowing what classifications were used by past societies. This can be a problem.

Key concepts and terms

agency
analogy
archaeological culture
biocultural profile
bioethnography
ethnoarchaeology
ethnocentrism
ethnographic analogy
etic
evolutionary theory
experimental archaeology
feminist theory
life history
normative approach
Marxism
materialism
middle-range theory
osteobiography
postprocessualism
processualism
queer theory
research design
systems theory

Chapter 10

Lives once lived
The anthropology of the dead

Bioarchaeologists study how humans were treated in both life and in death so that they may obtain information about past societies from an anthropological perspective. The data acquired directly from human remains can inform us about many details of the lives of individuals: their genetics, their metabolic and nutritional health, whether they had any diseases, whether they were victims of violence or were subjugated in some way, what kind of workload they had, whether they were mobile, and to some degree, whether their society took care of them when needed. But that is only part of the picture.

We are able to learn still more about a specific deceased person, and with an understanding of their treatment in the funerary system, a great deal can be learned about various aspects of their society. For example, pretreatment in preparation for sacrifice informs us not only about that person but also about the ritual system as a whole. Mortuary treatment of an individual can illuminate the nature of their status in a society. Grave goods can tell us about the status and profession of an individual and about the nature of those items in a society. Placement in a particular location within a cemetery can help us understand social systems. Commemorative behavior can shed light on belief systems and religion. It is important to keep in mind, however, that the rules governing a funerary system might be different from rules that manage the living and so may require different research approaches (e.g., Brown 1995:3).

Addressing anthropological questions

As with the rest of anthropology, bioarchaeologists are interested in learning everything they can about past societies. Broad categories of interest include social organization, political systems, religious systems, sex and gender roles, issues of inequality, paleodemography, health, and more. Many of these categories overlap, making it difficult to define a clear separation. There is a great deal to learn.

Exploring social organization

All societies have a system of rules and procedures by which they organize themselves into various social units. Among these units are kinship-based groups (people linked together as relatives) and nonkinship-based groups (people linked by status, profession, and/or religion). Each person in a society concurrently belongs to a number of such groups. As such, social organizations can range from fairly simple to fantastically complex.

Kinship is a fundamental aspect of any social organization. It is the system by which a person defines and organizes their relationships into groups, such as families, lineages, and clans. Often associated with kinship are rules that regulate marriage and post-marital residence.

How can bioarchaeologists reveal a kinship system? The process may begin with an analysis of biodistance (see Chapter 8) to postulate the relatedness of individuals. The locations of individuals within a cemetery may also provide clues. Perhaps a more accurate approach is analysis of the ancient DNA (aDNA) of burial populations where placement in a cemetery is known, in combination with genetic data (e.g., Dudar et al. 2003). Isotopic data can also sometimes be used in this endeavor. Thus, it is possible to reconstruct a kinship system and related marriage patterns. A good example of this line of research is the investigation into the family tree of the ancient Egyptian Pharaoh Tutankhamun (Metcalfe 2016), an issue not yet solved.

Within any society, all individuals occupy a place in both their kinship and nonkinship organizations. In small societies, social differentiation is typically **egalitarian**, based largely on age and skill. Larger societies with more complex social organizations often develop a hierarchical system of **social stratification**, with social strata based on status and/or class. Such systems are based on inequality among members of a specific population (discussed later).

Status is the social standing a person holds within a society. Status may have been **achieved** (based on personal actions) or **ascribed** (based on kinship). **Class** is a category of social status associated primarily with wealth, status, power, and/or an individual's profession. A common example of a class structure is a ruling class or the upper, middle, and lower classes in contemporary western societies. Peebles and Kus (1977) distinguished between vertical differentiation (social strata, top to bottom) and horizontal differentiation (standing within a stratum, such as sex, age, or membership in a clan) within stratified societies (such as at Moundville, see the following Case Study).

Overall, it is usually assumed that social status is reflected in the funerary system; that is, "that there is a direct relationship between the social status of the deceased and the relative amounts of treatments, grave goods, or energy expended in the burial of the individual" (Rakita and Buikstra 2005:4; also see Klaus et al. 2017). In essence, "who you are affects how you get buried and the separate bits that make up your identity get represented in different ways" (Parker Pearson 2003:29). This view follows the tenets of Saxe (1970) and Binford (1971) and is part of processual archaeology, still the predominant approach taken by most Americanist archaeologists (Rakita and Buikstra 2005:5).

Case study: social organization at Moundville, Alabama

The Moundville site in the area that is now west-central Alabama is one of the largest mound complexes in the southeastern United States. Covering about 370 acres, Moundville was situated within a palisade and had 29 large pyramidal mounds oriented around a central plaza (Figure 10.1). The site, which was founded ca. 1,100 BP, has been archaeologically investigated since the 1840s, with major work conducted in the early 1900s and 1930s (see Peebles and Black 1987; Knight and Steponaitis 2007; Blitz 1999; Wilson 2010).

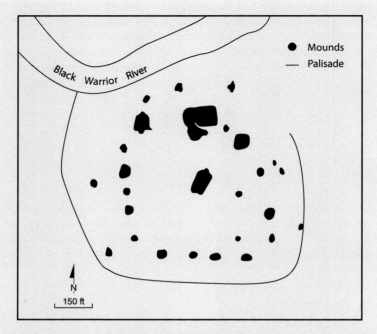

Figure 10.1 Map of the Moundville site, Alabama
Source: Author

At the time it was founded, Moundville was one of many small villages that were established within a region that was heavily populated and suffered from endemic warfare and resource stress (Knight and Steponaitis 2007:10). At about 950 BP, Moundville began its rise to prominence and a mound was built at the site. During this time (Moundville I), agriculture intensified, corn became more important, and site settlement was unstructured, with scattered dwellings (Knight and Steponaitis 2007:12, 15).

The size, character, and complexity of Moundville changed after about 800 BP (Moundville II). The palisade and additional mounds were constructed, the nearby population moved into the protected area, and many houses were built in an organized manner within the town walls. Nearby, many small, outlying sites were abandoned while several new, smaller mound sites were constructed, perhaps as secondary administrative centers to Moundville (Knight and Steponaitis 2007:16). By 700 BP, Moundville had become the largest polity in west-central Alabama.

Just after 700 BP (Moundville III), Moundville appears to have radically changed from a major town with a large population to a locality occupied by only a small number of elite people (Knight and Steponaitis 2007:18). The majority of the population was commoners who seem to have moved back to small farms in the countryside, and the palisade was no longer maintained. Three possible explanations have been proposed for the depopulation of Moundville (Knight and Steponaitis 2007:18–19): (1) the elite wanted the commoners to move to make the mound center more sacred, (2) local resources (e.g., farmland, fire-wood) had been exhausted, and/or (3) the need to keep people within a walled town no longer existed. The continued burial of high-status individuals within the site complex attests to its enduring ritual importance.

By about 600 BP (Moundville IV), some of the mounds at Moundville were apparently abandoned and a number of smaller mound sites were built in the vicinity (Knight and Steponaitis 2007:20). By about 550 BP, the influence of Moundville declined rapidly, and it was abandoned by about 350 BP (see Welch 1996; Knight and Steponaitis 2007:20).

During its heyday, it is believed that a small elite (upper) class at Moundville ruled the population. Evidence of residential occupation by commoners (the lower class) is present along the margins of the site, with relatively little activity in the center. Some of the mounds were likely used as residences for the elite (as wit-nessed by house foundations and debris), others as craft centers (as evidenced by the presence of manufacturing debris), some as burial mounds (as demonstrated by the existence of tombs), and others for display of the disinterred (secondary) remains of important people (as seen from pigments and other ritual materials).

The organization of space, mounds, and dwellings at Moundville could reflect the ordering of kinship organizations within the site. The food consumed by the elites was likely provided by commoners, as little evidence of food processing has been found in elite dwellings (Knight and Steponaitis 2007:16). In addition, analy-sis of the food remains from several elite households signifies the control of food resources and the status held by those households (Jackson and Scott 2003).

In an analysis of the grave goods recovered from 2,053 of the more than 3,000 burials excavated from Moundville, Peebles and Black (1987) offered an interpre-tation of the social structure at the site ca. 600 BP (Table 10.1). Seven burials, all apparently adult males, were found with copper axes and were interred at mounds in the center of the site. These seven individuals (classified as IA) were most likely of the highest status, perhaps the primary chiefs. The individuals with the next highest ranking (IB, n = 43) were all adult males and children (perhaps also males) and were buried in mounds (and other places) with copper earspools and other materials. The group with the third highest status (II, n = 67) consisted of individuals buried away from mounds with a variety of objects, including cop-per gorgets. These group II individuals were of both sexes and various ages, and probably represent the nobility. The remainder of the burials shows a descend-ing order of rank, as deduced from grave goods. The majority of the burials (n = 1,256, 61%) had no grave goods and likely represent the commoners. This pattern appears to reflect a patrilineal, hierarchical society with ascribed status.

Stratified social organizations are known from other Mississippian sites. For example, at Cahokia near St. Louis, Missouri, excavations at Mound 72 revealed 272

Table 10.1 Burial clusters and status ranks at the Moundville site

General status and percentage of society	Cluster	Number of individuals	Age and sex	Burial location	Grave goods
High (10.6%)	IA	7	adult males	all in mounds	copper axes, copper beads, pearl beads
	IB	43	adult males and children	mostly in mounds	copper earspools, copper gorgets, stone disks, bear tooth pendants, various minerals
Middle (12.7%)	II	67	all ages and sexes	near mounds	copper gorgets, shell beads, stone cubes
	III	211	all ages and sexes, but many children	near mounds	effigy ceramic vessels, shell gorgets, stone celts, animal bones
	IV	50	all ages and sexes	near mounds	projectile points, discoidals, bone awls
Low (76.7%)	V	55	mostly adults, but many children	away from mounds	certain types of ceramic bowls or jars
	VI	45	mostly adults	away from mounds	certain types of ceramic bowls or jars
	VII	55	mostly adults	away from mounds	certain types of ceramic water vessels
	VIII	70	mostly adults, but many children	away from mounds	certain types of ceramic water vessels
	IX	46	mostly adults	away from mounds	certain types of ceramic water vessels
	X	70	mostly adults	away from mounds	ceramic shards
	XI	1,256	both sexes and various ages, but many children	away from mounds	none

Source: Based on Peebles and Kus (1977:439, Figure 3)

burials. Included was the burial of a 40-year-old male laid on a bird-shaped platform and accompanied by some 20,000 shell beads. In the same mound, four mass graves were found that contained a total of 120 women between 15 and 25 years of age. These women exhibited poor skeletal health indicative of low status, suggesting human sacrifice (Iseminger 1996:35). Other individuals had been buried after their hands and heads had been removed. Dietary analysis showed that the lower-status people had diets primarily of corn, whereas higher-status individuals ate much more protein (Ambrose et al. 2003). Fish and deer were major protein staples, with elites apparently having greater access to such foods (Yerkes 2005).

Exploring political systems

All societies have some sort of political system, a way to maintain control in the population. In many prehistoric societies, political power was effectively the same as social standing, status, and class (if any). Power was often passed along kinship lines from generation to generation (royal succession being a good example). Thus, it is usually very difficult to separate social status from political power. Political leaders would have been members of the elite, and their funerals would have functioned as political events to reflect the power of those individuals within their society.

Exploring religion and ritual

Religion is a coherent system of shared beliefs in supernatural powers, beings, and forces based on faith. Religions function in part to explain the world, to prescribe values, to assert social control, and to ensure harmony between humans and the supernatural. Learning about the religious beliefs of a past society helps us gain a better understanding of the basic relationship of people with their environment, their value system, their treatment of others, and justifications for their actions and activities. Religion often includes some concept of the soul and an afterlife. In many cases, religious systems are highly integrated into the funerary system of a society, often to facilitate the transition of a deceased individual from one state (living) to another (the afterlife).

Ritual is a separate but related system. It is the performance of formalized, repetitive acts that people regard as meaningful. Rituals are commonly enacted during ceremonies and involve the use of ritual objects and places (see Kyriakidis 2007). Most religious activities have associated rituals, but not all rituals are religious in nature (consider, for example, the rituals conducted before the start of a contemporary sporting event). Material culture (e.g., artifacts) associated with religious and ritual behaviors tend to be nonutilitarian, making them more readily identified in the archaeological record.

Religious and ritual behaviors can be seen in the bioarchaeological record in a variety of ways, although it is sometimes difficult to separate religion from social or political systems. The process of human sacrifice, as seen in the Moche Sacrifice Ceremony (see the following Case Study) was highly ritualized and reflective of religious beliefs. The putative cannibalism in the American Southwest (see Case Study, page 133) was also probably highly ritualized.

A number of societies have included mourning ceremonies in their funerary system as part of commemorative behavior. Such ceremonies are usually conducted well after the death of a specific individual and may be performed for more than one individual, such as all the people that died in a specific year. In some cases, the ceremony has involved the destruction of property and/or representations of the dead, which would leave a distinct archaeological signature.

Case Study: the sacrifice ceremony of the Moche of Peru

The Moche were farmers and fishermen that lived along the north coast of Peru between about 1,900 and 1,200 years ago (Figure 10.2). They were superb artisans, working with metals (copper, gold, and silver), stone, and textiles. Their pottery was sometimes decorated with scenes of elaborately dressed people engaged in specific activities (Donnan 1976, 1990). One such activity

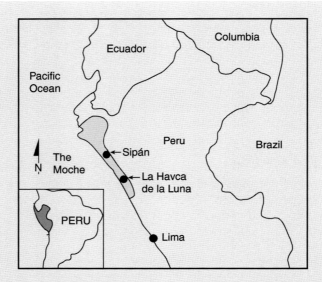

Figure 10.2 Location of the Moche along the northern coast of Peru

Source: Author

was the Sacrifice Ceremony, the iconography of which was detailed in a series of scenes depicted on pottery. The characters were unearthly, their dress and decoration were fantastically elaborate, and the activities were astounding. Four major "priests" were identified: Warrior Priest, Bird Priest, Priestess, and an unnamed priest. The four are shown decapitating and mutilating war captives and then drinking their blood from a cup. The entire story and imagery were interpreted as depictions of the Moche gods conducting supernatural activities, part of Moche art and mythology, and not as actual earthly practices.

Sadly, many Moche sites have been badly vandalized and looted. In 1987, vandals discovered and greatly damaged an intact royal tomb in a small mudbrick pyramid at the site of Sipán (Figure 10.3). Fortunately, police caught the looters and were able to recover some of the items stolen from the tomb. Archaeologist Walter Alva examined the confiscated objects and recognized some of them as depictions in Moche art. Alva realized the scientific value of the discovery and began an excavation to salvage whatever information might remain in the shattered site (Alva and Donnan 1994).

Alva excavated the pyramid and, remarkably, soon discovered the intact tomb (called Tomb 1) of a Moche lord (Alva 1988) (Figure 10.4). He found the burial of an adult male and many artifacts, some of which had never before been seen by archaeologists. Other burials associated with Tomb 1 were apparently sacrificial victims. The elaborate ornaments worn by the Moche lord were the same as those seen in the art depicting the Warrior Priest of the Sacrifice Ceremony (Donnan 1988).

Figure 10.3 The Moche site of Sipán, Peru

Source: Alamy Image ID: T7262F

Figure 10.4 The burial of the Moche Lord from Tomb 1, Sipán, Peru

Source: Alamy Image ID: ABJ4D6

A second tomb (Tomb 2) was discovered nearby and was excavated (Alva 1990). It also contained an adult male, but with different dress and ornamentation. A copper cup and a large copper headdress with an owl's head and large wings were found with the main burial, paraphernalia that corresponded with the Bird Priest of the Sacrifice Ceremony. The tomb of an individual identified as the Priestess of the Sacrifice Ceremony was later found in another Moche site (Donnan and Castillo 1992).

The Sacrifice Ceremony first identified on Moche pottery appears to have actually been practiced by the Moche. Warriors engaged in ritualized combat, and vanquished enemies were taken to Sipán as captives. They were stripped naked and bound, their clothing and weapons were bundled together, and they were brought before the Moche priests impersonating Moche deities. There they were sacrificed: decapitated, dismembered, their blood collected in cups and consumed in a ritual that was very important in Moche society.

Direct bioarchaeological evidence of the sacrifice of captives at Moche sites was found in the 1990s. Sacrificial victims were examined for age, sex, and trauma, and it was discovered that they were typically young males with healed injuries consistent with combat (Verano 2005; Verano and Phillips 2016). Cut marks on cervical vertebrae indicated that their throats had been slit, consistent with Moche ritual. Further, the bodies of the victims had been defleshed, dismembered, and buried in a manner not typical of Moche funerary practices. This indicated that the victims were captured enemy warriors, killed, and denied proper burials to exert power over them in death (Verano 2005:289).

Exploring sex and gender

Recall from Chapter 3 that there is an important difference between sex and gender, with the former being biological and the latter being one's role in a society. Beginning in the 1980s, investigations into gender became a major topic in archaeology (e.g., Conkey and Spector 1984; Wright 1996; Conkey and Gero 1997; Walker and Cook 1998; Schmidt and Voss 2000; Joyce 2008; Geller 2017a). Much of the work on gender in the past has now been subsumed under what has become known as "queer" archaeology, initially conceived as exploring homosexuality in the past (e.g., Dowson 2000). In actual practice, queer archaeology seeks to explore "diverse sexual behavior and sexualities in the past" (Rutecki and Blackmore 2016:9–10) and how such behaviors influence social identities and result in specific material remains (e.g., Voss 2008; Blackmore 2011; Holliman 2011; Sofaer and Stig Sørensen 2013; Geller 2017a).

In theory, different genders should be recognizable in the archaeological record through the analysis of skeletal data, mortuary treatments, grave goods, dietary data, and representational art (e.g., Soffer et al. 2000), all interpreted using ethnographic analogy. However, this is a difficult task (Rautman and Talalay 2000; Geller 2017a, 2019), and caution must be exercised when making assertions about socio-sexual identity (Geller 2019).

Using skeletal sex assignments and indications of activity patterns seen in bones, some gender assignments may be modeled. For example, if a male skeleton shows the same activity patterns as seen in females due to a sexual division of labor, it may suggest that the person engaged in activities more typical of females and perhaps occupied a woman's role in that society.

Mortuary treatments and grave goods are commonly employed to model gender assignments. As an example, if a male was buried in a manner typically associated with females and his grave contained artifacts thought to be associated with female tasks, a gender assignment could be posited. However, the criteria we use to make such gender assessments (e.g., burial position, grave goods) reflect the archaeologist's assumptions about past peoples' behaviors. To illustrate this point, the burial of a Viking warrior at a site in Sweden was assumed to be male, given the mortuary treatment and grave goods. Interestingly, however, aDNA revealed that the individual was female (Hedenstierna-Jonson et al. 2017; Price et al. 2019).

An analysis of grave goods (including perishables) with individuals of identified sex at the 8,200-year-old Windover site in Florida showed considerable crossover from what many would consider sex-specific artifact categories (Hamlin 2001), with both sexes having weaving artifacts and materials, fishing equipment, and projectile points. This suggests that, at least at Windover, grave goods alone were not sufficient to identify sex or gender.

In some cases, variability in gender identity might be hypothesized. For example, in the "weapons burials" of the early medieval period in England, many males were buried with weapons, suggesting they held the status of "warrior" (at least in death), whereas the absence of weapons in other male burials suggested the presence of a range of masculinities (Knüsel 2011:222).

In a study of late Holocene burials (N = 330) in the Ohio Valley region of North America, Wakefield-Murphy (2017) conducted two cluster analyses on the cemetery data from the site: one using traditional mortuary data (burial data by sex) and the second using biosocial data (burial data, skeletal data, sex, and age). An elite burial class identified during the Early Woodland period (ca. 3,000–2,200 BP) was interpreted as representing shamanistic practitioners, possibly constituting a separate gender. This pattern was not seen in later periods. Thus, a diachronic model of gender and social status was proposed to explore biosocial life among late Holocene Ohio Valley groups.

Case Study: sex and gender in central European burials

A study of cemetery populations from two sites dating to different time periods in central Europe was conducted to explore differences in sex and gender through time (Chapman 1997; Rega 1997). The first site, Mokrin, is located in present-day Serbia near the Romanian and Hungarian borders (Figure 10.5). Mokrin dates between 2,100 and 1,500 BC and is associated with the Early Bronze Age society known as Maros. Of the 268 excavated skeletons, 146 were identified to sex (Rega 1997:231).

Detecting differences in the orientation by sex of the Mokrin burials, Rega (1997:213) noted that "females in the cemetery are generally oriented with their

Figure 10.5 Location of the Mokrin and Tiszapolgár-Basatanya sites in central Europe
Source: Author

head to the south or southeast, on their right side facing east. The males are oriented with their head to the north or northwest on their left side, also facing east."
Artifact associations also appeared to be different. Multiple coil bracelets, bone
needles, and stone maces were found only in the graves of adult female skeletons,
whereas copper daggers and knives were found only with adult male skeletons
(Rega 1997:233, 235). On the other hand, the vast majority of graves contained
a mix of items, such as bowls, that were not exclusively associated with either
females or males. Thus, although biological sex – and its social significance in the
form of gendered identity – clearly played a role in some aspects of burial practices
(such as the orientation of the body), others (such as grave goods) appear to have
been mediated by gender roles but not exclusively determined by them.

The second site, Tiszapolgár-Basatanya, located in Hungary, is several hundred
miles north of Mokrin (see Figure 10.5). The site dates to the Copper Age,
between about 4,500 and 3,600 bc (Chapman 1997). At Tiszapolgár-Basatanya,
67 graves were identified from the Early Copper Age and 87 from the Middle
Copper Age (Chapman 1997:138). The Middle Copper Age was marked by the
introduction of domesticated animals, changing the subsistence pattern from the
earlier Early Copper Age occupation. Habitation practices also changed as Early
Copper Age people lived primarily in close quarters in villages, whereas Middle
Copper Age people moved into dispersed farmsteads (Chapman 1997:136–137).

Table 10.2 Diagnostic nonceramic artifacts from the Tiszapolgár-Basatanya cemetery by sex of the associated skeleton

Associated with Adult MALE Skeletons Only	Early Copper Age	wild animal bones, snails, complete dog, limestone disc, loom weight, ochre lumps
	Middle Copper Age	tusk, snails, cattle bones, antler artifacts, ground stone, clay funnel, copper awl, copper pin, copper dagger
Associated with Adult FEMALE Skeletons Only	Early Copper Age	deer tooth, bone spoon, pebble
	Middle Copper Age	shed antler, mussels, fish bone, bone awl, bone spoon, pebble, polished stone plate, polished stone hammer axe, spindle whorl, clay stud, copper bracelet, copper ingot

Source: Adapted from Chapman (1997)

It might be assumed that such drastic changes in lifestyle would also include changes in the relationships between and among men and women. Cemetery data from Tiszapolgár-Basatanya confirm that the changes in subsistence and habitation were accompanied by changes in material associated with social identity. As can be seen in Table 10.2, substantial differences in grave goods can be seen in both male and female burials between the two time periods.

It seems clear that in the Middle Copper Age, there was an increased emphasis on items made by humans as important grave goods. For the males, there is an exclusion of wild animal bones and an inclusion of domesticated animal bones (cattle), which may reflect a change in the importance of hunting in defining manhood (Chapman 1997:141). For the females, one change that can be seen is the decline in deer teeth and the rise in items such as spindle whorls associated with processing wool (Chapman 1997:141). What is clear is that significant changes in the material representations of maleness and femaleness were occurring during this period.

Exploring inequality

Inequalities exist in all human groups; even egalitarian societies recognize that infants are not equal to adults. The larger the society, the more complex it tends to be and the greater the inequalities among segments of the population (e.g., Danforth 1999). Such inequalities involve the development of stratified social structures, including higher-status people having greater access to good nutrition and health care, patterns that should be reflected in the archaeological record (e.g., Trinkaus 1995). Status could be manifested in various ways, whether it be achieved or ascribed and/or as factors such as sex, age, rank, kinship membership (e.g., lineage, clan, or moiety), profession, disability, gender, ethnicity, circumstance of death, and location of death. Inequality appears to be greater among agriculturalists, less so among horticulturalists and hunter-gatherers, and least among pastoralists. It can get complicated.

The following are several recent examples of research into inequality. Trinkaus and Buzhilova (2018) studied mortuary treatment of the early Upper Paleolithic people at Sunghir (Russia). They noted variation in the treatment and suggested the variation was associated with differential treatment based on pathological abnormalities.

Dong et al. (2019) demonstrated that during the late Dawenkou period (ca. 3,000–2,500 BC), at the site of Liangwangcheng in Jiangsu province, China, older adult females were afforded special mortuary treatment, and some consumed "preferred" foods. This suggests that the social status of women increased throughout their lives.

Justice and Temple (2019) studied juvenile late Holocene hunter-gatherer inhumations in northern Alaska and found that mortuary treatment varied with age and that body position, orientation, and grave good allocations changed several times after the age of three or four. This pattern was interpreted as reflecting changes in status as the individual matured, possibly related to concepts of personhood.

Schrader (2019) studied the skeletons of more than 800 individuals from Nubian communities occupied by the Egyptians ca. 2,000 BC. She revealed a bioarchaeology of everyday life and the inequality imposed upon the Nubians by their occupiers, such as the hard life of forced labor in quarries. Her study also revealed evidence of resistance by the Nubians and ultimately an accommodation between the two groups.

A topic of increasing interest among bioarchaeologists interested in understanding inequality is the study of violence (discussed in Chapter 7). Researchers analyzing traumatic injuries on human remains have shown that a person's social status and gender can have a significant impact on their exposure to violence. There are many researchers studying violence and exploring a range of different types of violent behavior among past (and modern) human societies, including intimate partner violence, child abuse, institutional abuse, torture, warfare, human sacrifice, and structural violence.

The transition to agriculture

About 10,000 years ago, people started to domesticate plants and animals, thus beginning a transition of some groups from hunting and gathering to agriculture. The process of the development and adoption of agriculture as the primary economic system brought about some major changes in the way societies were organized, how they operated, their population size, their subsistence systems, their settlement patterns, and their impact on the environment (e.g., Redman 1999; Bellwood 2005; Weisdorf 2005; Whitehouse and Kirleis 2014).

The shift to domesticated species resulted in a narrowing of the diet (fewer species used but some much more intensively), a growth in population, and an increase in sedentism. In addition to diet, other impacts included changes in people's morphology, activity, workload, mobility, and demography (Stock and Pinhasi 2011:6). Teeth became smaller as food became easier to chew (Pinhasi and Meiklejohn 2011) and jaws became shorter, resulting in the eventual congenital loss of the third molars (wisdom teeth), a process still ongoing.

In some areas, the consequence of this transition was a general decline in health, an increase in disease, and increased violence (e.g., Larsen 2006b; Larsen and Ruff 2011). In other areas, a general improvement in health can be seen, such as in Asia with the introduction of wet rice agriculture and the continued exploitation of protein-rich marine resources (Temple 2011).

Paleodemography

As articulated by Séguy and Buchet (2013:99), **paleodemography** seeks to "understand the population as it was, within a given socio-environmental context, where the individuals it comprised formed a dynamic group." Thus, paleodemography is the overall study of past populations: their size, birth rate, life span, population structure, growth, age and sex ratios, ethnicity, morbidity (prevalence of disease), mortality (age at death and cause of death), fertility, maternity, admixture, hazards, risk, aging, population profiles, migration, mobility, evolutionary change (mutation), biological response to changing environments, and other factors. Modern historical demographic studies have been developed in relation to census and insurance purposes, with "life tables" (Weiss 1973; Séguy and Buchet 2013:103–111) used to estimate the probability that a person of a particular age will die before their next birthday (to determine insurance premiums).

Most paleodemographic studies are based on the analysis of archaeological skeletal populations, which, in turn, are subject to a number of assumptions and limitations (e.g., Wood et al. 1992; Buikstra 1997; Bello et al. 2006; Chamberlain 2006; Konigsberg and Frankenberg 2012; Séguy and Buchet 2013; Milner et al. 2019; Steckel and Kjellström 2019). These include an assumption of the uniformity of biological processes between and among populations, an incomplete understanding of small-group population dynamics, archaeological sampling biases, and accuracy of sex and age-at-death estimates. Another critical concern in paleodemography is that many models were developed by demographers on the basis of analogies from modern data that may not be applicable to past populations (Weiss 1975; Séguy and Buchet 2013:13–18). Further, paleodemographic data are only samples of past populations, complicating the statistical confidence of a study. Nevertheless, Chamberlain (2006:177) argued that paleodemography is a well-established area of study that can produce "meaningful reconstructions of past population structures and processes."

Skeletal analysis is not without limitations, however. Many indicators of stress are nonspecific. Also, the older an individual was at death, the more difficult it is to determine age at death, so the ages of older individuals tend to be underestimated (see Schmitt 2004; Baker and Pearson 2006). Thus, population profiles can be skewed, with cohorts spanning longer and longer age ranges as they get older. Differences in preservation and/or mortuary treatment can also create sampling bias. These problems have suggested to some (e.g., Bocquet-Appel and Masset 1982, 1996) that paleodemography studies are not very useful.

Historical demography is conducted on extant populations using a variety of written records. For archaeological populations, no such records exist, so studies of paleodemography rely on accumulated data from the analyses of individuals. There is also an assumption that the "buried" population reflects the "burying" population; this is not necessarily the case, as a person who died of a disease is buried by people who had not died of the disease, possibly resulting in differences in morbidity, mortality, and mortuary treatment. In addition, some demographic studies assume homogeneity of the individuals in a population; in reality, each individual is unique and populations are highly heterogeneous. Further, it is important to include data on subadults to develop a complete picture of a population (Baker et al. 2005:4).

Some of the more difficult issues confronting paleodemographers are the accuracy of age and sex determinations. As noted earlier, such determinations can be quite difficult and, if incorrect, could greatly complicate any conclusions from a study. Obviously, considerable effort is expended in ensuring that those determinations are correct (Hoppa and Vaupel 2002; Storey 2006; Séguy and Buchet 2013).

Another issue in paleodemography is the selection of an appropriate model to use for the population analysis (Séguy and Buchet 2013). For example, a past population could be modeled as a stable one, where the group does not change through time. Alternatively, a population could be viewed as dynamic, perhaps due to migration (in or out) or to disease. In the latter case, it may be best to use a model focused on morbidity and mortality.

In the absence of human remains, other forms of archaeological data can be used as proxies in paleodemographic studies. Following Drennan et al. (2015), such data may include radiocarbon dates, number of sites (with estimates of site populations), number of houses within a site (with estimates of the number of house occupants), and measures of intensity of site occupation. Although these archaeological data sets can be informative and used to develop models, acquiring skeletal data is the most illustrative from a biological perspective. In an ideal world, the coupling of bioarchaeological and archaeological data sets would be the best (albeit rarest) scenario.

The osteological paradox

When human remains are analyzed, there is a general premise that paleodemographic profiles should look like modern profiles (Howell 1976). However, past populations are not modern ones, and this discrepancy results in what is called the **osteological paradox**, with three major issues (e.g., Wood et al. 1992; also see Wright and Yoder 2003; DeWitte and Stojanowski 2016). In addition, small sample size is always an issue.

The first issue is demographic nonstationarity; that is, the difference in the impact of fertility (birth) and mortality (death) in demographic profiles. Birth always occurs at the beginning of the profile, but death can happen at any point (time) in the profile. Given the generally high rates of infant mortality (including infanticide [Scott 2001; also see Scott 1999]) and the inevitability of death in old age, greater proportions of the young and old die relative to other ages. Thus, because birth occurs at the beginning of the profile and death can occur at any point, birth has a greater effect on a profile than death.

The second issue is selective mortality. For any condition or disease, we have only the individuals who died of it and not the ones who survived it and died from some other cause. Thus, we see individuals only at death and not in a dynamic trajectory of health.

The third issue is hidden heterogeneity. Skeletal series consist of a variety of individuals, each with unknowns such as genetics and susceptibility to disease. In addition, because skeletal series are often accumulations of people through time, it is difficult to create a demographic profile for any specific time, since detailed dating control is generally lacking.

In rare cases where multiple sets of remains date to the same specific time, the issue of heterogeneity is not a problem. For example, mass graves from diseases (e.g., plague pits) can contain a variety of people from a rather small geographic area who died within days of each other. Battlefield mass graves, such as at Towton in England (see pages 129–130) and Budeč in the Czech Republic (Štefan et al. 2016), can tell us a great deal about specific segments of a population, in this case military-aged males. In addition to combatants, other battlefields – such as the Bronze Age site on the Tollense River in Germany (Jantzen et al. 2011; also see Brinker et al. 2014; Curry 2016) – can contain the remains of civilian support personnel (including women and children; e.g., Tegtmeyer and Martin 2017b).

In some instances, an entire population of a town may have died at the same time. For example, the Early Neolithic mass grave discovered at Schöneck-Kilianstädten in Germany (Meyer et al. 2015) contained the remains of virtually the entire population of a small village that were killed in a raid, with the exception of the young women apparently taken as captives. An Anglican cemetery used between 1788 and 1853 was discovered during the construction of a mass transit station in London, resulting in the exhumation of as many as 40,000 individuals (this work was still ongoing as of 2019). Analysis of these remains could provide a remarkable window into the demographics of nineteenth-century London. Finally, a classic example of a complete demographic profile of a population is Crow Creek, South Dakota, where virtually everyone from the village, people of all ages, sexes, genders, statuses, and health conditions, were killed on the same day and thrown into a ditch (see the following Case Study).

Another example of the usefulness of a demographic study of a burial population is that of the cemetery at the 8,200-year-old Windover site in Florida, located in a peat bog. At Windover, 168 well-preserved bodies were discovered (e.g., Wentz 2012). The bodies represented various ages and both sexes, and the demographics and pathologies suggested a difficult life: 20% infant mortality, only 20% living into their forties, many broken arms and legs, arthritis, and some evidence of malnutrition. Analysis of the dental traits showed greater variability among females, suggesting the possibility of a patrilocal post-marital pattern (Tomczak and Powell 2003).

An understudied area of paleodemography is maternal mortality: death of the mother during childbirth (Stone 2016). There have been some examples of such occurrences from the archaeological record (e.g., Malgosa et al. 2004; Lieverse et al. 2015), but given the difficulty in determining cause of death, it is likely underreported. Other issues include a lack of recognition of an associated material culture, a lack of understanding about the ritual of a birth, and a lack of appreciation by archaeologists of the importance of childbirth as a social event (e.g., Beausang 2000).

Case study: the demographics of Crow Creek, South Dakota

In 1978, human remains were discovered eroding from the Crow Creek site on the Missouri River in south-central South Dakota (Figure 10.6) (Willey 1990; Willey and Emerson 1993; also see Bamforth and Nepstad-Thornberry 2007). Excavations revealed a large assemblage of commingled remains representing some 486 men, women, and children. The village had been attacked by unknown assailants some-time around AD 1325. Many of the individuals had been scalped, decapitated, and dismembered. The bodies were dumped together into a fortification ditch and were left exposed to the elements, and as a result, the bones had been skeletonized, scattered, and gnawed on by carnivores. They were later naturally covered by sediment.

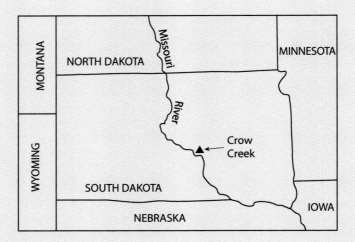

Figure 10.6 Location of the Crow Creek site
Source: Author

The Crow Creek site is a large (ca. 18 acres) village with at least 50 houses behind a palisade and fortification ditch, indicative of ongoing warfare. Based on the number of houses at the site and assumptions regarding house populations, it was estimated that the excavated sample from Crow Creek (N = 486) represented about 60% of the original population (Willey 1990:60); however, this is a very rough estimate and could have a considerable margin of error.

An analysis of the skeletal material was undertaken by Willey (1990; also see Willey and Emerson 1993). The number of victims (N = 486) was calculated by the greatest number of an identified element – the right temporal bones (Willey 1990:Table 2) – so it is possible that the true number was higher. The sample represented a population that died at a single point in time and from the same cause of death (trauma), rather than a cemetery population whose members had died at different times and from multiple causes of death.

A total of 181 adults was classified to sex (subadults were not sexed), with 99 males and 82 females (Willey 1990:48, Table 13), and some 337 individuals were classified by age (Willey 1990:43) (Table 10.3). When these data sets are combined, it is clear that the distribution varied from expected values, with more young men than young women and fewer older men than older women. Perhaps some individuals escaped or were not recovered archaeologically, or some young women may have been taken by the raiders.

Table 10.3 Crow Creek age and sex counts (adapted from Willey 1990:47, Table 13; Willey and Emerson 1993:Table 7)

Age interval (years of age at death)	Adult males (older than 15)	Adult females (older than 15)	Unsexed subadults (younger than 15)	Totals
0–1			10	10
1–4			38	38
5–9			79	79
10–14			29	29
15–19	24	12		36
20–24	19	7		26
25–29	11	4		15
30–34	10	6		16
35–39	11	11		22
40–44	4	3		7
45–49	6	13		19
50–54	7	12		19
55–59	7	14		21
unknown	unknown	unknown	unknown	149
Totals	99	82	156	486

Comparisons with regional cemetery samples revealed some interesting patterns (Willey 1990:51, Table 17). There were fewer subadults and more adults in the Crow Creek sample than in the cemetery populations, suggesting that the mortality distribution was not normal. This alone brings into question assumptions regarding what are "normal" age and sex ratios in prehistoric samples.

Using an analysis of craniometric data, the Crow Creek sample was compared to other regional samples in an attempt to determine biological affinity (Willey 1990). It was found that the Crow Creek people were most closely affiliated with the Arikara, an ethnographic Native American group living along the Missouri River to the north.

The health of past populations

Health has generally been seen from a biomedical perspective: the body's ability to function and ultimately to reproduce. Good health is seen as a normally functioning body coupled with adequate nutrition and an absence of disease and trauma. If these conditions are not met, poor health is the result. However, people can still function and reproduce in a state of poor health as long as it is not too poor. Overall health is also associated with mental and social well-being, although these factors are difficult to measure in bioarchaeological remains.

Case study: children's health in the prehistoric North American Southwest

Sobolik (2002) conducted a study of the health of children in the prehistoric American Southwest to explore the issue of children's health through time and across cultural boundaries. She compiled data on 9,703 inhumations from 61 cultural contexts (Ancestral Puebloan, Mogollon, Hohokam, and Sinagua; refer to Figure 7.5) from both large and small sites and from different time periods (AD 1 to the protohistoric period). She looked at mortality rates, evidence of metabolic stress (e.g., porotic hyperostosis, cribra orbitalia, linear enamel hypoplasias, and Harris lines) in children and adults, evidence of infection (periostosis) in children, and adult stature as a reflection of childhood health issues. Several other indicators of health were also considered, including the prevalence of tuberculosis, mastoiditis, and infections resulting from cranial deformation through the use of cradleboards (Sobolik 2002).

Mortality rates

Sobolik (2002) found that childhood mortality rates were very high: 42% for the combined sample. The rate was 38% for the Ancestral Puebloans, 51% for the Mogollon, 25% for the Hohokam, and 50% for the Sinagua. She also discovered that childhood mortality rates were higher during earlier time periods than later time periods, somewhat contrary to the general belief that children's health decreased through time as populations became more dependent on agriculture.

Metabolic stress

As noted in Chapter 5, metabolic stress results from the disruption of some biological function of the body. Although a metabolic disruption is generally nonspecific, it is commonly assumed to be related to some nutritional deficiency. The metabolic disruption pathologies investigated by Sobolik (2002) included porotic hyperostosis and cribra orbitalia on the skull, linear enamel hypoplasias on the teeth, and Harris lines on the long bones.

Porotic hyperostosis and cribra orbitalia

Recall from Chapter 5 that porotic hyperostosis and cribra orbitalia manifest as lesions and pitting on the surface of the bone, with the former on the surface of cranial bones and the latter on the roof of the eye orbits. These pathologies are frequently associated with anemia (but there may be other causes as well) and are often found in populations who are dependent on corn agriculture (El-Najjar et al. 1976; also see Larsen 2015). They tend to be found more frequently in children because their bones are thinner and not fully developed. If a child with such a pathology survives into adulthood, the lesions and pitting will eventually remodel and be less evident (e.g., Lewis 2018:194–197). Due to issues in the original documentation of these pathologies, Sobolik (2002) combined them into a single analytical category.

Given the inconsistencies in the original recordation, specific numbers are difficult to determine. Overall, however, it appears that both porotic hyperostosis and cribra orbitalia were widespread in the study populations (Sutton et al. 2010:Table 6.11). Among the Ancestral Puebloans, populations at smaller sites had significantly greater frequencies of these pathologies than at larger sites, and populations during earlier time periods had significantly greater rates than during later time periods (Sobolik 2002).

In an earlier study, El-Najjar et al. (1976) concluded that rates of porotic hyperostosis and cribra orbitalia were higher at sites in canyon regions where the populations were more dependent on agriculture and lower at sites in open regions where they would have had greater access to iron-rich animal products, suggestive of anemia as a causal factor in the pathologies. In a later study, Schultz et al. (2007) found that 50% of the children in their sample from Grasshopper Pueblo (N = 369) had evidence of anemia, interpreted as the consequence of a lack of food due to climatic and political changes.

Linear enamel hypoplasias

Linear enamel hypoplasias (LEH, see page 89) reflect a period of metabolic stress during childhood, generally viewed as a nutritional deficiency. As with porotic hyperostosis and cribra orbitalia, researchers have been inconsistent with how LEH was recorded, making comparisons difficult.

Nevertheless, Sobolik (2002) was able to establish a range of prevalence of LEH, finding the condition in 94% of secondary teeth in the individuals at the Ancestral Puebloan site of Hawikku to a low of 7% in the individuals at the Ancestral Puebloan site of Arroyo Hondo. The meaning of these differences is not clear, but may be related to the higher infant mortality rate at Arroyo Hondo, suggesting that LEH was not found on secondary teeth because the children did not live long enough to have developed such lesions. In more recent research, Ham (2018:114) reported that individuals without LEH had a higher likelihood of survival than those with LEH.

Harris lines

During times of metabolic or nutritional stress, normal bone growth of infants and adolescents may be interrupted, resulting in the formation of lines (or bands) of alternately thinner and denser mineralization in the growth areas of bones in children, called Harris lines (see page 87). Harris lines are only visible on radiographs, so they are not recognized in many skeletal analyses. Due to bone remodeling, Harris lines in adults are not discernible after about the age of 30.

Sobolik (2002) noted that only a few studies had included analyses of Harris lines. Danforth and Knick (1994:94) reported that 80% of the adults from the Ancestral Puebloan site of Carter Ranch had Harris lines. Hinkes (1983:133) reported that only 20% of the individuals from the Mogollon site of Grasshopper Pueblo had Harris lines but that there was an average of 7.4 lines (ranging from 1 to 27) per individual. Considerable evidence of Harris lines was also found at the Ancestral Puebloan sites of Hawikku and San Cristobal (Stodder 1990).

Periostosis

Sobolik (2002) examined the prevalence of periosteal lesions (see page 103) as an indicator of disease. However, limited data on such pathologies were available, so the prevalence of disease was difficult to determine. Earlier studies (e.g., Wade 1970; Hinkes 1983) had proposed the idea that disease was a major factor in infant deaths but there was little data to corroborate these claims. In support of this idea, Schultz et al. (2007) reported that the inflammatory disease referred to as meningeal irritation was diagnosed in more than 70% of the children examined in their study (N = 379).

Adult stature

Adult stature can be seen as a general measure of overall health and may reflect cumulative stress in childhood (Huss-Ashmore et al. 1982; Falkner and Tanner 1986). Sobolik (2002) compared adult stature in her sample and found that stature was similar throughout her study populations. The mean adult stature ranged between 147.7 cm for Carter Ranch females and 169.3 cm for Pueblo Bonito males (see Sutton et al. 2010:Tables 6.9 and 6.10). The greatest stature range for Southwest samples was males and females at Pueblo Bonito, seen as reflecting high-ranking status.

In examining skeletal samples from the Ancestral Puebloan sites of Pueblo Bonito and Hawikku, Ham (2018:100) found that males with below-average stature and/or body mass had an increased likelihood of survival. In addition, Ham (2018:108) reported that 42% of individuals up to ten years of age had active periosteal lesions and that individuals with healed lesions had a "survival advantage over those with active, mixed, or no lesions." Moreover, individuals with no LEH had a higher likelihood of survival than those with LEH (Ham 2018:114).

Discussion

Sobolik (2002) concluded that the children in the prehistoric and protohistoric agricultural groups of the American Southwest suffered from a pervasive pattern of high infant mortality, chronic malnutrition, and disease that seemed to function in a synergistic interaction. These issues do not appear to have improved over time, and it seems that increasing sedentism and dependence on agriculture exacerbated the problems. Even children of supposedly high-ranking lineages, such as seen at Pueblo Bonito, were not immune from these health risks (Palkovich 1984a).

One of the major questions about health in Southwest communities is the biological consequences of the adoption of corn agriculture, which many believe to be deleterious to health, a model supported by Sobolik (2002). It seems that a reliance on corn spawned an assortment of conditions that constituted a variety of challenges to health. The Southwest was (and is) a marginal environment for corn agriculture due to the frequency of droughts. Increasing dependence on corn resulted in a decrease in the use of other (wild) resources, thus decreasing the overall nutritional base. As agriculture became more important, settlements appear to have coalesced, populations became more sedentary, the people were weakened as malnutrition and parasitic infections increased (e.g., Paseka et al. 2018), and the opportunity for disease transmittal escalated. Moreover, some wild resources – such as hunted animals that provide iron-rich meat – would have been locally depressed due to hunting pressure, greatly impeding their procurement for an increasing human population and creating an "endemic nutritional inadequacy" (Palkovich 1984b:436; also see Stodder 1990). Children are particularly susceptible to these factors due to their nutritional needs for growth and development.

On the other hand, East (2008) argued that the health of children in the North American Southwest was not as bad as previously thought. She examined ante-natal and postnatal remains (N = 427) from three pueblo sites, with the largest sample (n = 334) coming from Grasshopper Pueblo. She compared her results to modern biomedical data on children with no pathologies and suggested that although the children of these three pueblos lived with mild to moderate chronic nutritional stress, their overall resilience was good, and they were able to bio-logically compensate for nutritional stress and infectious disease.

Recent research suggests that children's health may have been affected by concepts of personhood. Schillaci et al. (2011) examined patterns of infant and juvenile growth and pathologies in a diachronic (ca. AD 1300–1680) sample of Ancestral Puebloans from the Southwest. They observed poor growth in the first five years of life and a high mortality rate among infants and juveniles, often accompanied by porotic cranial lesions. They suggested that this pattern occurred prior to incorporating the child into the tribal ritual organization (Schillaci et al. 2011). Similarly, Nikitovic (2017) noted that among Ancestral Puebloans, high child mortality was common among infants and then increased between three and seven years of age. This was posited as reflecting a change in personhood when it was expected that children of that age cohort would develop greater independence.

Medical care

All past societies had some sort of interventional medical care to deal with acute issues, administered by specialists (e.g., shamans) skilled in the medical arts. Some treatments were spiritual or magical in nature. For example, the treatment of disease often involved the invocation of spirits or the use of magical potions, although some form of pharmacological treatment may have also been included. Such treatments usually leave little bioarchaeological evidence (one exception is hair from an archaeological context that may retain chemical traces of drugs).

In other cases, some form of empirically based treatment or direct physical intervention may have been involved, such as setting a broken bone, dressing a wound, or surgical intervention for bone infections (e.g., Toyne 2015c). In such cases, there would likely be some sort of bioarchaeological signature (see discussion of medical trauma on pages 137–138).

An interesting case of ancient health care is that of Ötzi, the Tyrolean Iceman (e.g., Dickson 2011; see Case Study, page 169). The skeletal analysis revealed healed trauma and recent illnesses, as well as several types of medicinal plants found in association with the body. In addition, a series of 61 tattoos in 19 clusters at joints and in the abdominal area suggested a form of medical treatment for arthritis and intestinal issues, perhaps marking acupuncture locations (Bahr 2015; also see Samadelli et al. 2015). Zink et al. (2019) argued that these data indicated that medical treatment and were was common by the early Bronze Age.

Disability and community health care

Like most societies, past communities made efforts to care for their members who had become disabled. Most people suffered occasional short-term disabilities (e.g., a sprained ankle) that could easily be accommodated. In some cases, however, severe impairments resulted in long-term or permanent disabilities. Under those conditions, how much effort would be expended to support those who could not contribute materially to the society? It is clear from the archaeological record that communities did indeed care for permanently disabled people (Hublin 2009; Byrnes and Muller 2017a). This form of medical treatment was afforded to severely disabled individuals who survived long after their impairment. In addition, as healthy people age, they require increasing levels of care.

Investigation into the bioarchaeology of health care is a relatively new approach (Tilley and Oxenham 2011; Tilley and Cameron 2014; Tilley 2015a; Redfern 2017a; Tilley and Schrenk 2017). Evidence of disability through disease and nonlethal trauma, along with evidence of how such stricken individuals were treated by their communities, can be detected in the archaeological record. How did past societies conceptualize disability (Boutin 2016)? Did disability create a new social identity (Byrnes and Muller 2017b:3)? How, and for how long, were such people cared for? Were they treated differently in death? The ability and willingness of a society to care for its disabled members and how they were treated in death can provide considerable insight into the social aspects of a society.

Tilley and Cameron (2014; also see Tilley 2017) introduced a four-stage "Index of Care" for bioarchaeologists to identify and interpret aspects of health care. The four steps are (1) identify and document any health-related issues in the remains; (2) assess any disability that might have resulted from such issues; (3) propose a strategy of caregiving for that individual; and (4) suggest social relations and practices related to the identity of the individual.

This model is widely applicable, although it is often difficult to empirically determine what level of care was needed and/or given to any specific individual, particularly if that person died of disease or trauma before any improvement (and thus implied care) would manifest in the remains. This perimortem issue is especially relevant with children given the fragility of their remains, but any differential mortuary treatment may be observable in cemeteries (see Oxenham and Willis 2017). Among the elderly, general disability could manifest slowly, with an increasing loss of mobility, memory deficits, and the inability to contribute materially to the community (e.g., Gowland 2017).

The archaeological record contains many examples of the care of disabled persons. One famous example is the Neandertal skeleton (Shanidar 1; Trinkaus 1983; Trinkaus and Villotte 2017) who suffered a number of traumatic injuries and became disabled, but was cared for (presumably by his family) for years after. Tilley and Oxenham (2011) described an adult individual with juvenile-onset quadriplegia in a Neolithic site (Man Bac) in Vietnam. Whereas other individuals were buried extended, this person was buried in a tightly flexed (fetal) position, likely his position in life due to his fused vertebrae that left him hunched over. He was diagnosed with Klippel-Feil syndrome, which would have paralyzed him from the waist down with little use of his arms. Although he would have required constant care, he survived for many years after the onset of his paralysis.

Tilley (2017; also see Tilley 2015b) reexamined the remains of Romito 2, a young (17 to 20 years old) probable male from southern Italy, dated to about 11,000 BP. Romito 2 had chondrodystrophic dwarfism that set him apart from his age cohort early on and caused some disabilities that prevented him from contributing to the group's economic activities, thus requiring some level of accommodation by his community. Despite these issues, Romito 2 was accorded the same mortuary treatment as the others in his community.

Lieverse et al. (2017) reported that a young adult male with a penetrating wound to one of his lumbar vertebrae had been recovered from an Early Neolithic site in southern Siberia. A projectile point had penetrated most of the way through the vertebral foramen, likely rendering the individual paraplegic. However, the community apparently cared for the individual long enough for the injury to heal, indicating both immediate and long-term care for disabled persons.

Tornberg and Jacobsson (2018) analyzed an individual from Neolithic Sweden who had suffered two severe antemortem skull traumas that likely resulted in brain injuries. They determined that the individual would have required short-term care for basic needs, as well as long-term care for cognitive impairment, both of which were apparently provided in that Neolithic society. They further argued that the availability of such care was necessary for a sustainable society.

A final example is an 18-year-old female from the Bronze Age site of Tell Abraq in the United Arab Emirates who was found to have suffered from paralysis. She was cared for in life, and when she died she was buried articulated in an ossuary, apparently a specialized treatment (Schrenk and Martin 2017).

Prosthetics

In some cases, a missing body part (e.g., limbs, eyes, feet, toes) was replaced with an artificial one, known as a prosthetic. Such replacements are indicative of ongoing medical treatment and continuing care of the affected individual. A number of prosthetic devices have been discovered in the archaeological record, including toes (Brier et al. 2015), thumbs, and feet (Bindera et al. 2016).

Chapter summary

Bioarchaeologists study human remains and their contexts to address anthropological questions. Understanding the life history of a person is the first step, and understanding the funerary system within which that individual was treated is the second step. Among the issues to address are social organization, political systems, religion and ritual, sex and gender, inequality, the transition to agriculture, paleodemography, health, and care.

Social organization is the manner in which a society is organized, with kinship being the prime component, but also including marriage patterns and post-marital residence. Some societies have simple egalitarian social organizations, whereas others have complex stratified social organizations based on status and/or class. Political systems exist to control the social aspects of a society; as such, it is often difficult to clearly separate the two systems.

Religion, the belief in supernatural forces, is a standard component in all facets of a funerary system and can provide considerable insight into a society. Funerary systems also include ritual behaviors, although not all are related to religion.

Investigations into sex and gender can reveal the considerable social and sexual diversity that existed in most past societies. Such studies are important to highlight the flaws in traditional western stereotypes about the roles of men and women. The study of inequality is related to sex, gender, and violence, and identifying inequality is an important part of understanding social and political organizations.

Some 10,000 years ago, humans began a transition from hunting and gathering to agriculture. This resulted in a series of changes to diet; sedentism; settlement patterns; social and political organizations; use of resources; changes to the environment; and importantly, changes to human morphology, morbidity, and mortality. Associated with such change is paleodemography, the study of the structure of populations. Paleodemography has its analytical problems, including the osteological paradox, small sample size, and dating. Nevertheless, in some cases, such as events where large groups of people died at the same time, it can be highly informative.

Bioarchaeologists are also interested in the health of past peoples, the impact of disease, and violence on both individuals and populations. The types of medical treatment and care afforded to disabled persons can provide information about the willingness and ability of a society to support its members.

Key concepts and terms

achieved status
ascribed status
class
egalitarian
kinship
osteological paradox
paleodemography
religion
ritual
social stratification
status

Chapter 11

Contemporary application

Forensic anthropology

Forensic anthropology has its roots in medicine and anatomy and is a subfield of anthropology "that incorporates a wide array of scientific techniques and skills modified from a multitude of disciplines and applies them to questions of medico-legal significance" (Grivas and Komar 2008:771). In essence, then, it deals with contemporary human remains "resulting from unexplained deaths" (Byers 2017:1). Forensic anthropology includes a number of specialties, such as forensic archaeology (e.g., Moran and Gold 2019), forensic science, dental analysis, and trauma analysis. The goal of this work is, in essence, to "reconstruct the specifics of a single event" (Connor and Scott 2001:3), rather than to investigate anthropological questions such as funerary systems, social structure, power relationships, and the like.

Forensic anthropology differs from bioarchaeology in that the focus of forensic anthropology is on recent materials and events in domestic and international settings in association with a medico-legal process, such as investigations of disasters or crimes (Martin and Anderson 2014b:4; also see Klepinger 2006; Dirkmaat et al. 2008; Komar and Buikstra 2008; Dirkmaat 2012; Crossland 2013; Blau and Ubelaker 2016; Byers 2017; Langley and Tersigni-Tarrant 2017; Boyd and Boyd 2018a; Moran and Gold 2019; Ubelaker 2019). This tends to be conflated with the "forensic" investigation of archaeological materials (e.g., Congram 2019). Further, it is vital that the forensic anthropologist has a firm grounding in osteology, law, and forensic science (Connor 2019:41).

For much of its history (see Komar and Buikstra 2008; Ubelaker 2018b), the major concentration of forensic anthropology was the identification of individuals, primarily from skeletal remains. More recently, however, a number of developments have expanded the field. The advent of DNA analysis has made identification easier, soft tissue analysis is becoming more common, and other analytical approaches have improved, including (1) better training focused on forensics; (2) new human comparative samples; (3) a greater understanding of taphonomy; (4) the use of archaeological methods; (5) enhanced trauma analysis; (6) improved quantitative statistical methods; and (7) the adoption of better rules regarding the admissibility of expert witness testimony. In addition, forensic anthropology has now undertaken a humanitarian function in the investigations of extralegal mass killings (Ubelaker 2018b).

For the most part, forensic anthropology has been viewed as an applied approach lacking its own body of theory (e.g., Adovasio 2012:684). Certainly, theory is used, such as evolutionary theory, as the basis of identification, but has often remained unstated (Boyd and Boyd 2018b:5). Boyd and Boyd (2018b:6–8; also see Boyd and Boyd 2011) proposed three interacting forms of theory that are applicable to forensic anthropology:

foundational, interpretive, and methodological. Foundational theory includes evolutionary theory that attempts to explain human variation and development. Interpretive theory (what archaeologists would call middle-range theory [e.g., Johnson 2019]) links empirical evidence to both premortem and postmortem behavior and events, such as the development of and responses to disease and trauma, or the taphonomic processes that affect a body after death. Methodological theory applies to the recovery and analysis of the remains, including statistical analyses. Each of these forms of theory interacts with and informs each other. However, this does not mean that a body contains infallible objective legal evidence (the "CSI" effect), as evidence "is always interpreted within specific contexts" (Steadman 2019:244).

Goals in forensic anthropology

The goals in forensic anthropology (Byers 2017:1–2; also see Ubelaker 2019) are first to establish whether the remains are human and, if so, determine the number of individuals present. Next, the remains are analyzed to estimate the age, sex, stature, and ancestry of the individual(s). Any trauma is noted for use in identification and to aid forensic pathologists in determining the manner and cause of death. An estimate of the time elapsed since death is made based on an analysis of the decomposition of a body. These data are compiled to establish a biocultural profile for use in identifying an individual. Any other evidence associated with the investigation would also be carefully collected.

For cremated remains, the identification of individuals is made more difficult due to distortion and fragmentation of the remains; however, the analytical goals remain the same (Schultz et al. 2015:93). For instance, the analysis of DNA may be possible, and the weight of the cremains might be used to estimate sex (Gonçalves et al. 2013). Discussions of burned human remains in forensic settings were provided by Schultz et al. (2015) and Symes et al. (2015).

Forensic anthropologists work with various entities and organizations. These include academia, medical examiners, police, government agencies on mass casualty events (e.g., air disasters, terrorist attacks), and international organizations on extralegal killings, the latter of which can be quite dangerous (Martin 2015:162; also see Klepinger 2006).

Discovery and recovery

Detecting and recovering recent human remains is conducted somewhat differently than in traditional archaeology (To 2017). The discovery of remains can be accomplished using a variety of methods, often informed by other factors such as criminal confession. A visual survey of the ground surface may be made as recent burial places could be more obvious than ancient ones. In some cases, geophysical methods (such as ground-penetrating radar [e.g., Schultz 2012]) may be used in suspected areas, and cadaver dogs may also be used (e.g., Rebmann et al. 2000; Oesterhelweg et al. 2008). In addition to locating the remains themselves, it is important to locate associated materials that would be useful in a forensic setting, such as blood-stained clothing and personal effects.

Once discovered, remains are then recovered by forensic archaeologists, specialists in field research who use archaeological methods and principles grounded in archaeological theory within a legal context (Dupras et al. 2006; Groen et al. 2015). Although there is a standardized methodology for assessing and processing sites, a variety of field techniques (e.g., mechanical and/or hand excavation) might be employed in the context of forensics, depending on the circumstances (Boyd and Boyd 2011, 2018b; also see Cox et al. 2013).

The exhumation of bodies for forensic investigation has been conducted for a long time, most commonly with war dead (Ferrándiz and Robben 2015). Such investigations are often constrained by the political hindrance of those who do not want the truth exposed, such as the fate of civilians killed in the Korean War (Kwon 2015), victims of the repressions in Chile and Argentina (Robben 2015), or the genocides in Cambodia and Rwanda (Lesley 2015). A brief history of forensic investigations of homicide victims was provided by Crossland and Joyce (2015).

Identification of remains

Various methods are employed to identify the remains of victims, but they should not be used in isolation (e.g., Christensen and Anderson 2017; Konigsberg and Jantz 2017). If possible, the fingerprints of the person can rapidly lead to their identification. Similarly, the presence of any birthmarks or body modifications, such as tattoos or piercings, could be compared to known people. The context of where the body was found (e.g., a battlefield or a basement) and the presence of any personal belongings or items found in association with the body (e.g., wallet or dog tags) would also be important.

For the remains themselves, the analysis of metric attributes to estimate age, sex, stature, and ancestry (see Chapter 3) creates a biological profile (Walsh-Henry and Boys 2015) to compare with specific known persons. It is important to keep in mind, however, that these attributes can only provide a probability of a match; the probability increases as more data sets are utilized.

Once the field of possibilities has been narrowed down using the methods noted earlier, other techniques, where applicable, may provide a more specific identification (or elimination of possibilities). Forensic odontologists can compare surviving dentition (tooth morphology, dental work, and appliances) to dental records (Edgar and Rautman 2016:340; Schmidt 2016; Zinni and Crowley 2017b). A number of possibly unique features could be assessed and compared to those of specific known individuals. Examples include radiographs of the skull that may reveal suture or sinus morphology and the presence of healed bones and/or orthopedic repairs (e.g., metal plates).

If the skull is intact and there are suspected matches, a photograph of the missing person can be superimposed on the skull to see if the features match (Stephan and Claes 2016). If there are no suspected matches, it may be possible to approximate (reconstruct) the face by using standard tissue–depth markers (e.g., Buti et al. 2017) or computer programs (e.g., Lindsay et al. 2015) to attempt a match to a missing person. The same techniques, sometimes along with historical data, are used to identify famous persons such as King Edward III of England (who died in AD 1485) (Nystrom 2017b). These methods can only be used as clues to identification and cannot be used for positive identification

The analysis of DNA is now a standard technique in identification when there is a specific deceased person who has been tentatively identified through the use of other methods and the family of that person can provide comparative samples. Since its development in the 1980s, the reliability of DNA testing has greatly improved (Ottoni et al. 2017; Edson et al. 2018). Commercially generated DNA profiles are now beginning to be used for identifying criminals. In addition to DNA, the isotopic analyses of tissues may indicate the geographic origin of a body or bodies, helping to narrow the possibilities (Bartelink et al. 2018; Chesson et al. 2018). The Federal Bureau of Investigation has compiled and maintains a database of DNA: the Combined DNA Index System (CODIS) for use in criminal investigations.

Identifying manner and cause of death

The identification of both the manner and cause of death of an individual is important in any investigation. The manner of death, such as homicide, suicide, accident, or natural cause, indicates the direction of any subsequent investigation. If the body is relatively intact, an autopsy is usually conducted. If not, skeletal indicators of trauma may be present to determine cause of death, such as those related to gunshots (e.g., Stefan 2014), blunt or sharp weapons, or other factors. Although forensic anthropologists can provide information on trauma and other aspects of a death, it is the legal responsibility of the pathologist (a medical doctor) to formally determine the cause of death.

Time since death

It is important to determine how much time has elapsed between the death of an individual and discovery of the remains so that such information can be made available for any investigation and legal proceeding (Wilson-Taylor and Dautartas 2017). An estimation of time since death is made based on a variety of taphonomic factors, including temperature, humidity, soil conditions, scavengers, insect activity, degree of skeletonization, and bone weathering, all of which influence the condition of the body. Other factors influencing taphonomy are toxicology (e.g., the presence of arsenic will inhibit decomposition) and trauma (e.g., fragmentation of the body will facilitate decomposition).

The various data sets used in making these estimations have been meticulously constructed by experiment and observation of the decomposition of donated bodies under controlled conditions, work begun in 1987 by William Bass at the University of Tennessee at a site colloquially known as the "**body farm**." There are now a number of such research programs at other universities.

Legal issues

Once evidence is collected, it must be safeguarded and maintained in an unbroken chain of custody by appropriate persons. Most jurisdictions require evidence based on scientific, definitive, or objective criteria, rather than presumptive, punitive, or circumstantial means (Walsh-Henry and Boys 2015:121).

Finally, once the analyses are complete, the forensic anthropologist completes an analytical report on the remains for legal purposes. They may also be called as an expert witness in a trial (see Klepinger 2006:133–137; Henneberg 2016), having to comply with the standard rules of scientific evidence (e.g., Grivas and Komar 2008; Boyd and Boyd 2018c).

Homicide cases

Forensic anthropologists become involved with diverse cases. Perhaps the most common are homicides, cases that may begin with the report of a missing person, although not all missing persons found dead are victims of homicides. The gathering of evidence from a crime scene (e.g., a murder) would hopefully be done in a detailed and meticulous manner by forensic anthropologists using archaeological field methods, and the laboratory analysis of the recovered materials would use the latest forensic methods.

The following (from Sutton 2013:357–358) is an example of such an investigation in Idaho. In 1995, four young men decided to teach a "friend" a lesson. The victim was bound and abused and eventually shot in the head with a 9-mm handgun. The murderers burned the body and covered the cremation with a thin layer of soil. The victim was reported missing by his family. Six months later, police were led to the site by one of the perpetrators who had confessed. The Forensic Services Division of the Idaho Department of Law Enforcement called the Idaho State archaeologist (Dr. Robert M. Yohe II), who had experience in dealing with cremated human remains.

The cremation site was excavated in the same manner as an archaeological site. First, a five-foot grid was established and each grid unit was carefully excavated by hand, with the soil screened and all recovered materials mapped. Burned bone fragments were quickly found, many of which were identified as human. In addition, a piece of burned fabric, a partially burned shoe, a belt buckle, and 9-mm bullets were found.

Some 1,200 bone fragments were recovered, most so badly burned and fragmented that they could not be identified to element. However, a fragment of the angle of the scapula with a partially fused epiphysis, a rib tip, and a fragmentary clavicle were identified and suggested an individual between 17 and 20 years of age. The robust characteristics of parts of the femur and mandible suggested a male. Thus, the data showed a young male, generally fitting the description of the missing person. When faced with this evidence, the perpetrators sought a plea deal and were sent to prison, and the family of the victim had some closure.

Mass death events

Other, fortunately less common, cases are mass death events. Many such events are disasters or accidents, such as earthquakes, tsunamis, and airplane crashes. In these cases, the primary goals are to recover and identify the victims, with little investigation regarding the cause of death (the manner being already known), although there are exceptions.

Purposeful mass death events include terrorist attacks, genocide, and war. For example, more than 3,000 people were killed in the terror attacks at the World Trade Center in Manhattan on September 11, 2001, and a number of forensic anthropologists were mobilized to contribute to the recovery efforts (MacKinnon and Mundorff 2006; Figura 2018).

Extralegal killings and mass graves

Extralegal killings include the intentional killing of prisoners and civilians in wartime, **genocide**, and human rights violations, and are subject to investigation and prosecution under international law (Crossland 2013; Guyomarc'h and Congram 2017). Such atrocities often result in the burial of the victims in concealed mass graves of varying sizes in the general location of their deaths (Anstett 2018:178). Haglund (2002:245) outlined five issues for the investigation of mass graves associated with extralegal killings: (1) the development of legal evidence, (2) identification of the dead, (3) creation of an accurate historical record, (4) advocating for the dead, and (5) recognizing the dignity of human life. In addition to the legal issues, the discovery of such places and the identification of victims is important for closure to the families and for national reconciliation, such as the murders of Chilean civilians by the Pinochet regime (DeVisser et al. 2014). However, not all mass graves are related to extralegal killings. Other examples include the burial of war dead or the dead from disasters (e.g., earthquakes or tsunamis) or diseases (e.g., bubonic plague) (Guyomarc'h and Congram 2017:337).

One of the most famous cases of mass murder of prisoners of war was the massacre of some 22,000 Polish officers by the Soviets in 1940 (Figure 11.1), many of whom were buried in the Katyn Forest in Russia. When the Germans discovered the graves in 1943, the Soviets accused the Germans, a story most people believed until a forensic investigation revealed that the men had been killed before the Germans had occupied the region (Materski 2008; Eyerman 2019). The Russians only recently admitted to the killings, and the event remains a major trauma to the Poles.

There are many examples of genocide, the most infamous being the Jewish Holocaust during World War II, when some 6 million people were murdered. In 1994, the Hutu majority government of Rwanda directed the murder of more than 500,000 Tutsi people, and mass graves from that event are still being found and investigated.

Figure 11.1 Bodies of Polish officers murdered in the Katyn Forest by the Soviets in 1940

Source: Public domain

In July 1995, Bosnian Serb forces killed as many 8,000 Muslim men and boys from the town of Srebrenica in the largest massacre in Europe since World War II. The case was brought to the International Criminal Tribunal for the Former Yugoslavia (ICTY) and the International Court of Justice (ICJ), and in 2016, the former Bosnian Serb leader Radovan Karadžić was found guilty of genocide and sentenced to 40 years in prison.

Most recently, the Islamic State of Iraq and Syria (ISIS) has committed mass murders of civilians in Iraq and Syria, burying the victims in numerous mass graves across the region. The discovery and investigations of these atrocities has only recently begun.

Sometimes forensic investigations can correct an existing historical record. For example, a mass grave containing seven Native American males was discovered in the city of Nephi, Utah (Rood 2006). The bodies all had gunshot wounds. The official historical record stated that on October 2, 1853, seven Native American males arrived at the fort in Nephi and that when questioned by the local Mormon leaders, "showed fight." The record stated that a skirmish then occurred, resulting in the deaths of the seven males and their interment in a mass grave. However, the forensic examination of the bodies revealed that each had been shot in the back of the head, likely while kneeling. Thus, they did not die in "a fight," but had been summarily executed.

Recovery of war dead

Soldiers who die during times of war are generally recovered soon afterward and are provided mortuary treatment. In some cases, however, the bodies are not recovered and are listed either as missing in action (MIA) or prisoner of war (POW). The United States makes a major effort to recover war dead through the Defense POW/MIA Accounting Agency (DPAA), which has facilities in Hawai'i, Nebraska, and Washington, D.C. As of 2018, there were about 82,000 Americans still listed as MIA/POW (41,000 having been lost at sea). When a location (e.g., a plane crash site) that might contain the remains of American MIA/POWs is identified, a team is dispatched to search for the remains using archaeological techniques. If such remains are located, they are collected, along with any artifacts (e.g., dog tags), and taken to a DPAA lab for identification and repatriation. Case studies on the recovery of U.S. war dead were presented in Sledge (2005) and Mann et al. (2009).

Other countries also have agencies that find, identify, and repatriate war dead. French war dead from as early as the Franco-Prussian War (1870–1871) have a special status of having died for France ('Mort pour la France') (Signoli and Védrines 2011:712). In addition, millions of foreign soldiers died in France and Belgium during World War I and II. When war dead are found in western Europe, agencies from France, Great Britain, and the United States attempt to identify the nationality based on artifact associations (e.g., weapons and uniforms). Germany has the private German War Graves Commission, but it mostly works in eastern Europe. Finally, Australia has fairly recently began a program to recover and identify their war dead (Donlon and Littleton 2011:635).

Not all war dead are repatriated to their country of origin. In some cases, formal cemeteries of known war dead are established in the areas where they died to commemorate their sacrifice (Renshaw 2013). Examples of this are the British and Commonwealth cemetery at Tyne Cot, Belgium, and the American cemetery in Normandy, France.

Case study: a tongue in cheek look at the preemptive forensics of the zombie apocalypse

The popular American stereotype of a "zombie" is a person who was infected by a virus that "killed" them but caused them to still be animate. These "dead" people then wander about the landscape seeking living humans to eat, being attracted to them by sound or smell. Once a living human is scratched or bitten by a zombie, they, too, are infected by the virus, "die," and become zombies themselves. By tradition, zombies have at least partially decayed soft tissues, move relatively slowly, and are easily recognized by the living. The only way to "kill" a zombie is to destroy their brain or to completely destroy their body, such as by cremating it.

So, how would a forensic anthropologist identify the remains of a zombie? If a body was sufficiently intact with soft tissue to be identified as a nonzombie, the cause of death would be established using standard techniques. If the body was sufficiently intact with soft tissue to be identified as a zombie, the cause of death of the human would be the virus. If the body had been destroyed, it would be necessary to determine whether it had been a zombie rather than a regular murder victim. If the body had been cremated, it is possible that some trauma could still be identified, and it may be possible to determine whether the virus was present in the cremains. If the body had been destroyed in a different manner, say a wood chipper, it may be possible to identify whether the virus was present and so identify the remains as that of a zombie. The nature of the cremation may also be a clue, as commercial cremations of regular people are done at high temperature and leave few cremains, whereas an impromptu cremation of a zombie would likely result in more and larger bone fragments.

If the remains were skeletonized, it would be necessary to determine whether they belonged to a regular human or a zombie. The presence of catastrophic trauma to the head would suggest a zombie but would not exclude a regular person who had been murdered. Trauma to other parts of the body would also be indicative. For example, trauma to the torso or extremities that would kill or immobilize a regular human would not kill a zombie but might slow them down a bit. If a leg or arm of a zombie had suffered trauma, say a compound fracture, the continued movement of the broken ends against each other would create a wear pattern (e.g., rounded edges of the fracture) not present on such an injury in a living human. A zombie skeleton might also show evidence of blunt or sharp force trauma that would have killed a regular human. Missing body parts could also be an indication of a zombie.

Thus, the cause of "death" for a zombie would be head trauma, although other skeletal indicators, such as other perimortem trauma with signs of wear, may be present. If a regular human died from massive head trauma, a homicide might be indicated. The identification of viral RNA or DNA (but be careful!!) might be required to close the case.

Chapter summary

Forensic anthropology is the practical application of the theory and method of bioarchaeology applied in a contemporary legal setting. The primary goals of forensic anthropologists are to identify victims of wars, disasters, and crimes, both to bring closure to families and to provide evidence for the prosecution of criminals, rather than to address anthropological questions.

Identification of specific individuals can be accomplished using a variety of methods not typically available with prehistoric remains, such as fingerprints, body modifications, personal items (e.g., a wallet), osteometric data or biological profile matches to known individuals, dental records, facial reconstruction, and DNA. Depending on the condition of the body, information on the manner and cause of death and time since death may be deduced. In all cases, a legal chain of custody must be maintained.

Important applications of forensic anthropology include disasters, terrorist attacks, extralegal killings, genocides, and homicides. Of particular importance is the recovery of war dead, and the United States expends considerable energy to accomplish that.

Key concepts and terms

body farms
extralegal killings
genocide

References

Achilli, Alessandro, Ugo A. Perego, Hovirag Lancioni, Anna Olivieri, Francesca Gandini, Baharak Hooshiar Kashani, Vincenza Battaglia, Viola Grugni, Norman Angerhofer, Mary P. Rogers, Rene J. Herrera, Scott R. Woodward, Damian Labuda, David Glenn Smith, Jerome S. Cybulski, Ornella Semino, Ripan S. Malhi, and Antonio Torroni 2013 Reconciling Migration Models to the Americas with the Variation of North American Native Mitogenomes. *Proceedings of the National Academy of Sciences* 110(35):14308–14313.

Adams, Dean C., F. James Rohlf, and Dennis E. Slice 2013 A Field Comes of Age: Geometric Morphometrics in the 21st Century. *Hystrix, the Italian Journal of Mammalogy* 24(1):7–14.

Adler, Christina J., Wolfgang Haak, Denise Donlon, Alan Cooper, and The Genographic Consortium 2010 Survival and Recovery of DNA from Ancient Teeth and Bones. *Journal of Archaeological Science* 38(5):956–964.

Adovasio, James M. 2012 An "Outsider" Look at Forensic Anthropology. In *A Companion to Forensic Anthropology*, edited by Dennis C. Dirkmaat, pp. 683–689. John Wiley & Sons, New York.

Adovasio, James M., D. Pedler, J. Donahue, and R. Stuckenrath 1999 No Vestiges of a Beginning nor Prospect for an End: Two Decades of Debate on Meadowcroft Rockshelter. In *Ice Age Peoples of North America*, edited by Robson Bonnichsen and Karen L. Turnmire, pp. 416–431. Center for the Study of the First Americans, Corvallis, OR.

Agarwal, Sabrina C. 2012 The Past of Sex, Gender, and Health: Bioarchaeology of the Aging Skeleton. *American Anthropologist* 114(2):322–335.

———— 2016 Bone Morphologies and Histories: Life Course Approaches in Bioarchaeology. *American Journal of Physical Anthropology, Supplement: Yearbook of Physical Anthropology* 159(S61):130–149.

Agarwal, Sabrina C., and Bonnie A. Glencross 2011 Building a Social Archaeology. In *Social Bioarchaeology*, edited by Sabrina C. Agarwal and Bonnie A. Glencross, pp. 1–11. Wiley-Blackwell, Oxford, UK.

Agarwal, Sabrina C., and Julie K. Wesp (eds.) 2017 *Exploring Sex and Gender in Bioarchaeology*. University of New Mexico Press, Albuquerque, NM.

Aldhouse-Green, Miranda 2015 *Bog Bodies Uncovered: Solving Europe's Ancient Mystery*. Thames & Hudson, London, UK.

Alekshin, V. A., Brad Bartel, Alexander B. Dolitsky, Antonio Gilman, Philip L. Kohl, D. Liversage, and Claude Masset 1983 Burial Customs as an Archaeological Source. *Current Anthropology* 24(2):137–149.

Alfonso-Durruty, Marta P. 2011 Experimental Assessment of Nutrition and Bone Growth's Velocity on Harris Line Formation. *American Journal of Physical Anthropology* 145(2):169–180.

AL-Khafif, Ghada Darwish, Rokia El-Banna, Nancy Khattab, Tamer Gad Rashed, and Salwa Dahesh 2018 The Immunodetection of Non-Falciparum Malaria in Ancient Egyptian Bones (Giza Necropolis). *BioMed Research International 2018* Article ID 9058108.

Allen, Mark W., and Terry L. Jones (eds.) 2014 *Violence and Warfare Among Hunter-Gatherers*. Left Coast Press, Walnut Creek, CA.

Alonso-Llamazares, Carmen, Carlos Gómez, Pablo García-Manrique, Antonio F. Pardiñas, and Belén López 2018 Medical Diagnostic Methods Applied to a Medieval Female with Vitamin D Deficiency from the North of Spain. *International Journal of Paleopathology* 22:109–120.

Alonzi, Elise 2016 SAA Repatriation Survey Analysis, Results of the Society for American Archaeology Repatriation Survey. *The SAA Archaeological Record* 16(4). Electronic document available at www.saa.org/Portals/0/SAA/GovernmentAffairs/SAA%20Repatriation%20Survey%20Results%20Report%2004.22.16.pdf.

Alpers, Michael P. 2007 A History of Kuru. *Papua and New Guinea Medical Journal* 50(1–2):10–19.

Altenmüller, Hartwig 2002 Funerary Boats and Boat Pits of the Old Kingdom. *Archiv orientální* 70:269–290.

Alva, Walter 1988 Discovering the New World's Richest Unlooted Tomb. *National Geographic* 174(4):510–549.

———— 1990 New Tomb of Royal Splendor. *National Geographic* 177(6):2–15.

Alva, Walter, and Christopher B. Donnan 1994 *Royal Tombs of Sipán* (2nd ed.). Fowler Museum of Cultural History, University of California, Los Angeles.

Ambrose, Stanley H., Jane E. Buikstra, and Harold W. Krueger 2003 Status and Gender Differences in Diet at Mound 72, Cahokia, Revealed by Isotopic Analysis of Bone. *Journal of Anthropological Archaeology* 22(3):217–226.

Ambrose, Stanley H., and Michael J. DeNiro 1987 Bone Nitrogen Isotope Composition and Climate. *Nature* 325:201.

Ammitzbøll, T., S. Ry Andersen, H. P. Andersson, J. Bodenhoff, M. Eiken, B. Eriksen, N. Foged, M. Ghisler, A. Gotfredsen, H. E. Hansen, J. P. Hart Hansen, J. Jakobsen, J. Balslev Jøgensen, T. Kobayasi, N. Kromann, K. J. Lyberth, L. Lyneborg, F. Mikkelsen, J. Møhl, R. Møller, J. Myhre, P. O. Pedersen, J. U. Prause, O. Sebbesen, E. Svejgaard, D. D. Thompson, V. Frølund Thomsen, and L. Vanggaard 1991 The People. In *The Greenland Mummies*, edited by Jens Peder Hart Hansen, Jørgen Meldgaard, and Jørgen Nordqvist, pp. 64–101. Smithsonian Institution Press, Washington, DC.

Andrus, C. Fred T., and Douglas E. Crowe 2000 Geochemical Analysis of *Crassostrea virginica* as a Method to Determine Season of Capture. *Journal of Archaeological Science* 27(1):33–42.

Andrushko, Valerie A., Kate A. S. Latham, Diane L. Grady, Alan G. Pastron, and Philip L. Walker 2005 Bioarchaeological Evidence for Trophy-Taking in Prehistoric Central California. *American Journal of Physical Anthropology* 127(4):375–384.

Angel, J. Lawrence 1966a Porotic Hyperostosis, Anemias, Malarias, and Marshes in the Prehistoric Eastern Mediterranean. *Science* 153(3737):760–763.

———— 1966b Early Skeletons from Tranquility, California. *Smithsonian Contributions to Anthropology* 2(1). Washington, DC.

———— 1969 Paleodemography and Evolution. *American Journal of Physical Anthropology* 31(3):343–353.

Anstett, Élisabeth 2018 What Is a Mass Grave? Toward an Anthropology of Human Remains in Contemporary Contexts of Mass Violence. In *A Companion to the Anthropology of Death*, edited by Antonius C. G. M. Robben, pp. 177–188. John Wiley & Sons, New York.

Antikas, T. G., and L. K. Wynn-Antikas 2016 New Finds from the Cremains in Tomb II at Aegae Point to Philip II and a Scythian Princess. *International Journal of Osteoarchaeology* 26(4):682–692.

Antoine, Daniel 2008 The Archaeology of "Plague." *Medical History* 52(S27):101–114.

Antoine, Daniel, Charles M. FitzGerlad, and Jerome C. Rose 2019 Incremental Structures in Teeth: Keys to Unlocking and Understanding Dental Growth and Development. In *Biological Anthropology of the Human Skeleton* (3rd ed.), edited by M. Anne Katzenberg and Anne L. Grauer, pp. 225–256. Wiley-Blackwell, New York.

Arens, William 1979 *The Man-Eating Myth: Anthropology and Anthropophagy*. Oxford University Press, New York.

Argent, Gala 2013 Inked: Human-Horse Apprenticeship, Tattoos, and Time in the Pazyryk World. *Society & Animals* 21(2):178–193.

Aris, Christopher, Pia Nystrom, and Elizabeth Craig-Atkins 2018 A New Multivariate Method for Determining Sex of Immature Human Remains Using the Maxillary First Molar. *American Journal of Physical Anthropology* 167(3):672–683.

Arkush, Elizabeth, and Mark W. Allen (eds.) 2006 *The Archaeology of Warfare: Prehistories of Raiding and Conquest*. University Press of Florida, Gainesville, FL.

Armelagos, George J., David S. Carlson, and Dennis P. Van Gerven 1982 The Theoretical Foundations and Development of Skeletal Biology. In *A History of American Physical Anthropology 1930–1980*, edited by Frank Spencer, pp. 305–328. Academic Press, New York.

Armelagos, George J., and Dennis P. Van Gerven 2017 *Life and Death on the Nile: A Bioethnography of Three Ancient Nubian Communities*. University Press of Florida, Gainesville, FL.

Armentano, Núria, Mercè Subirana, Albert Isidro, Oscar Escala, and Assumpció Malgosa 2012 An Ovarian Teratoma of Late Roman Age. *International Journal of Paleopathology* 2(4):236–239.

Arora, Manish 2005 *The Spatial Distribution of Lead in Teeth as a Biomarker of Prenatal and Neonatal Lead Exposure*. Unpublished Ph.D. dissertation, University of Sydney, Australia.

Artioli, Gilberto, Ivana Angelini, Günther Kaufmann, Caterina Canovaro, Gregorio Dal Sasso, and Igor Maria Villa 2017 Long-Distance Connections in the Copper Age: New Evidence from the Alpine Iceman's Copper Axe. *PLoS One* 12(7):e0179263.

Askenasy, Hans 1994 *Cannibalism: From Sacrifice to Survival*. Prometheus Books, Amherst, NY.

Associated Press 2017 German World War I Submarine Found with 23 Bodies Inside. *News Story*, September 19.

Atalay, Sonya 2008 Multivocality and Indigenous Archaeologies. In *Evaluating Multiple Narratives: Beyond Nationalist, Colonialist, Imperialist Archaeologies*, edited by Junko Habu, Clare Fawcett, and John M. Matsunaga, pp. 29–44. Springer, New York.

Atalay, Sonya, Lee Rains Clauss, Randall H. McGuire, and John R. Welsh (eds.) 2014 *Transforming Archaeology: Activist Practices and Prospects*. Left Coast Press, Walnut Creek, CA.

Aufderheide, Arthur C. 2003 *The Scientific Study of Mummies*. Cambridge University Press, Cambridge.

———— 2011 Soft Tissue Taphonomy: A Paleopathology Perspective. *International Journal of Paleopathology* 1(2):75–80.

———— 2013 A Brief History of Soft Tissue Paleopathology. In *The Dead Tell Tales: Essays in Honor of Jane E. Buikstra*, edited by María Cecilia Lozada and Barra O'Donnabhain, pp. 131–135. Cotsen Institute of Archaeology Press, Monograph 76. University of California, Los Angeles.

Aufderheide, Arthur C., Iván Muñoz, and Bernardo Arriaza 1993 Seven Chinchorro Mummies and the Prehistory of Northern Chile. *American Journal of Physical Anthropology* 91(2):189–201.

Aufderheide, Arthur C., Wilmar Salo, Michael Madden, John Streitz, Jane E. Buikstra, Felipe Guhl, Bernardo Arriaza, Colleen Renier, Lorentz E. Wittmers, Jr., Gino Fornaciari, and Marvin Allison 2004 A 9,000-Year Record of Chagas' Disease. *Proceedings of the National Academy of Sciences* 101(7):2,034–2,039.

Baadsgaard, Aubrey 2011 Mortuary Dress as Material Culture: A Case Study from the Royal Cemetery of Ur. In *Breathing New Life into the Evidence of Death*, edited by Aubrey Baadsgaard, Lexis T. Boutin, and Jane E. Buikstra, pp. 179–200. School for Advanced Research Press, Santa Fe, NM.

Bahn, Paul 2012 *Written in Bones: How Human Remains Unlock the Secrets of the Dead* (2nd ed.). Firefly Books, Buffalo, NY.

Bahr, Frank R. 2015 The New Examinations on the Man in the Ice "Ötzi" with the "Missing Link" as an Identification for the Development of Acupuncture in Europe. *Acupuncture & Auriculomedicine* 41(2):10–14.

Baker, Brenda J., and Sabrina C. Agarwal 2017 Stronger Together: Advancing a Global Bioarchaeology. *Bioarchaeology International* 1(1–2):1–18.

Baker, Brenda J., and Katelyn L. Bolhofner 2014 Biological and Social Implications of a Medieval Burial from Cyprus for Understanding Leprosy in the Past. *International Journal of Paleopathology* 4:17–24.

Baker, Brenda J., Tosha L. Dupras, and Matthew W. Tocheri 2005 *The Osteology of Infants and Children*. Texas A&M University Press, College Station, TX.

Baker, Jack, and Osbjorn M. Pearson 2006 Statistical Methods for Bioarchaeology: Applications of Age-Adjustment and Logistic Regression to Comparisons of Skeletal Populations with Differing Age-Structures. *Journal of Archaeological Science* 33(2):218–226.

Baker, Lori 2016 Biomolecular Applications. In *Handbook of Forensic Anthropology and Archaeology* (2nd ed.), edited by Soren Blau and Douglas H. Ubelaker, pp. 416–429. Routledge, New York.

Balabanova, Svetla, Wolfgang Pirsig, Franz Parsche, and Erhard Schneider 1995 Cocaine, Xanthine Derivatives and Nicotine in Cranial Hair of a Pre-Columbian Mummy. In *Proceedings of the First World Congress on Mummy Studies*, vol. 2, pp. 465–470. Museo Arqueológico Y Etnográfico de Tenerife, Canary Islands.

Bamforth, Douglas, and Curtis Nepstad-Thornberry 2007 Reconsidering the Occupational History of the Crow Creek Site (39BF11). *Plains Anthropologist* 52(202):153–173.

Barber, Elizabeth Wayland 1999 *The Mummies of Ürümchi*. W. W. Norton, New York.

Barber, Paul T. 1990 Cremation. In *Essays on Germanic Religion*, edited by Edgar C. Polomé, pp. 379–388. Journal of Indo-European Studies Monograph No. 6. The Institute for the Study of Man, Washington, DC.

Barker, Andrew, Jonathan Dombrosky, Barney Venables, and Steve Wolverton 2018 Taphonomy and Negative Results: An Integrated Approach to Ceramic-Bound Protein Residue Analysis. *Journal of Archaeological Science* 94:32–43.

Barker, Caroline, Esma Alicehajic, and Javier Naranjo Santana 2017 Post-Mortem Differential Preservation and Its Utility in Interpreting Forensic and Archaeological Mass Burials. In *Taphonomy of Human Remains: Forensic Analysis of the Dead and the Depositional Environment*, edited by Eline M. J. Schotsmans, Nicholas Márquez-Grant, and Shari L. Forbes, pp. 251–276. Wiley-Blackwell, Oxford, UK.

Barker, David J. P. 2012 Developmental Origins of Chronic Disease. *Public Health* 126(3):185–189.

Barkworth, Peter R. 1993 The Organization of Xerxes' Army. *Iranica Antiqua* 27:149–167.

Barrett, Autumn R., and Michael L. Blakey 2011 Life Histories of Enslaved Africans in Colonial New York: A Bioarchaeological Study of the New York African Burial Ground. In *Social Bioarchaeology*, edited by Sabrina C. Agarwal and Bonnie A. Glencross, pp. 212–251. Wiley-Blackwell, Oxford, UK.

Barrowclough, David 2014 *Time to Slay Vampire Burials? The Archaeological and Historical Evidence for Vampires in Europe*. Red Dagger Press, Cambridge, UK.

Bartelink, Eric J. 2006 *Resource Intensification in Pre-Contact Central California: A Bioarchaeological Perspective on Diet and Health Patterns Among Hunter-Gatherers from the Lower Sacramento Valley and San Francisco Bay*. Unpublished Ph.D. dissertation, Texas A&M University, College Station, TX.

Bartelink, Eric J., Gregory E. Berg, Lesley A. Chesson, Brett J. Tipple, Melanie M. Beasley, Julia R. Prince-Buitenhuys, Heather MacInnes, Amy T. MacKinnon, and Krista E. Latham 2018 Applications of Stable Isotope Forensics for Geolocating Unidentified Human Remains from Past Conflict Situations and Large-Scale Humanitarian Efforts. In *New Perspectives in Forensic Human Skeletal Identification*, edited by Krista E. Latham, Eric J. Bartelink, and Michael Finnegan, pp. 175–184. Academic Press, London, UK.

Bartelink, Eric J., Nikki A. Willits, and Kristin L. Chelotti 2014 A Probable Case of Acromegaly from the Windmiller Culture of Prehistoric Central California. *International Journal of Paleopathology* 4:37–46.

Bass, William M. 1987 *Human Osteology: A Laboratory and Field Manual* (3rd ed.). Missouri Archaeological Society Special Publication No. 2, Springfield, MI.

Bathurst, Rhonda R. 2005 Archaeological Evidence of Intestinal Parasites from Coastal Shell Middens. *Journal of Archaeological Science* 32(1):115–123.

Baud, C.-A., and Christiane Kramar 1991 Soft Tissue Calcifications in Paleopathology. In *Human Paleopathology: Current Syntheses and Future Options*, edited by Donald J. Ortner and Arthur C. Aufderheide, pp. 87–89. Smithsonian Institution Press, Washington, DC.

Bauer-Clapp, Heidi J., and Ventura R. Pérez 2014 Violence in Life, Violence in Death, Resiliency Through Repatriation: Bioarchaeological Analysis and Heritage Value of Yaqui Skeletal Remains from Sonora, Mexico. In *Biological and Forensic Perspectives on Violence: How Violent Death Is Interpreted from Skeletal Remains*, edited by Debra L. Martin and Cheryl P. Anderson, pp. 171–191. Cambridge University Press, Cambridge, UK.

Baustian, Kathryn M., Ryan P. Harrod, Anna J. Osterholtz, and Debra L. Martin 2012 Battered and Abused: Analysis of Trauma at Grasshopper Pueblo (AD 1275–1400). *International Journal of Paleopathology* 2(2–3):102–111.

Baxter, Jane Eva 2008 The Archaeology of Childhood. *Annual Review of Anthropology* 37:159–175.

Beasley, Melanie M., Antoinette M. Martinez, Dwight D. Simons, and Eric J. Bartelin 2013 Paleodietary Analysis of a San Francisco Bay Area Shellmound: Stable Carbon and Nitrogen Isotope Analysis of Late Holocene Humans from the Ellis Landing Site (CA-CCO-295). *Journal of Archaeological Science* 40(4):2084–2094.

Beatrice, Jared S., and Angela Soler 2016 Skeletal Indicators of Stress: A Component of the Biocultural Profile of Undocumented Migrants in Southern Arizona. *Journal of Forensic Sciences* 61(5):1164–1172.

Beaumont, Julia, Janet Montgomery, Jo Buckberry, and Mandy Jay 2015 Infant Mortality and Isotopic Complexity: New Approaches to Stress, Maternal Health, and Weaning. *American Journal of Physical Anthropology* 157(3):441–457.

Beausang, Elisabeth 2000 Childbirth in Prehistory: An Introduction. *European Journal of Archaeology* 3(1):69–87.

Beck, Lane A. 2006 Kidder, Hooton, Pecos, and the Birth of Bioarchaeology. In *Bioarchaeology: The Contextual Analysis of Human Remains*, edited by Jane A. Buikstra and Lane A. Beck, pp. 83–94. Elsevier Academic Press, Burlington, MA.

Beckett, Ronald G. 2015 Application and Limitations of Endoscopy in Anthropological and Archaeological Research. *The Anatomical Record* 298(6):1125–1134.

Bell, Lynne S. 2012 Histotaphonomy. In *Bone Histology: An Anthropological Perspective*, edited by Christian Crowder and Sam Stout, pp. 241–252. CRC Press, Boca Raton, FL.

Bello, Silvia M., Aminte Thomann, Michel Signoli, Olivier Dutour, and Peter Andrews 2006 Age and Sex Bias in the Reconstruction of Past Population Structures. *American Journal of Physical Anthropology* 129(1):24–38.

Bello, Silvia M., Rosalind Wallduck, Vesna Dimitrijević, Ivana Živaljević, and Chris B. Stringer 2016 Cannibalism Versus Funerary Defleshing and Disarticulation After a Period of Decay: Comparisons of Bone Modifications from Four Prehistoric Sites. *American Journal of Physical Anthropology* 161(4):722–743.

Bellwood, Peter S. 2005 *First Farmers: The Origins of Agricultural Societies*. Wiley-Blackwell, Malden, MA.

Benfer, Robert A., John T. Typpo, Vicki B. Graf, and Edward E. Pickett 1978 Mineral Analysis of Ancient Peruvian Hair. *American Journal of Physical Anthropology* 48(3):277–282.

Benson, L. V., E. M. Hattori, H. E. Taylor, S. R. Poulson, and E. A. Jolie 2006 Isotope Sourcing of Prehistoric Willow and Tule Textiles Recovered from Western Great Basin Rock Shelters and Caves – Proof of Concept. *Journal of Archaeological Science* 33(11):1588–1599.

Bentley, R. Alexander 2006 Strontium Isotopes from the Earth to the Archaeological Skeleton: A Review. *Journal of Archaeological Method and Theory* 13(3):136–187.

Bereczki, Zsolt, Maria Teschler-Nicola, Antonia Marcsik, Nicholas J. Meinzer, and Joerg Baten 2019 Growth Disruption in Children: Linear Enamel Hypoplasia. In *The Backbone of Europe: Health, Diet, Work, and Violence Over Two Millennia*, edited by Richard H. Steckel, Clark Spencer Larsen, Charlotte A. Roberts, and Joerg Baten, pp. 175–197. Cambridge University Press, Cambridge, UK.

Berger, Elizabeth, Liping Yang, and Wa Ye 2019 Foot Binding in a Ming Dynasty Cemetery Near Xi'an, China. *International Journal of Paleopathology* 24:79–88.

Bernal, Valeria 2007 Size and Shape Analysis of Human Molars: Comparing Traditional and Geometric Morphometric Techniques. *Homo* 58(4):279–296.

Bernard, H., L. Shoemaker, O. E. Craig, M. Rider, R. E. Parr, M. Q. Sutton, and R. M. Yohe II 2007 Introduction to the Analysis of Protein Residues in Archaeological Ceramics. In *Theory and Practice of Archaeological Residue Analysis*, edited by Hans Barnard and Jelmer W. Eerkens, pp. 216–231. BAR International Series 1650. Archaeo Press, Oxford, UK.

Berthon, William, Balázs Tihanyi, Luca Kis, László Révész, Hélène Coqueugniot, Olivier Dutour, and György Pálfi 2019 Horse Riding and the Shape of the Acetabulum: Insights from the Bioarchaeological Analysis of Early Hungarian Mounted Archers (10th Century). *International Journal of Osteoarchaeology* 29(1):117–126.

Bethard, Jonathan D. 2012 Isotopes. In *Research Methods in Human Skeletal Biology*, edited by Elizabeth A. DiGangi and Megan K. Moore, pp. 425–447. Elsevier Academic Press, Waltham, MA.

Bettinger, Robert L. 1993 Doing Great Basin Archaeology Recently: Coping with Variability. *Journal of Archaeological Research* 1(1):43–66.

Billman, Brian R., Patricia M. Lambert, and Banks L. Leonard 2000 Cannibalism, Warfare, and Drought in the Mesa Verde Region During the Twelfth Century A.D. *American Antiquity* 65(1):145–178.

Binder, Michaela, Charlotte Roberts, Neal Spencer, Daniel Antoine, and Caroline Cartwright 2014 On the Antiquity of Cancer: Evidence for Metastatic Carcinoma in a Young Man from Ancient Nubia (c. 1200 BC). *PloS One* 9(3):e90924.

Bindera, M., J. Eitler, J. Deutschmann, S. Ladstätter, F. Glaser, and D. Fiedler 2016 Prosthetics in Antiquity – An Early Medieval Wearer of a Foot Prosthesis (6th Century AD) from Hemmaberg/Austria. *International Journal of Paleopathology* 12:29–40.

Binford, Lewis R. 1962 Archaeology as Anthropology. *American Antiquity* 28(2):217–225.

———— 1964 A Consideration of Archaeological Research Design. *American Antiquity* 29(4):425–441.

———— 1965 Archaeological Systematics and the Study of Cultural Process. *American Antiquity* 31(2): 203–210.

———— 1971 Mortuary Practices: Their Study and Their Potential. In *Approaches to the Social Dimensions of Mortuary Practices*, edited by James A. Brown, pp. 6–29. Society for American Archaeology, Washington, DC.

Black, Jill, Susan Kerr, Lourdes Henebry-DeLeon, and Joseph G. Lorenz 2011 Dental Calculus as an Alternative Source of Mitochondrial DNA for Analysis of Skeletal Remains. In *Proceedings of the Society for California Archaeology*, vol. 25, edited by Don Laylander, Martin D. Rosen, Sharon A. Waechter, Shelly Davis-King, and Sherri Andrews, pp. 1–7. Society for California Archaeology, Chico, CA.

Blackmore, Chelsea 2011 How to Queer the Past Without Sex: Queer Theory, Feminisms and the Archaeology of Identity. *Archaeologies: Journal of the World Archaeological Congress* 7(1):75–96.

Blakely, Robert L. (ed.) 1977a *Biocultural Adaptation in Prehistoric America*. Proceedings of the Southern Anthropological Society No. 11. University of Georgia Press, Athens, GA.

———— 1977b Introduction. In *Biocultural Adaptation in Prehistoric America*, edited by Robert L. Blakely, pp. 1–9. Proceedings of the Southern Anthropological Society No. 11. University of Georgia Press, Athens, GA.

Blau, Soren, and Douglas H. Ubelaker (eds.) 2016 *Handbook of Forensic Anthropology and Archaeology* (2nd ed.). Routledge, New York.

Blitz, John H. 1999 Mississippian Chiefdoms and the Fission-Fusion Process. *American Antiquity* 64(4):577–592.

Blumenbach, Johann Friedrich 1776 *On the Natural Varieties of Mankind: De generis humani varietate native* (reprinted 1969). Bergman, New York.

Boas, Franz 1912 *Changes in Bodily Form of Descendants of Immigrants*. Columbia University Press, New York.

Bocquet-Appel, Jean-Pierre, and Claude Masset 1982 Farewell to Paleodemography. *Journal of Human Evolution* 11(4):321–333.

———— 1996 Paleodemography: Expectancy and False Hope. *American Journal of Physical Anthropology* 99(4):571–583.

Bogaard, Amy, and Alan K. Outram 2013 Palaeodiet and Beyond: Stable Isotopes in Bioarchaeology. *World Archaeology* 45(3):333–337.

Boldsen, Jesper L. 2001 Epidemiological Approach to the Paleopathological Diagnosis of Leprosy. *American Journal of Physical Anthropology* 115(4):380–387.

Boldsen, Jesper L., George R. Milner, Lyle W. Konigsberg, and James W. Wood 2002 Transition Analysis: A New Method for Estimating Age from Skeletons. In *Paleodemography: Age Distributions from Skeletal Samples*, edited by Robert D. Hoppa and James W. Vaupel, pp. 73–106. Cambridge University Press, Cambridge.

Bolhofner, Katelyn L. 2017 Identity Marker or Medical Treatment? An Exploration of the Practice and Purpose of Dental Ablation in Ancient Nubia. In *A World View of Bioculturally Modified Teeth*, edited by Scott E. Burnett and Joel D. Irish, pp. 48–61. University Press of Florida, Gainesville, FL.

Bonilla, Marta Díaz-Zorita, Jess Beck, Hervé Bocherens, and Pedro Díaz-del-Río 2018 Isotopic Evidence for Mobility at Large-Scale Human Aggregations in Copper Age Iberia: The Mega-Site of Marroquíes. *Antiquity* 92(364):991–1007.

Bonn-Muller, E. 2009 Entombed in Style: The Lavish Afterlife of a Chinese Noblewoman. *Archaeology* 62(3):40–43.

Bonnichsen, Robson, Larry Hodges, Walter Ream, Katharine G. Field, Donna L. Kirner, Karen Selsor, and R. E. Taylor 2001 Methods for the Study of Ancient Hair: Radiocarbon Dates and Gene Sequences from Individual Hairs. *Journal of Archaeological Science* 28(7):775–785.

Booth, Thomas J., Andrew T. Chamberlain, and Mike Parker Pearson 2015 Mummification in Bronze Age Britain. *Antiquity* 89(347):1155–1173.

Bourke, J. B. 1986 The Medical Investigation of Lindow Man. In *Lindow Man: The Body in the Bog*, edited by I. M. Stead, J. B. Bourke, and Don R. Brothwell, pp. 46–51. Cornell University Press, Ithaca, NY.

Boutin, Alexis T. 2016 Exploring the Social Construction of Disability: An Application of the Bioarchaeology of Personhood Model to a Pathological Skeleton from Ancient Bahrain. *International Journal of Paleopathology* 12:17–28.

Boyd, C. Clifford, and Donna C. Boyd 2011 Theory and the Scientific Basis for Forensic Anthropology. *Journal of Forensic Sciences* 58(6):1407–1415.

——— (eds.) 2018a *Forensic Anthropology: Theoretical Framework and Scientific Basis*. John Wiley & Sons, New York.

——— 2018b The Theoretical and Scientific Foundations of Forensic Anthropology. In *Forensic Anthropology: Theoretical Framework and Scientific Basis*, edited by C. Clifford Boyd and Donna C. Boyd, pp. 1–18. John Wiley & Sons, New York.

——— 2018c Forensic Anthropology, Scientific Evidence, and the Law: Why Theory Matters. In *Forensic Anthropology: Theoretical Framework and Scientific Basis*, edited by C. Clifford Boyd and Donna C. Boyd, pp. 307–323. John Wiley & Sons, New York.

Brace, C. Loring 1982 The Roots of the Race Concept in American Physical Anthropology. In *A History of American Physical anthropology 1930–1980*, edited by Frank Spencer, pp. 11–29. Academic Press, New York.

Bradley, Bruce, and Dennis Stanford 2004 The North Atlantic Ice-Edge Corridor: A Possible Palaeolithic Route to the New World. *World Archaeology* 36(4):459–478.

Bramanti, Barbara 2013 The Use of DNA Analysis in the Archaeology of Death and Burial. In *The Archaeology of Death and Burial*, edited by Sarah Tarlow and Liv Nilsson Stutz, pp. 99–122. Oxford University Press, Oxford, UK.

Braverman, Irwin M., Donald B. Redford, and Philip A. Mackowiak 2009 Akhenaten and the Strange Physiques of Egypt's 18th Dynasty. *Annals of Internal Medicine* 150(8):556–560.

Bresciani, J., W. Dansgaard, B. Fredskild, M. Ghisler, P. Grandjean, J. C. Hansen, J. P. Hart Hansen, N. Haarløv, B. Lorentzen, P. Nansen, A. M. Rørdam, and H. Tauber 1991 Living Conditions. In *The Greenland Mummies*, edited by Jens Peder Hart Hansen, Jørgen Meldgaard, and Jørgen Nordqvist, pp. 150–167. Smithsonian Institution Press, Washington, DC.

Brickley, Megan B. 2005 Rib Fractures in the Archaeological Record: A Useful Source of Sociocultural Information? *International Journal of Osteoarchaeology* 16(1):61–85.

——— 2018 Cribra Orbitalia and Porotic Hyperostosis: A Biological Approach to Diagnosis. *American Journal of Physical Anthropology* 167(4):896–902.

Brickley, Megan B., and Jo Buckberry 2015 Picking Up the Pieces: Utilizing the Diagnostic Potential of Poorly Preserved Remains. *International Journal of Paleopathology* 8:51–54.

Brickley, Megan B., and Rachel Ives 2005 Skeletal Manifestations of Infantile Scurvy. *American Journal of Physical Anthropology* 129(2):163–172.

Brickley, Megan B., Simon Mays, and Rachel Ives 2005 Skeletal Manifestations of Vitamin D Deficiency Osteomalacia in Documented Historical Collections. *International Journal of Osteoarchaeology*
15(6):389–403.

———— 2006 An Investigation of Skeletal Indicators of Vitamin D Deficiency in Adults: Effective Markers for Interpreting Past Living Conditions and Pollution Levels in 18th and 19th Century Birming-
ham, England. *American Journal of Physical Anthropology* 132(1):67–79.

Bridges, Patricia S. 1990 Osteological Correlates of Weapons Use. In *A Life in Science: Papers in Honor of
J. Lawrence Angel*, edited by Jane E. Buikstra, pp. 87–98. Center for American Archeology, Scientific
Paper 6, Kampsville, IL.

Brier, Bob, Phuong Vinh, Michael Schuster, Howard Mayforth, and Emily Johnson Chapin 2015
A Radiologic Study of an Ancient Egyptian Mummy with a Prosthetic Toe. *The Anatomical Record*
298(6):1047–1058.

Brinker, Ute, Stefan Flohr, Jürgen Piek, and Jörg Orschiedt 2014 Human Remains from a Bronze
Age Site in the Tollense Valley: Victims of a Battle? In *The Routledge Handbook of the Bioarchaeology of
Human Conflict*, edited by Christopher Knüsel and Martin J. Smith, pp. 146–160. Routledge, New
York.

Britton, Kate, Benjamin T. Fuller, Thomas Tütken, Simon Mays, and Michael P. Richards 2015 Oxygen
Isotope Analysis of Human Bone Phosphate Evidences Weaning Age in Archaeological Populations.
American Journal of Physical Anthropology 157(2):226–241.

Broca, P. 1871 *Memoires d'anthropologie*. C. Reinwald, Paris.

———— 1875 Instructions craniologiques et craniometriques. *Memoires de la Societe d Anthropologie de
Paris, Series 2* 2:1–203.

Brothwell, Don R., T. Holden, D. Liversage, B. Gottlieb, P. Bennike, and J. Boesen 1990 Establishing a
Minimum Damage Procedure for the Gut Sampling of Intact Human Bodies: The Case of the Huldremose Woman. *Antiquity* 64(245):830–835.

Brown, James A. (ed.) 1971 *Approaches to the Social Dimensions of Mortuary Practices*. Society for American
Archaeology, Washington, DC.

———— 1995 On Mortuary Analysis – With Special Reference to the Saxe-Binford Research Program.
In *Regional Approaches to Mortuary Analysis*, edited by Lane A. Beck, pp. 3–26. Plenum Press, New
York.

Brown, Terry, and Keri Brown 2011 *Biomolecular Archaeology: An Introduction*. Wiley-Blackwell, Oxford, UK.

Brück, Joanna 2014 Cremation, Gender, and Concepts of the Self in the British Early Bronze Age. In
Transformation by Fire: The Archaeology of Cremation in Cultural Context, edited by Ian Kuijt, Colin P.
Quinn, and Gabriel Cooney, pp. 119–139. University of Arizona Press, Tucson.

Bryant, Vaughn M., and Karl J. Reinhard 2012 Coprolites and Archaeology: The Missing Links in
Understanding Human Health. In *Vertebrate Coprolites*, edited by Adrian P. Hunt, Jesper Milàn, Spen-
cer G. Lucas, and Justin Alan Spielmann, pp. 379–387. New Mexico Museum of Natural History and
Science, Bulletin 57, Albuquerque, NM.

Buckberry, Jo 2015 The (Mis)use of Adult Age Estimates in Osteology. *Annals of Human Biology*
42(4):321–329.

Bugaj, Urszula, Mario Novak, and Maciej Trzeciecki 2013 Skeletal Evidence of a Post-Mortem Examination from the 18th/19th Century Radom, Central Poland. *International Journal of Paleopathology*
3(4):310–314.

Buikstra, Jane E. 1977 Biocultural Dimensions of Archaeological Study: A Regional Perspective. In
Biocultural Adaptation in Prehistoric America, edited by Robert L. Blakely, pp. 67–84. Proceedings of the
Southern Anthropological Society No. 11. University of Georgia Press, Athens, GA.

———— 1997 Paleodemography: Context and Promise. In *Integrating Archaeological Demography: Multidisciplinary Approaches to Prehistoric Population*, edited by Richard R. Paine, pp. 367–380. Center for
Archaeological Investigations, Carbondale, IL.

———— 2006a Preface. In *Bioarchaeology: The Contextual Analysis of Human Remains*, edited by Jane A.
Buikstra and Lane A. Beck, pp. xvii–xx. Elsevier Academic Press, Burlington, MA.

——— 2006b A Historical Introduction. In *Bioarchaeology: The Contextual Analysis of Human Remains*, edited by Jane E. Buikstra and Lane A. Beck, pp. 7–25. Elsevier Academic Press, Burlington, MA.

——— 2006c Introduction: Emerging Specialties. In *Bioarchaeology: The Contextual Analysis of Human Remains*, edited by Jane E. Buikstra and Lane A. Beck, pp. 195–205. Elsevier Academic Press, Burlington, MA.

——— 2006d Repatriation and Bioarchaeology: Challenges and Opportunity. In *Bioarchaeology: The Contextual Analysis of Human Remains*, edited by Jane E. Buikstra and Lane A. Beck, pp. 389–415. Elsevier Academic Press, Burlington, MA.

——— (ed.) 2019 *Ortner's Identification of Pathological Conditions in Human Skeletal Remains*. Academic Press, London, UK.

Buikstra, Jane E., Aubrey Baadsgaard, and Alexis T. Boutin 2011 Introduction. In *Breathing New Life into the Evidence of Death: Contemporary Approaches to Bioarchaeology*, edited by Aubrey Baadsgaard, Alexis T. Boutin, and Jane E. Buikstra, pp. 3–26. School for Advanced Research Press, Santa Fe, NM.

Buikstra, Jane E., and Lane A. Beck (eds.) 2006 *Bioarchaeology: The Contextual Analysis of Human Remains*. Elsevier Academic Press, Burlington, MA.

Buikstra, Jane E., Andrew Poznanski, Maria Lozada Cerna, Paul Goldstein, and Lisa M. Hoshower 1990 A Case of Juvenile Rheumatoid Arthritis from Pre-Columbian Peru. In *A Life in Science: Papers in Honor of J. Lawrence Angel*, edited by Jane E. Buikstra, pp. 99–137. Center for American Archeology, Scientific Paper 6, Kampsville, IL.

Buikstra, Jane E., and Charlotte A. Roberts (eds.) 2012 *The Global History of Paleopathology: Pioneers and Prospects*. Oxford University Press, New York.

Buikstra, Jane E., and Douglas H. Ubelaker (eds.) 1994 *Standards for Data Collection from Human Skeletal Materials*. Arkansas Archaeological Survey Research Series No. 44, Fayetteville, AR.

Burnett, Scott E. 2016 Crown Wear: Identification and Categorization. In *A Companion to Dental Anthropology*, edited by Joel D. Irish and G. Richard Scott, pp. 415–432. John Wiley & Sons, New York.

Burnett, Scott E., and Joel D. Irish 2017 Introduction to a World View of Bioculturally Modified Teeth. In *A World View of Bioculturally Modified Teeth*, edited by Scott E. Burnett and Joel D. Irish, pp. 1–16. University Press of Florida, Gainesville, FL.

Burridge, Alwyn 1996 Did Akhenaten Suffer from Marfan's Syndrome? *The Biblical Archaeologist* 59(2):127–128.

Burt, Nicole M., Dyan Semple, Kathryn Waterhouse, and Nancy C. Lovell 2013 *Identification and Interpretation of Joint Disease in Paleopathology and Forensic Anthropology*. Charles C Thomas Publisher Ltd., Springfield, IL.

Burton, James, and M. Anne Katzenberg 2019 Strontium Isotopes and the Chemistry of Bones and Teeth. In *Biological Anthropology of the Human Skeleton* (3rd ed.), edited by M. Anne Katzenberg and Anne L. Grauer, pp. 505–514. Wiley-Blackwell, New York.

Buti, Laura, Giorgio Gruppioni, and Stefano Benazzi 2017 Facial Reconstruction of Famous Historical Figures: Between Science and Art. In *Studies in Forensic Biohistory*, edited by Christopher M. Stojanowski and William N. Duncan, pp. 191–212. Cambridge University Press, Cambridge, UK.

Buzon, Michele R. 2012 The Bioarchaeological Approach to Paleopathology. In *A Companion to Paleopathology*, edited by Anne L. Grauer, pp. 58–75. Wiley-Blackwell, Oxford, UK.

Byard, Roger W. 2016 Forensic and Historical Aspects of Crucifixion. *Forensic Science, Medicine, and Pathology* 12(2):206–208.

Byers, Steven N. 2017 *Introduction to Forensic Anthropology* (5th ed.). Routledge, New York.

Byers, Steven N., and Rebecca Saunders 2018 Biodistance Among Four Louisiana Archaeological Sites from the Woodland Period. In *Bioarchaeology of the American Southeast: Approaches to Bridging Health and Identity in the Past*, edited by Shannon Chappell Hodge and Kristrina A. Shuler, pp. 17–35. The University of Alabama Press, Tuscaloosa, AL.

Byrnes, Jennifer F., and Jennifer L. Muller (eds.) 2017a *Bioarchaeology of Impairment and Disability*. Springer, Switzerland.

———— 2017b Mind the Gap: Bridging Disability Studies and Bioarchaeology – An Introduction. In *Bioarchaeology of Impairment and Disability*, edited by Jennifer F. Byrnes and Jennifer L. Muller, pp. 1–15. Springer, Switzerland.

Cabo, Luis L., Dennis C. Dirkmaat, James M. Adovasio, and Vicente C. Rozas 2012 Archaeology, Mass Graves, and Resolving Commingling Issues Through Spatial Analysis. In *A Companion to Forensic Anthropology*, edited by Dennis C. Dirkmaat, pp. 175–196. John Wiley & Sons, New York.

Cameron, M. E., H. Lapham, and C. Shaw 2018 Examining the Influence of Hide Processing on Native American Upper Limb Morphology. *International Journal of Osteoarchaeology* 28(3):332–342.

Cannon, Aubrey, and Katherine Cook 2015 Infant Death and the Archaeology of Grief. *Cambridge Archaeological Journal* 25(2):399–416.

Cappellini, Enrico, Ana Prohaska, Fernando Racimo, Frido Welker, Mikkel Winther Pedersen, Morten E. Allentoft, Peter de Barros Damgaard, Petra Gutenbrunner, Julie Dunne, Simon Hammann, Mélanie Roffet-Salque, Melissa Ilardo, J. Víctor Moreno-Mayar, Yucheng Wang, Martin Sikora, Lasse Vinner, Jürgen Cox, Richard P. Evershed, and Eske Willerslev 2018 Ancient Biomolecules and Evolutionary Inference. *Annual Review of Biochemistry* 87:1029–1060.

Carbone, Victor, and Bennie C. Keel 1985 Preservation of Plant and Animal Remains. In *The Analysis of Prehistoric Diets*, edited by Robert I. Gilbert, Jr. and James H. Mielke, pp. 1–20. Academic Press, New York.

Carlson, David S., and Dennis P. Van Gerven 1979 Diffusion, Biological Determinism, and Biocultural Adaptation in the Nubian Corridor. *American Anthropologist* 81(3):561–580.

Carmichael, David, Jane Hubert, and Brian Reeves 1994 Introduction. In *Sacred Sites, Sacred Places*, edited by David Charmichael, Jane Hubert, Brian Reeves, and Audhild Schanche, pp. 1–8. Routledge, London.

Carr, Christopher 1995 Mortuary Practices: Their Social, Philosophical-Religious, Circumstantial, and Physical Determinants. *Journal of Archaeological Method and Theory* 2(2):105–200.

Carroll, Gina M. A., Sarah A. Inskip, and Andrea Waters-Rist 2018 Pathophysiological Stable Isotope Fractionation: Assessing the Impact of Anemia on Enamel Apatite δ18O and δ13C Values and Bone Collagen δ15N and δ13C Values. *Bioarchaeology International* 2(2):117–146.

Cassman, Vicki, Nancy Odegaard, and Joseph Powell (eds.) 2006 *Human Remains: Guide for Museums and Academic Institutions*. AltaMira Press, Walnut Creek, CA.

Castex, Dominique, and Frédérique Blaizot 2017 Reconstructing the Original Arrangement, Organization and Architecture of Burials in Archaeology. In *Taphonomy of Human Remains: Forensic Analysis of the Dead and the Depositional Environment*, edited by Eline M. J. Schotsmans, Nicholas Márquez-Grant, and Shari L. Forbes, pp. 277–295. Wiley-Blackwell, Oxford, UK.

Cattaneo, Cristina, and Annalisa Cappella 2017 Distinguishing Between Peri- and Post-Mortem Trauma in Bone. In *Taphonomy of Human Remains: Forensic Analysis of the Dead and the Depositional Environment*, edited by Eline M. J. Schotsmans, Nicholas Márquez-Grant, and Shari L. Forbes, pp. 352–368. Wiley-Blackwell, Oxford, UK.

Cattaneo, Cristina, K. Gelsthorpe, P. Phillips, and R. J. Sokol 1993 Blood Residues on Stone Tools: Indoor and Outdoor Experiments. *World Archaeology* 25(1):29–43.

Cavalli-Sforza, Luigi L. 2000 *Genes, Peoples, and Languages*. Farrar, Straus & Giroux, New York.

Ceruti, Maria Constanza 2015 Frozen Mummies from Andean Mountaintop Shrines: Bioarchaeology and Ethnohistory of Inca Human Sacrifice. *BioMed Research International* Article ID 439428, 12 pages.

Chacon, Richard J., and David H. Dye (eds.) 2007 *The Taking and Displaying of Human Body Parts as Trophies by Amerindians*. Springer, New York.

Chamberlain, Andrew T. 2006 *Demography in Archaeology*. Cambridge University Press, New York.

Chamberlin, Andrew T., and Michael Parker Pearson 2001 *Earthly Remains: The History and Science of Preserved Human Bodies*. Oxford University Press, New York.

Chapman, John 1997 Changing Gender Relations in the Later Prehistory of Eastern Hungary. In *Invisible People and Processes: Writing Gender and Childhood into European Archaeology*, edited by Jenny Moore and Eleanor Scott, pp. 131–149. Leicester University Press, London.

────── 2005 Mortuary Analysis: A Matter of Time? In *Interacting with the Dead: Perspectives on Mortuary Archaeology for the New Millennium*, edited by Gordon F. M. Rakita, Jane E. Buikstra, Lane A. Beck, and Sloan R. Williams, pp. 25–40. University Press of Florida, Gainesville, FL.

Charles, Douglas K., and Jane E. Buikstra 1983 Archaic Mortuary Sites in the Central Mississippi Drainage: Distribution, Structure, and Behavioral Implications. In *Archaic Hunters and Gatherers in the American Midwest*, edited by James L. Phillips and James A. Brown, pp. 117–145. Academic Press, New York.

Chenal, Fanny, Bertrand Perrin, Hélène Barrand-Emam, and Bruno Boulestin 2015 A Farewell to Arms: A Deposit of Human Limbs and Bodies at Bergheim, France, c. 4000 BC. *Antiquity* 89(348): 1313–1330.

Cheng, Tsung O. 2012 Coronary Arteriosclerotic Disease Existed in China Over 2,200 Years Ago. *Methodist Debakey Cardiovasc Journal* 8(2):47–48.

Chesson, Lesley A., Brett J. Tipple, James R. Ehleringer, Todd Park, and Eric J. Bartelink 2018 Forensic Applications of Isotope Landscapes ("Isoscapes"): A Tool for Predicting Region-of-Origin in Forensic Anthropology Cases. In *Forensic Anthropology: Theoretical Framework and Scientific Basis*, edited by C. Clifford Boyd and Donna C. Boyd, pp. 127–148. John Wiley & Sons, New York.

Child, Angela M., and A. Mark Pollard 1992 A Review of the Applications of Immunochemistry to Archaeological Bone. *Journal of Archaeological Science* 19(1):39–47.

Christensen, Angi M., and Bruce E. Anderson 2017 Methods of Personal Identification. In *Forensic Anthropology: A Comprehensive Introduction* (2nd ed.), edited by Natalie R. Langley and Maria Teresa A. Tersigni-Tarrant, pp. 313–333. CRC Press, Boca Raton, FL.

Cohen, Mark N., and George J. Armelagos (eds.) 1984 *Paleopathology at the Origins of Agriculture*. Academic Press, Cambridge, UK.

────── 2013 *Paleopathology at the Origins of Agriculture* (2nd ed.). University Press of Florida, Gainesville, FL.

Colwell, Chip 2017 *Plundered Skulls and Stolen Spirits: Inside the Fight to Reclaim Native American's Culture*. University of Chicago Press, Chicago.

Congram, Derek 2019 Four-Field Forensic Archaeology. In *Forensic Archaeology: Multidisciplinary Perspectives*, edited by Kimberlee Sue Moran and Claire L. Gold, pp. 21–31. Springer, Switzerland.

Conkey, Margaret W., and Joan M. Gero 1997 Programme to Practice: Gender and Feminism in Archaeology. *Annual Review of Anthropology* 26:411–437.

Conkey, Margaret W., and Janet D. Spector 1984 Archaeology and the Study of Gender. In *Advances in Archaeological Method*, vol. 7, edited by Michael J. Schiffer, pp. 1–38. Academic Press, New York.

Connolly, R. C. 1986 The Anatomical Description of Lindow Man. In *Lindow Man: The Body in the Bog*, edited by I. M. Stead, J. B. Bourke, and Don R. Brothwell, pp. 54–62. Cornell University Press, Ithaca, NY.

Connolly, R. C., R. P. Evershed, G. Embery, J. B. Stanbury, D. Green, P. Beahan, and J. B. Shortall 1986 The Chemical Composition of some Body Tissues. In *Lindow Man: The Body in the Bog*, edited by I. M. Stead, J. B. Bourke, and Don R. Brothwell, pp. 72–76. Cornell University Press, Ithaca, NY.

Connor, Melissa A. 2019 Professionalism in Forensic Archaeology: Transitioning from "Cowboy of Science" to "Officer of the Court." In *Forensic Archaeology: Multidisciplinary Perspectives*, edited by Kimberlee Sue Moran and Claire L. Gold, pp. 33–42. Springer, Switzerland.

Connor, Melissa A., and D. D. Scott 2001 Paradigms and Perpetrators. *Historical Archaeology* 35(1):1–6.

Cook, Della Collins 2006 The Old Physical Anthropology and the New World: A Look at the Accomplishments of an Antiquated Paradigm. In *Bioarchaeology: The Contextual Analysis of Human Remains*, edited by Jane A. Buikstra and Lane A. Beck, pp. 27–71. Elsevier Academic Press, Burlington, MA.

Cook, Della Collins, and Mary Lucas Powell 2006 The Evolution of American Paleopathology. In *Bioarchaeology: The Contextual Analysis of Human Remains*, edited by Jane A. Buikstra and Lane A. Beck, pp. 281–322. Elsevier Academic Press, Burlington, MA.

Cook, Noble David 1998 *Born to Die: Disease and New World Conquest, 1492–1650*. Cambridge University Press, Cambridge, MA.

Cox, Margaret, Ambika Flavel, Ian Hanson, Joanna Laver, and Roland Wessling (eds.) 2013 *The Scientific Investigation of Mass Graves: Towards Protocols and Standard Operating Procedures* (2nd ed.). Cambridge University Press, New York.

Cox, Samantha L. 2015 A Critical Look at Mummy CT Scanning. *The Anatomical Record* 298(6):1099–1110.

Crandall, John J., and Haagen D. Klaus 2014 Advancements, Challenges, and Prospects in the Paleopathology of Scurvy: Current Perspectives on Vitamin C Deficiency in Human Skeletal Remains. *International Journal of Paleopathology* 5:1–8.

Crossland, Zoë 2013 Evidential Regimes of Forensic Archaeology. *Annual Review of Anthropology* 42:121–137.

Crossland, Zoë, and Rosemary A. Joyce 2015 Anthropological Perspectives on Disturbing Bodies: An Introduction. In *Disturbing Bodies: Perspectives on Forensic Anthropology*, edited by Zoë Crossland and Rosemary A. Joyce, pp. 3–27. School for Advanced Research Press, Santa Fe, NM.

Crowder, Christian M., Janna M. Andronowski, and Victoria M. Dominguez 2018a Bone Histology as an Integrated Tool in the Process of Human Identification. In *New Perspectives in Forensic Human Skeletal Identification*, edited by Krista E. Latham, Eric J. Bartelink, and Michael Finnegan, pp. 201–213. Academic Press, London, UK.

Crowder, Christian M., Jarred T. Heinrich, and Victoria M. Dominguez 2016 Histological Age Estimation. In *Handbook of Forensic Anthropology and Archaeology* (2nd ed.), edited by Soren Blau and Douglas H. Ubelaker, pp. 293–307. Routledge, New York.

Crowder, Christian M., Deborrah C. Pinto, Janna M. Andronowski, and Victoria M. Dominguez 2018b Theory and Histological Methods. In *Forensic Anthropology: Theoretical Framework and Scientific Basis*, edited by C. Clifford Boyd and Donna C. Boyd, pp. 113–126. John Wiley & Sons, New York.

Crowder, Christian M., and Sam Stout (eds.) 2012 *Bone Histology: An Anthropological Perspective*. CRC Press, Boca Raton, FL.

Crubzy, Eric, Pascal Murail, Louis Girard, and Jean-Pierre Bernadou 1998 False Teeth of the Roman World. *Nature* 391(6662):29.

Cunningham, Craig, Louise Scheuer, and Sue Black 2016 *Developmental Juvenile Osteology*. Academic Press, Amsterdam, Netherlands.

Curry, Andrew 2016 Slaughter at the Bridge: Uncovering a Colossal Bronze Age Battle. *Science* 351(6280):1384–1389.

Danely, Jason 2018 Mourning as Mutuality. In *A Companion to the Anthropology of Death*, edited by Antonius C. G. M. Robben, pp. 131–143. John Wiley & Sons, New York.

Danforth, Marie Elaine 1999 Nutrition and Politics in Prehistory. *Annual Review of Anthropology* 28:1–25.

Danforth, Marie Elaine, and Stanley G. Knick 1994 The Human Remains from Carter Ranch Pueblo, Arizona: Health in Isolation. *American Antiquity* 59(1):88–101.

Darling, J. Andrew 1998 Mass Inhumation and the Execution of Witches in the American Southwest. *American Anthropologist* 100(3):732–752.

Davies, Douglas J., and Lewis H. Mates (eds.) 2005 *Encyclopedia of Cremation*. Ashgate, Aldershot.

Davies-Barrett, Anna M., Daniel Antoine, and Charlotte A. Roberts 2019 Inflammatory Periosteal Reaction on Ribs Associated with Lower Respiratory Tract Disease: A Method for Recording Prevalence from Sites with Differing Preservation. *American Journal of Physical Anthropology* 168(3):530–542.

Davis, Donald A. 1991 *The Jeffrey Dahmer Story: An American Nightmare*. St. Martin's Paperbacks, New York.

Dawson, Heidi, and Kate Robson Brown 2012 Childhood Tuberculosis: A Probable Case from Late Mediaeval Somerset, England. *International Journal of Paleopathology* 2(1):31–35.

Dawson-Hobbis, Heidi 2017 Interpreting Cultural and Biological Markers of Stress and Status in Medieval Subadults from England. In *Children, Death and Burial: Archaeological Discourses*, edited by Eileen Murphy and Mélie Le Roy, pp. 211–226. Oxbow Books, Oxford, UK.

Day, Michael 1990 Archaeological Ethics and the Treatment of the Dead. *Anthropology Today* 6(1):15–16.

Dean, Katharine R., Fabienne Krauer, Lars Walløe, Ole Christian Lingjærde, Barbara Bramanti, Nils Chr Stenseth, and Boris V. Schmid 2018 Human Ectoparasites and the Spread of Plague in Europe During the Second Pandemic. *Proceedings of the National Academy of Sciences* 115(6):1304–1309.

De Boer, H. H., A. E. Van der Merwe, and G. J. R. Maat 2013 The Diagnostic Value of Microscopy in Dry Bone Palaeopathology: A Review. *International Journal of Paleopathology* 3(2):113–121.

DeLeon, Valerie B. 2006 Fluctuating Asymmetry and Stress in a Medieval Nubian Population. *American Journal of Physical Anthropology* 132(4):520–534.

Delgado-Darias, T., J. Velasco-Vásquez, M. Arnay-de-la-Rosa, E. Martín-Rodríquez, and E. González-Reimers 2006 Calculus, Periodontal Disease and Tooth Decay Among the Prehispanic Population from Gran Canaria. *Journal of Archaeological Science* 33(5):663–670.

Deter-Wolf, Aaron, Benoît Robitaille, Lars Krutak, and Sébastien Galliot 2016 The World's Oldest Tattoos. *Journal of Archaeological Science: Reports* 5:19–24.

DeVisser, Elizabeth M., Krista E. Latham, and Marisol Intriago Leiva 2014 The Contribution of Forensic Anthropology to a National Identity in Chile: A Case Study from Patio 29. In *Biological and Forensic Perspectives on Violence: How Violent Death Is Interpreted from Skeletal Remains*, edited by Debra L. Martin and Cheryl P. Anderson, pp. 216–235. Cambridge University Press, Cambridge, UK.

Devlin, Joanne Bennett, and Nicholas P. Herrmann 2017 Advanced Scene Topics – Fire and Commingling. In *Forensic Anthropology: A Comprehensive Introduction* (2nd ed.), edited by Natalie R. Langley and MariaTeresa A. Tersigni-Tarrant, pp. 347–364. CRC Press, Boca Raton, FL.

DeWitte, Sharon N. 2014 The Anthropology of Plague: Insights from Bioarcheological Analyses of Epidemic Cemeteries. *The Medieval Globe* 1(1):97–123.

——— 2019 Misconceptions About the Bioarchaeology of Plague. In *Bioarchaeologists Speak Out: Deep Time Perspectives on Contemporary Issues*, edited by Jane E. Buikstra, pp. 109–131. Springer, Switzerland.

DeWitte, Sharon N., and Christopher M. Stojanowski 2016 The Osteological Paradox 20 Years Later: Past Perspectives, Future Directions. *Journal of Archaeological Research* 23(4):397–450.

Dickson, James H. 2011 *Ancient Ice Mummies*. The History Press, Stroud, UK.

Dickson, James H., Klaus Oeggl, and Linda L. Handley 2005 The Iceman Reconsidered. *Scientific American* 15(1):4–10.

DiGangi, Elizabeth A., and Joseph T. Hefner 2012 Ancestry Estimation. In *Research Methods in Human Skeletal Biology*, edited by Elizabeth A. DiGangi and Megan K. Moore, pp. 117–149. Elsevier Academic Press, Waltham, MA.

DiGangi, Elizabeth A., and Megan K. Moore 2012a Introduction to Skeletal Biology. In *Research Methods in Human Skeletal Biology*, edited by Elizabeth A. DiGangi and Megan K. Moore, pp. 3–28. Elsevier Academic Press, Waltham, MA.

——— (eds.) 2012b *Research Methods in Human Skeletal Biology*. Elsevier Academic Press, Waltham, MA.

Dillehay, Tom D. 1997 *Monte Verde A Late Pleistocene Settlement in Chile, vol. 2, the Archaeological Context and Interpretation*. Smithsonian Institution Press, Washington, DC.

Dirkmaat, Dennis C. (ed.) 2012 *A Companion to Forensic Anthropology*. John Wiley & Sons, New York.

Dirkmaat, Dennis C., Luis L. Cabo, Stephen D. Ousley, and Steven A. Symes 2008 New Perspectives in Forensic Anthropology. *Yearbook of Physical Anthropology* 51:33–52.

Dittmar, Katharina 2009 Old Parasites for a New World: The Future of Paleoparasitological Research: A Review. *Journal of Parasitology* 95(2):365–372.

Dittrick, Jean, and Judy Myers Suchey 1986 Sex Determination of Prehistoric Central California Skeletal Remains Using Discriminant Analysis of the Femur and Humerus. *American Journal of Physical Anthropology* 70(1):3–9.

Dixon, Kelly, Shannon Novak, Gwen Robbins, Julie Schablitsky, Richard Scott, and Guy Tasa 2010 Men, Women, and Children Are Starving: Archaeology of the Donner Family Camp. *American Antiquity* 75(3):627–656.

Djukic, Ksenija, Natasa Miladinovic-Radmilovic, Marko Draskovic, and Marija Djuric 2018 Morphological Appearance of Muscle Attachment Sites on Lower Limbs: Horse Riders Versus Agricultural Population. *International Journal of Osteoarchaeology* 28(6):656–668.

Dobney, Keith, and Anton Ervynck 2000 Interpreting Developmental Stress in Archaeological Pigs: The Chronology of Linear Enamel Hypoplasia. *Journal of Archaeological Science* 27(7):597–607.

Dong, Yu, Liugen Lin, Xiaoting Zhu, Fengshi Luan, and Anne P. Underhill 2019 Mortuary Ritual and Social Identities During the Late Dawenkou Period in China. *Antiquity* 93(368):378–392.

Dongoske, Kurt E., Debra L. Martin, and T. J. Ferguson 2000 Critique of the Claim of Cannibalism at Cowboy Wash. *American Antiquity* 65(1):179–190.

Donlon, Denise, and Judith Littleton 2011 Australia. In *The Routledge Handbook of Archaeological Human Remains and Legislation*, edited by Nicholas Márquez-Grant and Linda Fibiger, pp. 632–645. Routledge, London.

Donnan, Christopher B. 1976 *Moche Art and Iconography*. University of California, Latin American Center Publications, Los Angeles.

——— 1988 Unravelling the Mystery of the Warrior-Priest. *National Geographic* 174(4):550–555.

——— 1990 Masterworks of Art Reveal a Remarkable Pre-Inca World. *National Geographic* 177(6):16–33.

Donnan, Christopher B., and Luis Jaime Castillo 1992 Finding the Tomb of a Moche Priestess. *Archaeology* 45(6):38–42.

D'Ortenzio, Lori, Tracy Prowse, Michael Inskip, Bonnie Kahlon, and Megan Brickley 2018 Age Estimation in Older Adults: Use of Pulp/Tooth Ratios Calculated from Tooth Sections. *American Journal of Physical Anthropology* 165(3):594–603.

D'Ortenzio, Lori, Isabelle Ribot, Emeline Raguin, Annabelle Schattmann, Benoit Bertrand, Bonnie Kahlon, and Megan Brickley 2016 The Rachitic Tooth: A Histological Examination. *Journal of Archaeological Science* 74:152–163.

Dowson, Thomas A. 2000 Why Queer Archaeology? An Introduction. *World Archaeology* 32(2):161–165.

Drennan, Robert D., C. Adam Berrey, and Christian E. Peterson 2015 *Regional Settlement Demography in Archaeology*. Eliot Werner Publications, Clinton Corners, NY.

Drucker, Dorothée G., and Hervé Bocherens 2004 Carbon and Nitrogen Stable Isotopes as Tracers of Change in Diet Breadth During Middle and Upper Palaeolithic in Europe. *International Journal of Osteoarchaeology* 14(3–4):162–177.

Dudar, J. C., J. S. Waye, and Shelley R. Saunders 2003 Determination of a Kinship System Using Ancient DNA, Mortuary Practice, and Historic Records in an Upper Canadian Pioneer Cemetery. *International Journal of Osteoarchaeology* 13(4):232–246.

Dufour, Elise, Chris Holmden, Wim Van Neer, Antoine Zazzo, William P. Patterson, Patrick Degryse, and Eddy Keppens 2007 Oxygen and Strontium Isotopes and Provenance Indicators of Fish at Archaeological Sites: The Case Study of Salalassos, SW Turkey. *Journal of Archaeological Science* 34(8):1226–1239.

Duncan, William N. 2005 Understanding Veneration and Violation in the Archaeological Record. In *Interacting with the Dead: Perspectives on Mortuary Archaeology for the New Millennium*, edited by Gordon F. M. Rakita, Jane E. Buikstra, Lane A. Beck, and Sloan R. Williams, pp. 207–227. University Press of Florida, Gainesville, FL.

Duncan, William N., and Kevin R. Schwarz 2014 Partible, Permeable, and Relational Bodies in a Maya Mass Grave. In *Commingled and Disarticulated Human Remains: Working Toward Improved Theory, Method, and Data*, edited by Anna J. Osterholtz, Kathryn M. Baustian, and Debra L. Martin, pp. 149–170. Springer, New York.

Dupras, Tosha L., John J. Schultz, Sandra M. Wheeler, and Lana J Williams 2006 *Forensic Recovery of Human Remains*. CRC Press, Boca Raton, FL.

Duray, Stephen M. 1990 Deciduous Enamel Defects and Caries Susceptibility in a Prehistoric Ohio Population. *American Journal of Physical Anthropology* 81(1):27–34.

Dutour, Olivier 2013 Paleoparasitology and Paleopathology: Synergies for Reconstructing the Past of Human Infectious Diseases and Their Pathocenosis. *International Journal of Paleopathology* 3(3):145–149.

East, Anna Louise 2008 *Reproduction and Prenatal Care in Arizona Prehistory: An Examination of Patterns of Health in Perinates and Children at Grasshopper, Point of Pines, and Turkey Creek Pueblos*. Unpublished Ph.D. dissertation, Department of Anthropology, University of New Mexico Albuquerque, NM.

Edgar, Heather J. H., and Anna L. M. Rautman 2016 Forensic Odontology. In *A Companion to Dental Anthropology*, edited by Joel D. Irish and G. Richard Scott, pp. 339–361. John Wiley & Sons, New York.

Edson, Suni M., Kimberly A. Root, Irene L. Kahline, Colleen A. Dunn, Bruché E. Trotter, and Jennifer A. O'Rourke 2018 Flexibility in Testing Skeletonized Remains for DNA Analysis Can Lead to Increased Success: Suggestions and Case Studies. In *New Perspectives in Forensic Human Skeletal Identification*, edited by Krista E. Latham, Eric J. Bartelink, and Michael Finnegan, pp. 141–156. Academic Press, London, UK.

Eerkens, Jelmer W., Eric J. Bartelink, Laura Brink, Richard T. Fitzgerald, Ramona Garibay, Gina A. Jorgenson, and Randy S. Wiberg 2016a Trophy Heads or Ancestor Veneration? Stable Isotope Perspectives on Disassociated and Modified Crania in Precontact Central California. *American Antiquity* 81(1):114–131.

Eerkens, Jelmer W., Eric J. Bartelink, Alex DeGregory, and Ramona Garibay 2016b C and N Stable Isotopes in Human Dental Calculus at CA-CCO-297, A Late Phase II Period Site on San Francisco Bay. In *Reconstructing Lifeways in Ancient California: Stable Isotope Evidence of Foraging Behavior, Life History Strategies, and Kinship Patterns*, edited by Alexandra M. Greenwald and Gregory B. Burns, pp. 101–107. Center for Archaeological Research at Davis, Publication No. 18. Davis, CA.

Eerkens, Jelmer W., Oleksandr Kovalyov, and Alex DeGeorgey 2016c Reconstructing Individual Mobility Based on Isotopic Patterns in Serial Samples of Apatite from Enamel and Dentine in Central California. In *Reconstructing Lifeways in Ancient California: Stable Isotope Evidence of Foraging Behavior, Life History Strategies, and Kinship Patterns*, edited by Alexandra M. Greenwald and Gregory B. Burns, pp. 47–56. Center for Archaeological Research at Davis, Publication No. 18, Davis, CA.

Eerkens, Jelmer W., Ruth V. Nichols, Gemma G. R. Murray, Katherine Perez, Engel Murga, Phil Kaijankoski, Jeffrey S. Rosenthal, Laurel Engbring, and Beth Shapiro 2018 A Probable Prehistoric Case of Meningococcal Disease from San Francisco Bay: Next Generation Sequencing of *Neisseria meningitidis* from Dental Calculus and Osteological Evidence. *International Journal of Paleopathology* 22:173–180.

Effros, Bonnie 2006 Grave Goods and the Ritual Expression of Identity. In *From Roman Provinces to Medieval Kingdoms*, edited by Thomas F. X. Noble, pp. 189–232. Routledge, New York.

Efremov, Ivan 1940 Taphonomy: A New Branch of Paleontology. *Pan-American Geologist* 74(2):81–93.

Ekengren, Fredrik 2013 Contextualizing Grave Goods: Theoretical Perspectives and Mythological Implications. In *The Archaeology of Death and Burial*, edited by Sarah Tarlow and Liv Nilsson Stutz, pp. 173–192. Oxford University Press, Oxford, UK.

Ekroth, Gunnel 2014 Animal Sacrifice in Antiquity. In *The Oxford Handbook of Animals in Classical Thought and Life*, edited by Gordon Lindsay Campbell, pp. 324–354. Oxford University Press, Oxford, UK.

El-Najjar, Mahmoud Y., Dennis J. Ryan, Christy G. Turner II, and Betsy Lozoff 1976 The Etiology of Porotic Hyperostosis Among the Prehistoric and Historic Anasazi Indians of the Southwestern United States. *American Journal of Physical Anthropology* 44(3):477–488.

Eriksson, Gunilla 2013 Stable Isotope Analysis of Humans. In *The Archaeology of Death and Burial*, edited by Sarah Tarlow and Liv Nilsson Stutz, pp. 123–146. Oxford University Press, Oxford, UK.

Errickson, David, I. Grueso, S. J. Griffith, J. M. Setchell, T. J. U. Thompson, C. E. L. Thompson, and Rebecca L. Gowland 2017 Towards a Best Practice for the Use of Active Non-Contact Surface Scanning to Record Human Skeletal Remains from Archaeological Contexts. *International Journal of Osteoarchaeology* 27(4):650–661.

Eshed, Vered, Avi Gopher, and Israel Hershkovitz 2006 Tooth Wear and Dental Pathology at the Advent of Agriculture: New Evidence from the Levant. *American Journal of Physical Anthropology* 130(2):145–159.

Eshraghian, Ahad, and Bart Loeys 2012 Loeys-Dietz Syndrome: A Possible Solution for Akhenaten's and His Family's Mystery Syndrome. *South African Medical Journal* 102(8):661–664.

Estalrrich, Almudena, José Antonio Alarcón, and Antonio Rosas 2017 Evidence of Toothpick Groove Formation in Neandertal Anterior and Posterior Teeth. *American Journal of Physical Anthropology* 162(4):747–756.

Evans, R. Paul, David M. Whitchurch, and Kerry Muhlestein 2015 Rethinking Burial Dates at a Graeco-Roman Cemetery: Fag el-Gamous, Fayoum, Egypt. *Journal of Archaeological Science Reports* 2:209–214.

Evershed, Richard P. 1990 Lipids from Samples of Skin from Seven Dutch Bog Bodies: Preliminary Report. *Archaeometry* 32(2):139–153.

——— 1993 Biomolecular Archaeology and Lipids. *World Archaeology* 25(1):74–93.

——— 2008 Organic Residue Analysis in Archaeology: The Archaeological Biomarker Revolution. *Archaeometry* 50(6):895–924.

Evershed, Richard P., and Robert C. Connolly 1994 Post-Mortem Transformations of Sterols in Bog Body Tissues. *Journal of Archaeological Science* 21(5):577–583.

Eyerman, Ron 2019 The Worst Was the Silence: The Unfinished Drama of the Katyn Massacre. In *Memory, Trauma, and Identity*, edited by Ron Eyerman, pp. 111–142. Palgrave Macmillan, Cham, Switzerland.

Faerman, Marina, Gila Kahila Bar-Gal, Dvora Filon, Charles L. Greenblatt, Lawrence Stager, Ariella Oppenheim, and Patricia Smith 1998 Determining the Sex of Infanticide Victims from the Late Roman Era Through Ancient DNA Analysis. *Journal of Archaeological Science* 25(9):861–865.

Falkner, Frank, and J. M. Tanner 1986 *Human Growth: A Comprehensive Treatise*, vol. 3 (2nd ed.). Plenum Press, New York.

Fankhauser, Barry 1994 Protein and Lipid Analysis of Food Residues. In *Tropical Archaeobotany: Applications and New Developments*, edited by Jon G. Hather, pp. 227–250. Routledge, London.

Faria, Miguel A. 2015 Neolithic Trepanation Decoded – A Unifying Hypothesis: Has the Mystery as to Why Primitive Surgeons Performed Cranial Surgery Been Solved? *Surgical Neurology International* 6. doi:10.4103/2152-7806.156634.

Ferrándiz, Francisco, and Antonius C. G. M. Robben 2015 *Necropolitics: Mass Graves and Exhumations in the Age of Human Rights*. University of Pennsylvania Press, Philadelphia.

Fiedel, Stuart J. 2017 The Anzick Genome Proves Clovis Is First, After All. *Quaternary International* 44(B):4–9.

Figura, Benjamin J. 2018 Advances in Disaster Victim Identification. In *New Perspectives in Forensic Human Skeletal Identification*, edited by Krista E. Latham, Eric J. Bartelink, and Michael Finnegan, pp. 333–341. Academic Press, London, UK.

Fiorato, Veronica, Anthea Boylston, and Christopher Knüsel (eds.) 2007 *Blood Red Roses: The Archaeology of a Mass Grave from the Battle of Towton AD 1461* (2nd ed.). Oxbow Books, Oxford, UK.

Fiorenza, Luca, Stefano Benazzi, Gregorio Oxilia, and Ottmar Kullmer 2018 Functional Relationship Between Dental Macrowear and Diet in Late Pleistocene and Recent Modern Human Populations. *International Journal of Osteoarchaeology* 28(2):153–161.

Fisher, Deborah L., Mitchell M. Holland, Lloyd G. Mitchell, Paul S. Sledzik, Allison Webb Wilcox, Mark Wadhams, and Victor W. Weedn 1993 Extraction, Evaluation, and Amplification of DNA from Decalcified and Undecalcified United States Civil War Bone. *Journal of Forensic Sciences* 38(1):60–68.

Flaherty, T., and T. J. Haigh 1986 Blood Groups in Mummies. In *Science in Egyptology*, edited by A. R. David, pp. 379–382. Manchester University Press, Manchester, UK.

Flohr, Stefan, Ute Brinker, Elena Spanagel, Annemarie Schramm, Jörg Orschiedt, and Uwe Kierdorf 2014 Killed in Action? A Biometrical Analysis of Femora of Supposed Battle Victims from the Middle Bronze Age Site of Weltzin 20, Germany. In *Biological and Forensic Perspectives on Violence: How Violent Death Is Interpreted from Skeletal Remains*, edited by Debra L. Martin and Cheryl P. Anderson, pp. 17–33. Cambridge University Press, Cambridge, UK.

Flohr, Stefan, and M. Schultz 2009 Osseous Changes Due to Mastoiditis in Human Skeletal Remains. *International Journal of Osteoarchaeology* 19(1):99–106.

Formicola, Vincenzo, and Marcello Franceschi 1996 Regression Equations for Estimating Stature from Long Bones of Early Holocene European Samples. *American Journal of Physical Anthropology* 100(1):83–88.

Fowler, Chris 2013 Identities in Transformation: Identities, Funerary Rites, and the Mortuary Process. In *The Archaeology of Death and Burial*, edited by Sarah Tarlow and Liv Nilsson Stutz, pp. 511–526. Oxford University Press, Oxford, UK.

France, Diane L. 2017 *Comparative Bone Identification: Human Subadult to Nonhuman*. CRC Press, Boca Raton, FL.

Frayer, David W., William A. Horton, Roberto Macchiarelli, and Margherita Mussi 1987 Dwarfism in an Adolescent from the Italian Late Upper Palaeolithic. *Nature* 330(6143):60–62.

Friedman, Renée, Daniel Antoine, Sahra Talamo, Paula J. Reimer, John H. Taylor, Barbara Wills, and Marcello A. Mannino 2018 Natural Mummies from Predynastic Egypt Reveal the World's Earliest Figural Tattoos. *Journal of Archaeological Science* 92:116–125.

Fritsch, Klaus O., Heshem Hamoud, Adel H. Allam, Alexander Grossmann, Abdel-Halim Nur El-Din, Gomaa Abdel-Maksoud, Muhammad Al-Tohamy Soliman, Ibrahim Badr, James D. Sutherland, M. Linda Sutherland, Mahmoud Akl, Caleb E Finch, Gregory S. Thomas, L. Samuel Wann, and Randall C. Thompson 2015 The Orthopedic Diseases of Ancient Egypt. *The Anatomical Record* 298(6):1036–1046.

Froehle, Andrew W., Corina M. Kellner, and Margaret J. Schoeninger 2012 Multivariate Carbon and Nitrogen Stable Isotope Model for the Reconstruction of Prehistoric Human Diet. *American Journal of Physical Anthropology* 147(3):352–369.

Fully, Georges 1956 Une Nouvelle Methode de Determination de la Taille. *Annales de Médicine Légale et de Criminologie* 36:266–273.

Galloway, Alison, and Vicki L. Wedel 2014 Bones of the Skull, the Dentition, and Osseous Structures of the Throat. In *Broken Bones: Anthropological Analysis of Blunt Force Trauma*, edited by Vicki L. Wedel and Alison Galloway, pp. 133–160. Charles C Thomas Publisher Ltd., Springfield, IL.

Galloway, Alison, Lauren Zephro, and Vicki L. Wedel 2014 Classification of Fractures. In *Broken Bones: Anthropological Analysis of Blunt Force Trauma*, edited by Vicki L. Wedel and Alison Galloway, pp. 59–72. Charles C Thomas Publisher Ltd., Springfield, IL.

Gardeła, Leszek, and Kamil Kajkowski 2013 Vampires, Criminals or Slaves? Reinterpreting "Deviant Burials" in Early Medieval Poland. *World Archaeology* 45(5):780–796.

Garland, Carey J., Laurie J. Reitsem, Clark Spencer Larsen, and David Hurst Thomas 2018 Early Life Stress at Mission Santa Catalina de Guale: An Integrative Analysis of Enamel Defects and Dentin Incremental Isotope Variation in Malnutrition. *Bioarchaeology International* 2(2):75–94.

Garvin, Heather M. 2012 Adult Sex Determination: Methods and Application. In *A Companion to Forensic Anthropology*, edited by Dennis C. Dirkmaat, pp. 239–247. John Wiley & Sons, New York.

Geller, Pamela L. 2011 Getting a Head Start in Life: Pre-Columbian Maya Cranial Modification from Infancy to Ancestorhood. In *The Bioarchaeology of the Human Head: Decapitation, Decoration, and Deformation*, edited by Michelle Bonogofsky, pp. 241–261. University Press of Florida, Gainesville, FL.

———— 2017a *The Bioarchaeology of Socio-Sexual Lives: Queering Common Sense About Sex, Gender, and Sexuality*. Springer, Switzerland.

———— 2017b Brave Old World: Ancient DNA Testing and Sex Determination. In *Exploring Sex and Gender in Bioarchaeology*, edited by Sabrina C. Agarwal and Julie K. Wesp, pp. 71–98. University of New Mexico Press, Albuquerque, NM.

———— 2019 The Fallacy of the Transgender Skeleton. In *Bioarchaeologists Speak Out: Deep Time Perspectives on Contemporary Issues*, edited by Jane E. Buikstra, pp. 231–242. Springer, Switzerland.

Gheggi, M. S., V. I. Williams, and M. B. Cremonte 2018 The Impact of the Inca Empire in Northwest Argentina: Assessment of Health Status and Food Consumption at Esquina de Huajra (Quebrada de Humahuaca, Argentina). *International Journal of Osteoarchaeology* 28(3):274–284.

Gilbert, M. Thomas P., Dennis L. Jenkins, Anders Gotherstrom, Nuria Naveran, Juan J. Sanchez, Michael Hofreiter, Philip Francis Thomsen, Joan Binladen, Thomas F. G. Higham, Robert M. Yohe II, Robert E. Parr, Linda Scott Cummings, and Eske Willerslev 2008 DNA from Pre-Clovis Human Coprolites in Oregon, North America. *Science* 320(5877):786–789.

Gilchrist, Roberta 2008 Magic for the Dead? The Archaeology of Magic in Later Medieval Burials. *Medieval Archaeology* 52(1):119–159.

Giles, Melanie 2013 Preserving the Body. In *The Archaeology of Death and Burial*, edited by Sarah Tarlow and Liv Nilsson Stutz, pp. 475–496. Oxford University Press, Oxford, UK.

Gill, George W., and Douglas W. Owsley 1985 Electron Microscopy of Parasite Remains on the Pitchfork Mummy and Possible Social Implications. *Plains Anthropologist* 30(107):45–50.

Giuffra, Valentina, Antonio Fornaciari, Simona Minozzi, Angelica Vitiello, and Gino Fornaciari 2016 Autoptic Practices in 16th–18th Century Florence: Skeletal Evidences from the Medici Family. *International Journal of Paleopathology* 15:21–30.

Gocha, Timothy P., Alexander G. Robling, and Sam D. Stout 2019 Histomorphometry of Human Cortical Bone: Applications to Age Estimation. In *Biological Anthropology of the Human Skeleton* (3rd ed.), edited by M. Anne Katzenberg and Anne L. Grauer, pp. 145–187. Wiley-Blackwell, New York.

Goepfert, Nicolas, Elise Dufour, Gabriel Prieto, and John Verano 2018 Herds for the Gods? Selection Criteria and Herd Management at the Mass Sacrifice Site of Huanchaquito-Las Llamas During the Chimú Period, Northern Coast of Peru. *Environmental Archaeology*, published online December.

Goldstein, Lynne G. 1980 *Mississippian Mortuary Practices: A Case Study of Two Cemeteries in the Lower Illinois Valley*. Northwestern University Archaeological Program, Evanston, IL.

———— 2013 Negotiating the Gateway: Working with Multiple Lines of Evidence to Determine Identity. In *The Dead Tell Tales: Essays in Honor of Jane E. Buikstra*, edited by María Cecilia Lozada and Barra O'Donnabhain, pp. 32–42. Cotsen Institute of Archaeology Press, Monograph 76. University of California, Los Angeles.

Gonçalves, David, Eugénia Cunha, and Tim JU Thompson 2013 Weight References for Burned Human Skeletal Remains from Portuguese Samples. *Journal of Forensic Sciences* 58(5):1134–1140.

Goodman, Alan H., Debra L. Martin, and George J. Armelagos 1984 Indicators of Stress from Bones and Teeth. In *Paleopathology at the Origins of Agriculture*, edited by Mark Nathan Cohen and George J. Armelagos, pp. 13–49. Academic Press, New York.

Goodman, Alan H., and Rhan-Ju Song 1999 Sources of Variation in Estimated Ages at Formation of Linear Enamel Hypoplasias. In *Human Growth in the Past: Studies from Bones and Teeth*, edited by Robert D. Hoppa and Charles M. Fitzgerald, pp. 210–240. Cambridge University Press, New York.

Goodwin, George. 2012 *Fatal Colours: Towton 1461-England's Most Brutal Battle*. W. W. Norton & Company, New York.

Goodwin, Sara, John D. McPherson, and W. Richard McCombie 2016 Coming of Age: Ten Years of Next-Generation Sequencing Technologies. *Nature Reviews Genetics* 17:333–351.

Gosman, James H. 2012 Growth and Development: Morphology, Mechanisms, and Abnormalities. In *Bone Histology: An Anthropological Perspective*, edited by Christian Crowder and Sam Stout, pp. 23–44. CRC Press, Boca Raton, FL.

Gould, Stephen Jay 1981 *The Mismeasure of Man*. W.W. Norton & Co., New York.

Gowland, Rebecca L. 2015 Entangled Lives: Implications of the Developmental Origins of Health and Disease Hypothesis for Bioarchaeology and the Life Course. *American Journal of Physical Anthropology* 158(4):530–540.

———— 2017 Growing Old: Biographies of Disability and Care in Later Life. In *New Developments in the Bioarchaeology of Care*, edited by Lorna Tilley and Alecia A. Schrenk, pp. 237–251. Springer, Switzerland.

Graham, Deborah D., and Jonathan D. Bethard 2019 Reconstructing the Origins of the Perrins Ledge Cremains Using Strontium Isotope Analysis. *Journal of Archaeological Science: Reports* 24:350–362.

Gramsch, Alexander 2013 Treating Bodies: Transformation and Communicative Practices. In *The Archaeology of Death and Burial*, edited by Sarah Tarlow and Liv Nilsson Stutz, pp. 459–474. Oxford University Press, Oxford, UK.

Grauer, Anne L. 2018 A Century of Paleopathology. *American Journal of Physical Anthropology* 165(4):904–914.

Greenwald, Alexandra M., Alex DeGeorgey, Marcos C. Martinez, Jelmer W. Eerkens, Eric C. Bartelink, Dwight Simons, Christina Alonzo, and Ramona Garibay 2016 Maternal Time Allocation and Parental Investment in an Intensive Hunter-Gatherer Subsistence Economy. In *Reconstructing Lifeways in Ancient California: Stable Isotope Evidence of Foraging Behavior, Life History Strategies, and Kinship Patterns*, edited by Alexandra M. Greenwald and Gregory B. Burns, pp. 11–22. Center for Archaeological Research at Davis, Publication No. 18, Davis, CA.

Gregoricka, Lesley A., Amy B. Scott, Tracy K. Betsinger, and Marek Polcyn 2017 Deviant Burials and Social Identity in a Postmedieval Polish Cemetery: An Analysis of Stable Oxygen and Carbon Isotopes from the "Vampires" of Drawsko. *American Journal of Physical Anthropology* 163:741–758.

Gresky, Julia, Elena Batieva, Alexandra Kitova, Alexey Kalmykov, Andrey Belinskiy, Sabine Reinhold, and Natalia Berezina 2016 New Cases of Trepanations from the 5th to 3rd Millennia BC in Southern Russia in the Context of Previous Research: Possible Evidence for a Ritually Motivated Tradition of Cranial Surgery? *American Journal of Physical Anthropology* 160(4):665–682.

Griggs, C. Wilfred (ed.) 1988 *Excavations at Seila, Egypt*. Religious Studies Center, Brigham Young University Press, Provo, UT.

Grivas, Christopher R., and Debra A. Komar 2008 Kumho, Daubert, and the Nature of Scientific Inquiry: Implications for Forensic Anthropology. *Journal of Forensic Science* 53(4):771–776.

Groen, W. J. Mike, Nicholas Márquez-Grant, and Robert C. Janaway (eds.) 2015 *Forensic Archaeology: A Global Perspective*. Wiley-Blackwell, Oxford, UK.

Grupe, Gisela, and Klaus Dörner 1989 Trace Elements in Excavated Human Hair. *Zeitschrift für Morphologie und Anthropologie* 77(3):297–308.

Guillén, Sonia E. 2005 Mummies, Cults, and Ancestors: The Chinchorro Mummies of the South Central Andes. In *Interacting with the Dead: Perspectives on Mortuary Archaeology for the New Millennium*, edited by Gordon F. M. Rakita, Jane E. Buikstra, Lane A. Beck, and Sloan R. Williams, pp. 142–149. University Press of Florida, Gainesville, FL.

Gülaçar, Fazil O., Alberto Susini, and Max Klohn 1990 Preservation and Post-Mortem Transformations of Lipids in Samples from a 4000-Year-Old Nubian Mummy. *Journal of Archaeological Science* 17(6):691–705.

Guo, Y., Y. Fan, Y. Hu, J. Zhu, and Michael P. Richards 2018 Diet Transition or Human Migration in the Chinese Neolithic? Dietary and Migration Evidence from the Stable Isotope Analysis of Humans and Animals from the Qinglongquan Site, China. *International Journal of Osteoarchaeology* 28(2):85–94.

Guyomarc'h, Pierre, and Derek Congram 2017 Mass Fatalities, Mass Graves, and the Forensic Investigation of International Crimes. In *Forensic Anthropology: A Comprehensive Introduction* (2nd ed.), edited by Natalie R. Langley and MariaTeresa A. Tersigni-Tarrant, pp. 335–345. CRC Press, Boca Raton, FL.

Haglund, William D. 2002 Recent Mass Graves: An Introduction. In *Advances in Forensic Taphonomy: Method, Theory and Archaeological Perspectives*, edited by William D. Haglund and Marcella H. Sorg, pp. 243–262. CRC Press, Boca Raton, FL.

Halcrow, Siân E., and Nancy Tayles 2011 The Bioarchaeological Investigation of Children and Childhood. In *Social Bioarchaeology*, edited by Sabrina C. Agarwal and Bonnie A. Glencross, pp. 333–360. Wiley-Blackwell, Oxford, UK.

Halcrow, Siân E., Nancy Tayles, Raelene Inglis, and Charles Higham 2012 Newborn Twins from Prehistoric Mainland Southeast Asia: Birth, Death and Personhood. *Antiquity* 86(333):838–852.

Hallam, Elizabeth, and Jenny Hockey 2001 *Death, Memory & Material Culture*. Berg Publishers, Oxford, UK.

Halperin, Edward C. 2004 Paleo-Oncology: The Role of Ancient Remains in the Study of Cancer. *Perspectives in Biology and Medicine* 47(1):1–14.

Halporn, Roberta 2002 F.A.Q. – A Question Wrapped in a Conundrum: Why Do Jews Put Pebbles on Gravestones? *Association for Gravestone Studies Quarterly* 26(1):4–5, 27.

Ham, Allison C. 2018 *Differential Survival and Systemic Stress in the Ancestral Pueblo Southwest: A Paleoepidemiological Study of Pueblo Bonito and Hawikku*. Master's thesis, George Mason University, Fairfax, VA.

Hamlin, Christine 2001 Sharing the Load: Gender and Task Division at the Windover Site. In *Gender and the Archaeology of Death*, edited by Bettina Arnold and Nancy L. Wicker, pp. 119–135. AltaMira Press, Walnut Creek, CA.

Hammerl, Emily 2012 Dental Anthropology. In *Research Methods in Human Skeletal Biology*, edited by Elizabeth A. DiGangi and Megan K. Moore, pp. 263–291. Elsevier Academic Press, Waltham, MA.

Hansen, Henrik B., Peter B. Damgaard, Ashot Margaryan, Jesper Stenderup, Niels Lynnerup, Eske Willerslev, and Morten E. Allentoft 2017 Comparing Ancient DNA Preservation in Petrous Bone and Tooth Cementum. *PloS One* 12(1):e0170940.

Hansen, Jens Peder Hart, Jørgen Meldgaard, and Jørgen Nordqvist (eds.) 1991 *The Greenland Mummies.* Smithsonian Institution Press, Washington, DC.

Hansen, Joyce, and Gary McGowan 1998 *Breaking Ground, Breaking Silence: The Story of New York's African Burial Ground.* Holt, New York.

Hardesty, Donald L. 1997 *The Archaeology of the Donner Party.* University of Nevada Press, Reno, NV.

Hargrave, Eve A., Shirley J. Schermer, Kristin M. Hedman, and Robin M. Little (eds.) 2015 *Transforming the Dead: Culturally Modified Bone in the Prehistoric Midwest.* The University of Alabama Press, Tuscaloosa, AL.

Harner, Michael 1977 The Ecological Basis for Aztec Sacrifice. *American Ethnologist* 4(1):117–135.

Harper, Kristin N., Paolo S. Ocampo, Bret M. Steiner, Robert W. George, Michael S. Silverman, Shelly Bolotin, Allan Pillay, Nigel J. Saunders, and George J. Armelagos 2008 On the Origin of the Treponematoses: A Phylogenetic Approach. *Public Library of Science, Neglected Tropical Diseases*, published online January 15.

Harold, Laura B., Jelmer W. Eerkens, and Candice Ralston 2016 Patrilocal Post-Marital Residence and Bride Service in the Early Period: Strontium Isotope Evidence from CA-SJO-112. In *Reconstructing Lifeways in Ancient California: Stable Isotope Evidence of Foraging Behavior, Life History Strategies, and Kinship Patterns*, edited by Alexandra M. Greenwald and Gregory B. Burns, pp. 33–44. Center for Archaeological Research at Davis, Publication No. 18, Davis, CA.

Harrington, Spencer P. M. 1993 Bones and Bureaucrats: New York's Great Cemetery Imbroglio. *Archaeology* 46(2):28–38.

Harris, Oliver J. T., Hannah Cobb, Colleen E. Batey, Janet Montgomery, Julia Beaumont, Héléna Gray, Paul Murtagh, and Phil Richardson 2017 Assembling Places and Persons: A Tenth-Century Viking Boat Burial from Swordle Bay on the Ardnamurchan Peninsula, Western Scotland. *Antiquity* 91(355):191–206.

Harrod, Ryan P. 2017 *The Bioarchaeology of Social Control: Assessing Conflict and Cooperation in Pre-Contact Puebloan Society.* Springer, Switzerland.

Harrod, Ryan P., and Debra L. Martin 2014a *Bioarchaeology of Climate Change and Violence: Ethical Considerations.* Springer, New York.

——— 2014b Signatures of Captivity and Subordination on Skeletonized Human Remains: A Bioarchaeological Case Study from the Ancient Southwest. In *Biological and Forensic Perspectives on Violence: How Violent Death Is Interpreted from Skeletal Remains*, edited by Debra L. Martin and Cheryl P. Anderson, pp. 103–119. Cambridge University Press, Cambridge, UK.

Hauswirth, William H., Cynthia D. Dickel, Glen H. Doran, Philip J. Laipis, and David N. Dickel 1991 8000-Year-Old Brain Tissue from the Windover Site: Anatomical, Cellular, and Molecular Analysis. In *Human Paleopathology: Current Syntheses and Future Options*, edited by Donald J. Ortner and Arthur C. Aufderheide, pp. 60–72. Smithsonian Institution Press, Washington, DC.

Hauswirth, William H., Cynthia D. Dickel, and David A. Lawlor 1994 DNA Analysis of the Windover Population. In *Ancient DNA: Recovery and Analysis of Genetic Material from Paleontological, Archaeological, Museum, Medical, and Forensic Specimens*, edited by Bernd Herrmann and Susanne Hummel, pp. 104–121. Springer-Verlag, Berlin.

Headland, Thomas, and Lawrence A. Reid 1989 Hunter-Gatherers and Their Neighbors from Prehistory to the Present. *Current Anthropology* 30(1):43–66.

Heaton, Tim H. E., John C. Vogel, Gertrud von la Chevallarie, and Gill Collett 1986 Climatic Influence on the Isotopic Composition of Bone Nitrogen. *Nature* 322:822–823.

Hedenstierna-Jonson, Charlotte, Anna Kjellström, Torun Zachrisson, Maja Krzewińska, Veronica Sobrado, Neil Price, Torsten Günther, Mattias Jakobsson, Anders Götherström, and Jan Storå 2017 A Female Viking Warrior Confirmed by Genomics. *American Journal of Physical Anthropology* 164(4):853–860.

Hegmon, Michelle 2003 Setting Theoretical Egos Aside: Issues and Theory in North American Archaeology. *American Antiquity* 68(2):213–243.

Heilen, Michael P. (ed.) 2012 *Uncovering Identity in Mortuary Analysis: Community-Sensitive Methods for Identifying Group Affiliation in Historical Cemeteries*. Left Coast Press, Walnut Creek, CA.

Hemphill, Brian E. 1999 Wear and Tear: Osteoarthritis as an Indicator of Mobility Among Great Basin Hunter-Gatherers. In *Prehistoric Lifeways in the Great Basin Wetlands: Bioarchaeological Reconstruction and Interpretation*, edited by Brian E. Hemphill and Clark Spencer Larsen, pp. 241–289. University of Utah Press, Salt Lake City, UT.

———— 2016 Assessing Odontometric Variation among Populations. In *A Companion to Dental Anthropology*, edited by Joel D. Irish and G. Richard Scott, pp. 311–336. John Wiley & Sons, New York.

Hemphill, Brian E., and Clark Spencer Larsen (eds.) 1999 *Prehistoric Lifeways in the Great Basin Wetlands: Bioarchaeological Reconstruction and Interpretation*. University of Utah Press, Salt Lake City, UT.

Hemphill, Brian E., and James P. Mallory 2004 Horse-Mounted Invaders from the Russo-Kazakh Steppe or Agricultural Colonists from Western Central Asia? A Craniometric Investigation of the Bronze Age Settlement of Xinjiang. *American Journal of Physical Anthropology* 124(3):199–222.

Henderson, Charlotte Yvette, Valentina Mariotti, F. Santos, Sébastien Villotte, and Cynthia A. Wilczak 2017 The New Coimbra Method for Recording Entheseal Changes and the Effect of Age-at-Death. *Bulletins et mémoires de la Société d'anthropologie de Paris* 29(3–4):140–149.

Henderson, Charlotte Yvette, and Efthymia Nikita 2016 Accounting for Multiple Effects and the Problem of Small Sample Sizes in Osteology: A Case Study Focusing on Entheseal Changes. *Archaeological and Anthropological Sciences* 8(4):805–817.

Henderson, Julian, John A. Evans, Hilary J. Sloane, Melanie J. Leng, and Chris Doherty 2005 The Use of Oxygen, Strontium and Lead Isotopes to Provenance Ancient Glasses in the Middle East. *Journal of Archaeological Science* 32(5):665–673.

Henneberg, Maciej 2016 The Expert Witness and the Court of Law. In *Handbook of Forensic Anthropology and Archaeology* (2nd ed.), edited by Soren Blau and Douglas H. Ubelaker, pp. 635–641. Routledge, New York.

Hershkovitz, I., and G. Edelson 1991 The First Identified Case of Thalassemia? *Human Evolution* 6(1):49–54.

Hertz, Robert 1960 *Death and the Right Hand*. Cohen & West, Oxford, UK.

Hildebolt, Charles F., Stephen Molnar, Memory Elvin-Lewis, and Jeffrey K. McKee 1988 The Effect of Geochemical Factors on Prevalences of Dental Diseases for Prehistoric Inhabitants of the State of Missouri. *American Journal of Physical Anthropology* 75(1):1–14.

Hillman, Gordon C. 1986 Plant Foods in Ancient Diet: The Archaeological Role of Palaeofaeces in General and Lindow Man's Gut Contents in Particular. In: *Lindow Man: The Body in the Bog*, edited by I. M. Stead, J. B. Bourke, and Don R. Brothwell, pp. 99–115. Cornell University Press, Ithaca, NY.

Hillson, Simon W. 1996 *Dental Anthropology*. Cambridge University Press, Cambridge, UK.

———— 2001 Recording Dental Caries in Archaeological Human Remains. *International Journal of Osteoarchaeology* 11(4):249–289.

———— 2005 *Teeth* (2nd ed.). Cambridge Manuals in Archaeology, Cambridge University Press, Cambridge, UK.

———— 2019 Dental Pathology. In *Biological Anthropology of the Human Skeleton* (3rd ed.), edited by M. Anne Katzenberg and Anne L. Grauer, pp. 295–333. Wiley-Blackwell, New York.

Hinkes, Madeleine Joyce 1983 *Skeletal Evidence of Stress in Subadults: Trying to Come of Age at Grasshopper Pueblo*. Unpublished Ph.D. dissertation, Department of Anthropology, University of Arizona, Tucson.

Hobert, Leah, and Emanuela Binello 2017 Trepanation in Ancient China. *World Neurosurgery* 101:451–456.

Hodge, Shannon Chappell 2018 Nonlethal Scalping in the Archaic: Violence, Trophy Taking, and Social Change. In *Bioarchaeology of the American Southeast: Approaches to Bridging Health and Identity in the Past*, edited by Shannon Chappell Hodge and Kristrina A. Shuler, pp. 95–114. The University of Alabama Press, Tuscaloosa, AL.

Holden, Timothy G. 1986 Preliminary Report on the Detailed Analyses of the Macroscopic Remains from the Gut of Lindow Man. In *Lindow Man: The Body in the Bog*, edited by I. M. Stead, J. B. Bourke, and Don R. Brothwell, pp. 116–125. Cornell University Press, Ithaca, NY.

——— 1994 Dietary Evidence from the Intestinal Contents of Ancient Humans with Particular Reference to Desiccated Remains from Northern Chile. In *Tropical Archaeobotany: Applications and New Developments*, edited by Jon G. Hather, pp. 65–85. Routledge, London.

Holland, Mitchell M., Deborah L. Fisher, Lloyd G. Mitchell, William C. Rodriquez, James J. Canik, Carl R. Merril, and Victor W. Weedn 1993 Mitrochondrial DNA Sequence Analysis of Human Skeletal Remains: Identification of Remains from the Vietnam War. *Journal of Forensic Sciences* 38(3):542–553.

Holliday, Diane Young 1993 Occipital Lesions: A Possible Cost of Cradleboards. *American Journal of Physical Anthropology* 90(3):283–290.

Holliman, Sandra E. 2011 Sex and Gender in Bioarchaeological Research: Theory, Method, and Interpretation. In *Social Bioarchaeology*, edited by Sabrina C. Agarwal and Bonnie A. Glencross, pp. 149–182. Wiley-Blackwell, Oxford, UK.

Holt, Brigitte, and Erin Whittey 2019 The Impact of Terrain on Lower Limb Bone Structure. *American Journal of Physical Anthropology* 168(4):729–743.

Honch, Noah V., T. F. G. Higham, John Chapman, B. Gaydarska, and Robert E. M. Hedges 2006 A Palaeodietary Investigation of Carbon (13C/12C) and Nitrogen (15N/14N) in Human and Faunal Bones from the Copper Age Cemeteries of Varna I and Durankulak, Bulgaria. *Journal of Archaeological Science* 33(11):1493–1504.

Hong, Mai-Linh K. 2017 "Get Your Asphalt Off My Ancestors!": Reclaiming Richmond's African Burial Ground. *Law, Culture and the Humanities* 13(1):81–103.

Hooton, Ernest A. 1918 On Certain Eskimo Characteristics in Icelandic Skulls. *American Journal of Physical Anthropology* 1(1):53–76.

——— 1930 *The Indians of Pecos Pueblo: A Study of Their Skeletal Remains*. Yale University Press, New Haven, CT.

Hoppa, Robert D., and James W. Vaupel (eds.) 2002 *Paleodemography: Age Distributions from Skeletal Samples*. Cambridge University Press, Cambridge, UK.

Horocholyn, Kalyna, and Megan B. Brickley 2017 Pursuit of Famine: Investigating Famine in Bioarchaeological Literature. *Bioarchaeology International* 1(3–4):101–115.

Howell, Nancy 1976 Toward a Uniformitarian Theory of Human Paleodemography. *Journal of Human Evolution* 5(1):25–40.

Hoy, Wendy E., and Jennifer L. Nicol 2019 The Barker Hypothesis Confirmed: Association of Low Birth Weight with All-Cause Natural Deaths in Young Adult Life in a Remote Australian Aboriginal Community. *Journal of Developmental Origins of Health and Disease* 10(1):55–62.

Hrdlička, Aleš 1910 Report on Skeletal Material from Missouri Mounds, Collected in 1906–1907 by Mr. Gerard Fowke. *Bureau of American Ethnology Bulletin* 37:103–319.

——— 1927 Anthropology and Medicine. *American Journal of Physical Anthropology* 10(1):1–9.

——— 1941 Diseases of and Artifacts on Skulls and Bones from Kodiak Island. *Smithsonian Miscellaneous Collections* 101(4).

Hu, Yaowu, Stanley H. Ambrose, and Changsui Wang 2006 Stable Isotopic Analysis of Human Bones from the Jiahu Site, Henan, China: Implications for the Transition to Agriculture. *Journal of Archaeological Science* 33(9):1319–1330.

Hubert, Jane 1994 Sacred Beliefs and Beliefs of Sacredness. In *Sacred Sites, Sacred Places*, edited by David Charmichael, Jane Hubert, Brian Reeves, and Audhild Schanche, pp. 9–19. Routledge, London.

Hublin, Jean-Jacques 2009 The Prehistory of Compassion. *Proceedings of the National Academy of Sciences of the United States of America* 106(16):6429–6430.

Hughes, C., D. J. A. Heylings, and C. Power 1996 Transverse (Harris) Lines in Irish Archaeological Remains. *American Journal of Physical Anthropology* 101(1):115–131.

Hughes, Stephen 2011 CT Scanning in Archaeology. In *Computed Tomography – Special Applications*, edited by Luca Saba, pp. 57–70. IntechOpen, London.

Hughes, Susan S., Andrew R. Millard, Sam J. Lucy, Carolyn A. Chenery, Jane A. Evans, Geoff Nowell, and D. Graham Pearson 2014 Anglo-Saxon Origins Investigated by Isotopic Analysis of Burials from Berinsfield, Oxfordshire, United Kingdom. *Journal of Archaeological Science* 42(1):81–92.

Humphrey, Louise T. 2016 Chemical and Isotopic Analyses of Dental Tissues. In *A Companion to Dental Anthropology*, edited by Joel D. Irish and G. Richard Scott, pp. 499–513. John Wiley & Sons, New York.

Hunt, Kathryn J., Charlotte Roberts, and Casey Kirkpatrick 2018 Taking Stock: A Systematic Review of Archaeological Evidence of Cancers in Human and Early Hominin Remains. *International Journal of Paleopathology* 21:12–26.

Huntley, Catherine, Angus Hodder, and Manoj Ramachandran 2015 Clinical and Historical Aspects of the Elephant Man: Exploring the Facts and the Myths. *Gene* 555(1):63–65.

Hurlbut, Sharon A. 2000 The Taphonomy of Cannibalism: A Review of Anthropogenic Bone Modification in the American Southwest. *International Journal of Osteoarchaeology* 10(1):4–26.

Huss-Ashmore, Rebecca, Alan H. Goodman, and George J. Armelagos 1982 Nutritional Inference from Paleopathology. In *Advances in Archaeological Method and Theory*, vol. 5, edited by Michael B. Schiffer, pp. 395–474. Academic Press, New York.

Hutchinson, Dale L., and Clark Spencer Larsen 2001 Enamel Hypoplasia and Stress in La Florida. In *Bioarchaeology of Spanish Florida: The Impact of Colonialism*, edited by Clark Spencer Larsen, pp. 181–206. University Press of Florida, Gainesville, FL.

Ikram, Salima, and Aidan Dodson 1998 *The Mummy in Ancient Egypt: Equipping the Dead for Eternity*. Thames & Hudson, London, UK.

Irish, Joel D. 2016a Terms and Terminology Used in Dental Anthropology. In *A Companion to Dental Anthropology*, edited by Joel D. Irish and G. Richard Scott, pp. 87–93. John Wiley & Sons, New York.

——— 2016b Assessing Dental Nonmetric Variation Among Populations. In *A Companion to Dental Anthropology*, edited by Joel D. Irish and G. Richard Scott, pp. 265–286. John Wiley & Sons, New York.

Irish, Joel D., and G. Richard Scott 2016 Introduction to Dental Anthropology. In *A Companion to Dental Anthropology*, edited by Joel D. Irish and G. Richard Scott, pp. 3–6. John Wiley & Sons, New York.

Iseminger, William R. 1996 Mighty Cahokia. *Archaeology* 49(3):30–37.

Ismail, Siti Sofo, Ian D. Bull, and Richard P. Evershed 2016 Interpreting Anthropogenic Signals from a Clandestine Grave Via Soil Lipid Biomolecular Analysis. *Transactions on Science and Technology* 3(3):501–506.

Ivanhoe, Francis 1985 Elevated Orthograde Skeletal Plasticity of Some Archaeological Populations from Mexico and the American Southwest: Direct Relation to Maize Phytate Nutritional Load. In *Health and Disease in the Prehistoric Southwest*, edited by Charles F. Merbs and Robert J. Miller, pp. 165–175. Arizona State University, Anthropological Research Papers No. 34, Tempe.

Ives, Rachel, and Megan B. Brickley 2014 New Findings in the Identification of Adult Vitamin D Deficiency Osteomalacia: Results from a Large-Scale Study. *International Journal of Paleopathology* 7:45–56.

Jackson, H. Edwin, and Susan L. Scott 2003 Patterns of Elite Faunal Utilization at Moundville, Alabama. *American Antiquity* 68(3):552–572.

Jacobsen, Thomas W., and Tracey Cullen 1990 The Work of J. L. Angel in the Eastern Mediterranean. In *A Life in Science: Papers in Honor of J. Lawrence Angel*, edited by Jane E. Buikstra, pp. 38–51. Center for American Archeology, Scientific Paper 6, Kampsville, IL.

Jantz, Richard L., and Stephen D. Ousley 2017 Introduction to Fordisc 3 and Human Variation Statistics. In *Forensic Anthropology: A Comprehensive Introduction* (2nd ed.), edited by Natalie R. Langley and MariaTeresa A. Tersigni-Tarrant, pp. 255–270. CRC Press, Boca Raton, FL.

Jantzen, Detlef, Ute Brinker, Jörg Orschiedt, and Jan Heinemeier 2011 A Bronze Age Battlefield? Weapons and Trauma in the Tollense Valley, North-Eastern Germany. *Antiquity* 85(328):417–433.

Jaouen, Klervia, Estelle Herrscher, and Vincent Balter 2017 Copper and Zinc Isotope Ratios in Human Bone and Enamel. *American Journal of Physical Anthropology* 162(3):491–500.

Jobling, Mark A., Rita Rasteiro, and Jon H. Wetton 2016 In the Blood: The Myth and Reality of Genetic Markers of Identity. *Journal of Ethnic and Racial Studies* 39(2):142–161.

Johnson, Matthew 2019 *Archaeological Theory: An Introduction* (3rd ed.). John Wiley & Sons, New York.

Jones, Joseph 1876 Explorations of the Aboriginal Remains of Tennessee. *Smithsonian Contributions to Knowledge* 22(259).

Jones, Michael 1990 The Temple of Apis in Memphis. *The Journal of Egyptian Archaeology* 76(1):141–147.

Joyce, Rosemary A. 2008 *Ancient Bodies, Ancient Lives: Sex, Gender, and Archaeology*. Thames & Hudson, New York.

———— 2015 Grave Responsibilities: Encountering Human Remains. In *Disturbing Bodies: Perspectives on Forensic Anthropology*, edited by Zoë Crossland and Rosemary A. Joyce, pp. 169–184. School for Advanced Research Press, Santa Fe, NM.

———— 2017 Sex, Gender, and Anthropology: Moving Bioarchaeology Outside the Subdiscipline. In *Exploring Sex and Gender in Bioarchaeology*, edited by Sabrina C. Agarwal and Julie K. Wesp, pp. 1–12. University of New Mexico Press, Albuquerque, NM.

Judd, Margaret 2004 Trauma in the City of Kerma: Ancient Versus Modern Injury Patterns. *International Journal of Osteoarchaeology* 14(1):34–51.

Junkins, Emily N., and David O. Carter 2017 Relationships Between Human Remains, Graves and the Depositional Environment. In *Taphonomy of Human Remains: Forensic Analysis of the Dead and the Depositional Environment*, edited by Eline M. J. Schotsmans, Nicholas Márquez-Grant, and Shari L. Forbes, pp. 145–154. Wiley-Blackwell, Oxford, UK.

Justice, Lauryn C., and Daniel H. Temple 2019 Bioarchaeological Evidence for Social Maturation in the Mortuary Ritual of Ipiutak and Tigara Hunter-Gatherers: Lifespan Perspectives on the Emergence of Personhood at Point Hope, Alaska. *American Antiquity* 84(2):234–251.

Kaestle, Frederika A., and David Glenn Smith 2001 Ancient Mitochondrial DNA Evidence for Prehistoric Population Movement: The Numic Expansion. *American Journal of Physical Anthropology* 115(1):1–12.

Kakaliouras, Ann M. 2017 NAGPRA and Repatriation in the Twenty-First Century: Shifting the Discourse from Benefits to Responsibilities. *Bioarchaeology International* 1(3–4):183–190.

Kappelman, John, Richard A. Ketcham, Stephen Pearce, Lawrence Todd, Wiley Akins, Matthew W. Colbert, Mulugeta Feseha, Jessica A. Maisano, and Adrienne Witzel 2016 Perimortem Fractures in Lucy Suggest Mortality from Fall Out of Tall Tree. *Nature* 537(7621):503–507.

Katzenberg, M. Anne 1993 Age Differences and Population Variation in Stable Isotope Values from Ontario Canada. In *Prehistoric Human Bone: Archaeology at the Molecular Level*, edited by Joseph B. Lambert and Gisela Grupe, pp. 39–62. Springer-Verlag, Berlin.

Katzenberg, M. Anne, and Andrea L. Waters-Rist 2019 Stable Isotope Analysis: A Tool for Studying Past Diet, Demography, and Life History. In *Biological Anthropology of the Human Skeleton* (3rd ed.), edited by M. Anne Katzenberg and Anne L. Grauer, pp. 469–504. Wiley-Blackwell, New York.

Keeley, Lawrence H. 1996 *War Before Civilization: The Myth of the Peaceful Savage*. Oxford University Press, Oxford, UK.

Kelly, Robert L. 1997 Late Holocene Great Basin Prehistory. *Journal of World Prehistory* 11(1):1–49.

———— 2001 *Prehistory of the Carson Desert and Stillwater Mountains*. University of Utah Anthropological Papers No. 123, Salt Lake City, UT.

Kemp, Brian M., Ripan S. Malhi, John McDonough, Deborah A. Bolnick, Jason A. Eshleman, Olga Rickards, Cristina Martinez-Labarga, John R. Johnson, Joseph G. Lorenz, E. James Dixon, Terence E. Fifield, Timothy H. Heaton, Rosita Worl, and David Glenn Smith 2007 Genetic Analysis of Early Holocene Skeletal Remains from Alaska and Its Implications for the Settlement of the Americas. *American Journal of Physical Anthropology* 132(4):605–621.

Kendell, Ashley, and P. Willey 2014 Crow Creek Bone Bed Commingling: Relationship Between Bone Mineral Density and Minimum Number of Individuals and Its Effect on Paleodemographic Analyses. In *Commingled and Disarticulated Human Remains: Working Toward Improved Theory, Method, and Data*, edited by Anna J. Osterholtz, Kathryn M. Baustian, and Debra L. Martin, pp. 85–104. Springer, New York.

Killion, Thomas W. 2008 *Opening Archaeology: Repatriation's Impact on Contemporary Research and Practice.* School for Advanced Research, Santa Fe, NM.

King, Charlotte L., Siân E. Halcrow, Andrew R. Millard, Darren R. Gröcke, Vivien G. Standen, Marco Portilla, and Bernardo T. Arriaza 2018 Let's Talk About Stress, Baby! Infant-Feeding Practices and Stress in the Ancient Atacama Desert, Northern Chile. *American Journal of Physical Anthropology* 166(1):139–155.

King, Thomas F. 2012 *Cultural Resource Laws and Practice* (4th ed.). AltaMira Press, Walnut Creek, CA.

Kirkpatrick, Casey L., Roselyn A. Campbell, and Kathryn J. Hunt 2018 Paleo-Oncology: Taking Stock and Moving Forward. *International Journal of Paleopathology* 21:3–11.

Kjellström, A. 2004 Evaluations of Sex Assessment Using Weighted Traits on Incomplete Skeletal Remains. *International Journal of Osteoarchaeology* 14(5):360–373.

Klaus, Haagen D. 2012 The Bioarchaeology of Structural Violence: A Theoretical Model and Case Study. In *The Bioarchaeology of Violence*, edited by Debra L. Martin, Ryan P. Harrod, and Ventura R. Pérez, pp. 29–62. University Press of Florida, Gainesville, FL.

———— 2018 Possible Prostate Cancer in Northern Peru: Differential Diagnosis, Vascular Anatomy, and Molecular Signaling in the Paleopathology of Metastatic Bone Disease. *International Journal of Paleopathology* 21:147–157.

Klaus, Haagen D., Mark Nathan Cohen, Marie Elaine Danforth, and Amanda R. Harvey 2017 Bioarchaeology and Social Complexity: Departing Reflections and Future Directions. In *Bones of Complexity: Bioarchaeological Case Studies of Social Organization and Skeletal Biology*, edited by Haagen D. Klaus, Amanda R. Harvey, and Mark N. Cohen, pp. 450–468. University Press of Florida, Gainesville, FL.

Klaus, Haagen D., and Connie M. Ericksen 2013 Paleopathology of an Ovarian Teratoma: Description and Diagnosis of an Exotic Abdominal Bone and Tooth Mass in a Historic Peruvian Burial. *International Journal of Paleopathology* 3(4):294–301.

Klepinger, Linda L. 2006 *Fundamentals of Forensic Anthropology*. John Wiley & Sons, New York.

Knight, Vernon J., Jr., and Vincas P. Steponaitis 2007 A New History of Moundville. In *Archaeology of the Moundville Chiefdom*, edited by Vernon J. Knight, Jr. and Vincas P. Steponaitis, pp. 1–25. The University of Alabama Press, Tuscaloosa, AL.

Knudson, Kelly J., Arthur E. Aufderheide, and Jane E. Buikstra 2007 Seasonality and Paleodiet in the Chiribaya Polity of Southern Peru. *Journal of Archaeological Science* 34(3):451–462.

Knudson, Kelly J., and Christopher M. Stojanowski 2008 New Directions in Bioarchaeology: Recent Contributions to the Study of Human Social Identities. *Journal of Archaeological Research* 16(4):397–432.

Knüsel, Christopher J. 2011 Men Take Up Arms for War: Sex and Status Distinctions of Humeral Medial Epicondylar Avulsion Fractures in the Archaeological Record. In *Breathing New Life into the Evidence of Death*, edited by Aubrey Baadsgaard, Lexis T. Boutin, and Jane E. Buikstra, pp. 221–249. School for Advanced Research Press, Santa Fe, NM.

Knüsel, Christopher, and Martin J. Smith (eds.) 2014 *The Routledge Handbook of the Bioarchaeology of Human Conflict*. Routledge, New York.

Komar, Debra A., and Jane E. Buikstra 2008 *Forensic Anthropology: Contemporary Theory and Practice*. Oxford University Press, New York.

Konigsberg, Lyle W. 2006 A Post-Neumann History of Biological and Genetic Distance Studies in Archaeology. In *Bioarchaeology: The Contextual Analysis of Human Remains*, edited by Jane E. Buikstra and Lane A. Beck, pp. 263–279. Elsevier Academic Press, Burlington, MA.

Konigsberg, Lyle W., and Susan R. Frankenberg 2012 Demography. In *Research Methods in Human Skeletal Biology*, edited by Elizabeth A. DiGangi and Megan K. Moore, pp. 293–322. Elsevier Academic Press, Waltham, MA.

Konigsberg, Lyle W., and Lee Meadows Jantz 2017 The Probabilistic Basic for Identifying Individuals in Biohistorical Research. In *Studies in Forensic Biohistory*, edited by Christopher M. Stojanowski and William N. Duncan, pp. 213–236. Cambridge University Press, Cambridge, UK.

——— 2018 Multivariate Regression Methods for the Analysis of Stature. In *New Perspectives in Forensic Human Skeletal Identification*, edited by Krista E. Latham, Eric J. Bartelink, and Michael Finnegan, pp. 87–104. Academic Press, London, UK.

Kornei, Katherine 2018 Life After War. *Discover* 39(4):70, 72.

Koudounaris, Paul 2011 *The Empire of Death: A Cultural History of Ossuaries and Charnel Houses.* Thames & Hudson, London, UK.

Kraft, John C., George Rapp, Jr., George J. Szemler, Christos Tziavos, and Edward W. Kase 1987 The Pass at Thermopylae, Greece. *Journal of Field Archaeology* 14(2):181–198.

Krause-Kyora, Ben, Julian Susat, Felix M. Key, Denise Kühnert, Esther Bosse, Alexander Immel, Christoph Rinne, Sabin-Christin Kornell, Diego Yepes, Sören Franzenburg, Henrike O. Heyne, Thomas Meier, Sandra Lösch, Harald Meller, Susanne Friederich, Nicole Nicklisch, Kurt W. Alt, Stefan Schreiber, Andreas Tholey, Alexander Herbig, Almut Nebel, and Johannes Krause 2018 Neolithic and Medieval Virus Genomes Reveal Complex Evolution of Hepatitis B. *Elife* 7: e36666.

Kreissl Lonfat, Bettina M., Ina Maria Kaufmann, and Frank Rühli 2015 A Code of Ethics for Evidence-Based Research with Ancient Human Remains. *The Anatomical Record* 298(6):1175–1181.

Kroeber, Albert L. 1927 Disposal of the Dead. *American Anthropologist* 29(3):308–315.

Krogman, Wilton Marion 1935 Life Histories Recorded in Skeletons. *American Anthropologist* 37(1):92–103.

Kroman, Anne M., and Steven A. Symes 2012 Investigation of Skeletal Trauma. In *Research Methods in Human Skeletal Biology*, edited by Elizabeth A. DiGangi and Megan K. Moore, pp. 219–239. Elsevier Academic Press, Waltham, MA.

Krueger, Kristin L. 2016 Dentition, Behavior, and Diet Determination. In *A Companion to Dental Anthropology*, edited by Joel D. Irish and G. Richard Scott, pp. 396–411. John Wiley & Sons, New York.

Kuckelman, Kristin A. 2017 Cranial Trauma and Victimization among Ancestral Pueblo Farmers of the Northern San Juan Region. In *Broken Bones, Broken Bodies: Bioarchaeological and Forensic Approaches for Accumulative Trauma and Violence*, edited by Caryn E. Tegtmeyer and Debra L. Martin, pp. 43–59. Lexington Books, Lanham, MD.

Kuckelman, Kristin A., Ricky R. Lightfoot, and Debra L. Martin 2002 The Bioarchaeology and Taphonomy of Violence at Castle Rock and Sand Canyon Pueblos, Southwestern Colorado. *American Antiquity* 67(3):486–513.

Kuijt, Ian, Colin P. Quinn, and Gabriel Cooney (eds.) 2014 *Transformation by Fire: The Archaeology of Cremation in Cultural Context.* University of Arizona Press, Tucson.

Kurin, Danielle S. 2013 Trepanation in South-Central Peru During the Early Late Intermediate Period (ca. AD 1000–1250). *American Journal of Physical Anthropology* 152(4):484–494.

Kusaka, Soichiro 2019 Stable Isotope Analysis of Human Bone Hydroxyapatite and Collagen for the Reconstruction of Dietary Patterns of Hunter-Gatherers from Jomon Populations. *International Journal of Osteoarchaeology* 29(1):36–47.

Kuzmina, E. E. 1998 Cultural Connections of the Tarim Basin People and Pastoralists of the Asian Steppes in the Bronze Age. In *The Bronze Age and Early Iron Age Peoples of Eastern Central Asia, vol. 1*, edited by Victor H. Mair, pp. 63–93. University of Pennsylvania Museum Publication, University Museum of Archaeology and Anthropology, Philadelphia.

Kuzminsky, Susan C., Jon M. Erlandson, and Tatiana Xifara 2016 External Auditory Exostoses and Its Relationship to Prehistoric Abalone Harvesting on Santa Rosa Island, California. *International Journal of Osteoarchaeology* 26(6):1014–1023.

Kwon, Heonik 2015 Korean War Mass Graves. In *Necropolitics: Mass Graves and Exhumations in the Age of Human Rights*, edited by Francisco Ferrándiz and Antonius C. G. M. Robben, pp. 76–91. University of Pennsylvania Press, Philadelphia.

Kyriakidis, Evangelos (ed.) 2007 *The Archaeology of Ritual.* University of California, Los Angeles, Cotsen Institute of Archaeology, Cotsen Advanced Seminars 3, Los Angeles.

Lahr, M. Mirazón, F. Rivera, R. K. Power, A. Mounier, B. Copsey, F. Crivellaro, J. E. Edung, J. M. Maillo Fernandez, C. Kiarie, J. Lawrence, A. Leakey, E. Mbua, H. Miller, A. Muigai, D. M.

Mukhongo, A. Van Baelen, R. Wood, J.-L. Schwenninger, R. Grün, H. Achyuthan, A. Wilshaw, and R. A. Foley 2016 Inter-Group Violence Among Early Holocene Hunter-Gatherers of West Turkana, Kenya. *Nature* 529:394–398.

Lallo, John W., George J. Armelagos, and Robert C. Mensforth 1977 The Role of Diet, Disease and Physiology in the Origin of Porotic Hyperostosis. *Human Biology* 49(3):471–483.

Lambert, Patricia M., Brian R. Billman, and Banks L. Leonard 2000 Explaining Variability in Mutilated Human Bone Assemblages from the American Southwest: A Case Study from the Southern Piedmont of Sleeping Ute Mountain, Colorado. *International Journal of Osteoarchaeology* 19(1):49–64.

Lambert, Patricia M., and Phillip L. Walker 2019 Bioarchaeological Ethics: Perspectives on the Use and Value of Human Remains in Scientific Research. In *Biological Anthropology of the Human Skeleton* (3rd ed.), edited by M. Anne Katzenberg and Anne L. Grauer, pp. 3–42. Wiley-Blackwell, New York.

Langdon, Frank W. 1881 The Madisonville Prehistoric Cemetery: Anthropological Notes. *Journal of the Cincinnati Society of Natural History* 4:237–257.

Langley, Natalie R. 2017 Stature Estimation. In *Forensic Anthropology: A Comprehensive Introduction* (2nd ed.), edited by Natalie R. Langley and MariaTeresa A. Tersigni-Tarrant, pp. 195–203. CRC Press, Boca Raton, FL.

Langley, Natalie R., Alice F. Gooding, and MariaTeresa A. Tersigni-Tarrant 2017 Age Estimation Methods. In *Forensic Anthropology: A Comprehensive Introduction* (2nd ed.), edited by Natalie R. Langley and MariaTeresa A. Tersigni-Tarrant, pp. 175–194. CRC Press, Boca Raton, FL.

Langley, Natalie R., and MariaTeresa A. Tersigni-Tarrant (eds.) 2017 *Forensic Anthropology: A Comprehensive Introduction* (2nd ed.). CRC Press, Boca Raton, FL.

Larsen, Clark Spencer 1985 Dental Modifications and Tool Use in the Western Great Basin. *American Journal of Physical Anthropology* 67(4):393–402.

———— 2001 *Bioarchaeology of Spanish Florida: The Impact of Colonialism*. Ripley P. Bullen Series. University Press of Florida, Gainesville, FL.

———— 2006a The Changing Face of Bioarchaeology: An Interdisciplinary Science. In *Bioarchaeology: The Contextual Analysis of Human Remains*, edited by Jane A. Buikstra and Lane A. Beck, pp. 359–374. Elsevier Academic Press, Burlington, MA.

———— 2006b The Agricultural Revolution as Environmental Catastrophe: Implications for Health and Lifestyle in the Holocene. *Quaternary International* 150(1):12–20.

———— 2015 *Bioarchaeology: Interpreting Behavior from the Human Skeleton* (2nd ed.). Cambridge University Press, Cambridge, UK.

———— 2018 Bioarchaeology in Perspective: From Classifications of the Dead to Conditions of the Living. *American Journal of Physical Anthropology* 165(4):865–878.

Larsen, Clark Spencer, and Dale L. Hutchinson 1999 Osteopathology of Carson Desert Foragers: Reconstructing Prehistoric Lifeways in the Western Great Basin. In *Bioarchaeology of the Stillwater Marsh: Prehistoric Human Adaptation in the Western Great Basin*, edited by Brian E. Hemphill and Clark Spencer Larsen, pp. 184–202. University of Utah Press, Salt Lake City, UT.

Larsen, Clark Spencer, and Robert L. Kelly (eds.) 1995 *Bioarchaeology of the Stillwater Marsh: Prehistoric Human Adaptation in the Western Great Basin*. Anthropological Papers of the American Museum of Natural History No. 77, New York.

Larsen, Clark Spencer, and George R. Milner (eds.) 1993 *In the Wake of Contact: Biological Responses to Conquest*. John Wiley and Sons, Hoboken, NJ.

Larsen, Clark Spencer, and Christopher B. Ruff 2011 "An External Agency of Considerable Importance": The Stresses of Agriculture in the Foraging-to-Farming Transition in Eastern North America. In *Human Bioarchaeology and the Transition to Agriculture*, edited by Ron Pinhasi and Jay T. Stock, pp. 293–315. Wiley-Blackwell, Oxford, UK.

Larsen, Clark Spencer, Christopher B. Ruff, and Robert L. Kelly 1995 Structural Analysis of the Stillwater Postcranial Human Remains: Behavioral Implications of Articular Joint Pathology and Long Bone Diaphyseal Morphology. In *Bioarchaeology of the Stillwater Marsh: Prehistoric Human Adaptation in* the *Western Great Basin*, edited by Clark Spencer Larsen and Robert L. Kelly, pp. 107–133, Anthropological Papers of the American Museum of Natural History No. 77, New York.

Larsen, Clark Spencer, Rebecca Shavit, and Mark C. Griffin 1991 Dental Caries Evidence for Dietary Change: An Archaeological Context. In *Advances in Dental Anthropology*, edited by Marc A. Kelley and Clark Spencer Larsen, pp. 179–202. Wiley-Liss, New York.

Larsen, Clark Spencer, and Philip L. Walker 2005 The Ethics of Bioarchaeology. In *Biological Anthropology and Ethics: From Repatriation to Genetic Identity*, edited by Trudy R. Turner, pp. 111–119. State University of New York Press, Albany, New York.

LeBlanc, Steven A. 1999 *Prehistoric Warfare in the American Southwest*. University of Utah Press, Salt Lake City, UT.

Lee, K. Alexandria 1996 Attitudes and Prejudices Towards Infanticide: Carthage, Rome, and Today. *Archaeological Review from Cambridge* 13(2):21–34.

Lee-Thorp, Julia A., and Matt Sponheimer 2006 Contributions of Biogeochemistry to Understanding Hominin Dietary Ecology. *American Journal of Physical Anthropology* 131(S43):131–148.

Legge, Scott S., and Anna M. Hardin 2016 The Pulp Cavity and Its Contents. In *A Companion to Dental Anthropology*, edited by Joel D. Irish and G. Richard Scott, pp. 191–203. John Wiley & Sons, New York.

Lehner, Mark 1997 *The Complete Pyramids*. Thames & Hudson, London, UK.

Leng, Melanie J., and Jonathan P. Lewis 2016 Oxygen Isotopes in Molluscan Shell: Applications in Environmental Archaeology. *Environmental Archaeology* 21(3):295–306.

Lesley, Elena 2015 Death on Display: Bones and Bodies in Cambodia and Rwanda. In *Necropolitics: Mass Graves and Exhumations in the Age of Human Rights*, edited by Francisco Ferrándiz and Antonius C. G. M. Robben, pp. 213–239. University of Pennsylvania Press, Philadelphia.

Lewis, J., D. DeGusta, M. R. Meyer, J. M. Monge, A. E. Mann, and R. L. Holloway 2011 The Mismeasure of Science: Stephen Jay Gould versus Samuel George Morton on Skulls and Bias. *Public Library of Science Biology* 9(6):e1001071.

Lewis, Mary E. 2004 Endocranial Lesions in Non-adult Skeletons: Understanding Their Aetiology. *International Journal of Osteoarchaeology* 14(2):82–97.

———— 2014 Sticks and Stones: Exploring the Nature and Significance of Child Trauma in the Past. In *The Routledge Handbook of the Bioarchaeology of Human Conflict*, edited by Christopher Knüsel and Martin J. Smith, pp. 39–63. Routledge, New York.

———— 2018 *Paleopathology of Children: Identification of Pathological Conditions in the Human Skeletal Remains of Non-Adults*. Academic Press, London, UK.

Lewis, Mary E., and Charlotte Roberts 1997 Growing Pains: The Interpretation of Stress Indicators. *International Journal of Osteoarchaeology* 7(6):581–586.

Li, Yu-Ning (ed.) 1975 *The First Emperor of China*. Routledge, London.

Lieverse, Angela R., Vladimir Ivanovich Bazaliiskii, and Andrzej W. Weber 2015 Death by Twins: A Remarkable Case of Dystocic Childbirth in Early Neolithic Siberia. *Antiquity* 89(343):23–38.

Lieverse, Angela R., D. M. L. Cooper, and Vladimir Ivanovich Bazaliiskii 2017 Penetrating Spinal Injury: An Extraordinary Case of Survival in Early Neolithic Siberia. *International Journal of Osteoarchaeology* 27(3):508–514.

Likovsky, Jakub, Markéta Urbanova, Martin Hájek, Viktor Černý, and Petr Čech 2006 Two Cases of Leprosy from Žatec (Bohemia), Dated to the Turn of the 12th Century and Confirmed by DNA Analysis for *Mycobacterium leprae*. *Journal of Archaeological Science* 33(9):1276–1283.

Lillie, Malcolm C., and Kenneth Jacobs 2006 Stable Isotope Analysis of 14 Individuals from the Mesolithic Cemetery of Vasilyevka II, Dnieper Rapids Region, Ukraine. *Journal of Archaeological Science* 33(6):880–886.

Lindo, John, Alessandro Achilli, Ugo A. Perego, David Archer, Cristina Valdiosera, Barbara Petzelt, Joycelynn Mitchell, Rosita Worl, E. James Dixon, Terence E. Fifield, Morten Rasmussen, Eske Willerslev, Jerome S. Cybulski, Brian M. Kemp, Michael DeGiorgio, and Ripan S. Malhi 2017 Ancient Individuals from the North American Northwest Coast Reveal 10,000 Years of Regional Genetic Continuity. *Proceedings of the National Academy of Sciences* 114(16):4093–4098.

Lindsay, Kaitlin E., Frank J. Rühli, and Valerie B. DeLeon 2015 Revealing the Face of an Ancient Egyptian: Synthesis of Current and Traditional Approaches to Evidence-Based Facial Approximation. *The Anatomical Record* 298(6):1144–1161.

Linke, Uli 2018 Death as Spectacle: Plastinated Bodies in Germany. In *A Companion to the Anthropology of Death*, edited by Antonius C. G. M. Robben, pp. 383–397. John Wiley & Sons, New York.

Liversidge, Helen M. 2016 Tooth Eruption and Timing. In *A Companion to Dental Anthropology*, edited by Joel D. Irish and G. Richard Scott, pp. 159–171. John Wiley & Sons, New York.

Llamas, Bastien, Lars Fehren-Schmitz, Guido Valverde, Julien Soubrier, Swapan Mallick, Nadin Rohland, Susanne Nordenfelt, Cristina Valdiosera, Stephen M. Richards, Adam Rohrlach, Maria Inés Barreto Romero, Isabel Flores Espinoza, Elsa Tomasto Cagigao, Lucía Watson Jiménez, Krzysztof Makowski, Ilán Santiago Leboreiro Reyna, Josefina Mansilla Lory, Julio Alejandro Ballivián Torrez, Mario A. Rivera, Richard L. Burger, Maria Constanza Ceruti, Johan Reinhard, R. Spencer Wells, Gustavo Politis, Calogero M. Santoro, Vivien G. Standen, Colin Smith, David Reich, Simon Y. W. Ho, Alan Cooper, and Wolfgang Haak 2016 Ancient Mitochondrial DNA Provides High-Resolution Time Scale of the Peopling of the Americas. *Science Advances* 2:e1501385.

Loe, Louise, Caroline Barker, and Richard Wright 2014 An Osteological Profile of Trench Warfare: Peri-Mortem Trauma Sustained by Soldiers Who Fought and Died in the Battle of Fromelles, 1916. In *The Routledge Handbook of the Bioarchaeology of Human Conflict*, edited by Christopher Knüsel and Martin J. Smith, pp. 575–601. Routledge, New York.

Lorentz, K. O. 2017 Marking Identity Through Cultural Cranial Modification Within the First Sedentary Communities (Ninth to Eighth Millennium BCE) in the Near East: Tepe Abdul Hosein, Iran. *International Journal of Osteoarchaeology* 27(6):973–983.

Lorkiewicz, W., J. Mietlińska, J. Karkus, E. Żądzińska, J. K. Jakubowski, and B. Antoszewski 2018 Over 4,500 Years of Trepanation in Poland: From the Unknown to Therapeutic Advisability. *International Journal of Osteoarchaeology* 28(6):626–635.

Love, Jennifer C. 2014 Postcranial Fractures in Child Abuse: Illustrated with a Case Study. In *Broken Bones: Anthropological Analysis of Blunt Force Trauma*, edited by Vicki L. Wedel and Alison Galloway, pp. 336–349. Charles C Thomas Publisher Ltd., Springfield, IL.

Love, Jennifer C., and Miriam E. Soto Martinez 2018 Theoretical Foundations of Child Abuse. In *Forensic Anthropology: Theoretical Framework and Scientific Basis*, edited by C. Clifford Boyd and Donna C. Boyd, pp. 201–211. John Wiley & Sons, New York.

Lovejoy, C. Owen, Richard S. Meindl, Robert P. Mensforth, and Thomas J. Barton 1985b Multifactorial Determination of Skeletal Age at Death: A Method and Blind Tests of Its Accuracy. *American Journal of Physical Anthropology* 68(1):1–14.

Lovejoy, C. Owen, Richard S. Meindl, Thomas R. Pryzbeck, and Robert P. Mensforth 1985a Chronological Metamorphosis of the Auricular Surface of the Ilium: A New Method for the Determination of Adult Skeletal Age at Death. *American Journal of Physical Anthropology* 68(1):15–28.

Lovell, Nancy C., and Anne L. Grauer 2019 Analysis and Interpretation of Trauma in Skeletal Remains. In *Biological Anthropology of the Human Skeleton* (3rd ed.), edited by M. Anne Katzenberg and Anne L. Grauer, pp. 335–383. Wiley-Blackwell, New York.

Lozada, María Cecilia 2011 Marking Ethnicity Through Perimortem Cranial Modification among the Pre-Inca Chiribaya, Peru. In *The Bioarchaeology of the Human Head: Decapitation, Decoration, and Deformation*, edited by Michelle Bonogofsky, pp. 228–240. University Press of Florida, Gainesville, FL.

Lucejko, Jeannette J., Jacopo La Nasa, Francesca Porta, Alessandro Vanzetti, Giuseppa Tanda, Claudio Filippo Mangiaracina, Alessandro Corretti, Maria Perla Colombini, and Erika Ribechini 2018 Long-lasting Ergot Lipids as New Biomarkers for Assessing the Presence of Cereals and Cereal Products in Archaeological Vessels. *Nature Scientific Reports* 8(1):3935.

Lukacs, John R. 1996 Sex Differences in Dental Caries Rates with the Origin of Agriculture in South Asia. *Current Anthropology* 37(1):147–153.

Lull, Vincente, Rafael Micó, Cristina Rihuete, and Robert Risch 2013 Taphonomy and Funerary Practices in Collective Cemeteries: A Prehistoric Case from Menorca (Balearic Islands, Spain). In

The Dead Tell Tales: Essays in Honor of Jane E. Buikstra, edited by María Cecilia Lozada and Barra O'Donnabhain, pp. 154–161. Cotsen Institute of Archaeology Press, Monograph 76. University of California, Los Angeles.

Luna, Leandro H. 2006 Evaluation of Uniradicular Teeth for Age-at-Death Estimations in a Sample from a Pampean Hunter-Gatherer Cemetery (Argentina). *Journal of Archaeological Science* 33(12):1706–1717.

Lyman, R. Lee 1994 *Vertebrate Taphonomy*. Cambridge University Press, Cambridge, UK.

Lyman, R. Lee, and Michael J. O'Brien 2004 A History of Normative Theory in Americanist Archaeology. *Journal of Archaeological Method and Theory* 11(4):369–396.

Lynnerup, Niels 2015a Bog Bodies. *The Anatomical Record* 298(6):1007–1012.

—— 2015b The Thule Inuit Mummies from Greenland. *The Anatomical Record* 298(6):1001–1006.

MacKinnon, Gaille, and Amy Z. Mundorff 2006 The World Trade Center – September 11, 2001. In *Forensic Human Identification: An Introduction*, edited by Tim Thompson and Sue Black, pp. 485–499. CRC Press, Boca Raton, FL.

Maggiano, Corey M. 2012 Making the Mold: A Microstructural Perspective on Bone Modeling During Growth and Mechanical Adaptation. In *Bone Histology: An Anthropological Perspective*, edited by Christian Crowder and Sam Stout, pp. 45–90. CRC Press, Boca Raton, FL.

Magli, Giulio 2015 *Archaeoastronomy: Introduction to the Science of Stars and Stones*. Springer, New York.

Mair, Victor H. 1995 Prehistoric Caucasoid Corpses of the Tarim Basin. *Journal of Indo-European Studies* 23(3–4):281–307.

Malgosa, Assumpció, A. Alesan, Santiago Safont, Madrona Ballbé, and María Manuela Ayala 2004 A Dystocic Childbirth in the Spanish Bronze Age. *International Journal of Osteoarchaeology* 14(2):98–103.

Mallory, James P., and Victor H. Mair 2000 *The Tarim Mummies*. Thames & Hudson, New York.

Malville, Nancy J. 2005 Mortuary Practices and Ritual Use of Human Bone in Tibet. In *Interacting with the Dead: Perspectives on Mortuary Archaeology for the New Millennium*, edited by Gordon F. M. Rakita, Jane E. Buikstra, Lane A. Beck, and Sloan R. Williams, pp. 190–206. University Press of Florida, Gainesville, FL.

Man, John 2009 *The Terra Cotta Army: China's First Emperor and the Birth of a Nation*. Da Capo Press, Cambridge, MA.

Mann, Robert W. 2017 *The Bone Book: A Photographic Lab Manual for Identifying and Siding Human Bones*. Charles C Thomas Publisher Ltd., Springfield, IL.

Mann, Robert W., Bruce E. Anderson, Thomas D. Holland, and Johnie E. Webb, Jr. 2009 Unusual "Crime" Scenes: The Role of Forensic Anthropology in Recovering and Identifying American MIAs. In *Hard Evidence: Case Studies in Forensic Anthropology*, edited by Dawnie Wolfe Steadman, pp. 133–140. Prentice Hall, Upper Saddle River, NJ.

Mann, Robert W., and David R. Hunt 2012 *Photographic Regional Atlas of Bone Disease: A Guide to Pathologic and Normal Variation in the Human Skeleton* (3rd ed.). Charles C Thomas Publisher Ltd., Springfield, IL.

Mann, Robert W., David R. Hunt, and Scott Lozanoff 2016 *Photographic Regional Atlas of Non-Metric Traits and Anatomical Variants in the Human Skeleton*. Charles C Thomas Publisher Ltd., Springfield, IL.

Marchi, Damiano, Vitale S. Sparacello, Brigitte M. Holt, and Vincenzo Formicola 2006 Biomechanical Approach to the Reconstruction of Activity Patterns in Neolithic Western Liguria, Italy. *American Journal of Physical Anthropology* 131(4):447–455.

Marden, Kerriann, Marcella H. Sorg, and William D. Haglund 2012 Taphonomy. In *Research Methods in Human Skeletal Biology*, edited by Elizabeth A. DiGangi and Megan K. Moore, pp. 241–262. Elsevier Academic Press, Waltham, MA.

Mariotti, Valentina, Micol Zuppello, Maria Elena Pedrosi, Matteo Bettuzzi, Rosa Brancaccio, Eva Peccenini, Maria Pia Morigi, and Maria Giovanna Belcastro 2015 Skeletal Evidence of Tuberculosis in a Modern Identified Human Skeletal Collection (Certosa Cemetery, Bologna, Italy). *American Journal of Physical Anthropology* 157(3):389–401.

Mark, S. 2017 A Review of the Evidence for Melanoma in Nine Inca Mummies. *International Journal of Osteoarchaeology* 27(4):573–579.

Marklein, Kathryn E., Rachael E. Leahy, and Douglas E. Crews 2016 In Sickness and in Death: Assessing Frailty in Human Skeletal Remains. *American Journal of Physical Anthropology* 161(2):208–225.

Marks, Murray K., Kerriann Marden, and Darinka Mileusnic-Polchan 2009 Forensic Osteology of Child Abuse. In *Hard Evidence: Case Studies in Forensic Anthropology*, edited by Dawnie Wolfe Steadman, pp. 205–220. Prentice Hall, Upper Saddle River, NJ.

Marlar, Richard A., Banks L. Leonard, Brian R. Billman, Patricia M. Lambert, and Jennifer E. Marlar 2000 Biochemical Evidence of Cannibalism at a Prehistoric Puebloan Site in Southwestern Colorado. *Nature* 407:74–78.

Márquez-Grant, Nicholas, and Linda Fibiger (eds.) 2011 *The Routledge Handbook of Archaeological Human Remains and Legislation*. Routledge, London.

Martin, Debra L. 1991 Bone Histology and Paleopathology: Methodological Considerations. In *Human Paleopathology: Current Syntheses and Future Options*, edited by Donald J. Ortner and Arthur C. Aufderheide, pp. 55–59. Smithsonian Institution Press, Washington, DC.

——— 2015 Excavating for Truths: Forensic Anthropology and Bioarchaeology as Ways of Making Meaning from Skeletal Evidence. In *Disturbing Bodies: Perspectives on Forensic Anthropology*, edited by Zoë Crossland and Rosemary A. Joyce, pp. 157–168. School for Advanced Research Press, Santa Fe, NM.

——— 2016 Hard Times in Dry Lands: Making Meaning of Violence in the Ancient Southwest. *Journal of Anthropological Research* 72(1):1–23.

Martin, Debra L., and Cheryl P. Anderson (eds.) 2014a *Biological and Forensic Perspectives on Violence: How Violent Death Is Interpreted from Skeletal Remains*. Cambridge University Press, Cambridge, UK.

——— 2014b Introduction: Interpreting Violence in the Ancient and Modern World When Skeletonized Bodies are All You Have. In *Biological and Forensic Perspectives on Violence: How Violent Death Is Interpreted from Skeletal Remains*, edited by Debra L. Martin and Cheryl P. Anderson, pp. 3–13. Cambridge University Press, Cambridge, UK.

Martin, Debra L., Nancy J. Akins, and H. Wolcott Toll 2014 Disarticulated and Disturbed, Processed and Eaten? Cautionary Notes from the La Plata Assemblage (AD 1000–1150). In *Commingled and Disarticulated Human Remains: Working Toward Improved Theory, Method, and Data*, edited by Anna J. Osterholtz, Kathryn M. Baustian, and Debra L. Martin, pp. 129–147. Springer, New York.

Martin, Debra L., and David W. Frayer (eds.) 1997 *Troubled Times: Violence and Warfare in the Past*. Gordon and Breach Publishers, Amsterdam, Netherlands.

Martin, Debra L., Alan H. Goodman, and George J. Armelagos 1985 Skeletal Pathologies as Indicators of Quality and Quantity of Diet. In *The Analysis of Prehistoric Diets*, edited by Robert I. Gilbert, Jr. and James H. Mielke, pp. 227–280. Academic Press, New York.

Martin, Debra L., Alan H. Goodman, George J. Armelagos, and Ann L. Magennis 1991 *Black Mesa Anasazi Health: Reconstructing Life from Patterns of Death and Disease*. Southern Illinois University at Carbondale, Center for Archaeological Investigations, Occasional Paper No. 14.

Martin, Debra L., Ryan P. Harrod, and Ventura R. Pérez (eds.) 2012a *The Bioarchaeology of Violence*. University Press of Florida, Gainesville, FL.

——— 2012b Introduction: Bioarchaeology and the Study of Violence. In *The Bioarchaeology of Violence*, edited by Debra L. Martin, Ryan P. Harrod, and Ventura R. Pérez, pp. 1–10. University Press of Florida, Gainesville, FL.

——— 2013 *Bioarchaeology: An Integrated Approach to Working with Human Remains*. Springer, New York.

Martin, Debra L., and Anne J. Osterholtz 2016 *Bodies and Lives in Ancient America: Health Before Columbus*. Routledge, London.

Martiniaková, M., B. Grosskopf, R. Omelka, K. Dammers, M. Vondráková, and M. Bauerová 2006 Histological Study of Compact Bone Tissue in Some Mammals: A Method for Species Determination. *International Journal of Osteoarchaeology* 17(1):82–90.

Massey, Gerald 2011 *The Natural Genesis (Two Volumes in One)*. Cosimo, New York (originally published in 1883).

Materski, Wojciech 2008 *Katyn: A Crime Without Punishment*. Yale University Press, New Haven.

Matheson, Carney D., and Margaret-AshleyVeall 2014 Presumptive Blood Test Using Hemastix® with EDTA in Archaeology. *Journal of Archaeological Science* 41:230–241.

Matisoo-Smith, Elizabeth, and K. Ann Horsburgh 2012 *DNA for Archaeologists*. Left Coast Press, Walnut Creek, CA.

Matsunami, Kodo 2010 *Funeral Customs of the World: A Comprehensive Guide to Practices and Traditions.* Buddhist Searchlight Center, Tochigi, Japan.

Mayes, Arion T., and Sarah B. Barber 2008 Osteobiography of a High-Status Burial from the Lower Rio Verde Valley of Oaxaca, Mexico. *International Journal of Osteoarchaeology* 18(6):573–588.

Mays, Simon 2002 The Relationship Between Molar Wear and Age in an Early 19th Century AD Archaeological Human Skeletal Series of Documented Age at Death. *Journal of Archaeological Science* 29(8):861–871.

———— 2010 *The Archaeology of Human Bones* (2nd ed.). Routledge, New York.

———— 2016 Estimation of Stature in Archaeological Human Skeletal Remains from Britain. *American Journal of Physical Anthropology* 161(4):646–655.

———— 2018 How Should We Diagnose Disease in Paleopathology? Some Epistemological Considera- tions. *International Journal of Paleopathology* 20:12–19.

Mays, Simon, and Megan B. Brickley 2018 Vitamin D Deficiency in Bioarchaeology and Beyond: The Study of Rickets and Osteomalacia in the Past. *International Journal of Paleopathology* 23:1–5.

Mays, Simon, and G. Michael Taylor 2003 A First Prehistoric Case of Tuberculosis from England. *International Journal of Osteoarchaeology* 13(4):189–196.

McCarthy, John P. 2006 African Community Identity at the Cemetery. In *African Re-Genesis: Confronting Social Issues in the Diaspora*, edited by Kevin C. MacDonald, pp. 176–183. Left Coast Press, Walnut Creek, CA.

McEwan, J. M., Simon Mays, and G. M. Blake 2005 The Relationship of Bone Mineral Density and Other Growth Parameters to Stress Indicators in a Medieval Juvenile Population. *International Journal of Osteoarchaeology* 15(3):155–163.

McGhee, Robert 2008 Aboriginalism and the Problems of Indigenous Archaeology. *American Antiquity* 73(4):579–597.

McIlvaine, Britney Kyle. 2015 Implications of Reappraising the Iron-Deficiency Anemia Hypothesis. *International Journal of Osteoarchaeology* 25(6):997–1000.

McKinley, Jacqueline I. 1997 Bronze Age "Barrows" and Funerary Rites and Rituals of Cremation. *Proceedings of the Prehistoric Society* 63:129–145.

———— 2013 Cremation: Excavation, Analysis, and Interpretation of Material from Cremation-Related Contexts. In *The Archaeology of Death and Burial*, edited by Sarah Tarlow and Liv Nilsson Stutz, pp. 147–171. Oxford University Press, Oxford, UK.

———— 2015 In the Heat of the Pyre. In *The Analysis of Burned Human Remains* (2nd ed.), edited by Christopher W. Schmidt and Steven A. Symes, pp. 181–202. Academic Press, Amsterdam, Netherlands.

McNeill, Judith R. 2005 Putting the Dead to Work: An Examination of the Use of Human Bone in Pre- historic Guam. In *Interacting with the Dead: Perspectives on Mortuary Archaeology for the New Millennium*, edited by Gordon F. M. Rakita, Jane E. Buikstra, Lane A. Beck, and Sloan R. Williams, pp. 305–315. University Press of Florida, Gainesville, FL.

Meigs, J. A. 1857 *Catalogue of Human Crania from the Collection of the Academy of Natural Sciences of Phila- delphia*. Merrihew and Thompson, Philadelphia.

Melbye, Jerry, and Scott I. Fairgrieve 1994 A Massacre and Possible Cannibalism in the Canadian Arctic: New Evidence from the Saunaktuk Site (NgTn-1). *Arctic Anthropology* 31(2):57–77.

Merbs, Charles F. 2012 Thumbprints of a Midwife: Birth and Death in an Ancient Pueblo Community. In *The Bioarchaeology of Individuals*, edited by Ann L. W. Stodder and Ann M. Palkovich, pp. 229–241. University Press of Florida, Gainesville, FL.

Metcalf, Peter, and Richard Huntington 1991 *Celebrations of Death: The Anthropology of Mortuary Ritual* (2nd ed.). Cambridge University Press, Cambridge, UK.

Metcalfe, Ryan 2016 Recent Identity and Relationship Studies, Including X-Rays and DNA. In *The Oxford Handbook of the Valley of the Kings*, edited by Richard H. Wilkinson and Kent R. Weeks, pp. 401–413. Oxford University Press, Oxford, UK.

Meyer, Christian, Christian Lohr, Detlef Gronenborn, and Kurt W. Alt 2015 The Massacre Mass Grave of Schöneck-Kilianstädten Reveals New Insights into Collective Violence in Early Neolithic Central Europe. *Proceedings of the National Academy of Sciences* 112(36):11217–11222.

Michael, Amy R., Gabriel D. Wrobel, and Jack Biggs 2018 Understanding Late Classic Maya Mortuary Ritual in Caves: Dental Evidence of Health from Macro- and Microscopic Defects and Caries. In *Bioarchaeology of Pre-Columbian Mesoamerica: An Interdisciplinary Approach*, edited by Cathy Willermet and Andrea Cucina, pp. 133–158. University Press of Florida, Gainesville, FL.

Michopoulou, Efrossyni, Efthymia Nikita, and Charlotte Yvette Henderson 2016 A Test of the Effectiveness of the Coimbra Method in Capturing Activity-Induced Entheseal Changes. *International Journal of Osteoarchaeology* 27(3):409–417.

Michopoulou, Efrossyni, Efthymia Nikita, and Efstratios D. Valakos 2015 Evaluating the Efficiency of Different Recording Protocols for Entheseal Changes in Regards to Expressing Activity Patterns Using Archival Data and Cross-Sectional Geometric Properties. *American Journal of Physical Anthropology* 158(4):557–568.

Mielke, James H., Lyle W. Konigsberg, and John H. Relethford 2006 *Human Biological Variation*. Oxford University Press, New York.

Milella, Marco, Maria Giovanna Belcastro, Christoph P. E. Zollikofer, and Valentina Mariotti 2012 The Effect of Age, Sex, and Physical Activity on Entheseal Morphology in a Contemporary Italian Skeletal Collection. *American Journal of Physical Anthropology* 148(3):379–388.

Miles, A. E. W. 2000 The Miles Method of Assessing Age from Tooth Wear Revisited. *Journal of Archaeological Science* 28(9):973–982.

Miller, Jay 2001 Keres: Engendered Key to the Pueblo Puzzle. *Ethnohistory* 48(3):495–514.

Milner, George R., Eve Anderson, and Virginia G. Smith 1991 Warfare in Late Prehistoric West-Central Illinois. *American Antiquity* 56(4):581–603.

Milner, George R., and Jesper L. Boldsen 2017 Life Not Death: Epidemiology from Skeletons. *International Journal of Paleopathology* 17:26–39.

Milner, George R., and Clark Spencer Larsen 1991 Teeth as Artifacts of Human Behavior: Intentional Mutilation and Accidental Modification. In *Advances in Dental Anthropology*, edited by Marc A. Kelley and Clark Spencer Larsen, pp. 357–378. Wiley-Liss, New York.

Milner, George R., James W. Wood, and Jesper L. Boldsen 2019 Paleodemography: Problems, Progress, and Potential. In *Biological Anthropology of the Human Skeleton* (3rd ed.), edited by M. Anne Katzenberg and Anne L. Grauer, pp. 593–633. Wiley-Blackwell, New York.

Mitchell, Piers D. 2013 The Origins of Human Parasites: Exploring the Evidence for Endoparasitism Throughout Human Evolution. *International Journal of Paleopathology* 3(3):191–198.

——— 2016 Parasites in European Populations from Prehistory to the Industrial Revolution. In *Sanitation, Latrines and Intestinal Parasites in Past Populations*, edited by Piers D. Mitchell, pp. 203–218. Routledge, New York.

——— 2017 Human Parasites in the Roman World: Health Consequences of Conquering an Empire. *Parasitology* 144(1):48–58.

Moghaddam, Negahnaz, Simone Mailler-Burcha, Levent Karab, Fabian Kanz, Christian Jackowski, and Sandra Lösch 2015 Survival After Trepanation – Early Cranial Surgery from Late Iron Age Switzerland. *International Journal of Paleopathology* 11:56–65.

Molnár, Erika, Antónia Marcsik, Zsolt Bereczki, Tyede H. Schmidt-Schultz, Michael Schultz, and György Pálfi 2009 Malignant Tumors in Osteoarchaeological Samples from Hungary. *Acta Biologica Szegediensis* 53(2):117–124.

Montgomery, Janet 2010 Passports from the Past: Investigating Human Dispersals Using Strontium Isotope Analysis of Tooth Enamel. *Annals of Human Biology* 37(3):325–346.

Montgomery, Janet, Christopher J. Knüsel, and Katie Tucker 2011 Identifying the Origins of Decapitated Male Skeletons from 3 Driffield Terrace, York, Through Isotope Analysis. In *The Bioarchaeology of the Human Head: Decapitation, Decoration, and Deformation*, edited by Michelle Bonogofsky, pp. 141–178. University of Florida Press, Gainesville, FL.

Moodie, Roy L. 1931 *Roentgenologic Studies of Egyptian and Peruvian Mummies*. Field Museum of Natural History, Anthropological Memoirs 3, Chicago, IL.

Moore, Keith L., T. V. N. Persaud, and Mark G. Torchia 2015 *The Developing Human*. Saunders, Philadelphia.

Moore, Megan K. 2012 Sex Estimation and Assessment. In *Research Methods in Human Skeletal Biology*, edited by Elizabeth A. DiGangi and Megan K. Moore, pp. 91–116. Elsevier Academic Press, Waltham, MA.

Moore, Megan K., and Ann H. Ross 2012 Stature Estimation. In *Research Methods in Human Skeletal Biology*, edited by Elizabeth A. DiGangi and Megan K. Moore, pp. 151–179. Elsevier Academic Press, Waltham, MA.

Mora, Alice, Bernardo T. Arriaza, Vivien G. Standen, Cristina Valdiosera, Agus Salim, and Colin Smith 2017 High-Resolution Palaeodietary Reconstruction: Amino Acid $\delta^{13}C$ Analysis of Keratin from Single Hairs of Mummified Human Individuals. *Quaternary International* 436(Part A):96–113.

Moran, Kimberlee Sue, and Claire L. Gold (eds.) 2019 *Forensic Archaeology: Multidisciplinary Perspectives*. Springer, Switzerland.

Moreno-Mayar, J. Víctor, Ben A. Potter, Lasse Vinner, Matthias Steinrücken, Simon Rasmussen, Jonathan Terhorst, John A. Kamm, Anders Albrechtsen, Anna-Sapfo Malaspinas, Martin Sikora, Joshua D. Reuther, Joel D. Irish, Ripan S. Malhi, Ludovic Orlando, Yun S. Song, Rasmus Nielsen, David J. Meltzer, and Eske Willerslev 2018 Terminal Pleistocene Alaskan Genome Reveals First Founding Population of Native Americans. *Nature* 553(7687):203–207.

Morris, Ian 1992 *Death-Ritual and Social Structure in Classical Antiquity*. Cambridge University Press, Cambridge, UK.

——— 2008 The Archaeology of Ancestors: The Saxe/Goldstein Hypothesis Revisited. *Cambridge Archaeological Journal* 1(2):147–169.

Morton, Samuel George 1839 *Crania Americana: A Comparative View of Skulls of Various Aboriginal Nations of North and South America*. J. Dobson, Philadelphia and London, Simpkin, Marshall & Co., London, UK.

Muhlestein, Kerry, and Bethany Jensen 2013 The Mummy Portraits of Fag el-Gamous. *Studia Antiqua* 12(1):51–64.

Muller, Jennifer L., Kristen E. Pearlstein, and Carlina de al Cova 2017 Dissection and Documented Skeletal Collections: Embodiments of Legalized Inequality. In *The Bioarchaeology of Dissection and Autopsy in the United States*, edited by Kenneth C. Nystrom, pp. 185–201. Springer, Switzerland.

Munsch, Sam 2019 Controversy Surrounding Human Remains from the First World War. In *The Public Archaeology of Death*, edited by Howard Williams, Benedict Wills-Eve, and Jennifer Osborne, pp. 133–140. Equinox, Sheffield, UK.

Murphy, Eileen, and Mélie Le Roy 2017a Introduction: Archaeological Children, Death and Burial. In *Children, Death and Burial: Archaeological Discourses*, edited by Eileen Murphy and Mélie Le Roy, pp. 1–18. Oxbow Books, Oxford, UK.

——— (eds.) 2017b *Children, Death and Burial: Archaeological Discourses*. Oxbow Books, Oxford, UK.

Murray, Carrie Ann (ed.) 2016 *Diversity of Sacrifice: Form and Function of Sacrificial Practices in the Ancient World and Beyond*. State University of New York Press, Albany, New York.

Nagar, Yossi 2011 Israel. In *The Routledge Handbook of Archaeological Human Remains and Legislation*, edited by Nicholas Márquez-Grant and Linda Fibiger, pp. 612–620. Routledge, London.

Nash, Stephen E. 2002 Archaeological Tree-Ring Dating at the Millennium. *Journal of Archaeological Research* 10(3):243–275.

Nawrocki, Stephen R., Krista E. Latham, and Eric J. Bartelink 2018 Human Skeletal Variation and Forensic Anthropology. In *New Perspectives in Forensic Human Skeletal Identification*, edited by Krista E. Latham, Eric. J. Bartelink, and Michael Finnegan, pp. 5–11. Elsevier Academic Press, London, UK.

Neely, Sharlotte, and Douglass W. Hume (eds.) 2020 *Native Nations: The Survival of Indigenous Peoples* (3rd ed.). JCharlton Publishing, Ltd., Vernon, BC.

Nehlich, Olaf 2015 The Application of Sulphur Isotope Analyses in Archaeological Research: A Review. *Earth-Science Reviews* 142:1–17.

Nell, Erin, and Clive Ruggles 2014 The Orientations of the Giza Pyramids and Associated Structures. *Journal for the History of Astronomy* 45(3):304–360.

Nelson, Andrew John, and Andrew David Wade 2015 Impact: Development of a Radiological Mummy Database. *The Anatomical Record* 298(6):941–948.

Nelson, Greg C. 2016 A Host of Other Dental Diseases and Disorders. In *A Companion to Dental Anthropology*, edited by Joel D. Irish and G. Richard Scott, pp. 465–483. John Wiley & Sons, New York.

Nerlich, Andreas G. 2018 Molecular Paleopathology and Paleo-Oncology – State of the Art, Potentials, Limitations and Perspectives. *International Journal of Paleopathology* 21:77–82.

Nicholas, George P., and Joe Watkins 2014 Indigenous Archaeologies in Archaeological Theory. In *Global Encyclopedia of Archaeology*, pp. 3777–3786. Springer, New York.

Nicklisch, Nicole, Veit Dresely, Jörg Orschiedt, Frank Ramsthaler, Björn Schlenker, Robert Ganslmeier, Susanne Friederich, Harald Meller, and Kurt W. Alt 2018 A Possible Case of Symbolic Trepanation in Neolithic Central Germany. *International Journal of Osteoarchaeology* 28(3):216–226.

Nielsen, Nina H., Bente Philippsen, Marie Kanstrup, and Jesper Olsen 2018 Diet and Radiocarbon Dating of Tollund Man: New Analyses of an Iron Age Bog Body from Denmark. *Radiocarbon* 60(5):1533–1545.

Nieves-Colón, Maria A., and Anne C. Stone 2019 Ancient DNA Analysis of Archaeological Remains. In *Biological Anthropology of the Human Skeleton* (3rd ed.), edited by M. Anne Katzenberg and Anne L. Grauer, pp. 515–544. Wiley-Blackwell, New York.

Nikita, Efthymia, and Efrossyni Michopoulou 2018 A Quantitative Approach for Sex Estimation Based on Cranial Morphology. *American Journal of Physical Anthropology* 165(3):507–517.

Nikitovic, Dejana 2017 *Embodiment of Puebloan Childhoods: Towards a Bioarchaeology of Childhood.* Unpublished Ph.D. dissertation, Department of Anthropology, University of Toronto.

Niven, Laura B., Charles P. Egeland, and Lawrence C. Todd 2004 An Inter-Site Comparison of Enamel Hypoplasia in Bison: Implications for Paleoecology and Modeling Late Plains Archaic Subsistence. *Journal of Archaeological Science* 31(12):1783–1794.

Njau, Jackson K., and Robert J. Blumenschine 2012 Crocodylian and Mammalian Carnivore Feeding Traces on Hominid Fossils from FLK 22 and FLK NN 3, Plio-Pleistocene, Olduvai Gorge, Tanzania. *Journal of Human Evolution* 63(2):408–417.

Nováček, Jan, Kristina Scheelen, and Michael Schultz 2017 The Wrestler from Ephesus: Osteobiography of a Man from the Roman Period Based on His Anthropological and Palaeopathological Record. In *Life & Death in Asia Minor in Hellenistic, Roman and Byzantine Times: Studies in Archaeology and Bioarchaeology*, edited by J. Rasmus Brandt, Erika Hagelberg, Gro Bjørnstad, and Sven Ahrens, pp. 318–338. Oxbow Books, Oxford, UK.

Nugent, Selin Elizabeth 2013 *Death on the Imperial Frontier: An Osteobiography of Roman Burial from Oğlanqala, Azerbaijan.* Master's thesis, Department of Anthropology, The Ohio State University.

Nuzzolese, Emilio, and Matteo Borrini 2010 Forensic Approach to an Archaeological Casework of "Vampire" Skeletal Remains in Venice: Odontological and Anthropological Prospectus. *Journal of Forensic Sciences* 55(6):1634–1637.

Nystrom, Kenneth C. 2011 Postmortem Examinations and the Embodiment of Inequality in 19th Century United States. *International Journal of Paleopathology* 1(3–4):164–172.

——— (ed.) 2017a *The Bioarchaeology of Dissection and Autopsy in the United States.* Springer, Switzerland.

——— 2017b The Biohistory of Prehistory: Mummies and the Forensic Creation of Identity. In *Studies in Forensic Biohistory*, edited by Christopher M. Stojanowski and William N. Duncan, pp. 143–166. Cambridge University Press, Cambridge, UK.

———— 2019 Contributions of Mummy Science to Public Perception of the Past. In *Bioarchaeologists Speak Out: Deep Time Perspectives on Contemporary Issues*, edited by Jane E. Buikstra, pp. 257–282. Springer, Switzerland.

O'Connell, James F. 1995 Ethnoarchaeology Needs a General Theory of Behavior. *Journal of Archaeological Research* 3(3):205–255.

O'Connell, Robert L. 2010 *The Ghosts of Cannae: Hannibal and the Darkest Hour of the Roman Republic.* Random House, New York.

Odes, Edward J., Patrick S. Randolph-Quinney, Maryna Steyn, Zach Throckmorton, Jacqueline S. Smilg, Bernhard Zipfel, Tanya N. Augustine, Frikkie de Beer, Jakobus W. Hoffman, Ryan D. Franklin, and Lee R. Berger 2016 Earliest Hominin Cancer: 1.7-Million-Year-Old Osteosarcoma from Swartkrans Cave, South Africa. *South African Journal of Science* 112(7–8):1–5.

Oesterhelweg, Lars, S. Kröber, K. Rottmann, J. Willhöft, C. Braun, N. Thies, K. Püschel, J. Silkenath, and A. Gehl 2008 Cadaver Dogs – A Study on Detection of Contaminated Carpet Squares. *Forensic Science International* 174(1):35–39.

Oestigaard, Terje 2013 Cremations in Culture and Cosmology. In *The Archaeology of Death and Burial*, edited by Sarah Tarlow and Liv Nilsson Stutz, pp. 497–509. Oxford University Press, Oxford, UK.

Ogilvie, Marsha D., and Charles E. Hilton 2000 A Case of Ritualized Violence in the Prehistoric American Southwest. *International Journal of Osteoarchaeology* 10(1):27–48.

Oliveira, R. N., S. F. S. M. Silva, A. Kawano, and J. L. F. Antunes 2006 Estimating Age by Tooth Wear of Prehistoric Human Remains in Brazilian Archaeological Sites. *International Journal of Osteoarchaeology* 16(5):407–414.

Oppenheimer, Stephen, Bruce Bradley, and Dennis Stanford 2014 Solutrean Hypothesis: Genetics, the Mammoth in the Room. *World Archaeology* 46(5):752–774.

Orofino, Vincenzo, and Paolo Bernardini 2016 Archaeoastronomical Study of the Main Pyramids of Giza, Egypt: Possible Correlations with the Stars? *Archaeological Discovery* 4(1):1–10.

Ortiz de Montellano, Bernard R. 1978 Aztec Cannibalism: An Ecological Necessity? *Science* 200(4342):611–617.

Ortner, Donald J. 2003 *Identification of Pathological Conditions in Human Skeletal Remains* (2nd ed.). Academic Press, Amsterdam, Netherlands.

———— 2011 Human Skeletal Paleopathology. *International Journal of Paleopathology* 1(1):4–11.

Ortner, Donald J., and Walter G. J. Putschar 1981 *Identification of Pathological Conditions in Human Skeletal Remains*. Smithsonian Contributions to Anthropology No. 2, Washington, DC.

Ortner, Sherry B. 2006 *Anthropology and Social Theory: Culture, Power, and the Acting Subject.* Duke University Press, Durham, NC.

Osterholtz, Anna J. 2012 The Social Role of Hobbling and Torture: Violence in the Prehistoric Southwest. *International Journal of Paleopathology* 2(2–3):148–155.

———— (ed.) 2016a *Theoretical Approaches to Analysis and Interpretation of Commingled Human Remains.* Springer, Switzerland.

———— 2016b Patterned Processing and Performance Violence. In *Theoretical Approaches to Analysis and Interpretation of Commingled Human Remains*, edited by Anna J. Osterholtz, pp. 125–138. Springer, Switzerland.

Osterholtz, Anna J., Kathryn M. Baustian, and Debra L. Martin (eds.) 2014a *Commingled and Disarticulated Human Remains: Working Toward Improved Theory, Method, and Data.* Springer, New York.

Osterholtz, Anna J., Kathryn M. Baustian, Debra L. Martin, and Daniel T. Potts 2014b Commingled Human Skeletal Assemblages: Integrative Techniques in Determination of the MNI/MNE. In *Commingled and Disarticulated Human Remains: Working Toward Improved Theory, Method, and Data*, edited by Anna J. Osterholtz, Kathryn M. Baustian, and Debra L. Martin, pp. 35–50. Springer, New York.

Osterholtz, Anna J., and Debra L. Martin 2017 The Poetics of Annihilation: On the Presence of Women and Children at Massacre Sites in the Ancient Southwest. In *Bioarchaeology of Women and Children in Times of War*, edited by Caryn E. Tegtmeyer and Debra L. Martin, pp. 111–128. Springer, Switzerland.

Otterbein, Keith F. 2000 Killing of Captured Enemies: A Cross-Cultural Study. *Current Anthropology* 41(3):439–443.

Ottoni, Claudio, Bram Bekaert, and Ronny Decorte 2017 DNA Degration: Current Knowledge and Progress in DNA Analysis. In *Taphonomy of Human Remains: Forensic Analysis of the Dead and the Depositional Environment*, edited by Eline M. J. Schotsmans, Nicholas Márquez-Grant, and Shari L. Forbes, pp. 65–80. Wiley-Blackwell, Oxford, UK.

Ousley, Stephen D. 2012 Estimating Stature. In *A Companion to Forensic Anthropology*, edited by Dennis C. Dirkmaat, pp. 330–334. John Wiley & Sons, New York.

Ousley, Stephen D., William T. Billeck, and R. Eric Hollinger 2006 Federal Repatriation Legislation and the Role of Physical Anthropology in Repatriation. *Yearbook of Physical Anthropology* 48:2–32.

Ousley, Stephen D., and Richard L. Jantz 2012 Fordisc 3 and Statistical Methods for Estimating Sex and Ancestry. In *A Companion to Forensic Anthropology*, edited by Dennis C. Dirkmaat, pp. 311–329. John Wiley & Sons, New York.

Ousley, Stephen D., Richard L. Jantz, and Joseph T. Hefner 2018 From Blumenbach to Howells: The Slow, Painful Emergence of Theory Through Forensic Race Estimation. In *Forensic Anthropology: Theoretical Framework and Scientific Basis*, edited by C. Clifford Boyd and Donna C. Boyd, pp. 67–97. John Wiley & Sons, New York.

Outram, Alan K. 2008 Introduction to Experimental Archaeology. *World Archaeology* 40(1):1–6.

Owsley, Douglas W., and Richard L. Jantz 2001 Archaeological Politics and Public Interest in Paleoamerican Studies: Lessons from Gordon Creek Woman and Kennewick Man. *American Antiquity* 66(4):565–575.

——— (eds.) 2014 *Kennewick Man: The Scientific Investigation of an Ancient American Skeleton*. Texas A&M University Press, College Station, TX.

Oxenham, Marc F., and Anna Willis 2017 Toward a Bioarchaeology of the Care of Children. In *New Developments in the Bioarchaeology of Care*, edited by Lorna Tilley and Alecia A. Schrenk, pp. 219–236. Springer, Switzerland.

Oxilia, Gregorio, Flavia Fiorillo, Francesco Boschin, Elisabetta Boaretto, Salvatore A. Apicella, Chiara Matteucci, Daniele Panetta, Rossella Pistocchi, Franca Guerrini, Cristiana Margherita, Massimo Andretta, Rita Sorrentino, Giovanni Boschian, Simona Arrighi, Irene Dori, Giuseppe Mancuso, Jacopo Crezzini, Alessandro Riga, Maria C. Serrangeli, Antonino Vazzana, Piero A. Salvadori, Mariangela Vandini, Carlo Tozzi, Adriana Moroni, Robin N. M. Feeney, John C. Willman, Jacopo Moggi-Cecchi, and Stefano Benazzi 2017 The Dawn of Dentistry in the Late Upper Paleolithic: An Early Case of Pathological Intervention at Riparo Fredian. *American Journal of Physical Anthropology* 163(3):446–461.

Özbek, Metin 2012 Auditory Exostoses Among the Prepottery Neolithic Inhabitants of Çayönü and Aşıklı, Anatolia: Its Relation to Aquatic Activities. *International Journal of Paleopathology* 2(4):181–186.

Özkaya, Nihat, Dawn Leger, David Goldsheyder, and Margareta Nordin 2017 *Fundamentals of Biomechanics: Equilibrium, Motion, and Deformation* (4th ed.). Springer, Switzerland.

Pabst, M. A., I. Letofsky-Papst, E. Bock, M. Moser, L. Dorfer, E. Egarter-Vigl, and F. Hofer 2009 The Tattoos of the Tyrolean Iceman: A Light Microscopical, Ultrastructural and Element Analytical Study. *Journal of Archaeological Science* 36(10):2335–2341.

Palkovich, Ann M. 1984a Disease and Mortality Patterns in the Burial Rooms of Pueblo Bonito: Preliminary Considerations. In *Recent Research in Chaco Prehistory*, no. 8, edited by W. James Judge and John D. Schelberg, pp. 103–113. Division of Cultural Research, U.S. Department of the Interior, National Park Service, Albuquerque, NM.

——— 1984b Agriculture, Marginal Environments, and Nutritional Stress in the Prehistoric Southwest. In *Paleopathology at the Origins of Agriculture*, edited by Mark Nathan Cohen and George J. Armelagos, pp. 425–438. Academic Press, Orlando, FL.

——— 2012 Community Violence and Everyday Life: Death at Arroyo Hondo. In *The Bioarchaeology of Violence*, edited by Debra L. Martin, Ryan P. Harrod, and Ventura R. Pérez, pp. 111–120. University Press of Florida, Gainesville, FL.

Pankowská, A., P. Spěváčková, H. Kašparová, and J. Šneberger 2017 Taphonomy of Burnt Burials: Spatial Analysis of Bone Fragments in Their Secondary Deposition. *International Journal of Osteoarchaeology* 27(2):143–154.

Panzer, Stephanie, Sieglinde Ketterl, Roxane Bicker, Sylvia Schoske, and Andreas G. Nerlich 2019 How to CT Scan Human Mummies: Theoretical Considerations and Examples of Use. *International Journal of Paleopathology* 26:22–134.

Panzer, Stephanie, Oliver Peschel, Brigitte Haas-Gebhard, Beatrice E. Bachmeier, Carsten M. Pusch, and Andreas G. Nerlich 2014 Reconstructing the Life of an Unknown (ca. 500 Years-Old South American Inca) Mummy – Multidisciplinary Study of a Peruvian Inca Mummy Suggests Severe Chagas Disease and Ritual Homicide. *PLoS One* 9(2):e89528.

Papageorgopoulou, Christina, Natallia Shved, Johann Wanek, and Frank J. Rühli 2015 Modeling Ancient Egyptian Mummification on Fresh Human Tissue: Macroscopic and Histological Aspects. *The Anatomical Record* 298(6):974–987.

Papageorgopoulou, Christina, Susanne K. Suter, Frank J. Rühli, and Frank Siegmund 2011 Harris Lines Revisited: Prevalence, Comorbidities, and Possible Etiologies. *American Journal of Human Biology* 23(3):381–391.

Papathanasiou, Anastasia 2003 Stable Isotope Analysis in Neolithic Greece and Possible Implications on Human Health. *International Journal of Osteoarchaeology* 13(5):314–324.

Papathanasiou, Anastasia, Nicholas J. Meinzer, Kimberly D. Williams, and Clark Spencer Larsen 2019 History of Anemia and Related Nutritional Deficiencies: Evidence from Cranial Porosities. In *The Backbone of Europe: Health, Diet, Work, and Violence over Two Millennia*, edited by Richard H. Steckel, Clark Spencer Larsen, Charlotte A. Roberts, and Joerg Baten, pp. 198–230. Cambridge University Press, Cambridge, UK.

Pardoe, Colin 2013 Repatriation, Reburial, and Biological Research in Australia. In *The Archaeology of Death and Burial*, edited by Sarah Tarlow and Liv Nilsson Stutz, pp. 733–761. Oxford University Press, Oxford, UK.

Parker Pearson, Mike 2003 *The Archaeology of Death and Burial* (2nd ed.). The History Press, Shroud, UK.

Parsche, Franz, Svetlana Balabanova, and Wolfgang Pirsig 1993 Drugs in Ancient Populations. *The Lancet* 341(8843):503.

Paseka, Rachel E., Carrie C. Heitman, and Karl J. Reinhard 2018 New Evidence of Ancient Parasitism Among Late Archaic and Ancestral Puebloan Residents of Chaco Canyon. *Journal of Archaeological Science: Reports* 18:51–58.

Passalacqua, Nicholas V., and Christopher W. Rainwater (eds.) 2015 *Skeletal Trauma Analysis: Case Studies in Context*. John Wiley & Sons, New York.

Pavelka, Jaroslav, Ladislav Smejda, Radovan Hynek, and Stepanka Hrdlickova Kuckova 2016 Immunological Detection of Denatured Proteins as a Method for Rapid Identification of Food Residues on Archaeological Pottery. *Journal of Archaeological Science* 73:25–35.

Pearson, Osbjorn M., and Jane E. Buikstra 2006 Behavior and the Bones. In *Bioarchaeology: The Contextual Analysis of Human Remains*, edited by Jane A. Buikstra and Lane A. Beck, pp. 207–225. Elsevier Academic Press, Burlington, MA.

Peebles, Christopher S., and Glenn A. Black 1987 Moundville from 1000 to 1500 AD as Seen from 1840 to 1985 AD. In *Chiefdoms in the Americas*, edited by Robert D. Drennan and Carlos A. Uribe, pp. 21–41. University Press of America, Lanham, MD.

Peebles, Christopher S., and Susan M. Kus 1977 Some Archaeological Correlates of Ranked Societies. *American Antiquity* 42(3):421–448.

Pérez, Ventura R. 2012 The Politicization of the Dead: Violence as Performance, Politics as Usual. In *The Bioarchaeology of Violence*, edited by Debra L. Martin, Ryan P. Harrod, and Ventura R. Pérez, pp. 13–28. University Press of Florida, Gainesville, FL.

Phenice, T. W. 1969 A Newly Developed Visual Method of Sexing the Os Pubis. *American Journal of Physical Anthropology* 30(2):297–302.

Pickering, Michael P. 1989 Food for Thought: An Alternative to "Cannibalism in the Neolithic." *Australian Archaeology* 28(1):35–39.

Pietrusewsky, Michael 2019 Traditional Morphometrics and Biological Distance: Methods and an Example. In *Biological Anthropology of the Human Skeleton* (3rd ed.), edited by M. Anne Katzenberg and Anne L. Grauer, pp. 547–591. Wiley-Blackwell, New York.

Pinhasi, Ron, and Christopher Meiklejohn 2011 Dental Reduction and the Transition to Agriculture in Europe. In *Human Bioarchaeology and the Transition to Agriculture*, edited by Ron Pinhasi and Jay T. Stock, pp. 451–474. Wiley-Blackwell, Oxford, UK.

Pinotti, Thomaz, Anders Bergström, Maria Geppert, Matt Bawn, Dominique Ohasi, Wentao Shi, Daniela R. Lacerda, Arne Solli, Jakob Norstedt, Kate Reed, Kim Dawtry, Fabricio González-Andrade, Cesar Paz-y-Miño, Susana Revollo, CinthiaCuellar, Marilza S. Jota, José E. Santos Jr., Qasim Ayub, and ChrisTyler-Smith 2019 Y Chromosome Sequences Reveal a Short Beringian Standstill, Rapid Expansion, and Early Population Structure of Native American Founders. *Current Biology* 29(1):149–157.

Piombino-Mascali, Dario, Heather Gill-Ferking, and Ronald G. Beckett 2017 The Taphonomy of Natural Mummies. In *Taphonomy of Human Remains: Forensic Analysis of the Dead and the Depositional Environment*, edited by Eline M. J. Schotsmans, Nicholas Márquez-Grant, and Shari L. Forbes, pp. 101–119. Wiley-Blackwell, Oxford, UK.

Piombino-Mascali, Dario, and Albert R. Zink 2011 Italy. In *The Routledge Handbook of Archaeological Human Remains and Legislation*, edited by Nicholas Márquez-Grant and Linda Fibiger, pp. 220–232. Routledge, London.

Pluskowski, Aleksander (ed.) 2012 *The Ritual Killing and Burial of Animals: European Perspectives*. Oxbow Books, Oxford, UK.

Pollard, A. Mark 2011 Isotopes and Impact: A Cautionary Tale. *Antiquity* 85(328):631–638.

Polosmak, N., and C. O'Rear 1994 A Mummy Unearthed from the Pastures of Heaven. *National Geographic* 186(4):80–101.

Portal, Jane 2007 *The First Emperor: China's Terracotta Army*. Harvard University Press, Cambridge, MA.

Powell, Mary L. 1985 The Analysis of Dental Wear and Caries for Dietary Reconstruction. In *The Analysis of Prehistoric Diets*, edited by Robert I. Gilbert, Jr. and James H. Mielke, pp. 307–338. Academic Press, New York.

Powell, Mary L., Della Collins Cook, Georgieann Bogdan, Jane E. Buikstra, Mario M. Castro, Patrick D. Horne, David R. Hunt, Richard T. Koritzer, Sheila Ferraz Mendonça de Souza, Mary Kay Sandford, Laurie Saunders, Glaucia Aparecida Malerba Sene, Lynne Sullivan, and John J. Swetnam 2006 Invisible Hands: Women in Bioarchaeology. In *Bioarchaeology: The Contextual Analysis of Human Remains*, edited by Jane A. Buikstra and Lane A. Beck, pp. 131–194. Elsevier Academic Press, Burlington, MA.

Power, Ronika K., and Yann Tristant 2016 From Refuse to Rebirth: Repositioning the Pot Burial in the Egyptian Archaeological Record. *Antiquity* 90(354):1474–1488.

Praetzellis, Adrian 2015 *Archaeological Theory in a Nutshell*. Routledge, London.

Prates, Carlos, Sandra Sousa, Carlos Oliveira, and Salima Ikram 2011 Prostate Metastatic Bone Cancer in an Egyptian Ptolemaic Mummy, a Proposed Radiological Diagnosis. *International Journal of Paleopathology* 1(2):98–103.

Prevedorou, E., and Christopher M. Stojanowski 2017 Biological Kinship, Postmarital Residence and the Emergence of Cemetery Formalisation at Prehistoric Marathon: Cemetery Structure at Tsepi. *International Journal of Osteoarchaeology* 27(4):580–597.

Price, Neil, Charlotte Hedenstierna-Jonson, Torun Zachrisson, Anna Kjellström, Jan Storå, Maja Krzewińska, Torsten Günther, Verónica Sobrado, Mattias Jakobsson, and Anders Götherström 2019 Viking Warrior Women? Reassessing Birka Chamber Grave Bj.581. *Antiquity* 93(367):181–198.

Price, T. Douglas, James H. Burton, Paul D. Fullagar, Lori E. Wright, Jane E. Buikstra, and Vera Tiesler 2014 Strontium Isotopes and the Study of Human Mobility Among the Ancient Maya. In *Archaeology and Bioarchaeology of Population Movement Among the Prehispanic Maya*, edited by Andrea Cucina, pp. 119–132. Springer, New York.

Pringle, Heather 2001 The Incorruptibles. *Discover* 22(6):66–71.

Průchová, E., L. Chroustovský, and P. Kacl 2017 Maximizing Skeletal Data Collection in Commercial Archaeology. *International Journal of Osteoarchaeology* 27(4):527–536.

Putnam, Frederic W. 1884 Abnormal Human Skull from Stone Graves in Tennessee. *Proceedings of the American Association for the Advancement of Science* 32:390–392.

Quigley, Christine 1998 *Modern Mummies*. McFarland & Company, Inc., Jefferson County, NC.

Quinn, Colin P., Ian Kuijt, and Gabriel Cooney 2014a Introduction. In *Transformation by Fire: The Archaeology of Cremation in Cultural Context*, edited by Ian Kuijt, Colin P. Quinn, and Gabriel Cooney, pp. 3–21. University of Arizona Press, Tucson.

Quinn, Colin P., Lynne Goldstein, Gabriel Cooney, and Ian Kuijt 2014a Perspectives – Complexities of Terminologies and Intellectual Frameworks in Cremation Studies. In *Transformation by Fire: The Archaeology of Cremation in Cultural Context*, edited by Ian Kuijt, Colin P. Quinn, and Gabriel Cooney, pp. 27–32. University of Arizona Press, Tucson.

Radimilahy, Chantal 1994 Sacred Sites in Madagascar. In *Sacred Sites, Sacred Places*, edited by David Charmichael, Jane Hubert, Brian Reeves, and Audhild Schanche, pp. 82–88. Routledge, London.

Radini, Anita, Efthymia Nikita, Stephen Buckley, Les Copeland, and Karen Hardy 2017 Beyond Food: The Multiple Pathways for Inclusion of Materials into Ancient Dental Calculus. *American Journal of Physical Anthropology* 162(1):71–83.

Radosavljevich, Paul R. 1911 Professor Boas' New Theory of the Head – A Critical Contribution to School Anthropology. *American Anthropologist* 13(3):394–436.

Raff, Jennifer A., and Deborah A. Bolnick 2014 Palaeogenomics: Genetic Roots of the First Americans. *Nature* 506:162–163.

Raghavan, M., M. Steinrücken, K. Harris, S. Schiffels, S. Rasmussen, M. DeGiorgio, A. Albrechtsen, C. Valdiosera, M. C. Ávila-Arcos, A. Malaspinas, A. Eriksson, I. Moltke, M. Metspalu, J. R. Homburger, J. Wall, O. E. Cornejo, J. V. Moreno-Mayar, T. S. Korneliussen, T. Pierre, M. Rasmussen, P. F. Campos, P. de Barros Damgaard, M. E. Allentoft, J. Lindo, E. Metspal, R. Rodríguez-Varel, J. Mansilla, C. Henrickson, A. Seguin-Orlando, H. Malmström, T. Stafford Jr., S. S. Shringarpure, A. Moreno-Estrada, M. Karmin, K. Tambets, A. Bergström, Y. Xue, V. Warmuth, A. D. Friend, J. Singarayer, P. Valdes, F. Balloux, I. Leboreiro, J. L. Vera, H. Rangel-Villalobos, D. Pettener, D. Luiselli, L. G. Davis, E. Heyer, C. P. E. Zollikofer, M. S. Ponce de León, C. I. Smith, V. Grimes, K. Pike, M. Deal, B. T. Fuller, B. Arriaza, V. Standen, M. F. Luz, F. Ricaut, N. Guidon, L. Osipova, M. I. Voevoda, O. L. Posukh, O. Balanovsky, M. Lavryashina, Y. Bogunov, E. Khusnutdinova, M. Gubina, E. Balanovska, S. Fedorova, S. Litvinov, B. Malyarchuk, M. Derenko, M. J. Mosher, D. Archer, J. Cybulski, B. Petzelt, J. Mitchell, R. Worl, P. J. Norman, P. Parham, B. M. Kemp, T. Kivisild, C. Tyler-Smith, M. S. Sandhu, M. Crawford, R. Villems, and D. G. Smith 2015 Genomic Evidence for the Pleistocene and Recent Population History of Native Americans. *Science* 349(6250):3881–3810.

Ragir, Sonia 1972 *The Early Horizon in Central California Prehistory*. Contributions of the University of California Archaeological Research Facility No. 15, Berkeley.

Rakita, Gordon F. M., and Jane E. Buikstra 2005 Introduction. In *Interacting with the Dead: Perspectives on Mortuary Archaeology for the New Millennium*, edited by Gordon F. M. Rakita, Jane E. Buikstra, Lane A. Beck, and Sloan R. Williams, pp. 1–11. University Press of Florida, Gainesville, FL.

Rasmussen, Simon, Morten Erik Allentoft, Kasper Nielsen, Ludovic Orlando, Martin Sikora, Karl-Göran Sjögren, Anders Gorm Pedersen, Mikkel Schubert, Alex Van Dam, Christian Moliin Outzen Kapel, Henrik Bjørn Nielsen, Søren Brunak, Pavel Avetisyan, Andrey Epimakhov, Mikhail Viktorovich Khalyapin, Artak Gnuni, Aivar Kriiska, Irena Lasak, Mait Metspalu, Vyacheslav Moiseyev, Andrei Gromov, Dalia Pokutta, Lehti Saag, Liivi Varul, Levon Yepiskoposyan, Thomas Sicheritz-Pontén, Robert A. Foley, Marta Mirazón Lahr, Rasmus Nielsen, Kristian Kristiansen, and Eske Willerslev 2015 Early Divergent Strains of *Yersinia pestis* in Eurasia 5,000 Years Ago. *Cell* 163(3):571–582.

Rautman, Alison E., and Todd W. Fenton 2005 A Case of Historic Cannibalism in the American West: Implications for Southwestern Archaeology. *American Antiquity* 70(2):321–341.

Rautman, Alison E., and Lauren E. Talalay 2000 Introduction: Diverse Approaches to the Study of Gender in Archaeology. In *Reading the Body: Representations and Remains in the Archaeological Record*, edited
by Alison E. Rautman, pp. 1–12. University of Pennsylvania Press, Philadelphia.

Raxter, Michelle H., and Christopher B. Ruff 2018 Full Skeleton Stature Estimation. In *New Perspectives in Forensic Human Skeletal Identification*, edited by Krista E. Latham, Eric J. Bartelink, and Michael
Finnegan, pp. 105–113. Academic Press, London, UK.

Raymond, Anan W., and Virginia M. Parks 1990 Archaeological Sites Exposed by Recent Flooding of
Stillwater Marsh, Carson Desert, Churchill County, Nevada. In *Wetlands Adaptation in the Great Basin*,
edited by Joel C. Janetski and David B. Madsen, pp. 33–61. Brigham Young University, Museum of
Peoples and Cultures, Occasional Paper No. 1, Provo, UT.

Read, Piers Paul 1974 *Alive: The Story of the Andes Survivors*. J.B. Lippincott Co., Philadelphia.

Rebmann, Andrew, Edward David, and Marcella H. Sorg 2000 *Cadaver Dog Handbook: Forensic Training
and Tactics for the Recovery of Human Remains*. CRC Press, Boca Raton, FL.

Redfern, Rebecca C. 2017a *Injury and Trauma in Bioarchaeology: Interpreting Violence in Past Lives*. Cambridge University Press, Cambridge, UK.

———— 2017b Identifying and Interpreting Domestic Violence in Archaeological Human Remains:
A Critical Review of the Evidence. *International Journal of Osteoarchaeology* 27(1):13–34.

Redman, Charles L. 1999 *Human Impact on Ancient Environments*. University of Arizona Press, Tucson.

Redman, Samuel J. 2016 *Bone Rooms: From Scientific Racism to Human Prehistory in Museums*. Harvard
University Press, Cambridge, MA.

Rega, Elizabeth 1997 Age, Gender and Biological Reality in the Early Bronze Age Cemetery at Mokrin.
In *Invisible People and Processes: Writing Gender and Childhood into European Archaeology*, edited by Jenny
Moore and Eleanor Scott, pp. 229–247. Leicester University Press, London.

Reinhard, Johan, and Maria Constanza Ceruti 2010 *Inca Rituals and Sacred Mountains: A Study of the
World's Highest Archaeological Sites*. University of California, Cotsen Institute of Archaeology Press,
Los Angeles.

Reinhard, Karl J. 1992 Parasitology as an Interpretive Tool in Archaeology. *American Antiquity*
57(2):231–245.

———— 2006 A Coprological View of Ancestral Pueblo Cannibalism. *American Scientist* 94(3):254–261.

———— 2017 Reestablishing Rigor in Archaeological Parasitology. *International Journal of Paleopathology*
19:124–134.

Reinhard, Karl J., and Vaughn M. Bryant, Jr. 1992 Coprolite Analysis: A Biological Perspective on
Archaeology. In *Archaeological Method and Theory*, vol. 4, edited by Michael B. Schiffer, pp. 245–288.
University of Arizona Press, Tucson.

———— 1995 Investigating Mummified Intestinal Contents: Reconstructing Diet and Parasitic Disease.
In *Proceedings of the First World Congress on Mummy Studies*, vol. 1, pp. 403–408. Museo Arqueológico
Y Etnográfico de Tenerife, Canary Islands.

Reinhard, Karl J., and Dennis R. Danielson 2005 Pervasiveness of Phytoliths in Prehistoric Southwestern Diet and Implications for Regional and Temporal Trends for Dental Microwear. *Journal of
Archaeological Science* 32(7):981–988.

Reinhard, Karl J., Phil R. Geib, Martha M. Callahan, and Richard H. Hevly 1992 Discovery of Colon
Contents in a Skeletonized Burial: Soil Sampling for Dietary Remains. *Journal of Archaeological Science*
19(6):697–705.

Reitsema, Laurie J., and Samantha Holder 2018 Stable Isotope Analysis and the Study of Human Stress,
Disease, and Nutrition. *Bioarchaeology International* 2(2):63–74.

Renshaw, Layla 2013 The Archaeology and Material Culture of Modern Military Death. In *The Archaeology of Death and Burial*, edited by Sarah Tarlow and Liv Nilsson Stutz, pp. 763–779. Oxford University Press, Oxford, UK.

Reynolds, Amanda C., Julio L. Betancourt, Jay Quade, P. Jonathan Patchett, Jeffrey S. Dean, and John
Stein 2005 $^{87}Sr/^{86}Sr$ Sourcing of Ponderosa Pine Used in Anasazi Great House Construction at Chaco
Canyon, New Mexico. *Journal of Archaeological Science* 32(7):1061–1075.

Reznek, R. H., M. G. Hallett, and M. Charlesworth 1986 Computed Tomography of Lindow Man. In *Lindow Man: The Body in the Bog*, edited by I. M. Stead, J. B. Bourke, and Don R. Brothwell, pp. 63–65. Cornell University Press, Ithaca, NY.

Rivera, Frances, and Marta Mirazón Lahr 2017 New Evidence Suggesting a Dissociated Etiology for *Cribra Orbitalia* and Porotic Hyperostosis. *American Journal of Physical Anthropology* 164(1):76–96.

Rivollat, Maïté, Dominique Castex, Laurent Hauret, and Anne-Marie Tilliera 2015 Ancient Down Syndrome: An Osteological Case from Saint-Jean-des-Vignes, Northeastern France, from the 5–6th Century AD. *International Journal of Paleopathology* 7:8–14.

Robben, Antonius C. G. M. 2015 Exhumations, Territoriality, and Necropolitics in Chile and Argentina. In *Necropolitics: Mass Graves and Exhumations in the Age of Human Rights*, edited by Francisco Ferrándiz and Antonius C. G. M. Robben, pp. 53–75. University of Pennsylvania Press, Philadelphia.

Roberts, Charlotte A. 2006 A View from Afar: Bioarchaeology in Britain. In *Bioarchaeology: The Contextual Analysis of Human Remains*, edited by Jane A. Buikstra and Lane A. Beck, pp. 417–439. Elsevier Academic Press, Burlington, MA.

——— 2009 *Human Remains in Archaeology: A Handbook*. Council for British Archaeology, York, UK.

——— 2011 The Bioarchaeology of Leprosy and Tuberculosis: A Comparative Study of Perceptions, Stigma, Diagnosis, and Treatment. In *Social Bioarchaeology*, edited by Sabrina C. Agarwal and Bonnie A. Glencross, pp. 252–281. Wiley-Blackwell, Oxford, UK.

——— 2013 Social Aspects of the Bioarchaeology of Leprosy. In *The Dead Tell Tales: Essays in Honor of Jane E. Buikstra*, edited by María Cecilia Lozada and Barra O'Donnabhain, pp. 136–144. Cotsen Institute of Archaeology Press, Monograph 76. University of California, Los Angeles.

Roberts, Charlotte A., and Keith Manchester 2007 *The Archaeology of Disease* (3rd ed.). Cornell University Press, Ithaca, NY.

Roffey, Simon, Katie Tucker, Kori Filipek-Ogden, Janet Montgomery, Jamie Cameron, Tamsin O'Connell, Jane Evans, Phil Marter, and G. Michael Taylor 2017 Investigation of a Medieval Pilgrim Burial Excavated from the Leprosarium of St Mary Magdalen Winchester, UK. *PLoS Neglected Tropical Diseases* 11(1):e0005186.

Rogers, Alexander K., and Daron Duke 2011 An Archaeologically Validated Protocol for Computing Obsidian Hydration Rates from Laboratory Data. *Journal of Archaeological Science* 38(6):1340–1345.

Roizen, Nancy J., and David Patterson 2003 Down's Syndrome. *Lancet* 361(9365):1281–1289.

Rood, Ronald J. 2006 *Archaeological Excavation of 42JB1470*. Utah Division of State History, Archaeology/Antiquities Section, Salt Lake City, UT.

Rorabaugh, Adam N., and Kate A. Shantry 2017 From Labrets to Cranial Modification: Credibility Enhancing Displays and the Changing Expression of Coast Salish Resource Commitments. *The Journal of Island and Coastal Archaeology* 12(3):380–397.

Rose, Jerome C., and Dolores L. Burke 2006 The Dentist and the Archaeologist: The Role of Dental Anthropology in North American Bioarchaeology. In *Bioarchaeology: The Contextual Analysis of Human Remains*, edited by Jane A. Buikstra and Lane A. Beck, pp. 323–346. Elsevier Academic Press, Burlington, MA.

Rose, Jerome C., Thomas J. Green, and Victoria D. Green 1996 NAGPRA Is Forever: Osteology and the Repatriation of Skeletons. *Annual Review of Anthropology* 25:81–103.

Ross, Ann H., and Suzanne M. Abel 2011 *The Juvenile Skeleton in Forensic Abuse Investigations*. Humana Press, New York.

Ross, Zoe Patterson, Jennifer Klunk, Gino Fornaciari, Valentina Giuffra, Sebastian Duchêne, Ana T. Duggan, Debi Poinar, Mark W. Douglas, John-Sebastian Eden, Edward C. Holmes, and Hendrik N. Poinar 2018 The Paradox of HBV Evolution as Revealed from a 16th Century Mummy. *PLoS Pathogens*. doi.org/10.1371/journal.ppat.1006750.

Rothhammer, Francisco, Marvin J. Allison, Lautaro Núñez, Vivien Standen, and Bernardo Arriaza 1985 Chagas' Disease in Pre-Columbian South America. *American Journal of Physical Anthropology* 68(4):495–498.

Rothschild, Bruce M., I. Hershkovitz, O. Dutour, B. Latimer, Christine Rothschild, and L. M. Jellema 1997 Recognition of Leukemia in Skeletal Remains: Report and Comparison of Two Cases. *American Journal of Physical Anthropology* 102(4):481–496.

Rothschild, Bruce M., and Christine Rothschild 1997 Congenital Syphilis in the Archaeological Record: Diagnostic Insensitivity of Osseous Lesions. *International Journal of Osteoarchaeology* 7(1):39–42.

Rowbotham, Samantha K. 2016 Anthropological Estimation of Sex. In *Handbook of Forensic Anthropology and Archaeology* (2nd ed.), edited by Soren Blau and Douglas H. Ubelaker, pp. 261–272. Routledge, New York.

Rubenstein, Steven Lee 2007 Circulation, Accumulation, and the Power of Shuar Shrunken Heads. *Cultural Anthropology* 22(3):357–399.

Ruff, Christopher B. 2019 Biomechanical Analyses of Archaeological Human Skeletons. In *Biological Anthropology of the Human Skeleton* (3rd ed.), edited by M. Anne Katzenberg and Anne L. Grauer, pp. 189–224. Wiley-Blackwell, New York.

Ruff, Christopher B., Brigitte M. Holt, Markku Niskanen, Vladimir Sladék, Margit Berner, Evan Garofalo, Heather M. Garvin, Martin Hora, Heli Maijanen, Sirpa Niinimäki, Kati Salo, Eliška Schuplerová, and Dannielle Tompkins 2012 Stature and Body Mass Estimation from Skeletal Remains in the European Holocene. *American Journal of Physical Anthropology* 148(4):601–617.

Ruff, Christopher B., Markku Niskanen, Heli Maijanen, and Simon Mays 2019 Effects of Age and Body Proportions on Stature Estimation. *American Journal of Physical Anthropology* 168(2):370–377.

Rufino, A. I., M. T. Ferreira, and S. N. Wasterlain 2017 Periapical Lesions in Intentionally Modified Teeth in a Skeletal Sample of Enslaved Africans (Lagos, Portugal). *International Journal of Osteoarchaeology* 27(2):288–297.

Rühli, Frank J. 2015 Short Review: Magnetic Resonance Imaging of Ancient Mummies. *The Anatomical Record* 298(6):1111–1115.

Rühli, Frank J., and Salima Ikram 2014 Purported Medical Diagnoses of Pharaoh Tutankhamun, c. 1325 BC. *HOMO: Journal of Comparative Human Biology* 65(1):51–63.

Rutecki, Dawn M., and Chelsea Blackmore 2016 Towards an Inclusive Queer Archaeology. *SAA Archaeological Record* 9–11, January.

Rylander, Kate Aasen 1994 Corn Preparation Among the Basketmaker Anasazi: A Scanning Electron Microscope Study of *Zea Mays* Remains from Coprolites. In *Paleonutrition: The Diet and Health of Prehistoric Americans*, edited by Kristin D. Sobolik, pp. 115–133. Southern Illinois University, Center for Archaeological Investigations, Occasional Paper No. 22, Carbondale, IL.

Salanova, Laure, Philippe Chambon, Jean-Gabriel Pariat, Anne-Sophie Marçais, and Frédérique Valentin 2017 From One Ritual to Another: The Long-Term Sequence of the Bury Gallery Grave (Northern France, Fourth – Second Millennia BC). *Antiquity* 91(355):57–73.

Samadelli, Marco, Marcello Melis, Matteo Miccoli, Eduard Egarter Vigl, and Albert R. Zink 2015 Complete Mapping of the Tattoos of the 5300-Year-Old Tyrolean Iceman. *Journal of Cultural Heritage* 16(5):753–758.

Sandford, Mary K. 1984 *Diet, Disease, and Nutritional Stress: An Elemental Analysis of Human Hair from Kulubnarti, A Medieval Sudanese Nubian Population.* Unpublished Ph.D. dissertation, University of Colorado Press, Boulder, CO.

Sandford, Mary K., and Grace E. Kissling 1993 Chemical Analyses of Human Hair: Anthropological Applications. In *Investigations of Ancient Human Tissue: Chemical Analyses in Anthropology*, edited by Mary K. Sandford, pp. 131–166. Gordon and Breach, Langhorne, PA.

Sandford, Mary K., Dennis P. Van Gerven, and Robert R. Meglen 1983 Elemental Hair Analysis: New Evidence on the Etiology of Cribra Orbitalia in Sudanese Nubia. *Human Biology* 55(4):831–844.

Sanson, Gordon D., Stuart A. Kerr, and Karlis A. Gross 2007 Do Silica Phytoliths Really Wear Mammalian Teeth? *Journal of Archaeological Science* 34(4):526–531.

Santana, Jonathan, Francisco Javier Rodríguez-Santos, María Dolores Camalich-Massieu, Dimas Martín-Socas, and Rosa Fregel 2019 Aggressive or Funerary Cannibalism? Skull-Cup and Human Bone Manipulation in Cueva de El Toro (Early Neolithic, Southern Iberia). *American Journal of Physical Anthropology* 169(1):31–54.

Sapir-Hen, L., M. A. S. Martin, and I. Finkelstein 2017 Food Rituals and Their Social Significance in the Mid-Second Millennium BC in the Southern Levant: A View from Megiddo. *International Journal of Osteoarchaeology* 27(6):1048–1058.

Saul, Frank P. 1972 The Human Skeletal Remains of Altar de Sacrificios: An Osteobiographic Analysis. *Harvard University, Papers of the Peabody Museum* 63(2).

Saunders, Nicholas J. 2007 *Killing Time: Archaeology and the First World War*. Sutton Publishing, Thrupp, UK.

———— 2017 *Beyond the Dead Horizon: Studies in Modern Conflict Archaeology*. Oxbow Books, Oxford, UK.

Saxe, Arthur A. 1970 *Social Dimensions of Mortuary Practices*. Unpublished Ph.D. dissertation, Department of Anthropology, University of Michigan, Ann Arbor.

Sayer, Duncan 2017 *Ethics and Burial Archaeology*. Duckworth, London.

Scarre, Geoffrey 2003 Archaeology and Respect for the Dead. *Journal of Applied Philosophy* 20(3):237–249.

———— 2006 Can Archaeology Harm the Dead? In *The Ethics of Archaeology: Philosophical Perspectives on Archaeological Practice*, edited by Chris Scarre and Geoffrey Scarre, pp. 181–198. Cambridge University Press, Cambridge, UK.

———— 2013 "Sapient Trouble-Tombs"? In *The Archaeology of Death and Burial*, edited by Sarah Tarlow and Liv Nilsson Stutz, pp. 665–676. Oxford University Press, Oxford, UK.

Schaefer, Maureen, Sue Black, and Louise Scheuer 2009 *Juvenile Osteology: A Laboratory and Field Manual*. Elsevier Academic Press, Burlington, MA.

Schaefer, Maureen, Nicole Geske, and Craig Cunningham 2018 A Decade of Development of Juvenile Aging. In *New Perspectives in Forensic Human Skeletal Identification*, edited by Krista E. Latham, Eric J. Bartelink, and Michael Finnegan, pp. 45–60. Academic Press, London, UK.

Scheib, C. L., Hongjie Li, Tariq Desai, Vivian Link, Christopher Kendall, Genevieve Dewar, Peter William Griffith, Alexander Mörseburg, John R. Johnson, Amiee Potter, Susan L. Kerr, Phillip Endicott, John Lindo, Marc Haber, Yali Xue, Chris Tyler-Smith, Manjinder S. Sandhu, Joseph G. Lorenz, Tori D. Randall, Zuzana Faltyskova, Luca Pagani, Petr Danecek, Tamsin C. O'Connell, Patricia Martz, Alan S. Boraas, Brian F. Byrd, Alan Leventhal, Rosemary Cambra, Ronald Williamson, Louis Lesage, Brian Holguin, Ernestine Ygnacio-De Soto, JohnTommy Rosas, Mait Metspalu, Jay T. Stock, Andrea Manica, Aylwyn Scally, Daniel Wegmann, Ripan S. Malhi, and Toomas Kivisild 2018 Ancient Human Parallel Lineages Within North America Contributed to a Coastal Expansion. *Science* 360(6392):1024–1027.

Schermer, Shirley J., Eve A. Hargrave, Kristin M. Hedman, and Robin M. Little 2015 Transforming the Dead. In *Transforming the Dead: Culturally Modified Bone in the Prehistoric Midwest*, edited by Eve A. Hargrave, Shirley J. Schermer, Kristin M. Hedman, and Robin M. Little, pp. 1–12. The University of Alabama Press, Tuscaloosa, AL.

Scheuer, Louise, and Sue Black 2004 *The Juvenile Skeleton*. Elsevier Academic Press, Burlington, MA.

Schiffer, Michael B. 2010 *Behavioral Archaeology: Principles and Practice*. Equinox, Sheffield, UK.

Schillaci, Michael A., Dejana Nikitovic, Nancy J. Akins, Lianne Tripp, and Ann M. Palkovich 2011 Infant and Juvenile Growth in Ancestral Pueblo Indians. *American Journal of Physical Anthropology* 145(2):318–326.

Schiller, Francis 1992 *Paul Broca: Founder of French Anthropology, Explorer of the Brain*. Oxford University Press, Oxford, UK.

Schmidt, Christopher W. 2015 Burned Human Teeth. In *The Analysis of Burned Human Remains* (2nd ed.), edited by Christopher W. Schmidt and Steven A. Symes, pp. 61–81. Academic Press, Amsterdam, Netherlands.

———— 2016 Estimating Age, Sex, and Individual ID from Teeth. In *A Companion to Dental Anthropology*, edited by Joel D. Irish and G. Richard Scott, pp. 362–376. John Wiley & Sons, New York.

Schmidt, Christopher W., and Amber E. Osterholt 2014 Middle and Late Archaic Trophy Taking in Indiana. In *Violence and Warfare Among Hunter-Gatherers*, edited by Mark W. Allen and Terry L. Jones, pp. 241–256. Left Coast Press, Walnut Creek, CA.

Schmidt, Christopher W., Robin Quataert, Fatma Zalzala, and Ruggero D'Anastasio 2017 Taphonomy of Teeth. In *Taphonomy of Human Remains: Forensic Analysis of the Dead and the Depositional Environment*, edited by Eline M. J. Schotsmans, Nicholas Márquez-Grant, and Shari L. Forbes, pp. 92–100. Wiley-Blackwell, Oxford, UK.

Schmidt, Christopher W., Ashley Remy, Rebecca Van Sessen, John Willman, Kristin Krueger, Rachel Scott, Patrick Mahoney, Jeremy Beach, Jaqueline McKinley, Ruggero D'Anastasio, Laura Chiu, Michele Buzon, J. Rocco De Gregory, Susan Sheridan, Jacqueline Eng, James Watson, Haagen Klaus, Pedro Da-Gloria, Jeremy Wilson, Abigail Stone, Paul Sereno, Jessica Droke, Rose Perash, Christopher Stojanowski, and Nicholas Herrmann 2019 Dental Microwear Texture Analysis of *Homo sapiens sapiens*: Foragers, Farmers, and Pastoralists. *American Journal of Physical Anthropology* 169(2):207–226.

Schmidt, Christopher W., and Steven A. Symes (eds.) 2015 *The Analysis of Burned Human Remains* (2nd ed.). Academic Press, Amsterdam, Netherlands.

Schmidt, Robert A., and Barbara L. Voss (eds.) 2000 *Archaeologies of Sexuality*. Routledge, London.

Schmitt, Aurore 2004 Age at Death Assessment Using the Os Pubis and the Auricular Surface of the Ilium: A Test on an Identified Asian Sample. *International Journal of Osteoarchaeology* 14(1):1–6.

Schoeninger, Margaret J. 1999 Prehistoric Subsistence Strategies in the Stillwater Marsh Region of the Carson Desert. In *Prehistoric Lifeways in the Great Basin Wetlands: Bioarchaeological Reconstruction and Interpretations*, edited by Brian E. Hemphill and Clark Spencer Larsen, pp. 151–166. University of Utah Press, Salt Lake City, UT.

Schoeninger, Margaret J., Holly Reeser, and Kris Hallin 2003 Paleoenvironment of *Australopithecus anamensis* at Allia Bay, East Turkana, Kenya: Evidence from Mammalian Herbivore Enamel Stable Isotopes. *Journal of Anthropological Archaeology* 22(3):200–207.

Schotsmans, Eline M. J., Nicholas Márquez-Grant, and Shari L. Forbes (eds.) 2017a Introduction. In *Taphonomy of Human Remains: Forensic Analysis of the Dead and the Depositional Environment*, edited by Eline M. J. Schotsmans, Nicholas Márquez-Grant, and Shari L. Forbes, pp. 1–8. Wiley-Blackwell, Oxford, UK.

——— (eds.) 2017b *Taphonomy of Human Remains: Forensic Analysis of the Dead and the Depositional Environment*. Wiley-Blackwell, Oxford, UK.

Schrader, Sarah 2019 *Activity, Diet and Social Practice: Addressing Everyday Life in Human Skeletal Remains*. Springer, Switzerland.

Schrenk, Alecia A., and Debra L. Martin 2017 Applying the Index of Care to the Case of a Bronze Age Teenager Who Lived with Paralysis: Moving from Speculation to Strong Inference. In *New Developments in the Bioarchaeology of Care*, edited by Lorna Tilley and Alecia A. Schrenk, pp. 47–64. Springer, Switzerland.

Schulting, Rick J., Stella M. Blockley, Hervé Bocherens, Dorothée Drucker, and Mike Richards 2008 Stable Carbon and Nitrogen Isotope Analysis on Human Remains from the Early Mesolithic Site of La Vergne (Charente-Maritime, France). *Journal of Archaeological Science* 35(3):763–772.

Schulting, Rick J., and Michael P. Richards 2001 Dating Women and Becoming Farmers: New Paleodietary and AMS Dating Evidence from the Breton Mesolithic Cemeteries of Téviec and Hoëdic. *Journal of Anthropological Archaeology* 20(3):314–344.

Schultz, John J. 2012 The Application of Ground Penetrating Radar for Forensic Grave Detection. In *A Companion to Forensic Anthropology*, edited by Dennis C. Dirkmaat, pp. 85–100. John Wiley & Sons, New York.

Schultz, John J., Michael W. Warren, and John S. Krigbaum 2015 Analysis of Human Cremains. In *The Analysis of Burned Human Remains* (2nd ed.), edited by Christopher W. Schmidt and Steven A. Symes, pp. 83–103. Academic Press, Amsterdam, Netherlands.

Schultz, Michael, U. Timme, and T. H. Schmidt-Schultz 2007 Infancy and Childhood in the Pre-Columbian North American Southwest – First Results of the Palaeopathological Investigation of the Skeletons from the Grasshopper Pueblo, Arizona. *International Journal of Osteoarchaeology* 17(4):369–379.

Schurr, Mark R. 2018 Exploring Ideas About Isotopic Variation in Breastfeeding and Weaning Within and Between Populations: Case Studies from the American Midcontinent. *International Journal of Osteoarchaeology* 28(5):479–491.

Schurr, Mark R., Robert G. Hayes, and Della C. Cook 2015 Thermally Induced Changes. In *The Analysis of Burned Human Remains* (2nd ed.), edited by Christopher W. Schmidt and Steven A. Symes, pp. 105–118. Academic Press, Amsterdam, Netherlands.

Schurr, Theodore G. 2015 Tracing Human Movements from Siberia to the Americas: Insights from Genetic Studies. In *Mobility and Ancient Society in Asia and the Americas*, edited by Michael David Frachetti and Robert N. Spengler III, pp. 23–47. Springer, Switzerland.

Schwarcz, Henry P., and Christine D. White 2004 The Grasshopper or the Ant? Cultigen-Use Strategies in Ancient Nubia from C-13 Analyses of Human Hair. *Journal of Archaeological Science* 31(6):753–762.

Schwartz, Glenn M. 2017 The Archaeological Study of Sacrifice. *Annual Review of Anthropology* 46:223–240.

Schwitalla, Al W. 2013 *Global Warming in California: A Lesson from the Medieval Climatic Anomaly (A.D. 800–1350).* Center for Archaeological Research at Davis, Publication No. 17, Davis, CA.

Schwitalla, Al W., Terry L. Jones, Randy S. Wiberg, Martin A. Pilloud, Brian F. Codding, and Eric C. Strother 2014 Archaic Violence in Western North America: The Bioarchaeological Record of Dismemberment, Human Bone Artifacts, and Trophy Skulls from Central California. In *Violence and Warfare among Hunter-Gatherers*, edited by Mark W. Allen and Terry L. Jones, pp. 273–295. Left Coast Press, Walnut Creek, CA.

Scott, Eleanor 1999 *The Archaeology of Infancy and Infant Death.* British Archaeological Reports International Series 819. Archaeo Press, Oxford, UK.

———— 2001 Killing the Female? Archaeological Narratives of Infanticide. In *Gender and the Archaeology of Death*, edited by Bettina Arnold and Nancy L. Wicker, pp. 3–21. AltaMira Press, Walnut Creek, CA.

Scott, G. Richard 2016 A Brief History of Dental Anthropology. In *A Companion to Dental Anthropology*, edited by Joel D. Irish and G. Richard Scott, pp. 7–17. John Wiley & Sons, New York.

Scott, G. Richard, Christopher Maier, and Kelly Heim 2016 Identifying and Recording Key Morphological (Nonmetric) Crown and Root Traits. In *A Companion to Dental Anthropology*, edited by Joel D. Irish and G. Richard Scott, pp. 247–264. John Wiley & Sons, New York.

Scott, G. Richard, and Marin A. Pilloud 2019 Dental Morphology. In *Biological Anthropology of the Human Skeleton* (3rd ed.), edited by M. Anne Katzenberg and Anne L. Grauer, pp. 257–292. Wiley-Blackwell, New York.

Scott, G. Richard, Christy G. Turner II, Grant C. Townsend, and María Martinón-Torres 2018 *The Anthropology of Modern Human Teeth: Dental Morphology and Its Variation in Recent and Fossil Homo sapiens* (2nd ed.). Cambridge University Press, Cambridge, UK.

Seeman, Mark F. 1988 Ohio Hopewell Trophy-Skull Artifacts as Evidence for Competition in Middle Woodland Societies Circa 50 B.C.–A.D. 350. *American Antiquity* 53(3):565–577.

Séguy, Isabelle, and Luc Buchet 2013 *Handbook of Palaeodemography.* Springer, New York.

Seo, Min, Jong-Yil Chai, Myeung Ju Kim, Sang Yuk Shim, Ho Chul Ki, and Dong Hoon Shin 2016 Detection Trend of Helminth Eggs in the Strata Soil Samples from Ancient Historic Places of Korea. *The Korean Journal of Parasitology* 54(5):555.

Shapiro, H. L. 1959 The History and Development of Physical Anthropology. *American Anthropologist* 61(3):371–379.

Sharapova, Svetlana, and Dmitry Razhev 2011 Skull Deformation During the Iron Age in Trans-Urals and Western Siberia. In *The Bioarchaeology of the Human Head: Decapitation, Decoration, and Deformation*, edited by Michelle Bonogofsky, pp. 202–227. University Press of Florida, Gainesville, FL.

Shay, Talia 1985 Differentiated Treatment of Deviancy at Death as Revealed in Anthropological and Archeological Material. *Journal of Anthropological Archaeology* 4(3):221–241.

Shellis, R. Peter, and Martin Addy 2014 The Interactions Between Attrition, Abrasion and Erosion in Tooth Wear. In *Erosive Tooth Wear: From Diagnosis to Therapy*, edited by A. Lussi and C. Ganss, pp. 32–45. Monographs in Oral Science No. 25. Karger, Basel, Switzerland.

Shellis, R. Peter, J. D. B. Featherstone, and A. Lussi 2014 Understanding the Chemistry of Dental Erosion. In *Erosive Tooth Wear: From Diagnosis to Therapy*, edited by A. Lussi and C. Ganss, pp. 163–179. Monographs in Oral Science No. 25. Karger, Basel, Switzerland.

Shimada, Izumi, Haggen D. Klaus, Rafael A. Segura, and Go Matsumoto 2015 Living with the Dead: Conceptions and Treatment of the Dead on the Peruvian Coast. In *Living with the Dead in the Andes*, edited by Izumi Shimada and James L. Fitzsimmons, pp. 101–172. University of Arizona Press, Tucson.

Shishlina, N., S. Pankova, V. Sevastyanov, O. Kuznetsova, and Yu Demidenko 2016 Pastoralists and Mobility in the Oglakhty Cemetery of Southern Siberia: New Evidence from Stable Isotopes. *Antiquity* 90(351):679–694.

Signoli, Michel, and Guillaume de Védrines 2011 Burials Related to Recent Military Conflicts: Case Studies from France. In *The Routledge Handbook of Archaeological Human Remains and Legislation*, edited by Nicholas Márquez-Grant and Linda Fibiger, Appendix 3, pp. 711–717. Routledge, London.

Skedros, John G. 2012 Interpreting Load History in Limb-Bone Diaphyses: Important Considerations in Their Biomechanical Foundations. In *Bone Histology: An Anthropological Perspective*, edited by Christian Crowder and Sam Stout, pp. 153–220. CRC Press, Boca Raton, FL.

Skinner, Mark 1996 Developmental Stress in Immature Hominines from Late Pleistocene Eurasia: Evidence from Enamel Hypoplasia. *Journal of Archaeological Science* 23(6):833–852.

———— 1997 Dental Wear in Immature Late Pleistocene European Hominines. *Journal of Archaeological Science* 24(8):677–700.

Skoglund, Pontus, Jan Storå, Anders Götherström, and Mattias Jakobsson 2013 Accurate Sex Identification of Ancient Human Remains Using DNA Shotgun Sequencing. *Journal of Archaeological Science* 40:4477–4482.

Sládek, Vladimír, Jiří Macháček, Christopher B. Ruff, Eliška Schuplerová, Renáta Přichystalová, and Martin Hora 2015 Population-Specific Stature Estimation from Long Bones in the Early Medieval Pohansko (Czech Republic). *American Journal of Physical Anthropology* 158(2):312–324.

Slater, Philip A., Kristin M. Hedman, and Thomas E. Emerson 2014 Immigrants at the Mississippian Polity of Cahokia: Strontium Isotope Evidence for Population Movement. *Journal of Archaeological Science* 44:117–127.

Slavinsky, Vyacheslav Sergeyevich, Konstantin Vladimirovich Chugunov, Alexander Alekseevich Tsybankov, Sergey Nikolaevich Ivanov, Alisa Vladimirovna Zubova, and Sergey Mikhailovich Slepchenko 2018 *Trichuris trichiura* in the Mummified Remains of Southern Siberian Nomads. *Antiquity* 92(362):410–420.

Sledge, Michael 2005 *Soldier Dead: How We Recover, Identify, Bury, and Honor Our Military Fallen.* Columbia University Press, New York.

Slepchenko, S. M., A. V. Vybornov, V. S. Slavinsky, A. A. Tsybankov, and V. E. Matveev 2017 Ante Mortem Cranial Trepanation in the Late Bronze Age in Western Siberia. *International Journal of Osteoarchaeology* 27(3):356–364.

Slon, Viviane, Charlotte Hopfe, Clemens L. Weiß, Fabrizio Mafessoni, Marco de la Rasilla, Carles Lalueza-Fox, Antonio Rosas, Marie Soressi, Monika V. Knul, Rebecca Miller, John R. Stewart, Anatoly P. Derevianko, Zenobia Jacobs, Bo Li1, Richard G. Roberts, Michael V. Shunkov, Henry de Lumley, Christian Perrenoud, Ivan Gušić, Željko Kućan, Pavao Rudan, Ayinuer Aximu-Petri, Elena Essel, Sarah Nagel, Birgit Nickel, Anna Schmidt, Kay Prüfer, Janet Kelso, Hernán A. Burbano, Svante Pääbo, and Matthias Meyer 2017 Neandertal and Denisovan DNA from Pleistocene Sediments. *Science* 356(6338):605–608.

Smith, David Glenn, Robert L. Bettinger, and Becky K. Rolfs 1995 Serum Albumin Phenotypes at Stillwater: Implications for Population History in the Great Basin. In *Bioarchaeology of the Stillwater Marsh: Prehistoric Human Adaptation in the Western Great Basin*, edited by Clark Spencer Larsen and Robert L. Kelly, pp. 68–72. American Museum of Natural History, Anthropological Papers 77, New York.

Smith, Linda Tuhiwai 2012 *Decolonizing Methodologies: Research and Indigenous Peoples* (2nd ed.). Zed Books, London.

Smith, Maria Ostendorf 2012 Paleopathology. In *Research Methods in Human Skeletal Biology*, edited by Elizabeth A. DiGangi and Megan K. Moore, pp. 181–217. Elsevier Academic Press, Waltham, MA.

Smith, Patricia, and Gal Avishai 2005 The Use of Dental Criteria for Estimating Postnatal Survival in Skeletal Remains of Infants. *Journal of Archaeological Science* 32(1):83–89.

Smith, Patricia, and Gila Kahila 1992 Identification of Infanticide in Archaeological Sites: A Case Study from the Late Roman-Early Byzantine Periods at Ashkelon, Israel. *Journal of Archaeological Science* 19(6):667–675.

Smith, Scott C. 2016 *Landscape and Politics in the Ancient Andes: Biographies of Place at Khonkho Wankane.* University of New Mexico Press, Albuquerque, NM.

Smith-Guzmán, Nicole E. 2015 The Skeletal Manifestation of Malaria: An Epidemiological Approach Using Documented Skeletal Collections. *American Journal of Physical Anthropology* 158(4):624–635.

Snoddy, Anne Marie E., Hallie R. Buckley, Gail E. Elliott, Vivien G. Standen, Bernardo T. Arriaza, and Siân E. Halcrow 2018 Macroscopic Features of Scurvy in Human Skeletal Remains: A Literature Synthesis and Diagnostic Guide. *American Journal of Physical Anthropology* 167(4):876–895.

Snoddy, Anne Marie E., Hallie R. Buckley, and Siân E. Halcrow 2016 More Than Metabolic: Considering the Broader Paleoepidemiological Impact of Vitamin D Deficiency in Bioarchaeology. *American Journal of Physical Anthropology* 160(2):183–196.

Snoeck, Christophe, John Pouncett, Greer Ramsey, Ian G. Meighan, Nadine Mattielli, Steven Goderis, Julia A. Lee-Thorp, and Rick J. Schulting 2016 Mobility During the Neolithic and Bronze Age in Northern Ireland Explored Using Strontium Isotope Analysis of Cremated Human Bone. *American Journal of Physical Anthropology* 160(3):397–413.

Sobolik, Kristin D. 2002 Children's Health in the Prehistoric Southwest. In *Children in the Prehistoric Puebloan Southwest*, edited by Kathryn A. Kamp, pp. 125–151. University of Utah Press, Salt Lake City, UT.

———— 2003 *Archaeobiology.* AltaMira Press, Walnut Creek, CA.

Sobolik, Kristin D., and Deborah J. Gerick 1992 Prehistoric Medicinal Plant Usage: A Case Study from Coprolites. *Journal of Ethnobiology* 12(2):203–211.

Sobolik, Kristin D., Kristen J. Gremillion, Patricia L. Whitten, and Patty Jo Watson 1996 Technical Note: Sex Determination of Prehistoric Human Paleofeces. *American Journal of Physical Anthropology* 101(2):283–290.

Sofaer, Joanna R. 2006 *The Body as Material Culture: A Theoretical Osteoarchaeology.* Cambridge University Press, Cambridge, UK.

Sofaer, Joanna R., and Marie Louise Stig Sørensen 2013 Death and Gender. In *The Archaeology of Death and Burial*, edited by Sarah Tarlow and Liv Nilsson Stutz, pp. 527–541. Oxford University Press, Oxford, UK.

Soffer, Olga, James M. Adovasio, and David C. Hyland 2000 The "Venus" Figurines: Textiles, Basketry, Gender, and Status in the Upper Paleolithic. *Current Anthropology* 41(4):511–537.

Soren, David 2003 Can Archaeologists Excavate Evidence of Malaria? *World Archaeology* 35(2):193–209.

Sparacello, Vitale Stefano, Charlotte A. Roberts, Alessandro Canci, Jacopo Moggi-Cecchi, and Damiano Marchi 2016 Insights on the Paleoepidemiology of Ancient Tuberculosis from the Structural Analysis of Postcranial Remains from the Ligurian Neolithic (Northwestern Italy). *International Journal of Paleopathology* 15:50–64.

Spence, Michael W., Michael J. Shkrum, Alison Ariss, and John Regan 1999 Craniocervical Injuries in Judicial Hangings: An Anthropologic Analysis of Six Cases. *The American Journal of Forensic Medicine and Pathology* 20(4):309–322.

Spradley, M. Katherine, and Richard L. Jantz 2011 Sex Estimation in Forensic Anthropology: Skull Versus Postcranial Elements. *Journal of Forensic Sciences* 56(2):289–296.

———— 2016 Ancestry Estimation in Forensic Anthropology: Geometric Morphometric Versus Standard and Nonstandard Interlandmark Distances. *Journal of Forensic Sciences* 61(4):892–897.

Spradley, M. Katherine, and Kyra E. Stull 2018 Advancements in Sex and Ancestry Estimation. In *New Perspectives in Forensic Human Skeletal Identification*, edited by Krista E. Latham, Eric J. Bartelink, and Michael Finnegan, pp. 13–21. Academic Press, London, UK.

Spradley, M. Katherine, and Katherine Weisensee 2017 Ancestry Estimation: The Importance, the History, and the Practice. In *Forensic Anthropology: A Comprehensive Introduction* (2nd ed.), edited by Natalie R. Langley and MariaTeresa A. Tersigni-Tarrant, pp. 163–174. CRC Press, Boca Raton, FL.

Sprague, Roderick 2005 *Burial Terminology: A Guide for Researchers*. AltaMira Press, Walnut Creek, CA.

Stacey, Rebecca J., Carl Heron, and Mark Q. Sutton 1998 The Chemistry, Archaeology, and Ethnography of a Native American Insect Resin. *Journal of California and Great Basin Anthropology* 20(1):53–71.

Standen, Vivien G., and Bernardo T. Arriaza 2000 Trauma in the Preceramic Coastal Populations of Northern Chile: Violence or Occupational Hazards? *American Journal of Physical Anthropology* 112(3):239–249.

Stanford, Dennis J., and Bruce A. Bradley 2012 *Across Atlantic Ice: The Origin of America's Clovis Culture*. University of California Press, Berkeley.

Steadman, Dawnie W. 2019 The Body-as-Evidence Paradigm in Domestic and International Forensic Anthropology. In *Bioarchaeologists Speak Out: Deep Time Perspectives on Contemporary Issues*, edited by Jane E. Buikstra, pp. 243–255. Springer, Switzerland.

Steckel, Richard H., and Anna Kjellström 2019 Measuring Community Health Using Skeletal Remains: A Health Index for Europe. In *The Backbone of Europe: Health, Diet, Work, and Violence Over Two Millennia*, edited by Richard H. Steckel, Clark Spencer Larsen, Charlotte A. Roberts, and Joerg Baten, pp. 52–83. Cambridge University Press, Cambridge, UK.

Steckel, Richard H., and Jerome C. Rose (eds.) 2005 *The Backbone of History: Health and Nutrition in the Western Hemisphere* (revised ed.). Cambridge University Press, Cambridge, UK.

Štefan, Ivo, Petra Stránská, and Hana Vondrová 2016 The Archaeology of Early Medieval Violence: The Mass Grave at Budeč, Czech Republic. *Antiquity* 90(351):759–776.

Stefan, Vincent H. 2014 The Determination of Homicide vs. Suicide in Gunshot Wounds. In *Biological and Forensic Perspectives on Violence: How Violent Death Is Interpreted from Skeletal Remains*, edited by Debra L. Martin and Cheryl P. Anderson, pp. 51–62. Cambridge University Press, Cambridge, UK.

Steinbock, R. Ted 1985 The History, Epidemology, and Paleopathology of Kidney and Bladder Stone Disease. In *Health and Disease in the Prehistoric Southwest*, edited by Charles F. Merbs and Robert J. Miller, pp. 177–209. Arizona State University, Anthropological Research Papers No. 34, Tempe.

Stephan, Carl N., and Peter Claes 2016 Craniofacial Identification: Techniques of Facial Approximation and Craniofacial Superimposition. In *Handbook of Forensic Anthropology and Archaeology* (2nd ed.), edited by Soren Blau and Douglas H. Ubelaker, pp. 402–415. Routledge, New York.

Stevens, Susan T. 1991 Charon's Obol and Other Coins in Ancient Funerary Practice. *Phoenix* 45(3):215–229.

Stewart, Marissa C., and Giuseppe Vercellotti 2017 Application of Geographic Information Systems to Investigating Associations Between Social Status and Burial Location in Medieval Trino Vercellese (Piedmont, Italy). *American Journal of Physical Anthropology* 164(1):11–29.

Stewart, T. D. 1947 *Hrdlička's Practical Anthropometry*. Wistar Press, Philadelphia.

Stichelbaut, Birger, and David Chielens 2016 The Aerial Perspective in a Museum Context: Above Flanders Fields 1914–1918. In *Conflict Landscapes and Archaeology from Above*, edited by B. Stichelbaut and D. Cowley, pp. 279–291. Ashgate, Routledge, Farnham.

Stichelbaut, Birger, Wouter Gheyle, Veerle Van Eetvelde, Marc Van Meirvenne, Timothy Saey, Nicolas Note, Hanne Van den Berghe, and Jean Bourgeois 2017 The Ypres Salient 1914–1918: Historical Aerial Photography and the Landscape of War. *Antiquity* 91(355):235–249.

Stirland, Ann 2012 The Men of the Mary Rose. In *The Social History of English Seamen, 1485–1649*, edited by Cheryl A. Fury, pp. 47–73. Boydell & Brewer, Woodbridge, UK.

Stock, Jay T., and Ron Pinhasi 2011 Introduction: Changing Paradigms in Our Understanding of the Transition to Agriculture: Human Bioarchaeology, Behaviour and Adaptation. In *Human Bioarchaeology and the Transition to Agriculture*, edited by Ron Pinhasi and Jay T. Stock, pp. 1–13. Wiley-Blackwell, Oxford, UK.

Stodder, Ann L. W. 1990 *Paleoepidemiology of Eastern and Western Pueblo Communities in Protohistoric New Mexico.* Unpublished Ph.D. dissertation, Department of Anthropology, University of Colorado Press, Boulder, CO.

———— 2019 Taphonomy and the Nature of Archaeological Assemblages. In *Biological Anthropology of the Human Skeleton* (3rd ed.), edited by M. Anne Katzenberg and Anne L. Grauer, pp. 547–591. Wiley-Blackwell, New York.

Stodder, Ann L. W., and Ann M. Palkovich 2012 Osteobiography and Bioarchaeology. In *The Bioarchaeology of Individuals*, edited by Ann L. W. Stodder and Ann M. Palkovich, pp. 1–8. University Press of Florida, Gainesville, FL.

Stojanowski, Christopher M. 2013 Ethnogenetic Theory and New Directions in Biodistance Research. In *The Dead Tell Tales: Essays in Honor of Jane E. Buikstra*, edited by María Cecilia Lozada and Barra O'Donnabhain, pp. 71–82. Cotsen Institute of Archaeology Press, Monograph 76. University of California, Los Angeles.

———— 2019 Ancient Migrations: Biodistance, Genetics, and the Persistence of Typological Thinking. In *Bioarchaeologists Speak Out: Deep Time Perspectives on Contemporary Issues*, edited by Jane E. Buikstra, pp. 181–200. Springer, Switzerland.

Stojanowski, Christopher M., and Ryan M. Seidemann 1999 A Reevaluation of the Sex Prediction Accuracy of the Minimum Supero-Interior Femoral Neck Diameter for Modern Individuals. *Journal of Forensic Sciences* 44(6):1215–1218.

Stojanowski, Christopher M., Kent M. Johnson, Kathleen S. Paul, and Charisse L. Carver 2016a Indicators of Idiosyncratic Behavior in the Dentition. In *A Companion to Dental Anthropology*, edited by Joel D. Irish and G. Richard Scott, pp. 377–395. John Wiley & Sons, New York.

Stojanowski, Christopher M., Andrew C. Seidel, Laura C. Fulginiti, Kent M. Johnson, and Jane E. Buikstra 2016b Contesting the Massacre at Nataruk. *Nature* 539:E8–E10.

Stone, Pamela K. 2012 Binding Women: Ethnology, Skeletal Deformations, and Violence Against Women. *International Journal of Paleopathology* 2(2–3):53–60.

———— 2016 Biocultural Perspectives on Maternal Mortality and Obstetrical Death from the Past to the Present. *American Journal of Physical Anthropology* 159(S61):150–171.

Stone, Pamela K. (ed.) 2018 *Bioarchaeological Analyses and Bodies: New Ways of Knowing Anatomical and Archaeological Skeletal Collections.* Springer, Switzerland.

Storey, Rebecca 2006 An Elusive Paleodemography? A Comparison of Two Methods for Estimating the Adult Age Distribution of Deaths at Late Classic Copan, Honduras. *American Journal of Physical Anthropology* 132(1):40–47.

———— 2014 Classic Maya Warfare and Skeletal Trophies: Victims and Aggressors. In *Biological and Forensic Perspectives on Violence: How Violent Death Is Interpreted from Skeletal Remains*, edited by Debra L. Martin and Cheryl P. Anderson, pp. 120–133. Cambridge University Press, Cambridge, UK.

Stout, Sam 1989 Histomorphometric Analysis of Human Skeletal Remains. In *Reconstruction of Life from the Skeleton*, edited by Mehmet Y. İşcan and Kenneth A. R. Kennedy, pp. 41–52. Alan R. Liss, Inc., New York.

Stout, Sam, and Christian Crowder 2012 Bone Remodeling, Histomorphology, and Histomorphometry. In *Bone Histology: An Anthropological Perspective*, edited by Christian Crowder and Sam Stout, pp. 1–22. CRC Press, Boca Raton, FL.

Streeter, Margaret 2012 Histological Age-at-Death Estimations. In *Bone Histology: An Anthropological Perspective*, edited by Christian Crowder and Sam Stout, pp. 135–152. CRC Press, Boca Raton, FL.

Stutz, Liv Nilsson 2018 From Here and to Death: The Archaeology of the Human Body. In *A Companion to the Anthropology of Death*, edited by Antonius C. G. M. Robben, pp. 323–335. John Wiley & Sons, New York.

Suchey, Judy M., and Sheilagh T. Brooks 1986a *Instruction for Use of Suchey-Brooks System for Age Determination of the Male Os Pubis.* Instructional Materials Accompanying Male Pubic Symphyseal Models of the Suchey-Brooks System. France Casting, Fort Collins, CO.

———— 1986b *Instruction for Use of Suchey-Brooks System for Age Determination of the Female Os Pubis.* Instructional Materials Accompanying Female Pubic Symphyseal Models of the Suchey-Brooks System. France Casting, Fort Collins, CO.

Sundstrom, Linea 2015 The Meaning of Scalping in Native North America. In *Transforming the Dead: Culturally Modified Bone in the Prehistoric Midwest*, edited by Eve A. Hargrave, Shirley J. Schermer, Kristin M. Hedman, and Robin M. Little, pp. 249–261. The University of Alabama Press, Tuscaloosa, AL.

Sutter, Richard C., and Rosa J. Cortez 2005 The Nature of Moche Human Sacrifice: A BioArchaeological Perspective. *Current Anthropology* 46(4):521–549.

Sutton, Mark Q. 1988a Dental Modification in a Burial from the Southern San Joaquin Valley, California. In *Human Skeletal Biology: Contributions to the Understanding of California's Prehistoric Populations*, edited by Gary D. Richards, pp. 91–96. Coyote Press Archives of California Prehistory No. 24, Salinas, CA.

———— 1988b *Insects as Food: Aboriginal Entomophagy in the Great Basin*. Ballena Press Anthropological Papers No. 33, Socorro, NM.

———— 1994 Indirect Studies in Paleonutrition Studies. In *Paleonutrition: The Diet and Health of Prehistoric Americans*, edited by Kristin D. Sobolik, pp. 98–111. Center for Archaeological Investigations, Occasional Paper No. 22. Southern Illinois University, Carbondale, IL.

———— 1995 Archaeological Aspects of Insect Use. *Journal of Archaeological Method and Theory* 2(3):253–298.

———— 2013 *Archaeology: The Science of the Human Past* (4th ed.). Routledge, New York.

———— 2017a Voices from the Past: Conceptualizing a "Fifth World." *Journal of Anthropology and Archaeology* 5(1):17–19.

———— 2017b The "Fishing Link": Salmonids and the Initial Peopling of the Americas. *PaleoAmerica* 3(3):231–259.

Sutton, Mark Q., Minnie Malik, and Andrew Ogram 1996 Experiments on the Determination of Gender from Coprolites by DNA Analysis. *Journal of Archaeological Science* 23(2):263–267.

Sutton, Mark Q., and Karl J. Reinhard 1995 Cluster Analysis of the Coprolites from Antelope House: Implications for Anasazi Diet and Cuisine. *Journal of Archaeological Science* 22(6):741–750.

Sutton, Mark Q., Kristin D. Sobolik, and Jill K. Gardner 2010 *Paleonutrition*. University of Arizona Press, Tucson.

Symes, Steven A., Christopher W. Rainwater, Erin N. Chapman, Desina R. Gipson, and Andrea L. Piper 2015 Patterned Thermal Destruction in a Forensic Setting. In *The Analysis of Burned Human Remains* (2nd ed.), edited by Christopher W. Schmidt and Steven A. Symes, pp. 17–59. Academic Press, Amsterdam, Netherlands.

Szpak, Paul, Jean-François Millaire, Christine D. White, Steve Bourget, and Fred Longstaffe 2016 Life Histories of Sacrificed Camelids from Huancaco (Virú Valley). In *Ritual Violence in the Ancient Andes: Reconstructing Sacrifice on the North Coast of Peru*, edited by Haagen D. Klaus and J. Marla Toyne, pp. 319–341. University of Texas Press, Austin, TX.

Tafuri, M. A., M. Rottoli, M. Cupitò, M. L. Pulcini, G. Tasca, N. Carrara, F. Bonfanti, L. Salzani, and A. Canci 2018 Estimating C_4 Plant Consumption in Bronze Age Northeastern Italy Through Stable Carbon and Nitrogen Isotopes in Bone Collagen. *International Journal of Osteoarchaeology* 28(2):131–142.

Tarlow, Sarah, and Liv Nilsson Stutz (eds.) 2013 *The Archaeology of Death and Burial*. Oxford University Press, Oxford, UK.

Taylor, G. Michael, Stephanie Widdison, Ivor N. Brown, and Douglas B. Young 2000 A Mediaeval Case of Lepromatous Leprosy from 13–14th Century Orkney, Scotland. *Journal of Archaeological Science* 27(12):1133–1138.

Taylor, R. E., and Ofer Bar-Yosef 2014 *Radiocarbon Dating: An Archaeological Perspective* (2nd ed.). Routledge, London.

Taylor, Walter W. 1948 *A Study of Archeology*. Memoirs of the American Anthropological Association No. 69, Menasha, WI.

Teaford, Mark F., Clark Spencer Larsen, Robert F. Pastor, and Vivian E. Noble 2001 Pits and Scratches: Microscopic Evidence of Tooth Use and Masticatory Behavior in La Florida. In *Bioarchaeology of Spanish Florida: The Impact of Colonialism*, edited by Clark Spencer Larsen, pp. 82–112. University Press of Florida, Gainesville, FL.

Tegtmeyer, Caryn E., and Debra L. Martin (eds.) 2017a *Broken Bones, Broken Bodies: Bioarchaeological and Forensic Approaches for Accumulative Trauma and Violence*. Lexington Books, Lanham, MD.
———— 2017b *Bioarchaeology of Women and Children in Times of War*. Springer, Switzerland.
Tegtmeyer, Caryn E., and Debra L. Martin 2017c The Bioarchaeology of Women, Children, and Other Vulnerable Groups in Times of War. In *Bioarchaeology of Women and Children in Times of War*, edited by Caryn E. Tegtmeyer and Debra L. Martin, pp. 1–14. Springer, Switzerland.
Temple, Daniel H. 2011 Evolution of Postcranial Morphology During the Agricultural Transition in Prehistoric Japan. In *Human Bioarchaeology and the Transition to Agriculture*, edited by Ron Pinhasi and Jay T. Stock, pp. 235–262. Wiley-Blackwell, Oxford, UK.
———— 2016 Caries: The Ancient Scourge. In *A Companion to Dental Anthropology*, edited by Joel D. Irish and G. Richard Scott, pp. 433–449. John Wiley & Sons, New York.
Temple, Daniel H., and Alan H. Goodman 2014 Bioarcheology Has a "Health" Problem: Conceptualizing "Stress" and "Health" in Bioarchaeological Research. *American Journal of Physical Anthropology* 155(2):186–191.
Testart, Alain 1988 Some Major Problems in the Social Anthropology of Hunter-Gatherers. *Current Anthropology* 29(1):1–31.
Theodorakou, C., and Michael J. Farquharson 2008 Human Soft Tissue Analysis Using X-Ray or Gamma-Ray Techniques. *Physics in Medicine & Biology* 53(11):R111.
Thomas, David Hurst 2000 *Skull Wars: Kennewick Man, Archaeology, and the Battle for Native American Identity*. Basic Books, New York.
Thomas, Geoffrey P. 2016 An 8000-Year-Old Case of Thalassemia from the Windover, Florida Skeletal Population. *International Journal of Paleopathology* 14(1):81–90.
Thompson, Tim J. U., David Gonçalves, Kristy Squires, and Priscilla Ulguim 2017 Thermal Alteration to the Body. In *Taphonomy of Human Remains: Forensic Analysis of the Dead and the Depositional Environment*, edited by Eline M. J. Schotsmans, Nicholas Márquez-Grant, and Shari L. Forbes, pp. 318–334. Wiley-Blackwell, Oxford, UK.
Thompson, Tim J. U., and Priscilla F. Ulguim 2016 Burned Human Remains. In *Handbook of Forensic Anthropology and Archaeology* (2nd ed.), edited by Soren Blau and Douglas H. Ubelaker, pp. 391–401. Routledge, New York.
Tiesler, Vera 2014 *The Bioarchaeology of Artificial Cranial Modifications: New Approaches to Head Shaping and Its Meanings in Pre-Columbian Mesoamerica and Beyond*. Springer, New York.
Tilley, Lorna 2015a *Theory and Practice in the Bioarchaeology of Care*. Springer, New York.
———— 2015b Accommodating Difference in the Prehistoric Past: Revisiting the Case of Romito 2 from a Bioarchaeology of Care Perspective. *International Journal of Paleopathology* 8:64–74.
———— 2017 Showing That They Cared: An Introduction to Thinking, Theory and Practice in the Bioarchaeology of Care. In *New Developments in the Bioarchaeology of Care*, edited by Lorna Tilley and Alecia A. Schrenk, pp. 11–43. Springer, Switzerland.
Tilley, Lorna, and Tony Cameron 2014 Introducing the Index of Care: A Web-Based Application Supporting Archaeological Research into Health-Related Care. *International Journal of Paleopathology* 6:5–9.
Tilley, Lorna, and Marc F. Oxenham 2011 Survival Against the Odds: Modeling the Social Implications of Care Provision to Seriously Disabled Individuals. *International Journal of Paleopathology* 1(1):35–42.
Tilley, Lorna, and Alecia A. Schrenk (eds.) 2017 *New Developments in the Bioarchaeology of Care: Further Case Studies and Expanded Theory*. Springer, Switzerland.
Tito, Raul Y., Samuel L. Belknap, Kristin D. Sobolik, Robert C. Ingraham, Lauren M. Cleeland, and Cecil M. Lewis, Jr. 2011 Brief Communication: DNA from Early Holocene American Dog. *American Journal of Physical Anthropology* 145(4):653–657.
Tjelldén, A. K. E., S. M. Kristiansen, H. Birkedal, and M. M. E. Jans 2018 The Pattern of Human Bone Dissolution – A Histological Study of Iron Age Warriors from a Danish Wetland Site. *International Journal of Osteoarchaeology* 28(4):407–418.

To, Denise 2017 Forensic Archaeology: Survey Methods, Scene Documentation, Excavation, and Recovery Methods. In *Forensic Anthropology: A Comprehensive Introduction* (2nd ed.), edited by Natalie R. Langley and MariaTeresa A. Tersigni-Tarrant, pp. 35–56. CRC Press, Boca Raton, FL.

Tocheri, Matthew W., and J. Eldon Molto 2002 Aging Fetal and Juvenile Skeletons from Roman Period Egypt Using Basiocciput Osteometrics. *International Journal of Osteoarchaeology* 12(5):356–363.

Tomczak, Paula D., and Joseph F. Powell 2003 Postmarital Residence Practices in the Windover Population: Sex-Based Dental Variation as an Indicator of Patrilocality. *American Antiquity* 68(1):93–108.

Tomczyk, J., P. Palczewski, H. Mańkowska-Pliszka, T. Płoszaj, K. Jędrychowska-Dańska, and H. Witas 2016 Anaemia (Thalassaemia) in the Middle Euphrates Valley of Syria in the Second – Fourth Centuries AD? *Antiquity* 90(349):157–171.

Tornberg, Anna, and Lars Jacobsson 2018 Care and Consequences of Traumatic Brain Injury in Neolithic Sweden: A Case Study of Ante Mortem Skull Trauma and Brain Injury Addressed Through the Bioarchaeology of Care. *International Journal of Osteoarchaeology* 28(2):188–198.

Torres-Rouff, Christina 2011 Piercing the Body: Labret Use, Identity, and Masculinity in Prehistoric Chile. In *Breathing New Life into the Evidence of Death*, edited by Aubrey Baadsgaard, Lexis T. Boutin, and Jane E. Buikstra, pp. 153–178. School for Advanced Research Press, Santa Fe, NM.

Torres-Rouff, Christina, and Laura M. King 2014 Face Me Like a Man! (or, Like a Woman): Antemortem Nasal Fractures in Pre-Columbian San Pedro de Atacama. In *Biological and Forensic Perspectives on Violence: How Violent Death Is Interpreted from Skeletal Remains*, edited by Debra L. Martin and Cheryl P. Anderson, pp. 134–147. Cambridge University Press, Cambridge, UK.

Townsend, G. C., and T. Brown 1981 The Carabelli Trait in Australian Aboriginal Dentition. *Archives of Oral Biology* 26(10):809–814.

Toyne, J. Marla 2015a The Body Sacrificed: A Bioarchaeological Analysis of Ritual Violence in Ancient Túcume, Peru. *Journal of Religion and Violence* 3(1):137–171.

—— 2015b Ritual Violence and Human Offerings at the Temple of the Sacred Stone, Túcume, Peru. In *Living with the Dead in the Andes*, edited by Izumi Shimada and James L. Fitzsimmons, pp. 173–199. University of Arizona Press, Tucson.

—— 2015c Tibial Surgery in Ancient Peru. *International Journal of Paleopathology* 8:29–35.

Toyne, J. Marla, Christine D. White, John W. Verano, Santiago Uceda Castillo, Jean François Millaire, and Fred J. Longstaffe 2014 Residential Histories of Elites and Sacrificial Victims at Huacas de Moche, Peru, as Reconstructed from Oxygen Isotopes. *Journal of Archaeological Science* 42(1):15–28.

Trammel, Lindsay H., and Anne M. Kroman 2012 Bone and Dental Histology. In *Research Methods in Human Skeletal Biology*, edited by Elizabeth A. DiGangi and Megan K. Moore, pp. 361–395. Elsevier Academic Press, Waltham, MA.

Trautmann, B., C. Wißing, M. Díaz-Zorita Bonilla, C. Bis-Worch, and H. Bocherens 2017 Reconstruction of Socioeconomic Status in the Medieval (14th–15th Century) Population of Grevenmacher (Luxembourg) Based on Growth, Development and Diet. *International Journal of Osteoarchaeology* 27(6):947–957.

Trigg, Heather B., Richard I. Ford, John G. Moore, and Louise D. Jessop 1994 Coprolite Evidence for Prehistoric Foodstuffs, Condiments, and Medicines. In *Eating on the Wild Side: The Pharmacologic, Ecological, and Social Implications of Using Noncultigens*, edited by Nina L. Etkin, pp. 210–223. University of Arizona Press, Tucson.

Trinkaus, Erik 1983 *The Shanidar Neandertals*. Academic Press, New York.

Trinkaus, Erik, and Alexandra P. Buzhilova 2018 Diversity and Differential Disposal of the Dead at Sunghir. *Antiquity* 92(361):7–21.

Trinkaus, Erik, and Sébastien Villotte 2017 External Auditory Exostoses and Hearing Loss in the Shanidar 1 Neandertal. *PLoS One* 12(10):e0186684.

Trinkaus, Kathryn M. 1995 Mortuary Behavior, Labor Organization, and Social Rank. In *Regional Approaches to Mortuary Analysis*, edited by Lane A. Beck, pp. 53–75. Plenum Press, New York.

Trotter, Mildred 1970 Estimation of Stature from Intact Long Limb Bones. In *Personal Identification in Mass Disasters*, edited by T. D. Stewart, pp. 71–83. Smithsonian Institution, Washington, DC.

Trotter, Mildred, and Goldine C. Gleser 1952 Estimation of Stature from Long Bones of American Whites and Negroes. *American Journal of Physical Anthropology* 10(4):463–514.

Tschauner, Hartmut 1996 Middle-Range Theory, Behavioral Archaeology, and Postempiricist Philosophy of Science in Archaeology. *Journal of Archaeological Method and Theory* 3(1):1–30.

Tsutaya, Takumi 2017 Post-Weaning Diet in Archaeological Human Populations: A Meta-Analysis of Carbon and Nitrogen Stable Isotope Ratios of Child Skeletons. *American Journal of Physical Anthropology* 164(3):546–557.

Tucker, Katie 2014 The Osteology of Decapitation Burials from Roman Britain. In *The Routledge Handbook of the Bioarchaeology of Human Conflict*, edited by Christopher Knüsel and Martin J. Smith, pp. 213–236. Routledge, New York.

Tung, Tiffiny A. 2012 Violence Against Women: Differential Treatment of Local and Foreign Females in the Heartland of the Wari Empire, Peru. In *Biological and Forensic Perspectives on Violence: How Violent Death Is Interpreted from Skeletal Remains*, edited by Debra L. Martin and Cheryl P. Anderson, pp. 180–198. Cambridge University Press, Cambridge, UK.

———— 2016 Commingled Bodies and Mixed and Communal Identities. In *Theoretical Approaches to Analysis and Interpretation of Commingled Human Remains*, edited by Anna J. Osterholtz, pp. 243–251. Springer, Switzerland.

Turner, Christy G. II 1971 Three-Rooted Mandibular First Permanent Molars and the Question of American Indian Origins. *American Journal of Physical Anthropology* 34(2):229–241.

———— 1983 Taphonomic Reconstructions of Human Violence and Cannibalism Based on Mass Burials in the American Southwest. In *Carnivores, Human Scavengers, and Predators: A Question of Bone Technology*, edited by G. M. LeMoine and A. S. MacEachern, pp. 219–240. Archaeological Association of the University of Calgary, Calgary.

———— 1994 Relating Eurasian and Native American Populations Through Dental Morphology. In *Method and Theory for Investigating the Peopling of the Americas*, edited by Robson Bonnichsen and D. Gentry Steele, pp. 131–140. Center for the Study of the First Americans, Oregon State University, Corvallis, OR.

Turner, Christy G. II, and Nancy T. Morris 1970 A Massacre at Hopi. *American Antiquity* 35(3):320–331.

Turner, Christy G. II, and Jacqueline A. Turner 1999 *Man Corn: Cannibalism and Violence in the Prehistoric American Southwest*. University of Utah Press, Salt Lake City, UT.

Ubelaker, Douglas H. 2006 The Changing Role of Skeletal Biology at the Smithsonian. In *Bioarchaeology: The Contextual Analysis of Human Remains*, edited by Jane A. Buikstra and Lane A. Beck, pp. 73–81. Elsevier Academic Press, Burlington, MA.

———— 2011 United States of America. In *The Routledge Handbook of Archaeological Human Remains and Legislation*, edited by Nicholas Márquez-Grant and Linda Fibiger, pp. 532–540. Routledge, London.

———— 2018a Estimation of Immature Age from Dentition. In *New Perspectives in Forensic Human Skeletal Identification*, edited by Krista E. Latham, Eric J. Bartelink, and Michael Finnegan, pp. 61–64. Academic Press, London, UK.

———— 2018b A History of Forensic Anthropology. *American Journal of Physical Anthropology* 165(4):915–923.

———— 2019 Forensic Anthropology: Methodology and Applications. In *Biological Anthropology of the Human Skeleton* (3rd ed.), edited by M. Anne Katzenberg and Anne L. Grauer, pp. 43–71. Wiley-Blackwell, New York.

Uhl, Natalie M. 2012 Age-at-Death Estimation. In *Research Methods in Human Skeletal Biology*, edited by Elizabeth A. DiGangi and Megan K. Moore, pp. 63–90. Elsevier Academic Press, Waltham, MA.

Upadhyay, Ram Ballabh, Juhi Upadhyay, Pankaj Agrawal, and Nirmala N. Rao 2012 Analysis of Gonial Angle in Relation to Age, Gender, and Dentition Status by Radiological and Anthropometric Methods. *Journal of Forensic Dental Sciences* 4(1):29–33.

Valentin, F., Hervé Bocherens, B. Gratuze, and C. Sand 2006 Dietary Patterns During the Late Prehistoric/Historic Period in Cikobia Island (Fiji): Insights from Stable Isotopes and Dental Pathologies. *Journal of Archaeological Science* 33(10):1396–1410.

Van Asch, Barbara, Ai-bing Zhang, Mattias C. R. Oskarsson, Cornelya F. C. Klutsch, Antonio Amorim, and Peter Savolainen 2013 Pre-Columbian Origins of Native American Dog Breeds, with Only Limited Replacement by European Dogs, Confirmed by mtDNA Analysis. *Proceedings of the Royal Society B* 280(1766).

Van Gerven, Dennis P., J. Hummert, K. Pendergast-Moore, and Mary Kay Sandford 1990 Nutrition, Disease, and the Human Life Cycle: A Bioethnography of a Medieval Nubian Community. In *Primate Life History and Evolution*, edited by Carol Jean DeRousseau, pp. 297–324. Wiley, New York.

Van Wolputte, Steven 2004 Hang on to Your Self: Of Bodies, Embodiment, and Selves. *Annual Review of Anthropology* 33:251–269.

VanPool, Christine S., and Todd L. VanPool 1999 The Scientific Nature of Postprocessualism. *American Antiquity* 64(1):33–53.

Velasco-Vázquez, J., T. Delgado-Darias, and V. Alberto-Barroso 2018 Violence Targeting Children or Violent Society? Craniofacial Injuries Among the Pre-Hispanic Subadult Population of Gran Canaria (Canary Islands). *International Journal of Osteoarchaeology* 28(4):388–396.

Vencl, S. 1984 War and Warfare in Archaeology. *Journal of Anthropological Archaeology* 3(2):116–132.

Verano, John W. 2000 Paleonthological Analysis of Sacrificial Victims at the Pyramid of the Moon, Moche River Valley, Northern Peru. *Chungará (Arica)* 32(1):61–70.

——— 2005 Human Sacrifice and Postmortem Modification at the Pyramid of the Moon, Moche Valley, Peru. In *Interacting with the Dead: Perspectives on Mortuary Archaeology for the New Millennium*, edited by Gordon F. M. Rakita, Jane E. Buikstra, Lane A. Beck, and Sloan R. Williams, pp. 277–289. University Press of Florida, Gainesville, FL.

——— 2016 *Holes in the Head: The Art and Archaeology of Trepanation in Ancient Peru*. Studies in Pre-Columbian Art and Archaeology No. 38. Dumbarton Oaks, Washington, DC.

Verano, John W., and Sara A. Phillips 2016 The Killing of Captives on the North Coast of Peru in Pre-Hispanic Times: Iconographic and Bioarchaeological Evidence. In *Ritual Violence in the Ancient Andes: Reconstructing Sacrifice on the North Coast of Peru*, edited by Haagen D. Klaus and J. Marla Toyne, pp. 244–265. University of Texas Press, Austin, TX.

Verdugo, C., K. Kassadjikova, E. Washburn, K. M. Harkins, and L. Fehren-Schmitz 2017 Ancient DNA Clarifies Osteological Analyses of Commingled Remains from Midnight Terror Cave, Belize. *International Journal of Osteoarchaeology* 27(3):495–499.

Verlinden, Petra, and Mary E. Lewis 2015 Childhood Trauma: Methods for the Identification of Physeal Fractures in Nonadult Skeletal Remains. *American Journal of Physical Anthropology* 157(3):411–420.

Virchow, R. 1896 Heredity and the Formation of Race. Translated and reprinted in *This Is Race* (1950), edited by E. W. Count, pp. 178–193. Schuman, New York.

Voas, Maddeline 2018 Tiny Graves: Mortality, Health, and Personhood in the Early Stages of Life. *Society* 55(4):349–355.

von Hunnius, Tanya E., Charlotte A. Roberts, Anthea Boylston, and Shelley R. Saunders 2006 Histological Identification of Syphilis in Pre-Columbian England. *American Journal of Physical Anthropology* 129(4):559–566.

Voss, Barbara L. 2008 Sexuality Studies in Archaeology. *Annual Review of Anthropology* 37:317–336.

Vyhnanek, Lubos, and Milan Stoukal 1991 Harris Lines in Adults: An Open Problem. In *Human Paleopathology: Current Syntheses and Future Options*, edited by Donald J. Ortner and Arthur C. Aufderheide, pp. 92–94. Smithsonian Institution Press, Washington, DC.

Wade, Andrew D., Ronald G. Beckett, Gerald J. Conlogue, Ramon Gonzalez, Ronn Wade, and Bob Brier 2015 MUMAB: A Conversation with the Past. *The Anatomical Record* 298(6):954–973.

Wade, William Dexter 1970 *Skeletal Remains of a Prehistoric Population from the Puerco Valley, Eastern Arizona*. University of Colorado Press, Denver, CO.

Wadea, Andrew D., Ronald Beckett, Gerald Conlogue, Greg Garvin, Sahar Saleem, Gianfranco Natale, Davide Caramella, and Andrew Nelson 2019 Diagnosis by Consensus: A Case Study in the Importance of Interdisciplinary Interpretation of Mummified Remains. *International Journal of Paleopathology* 24:144–153.

Wakefield-Murphy, Robyn 2017 *The Bioarchaeology of Gendered Social Processes Among Pre- and Post-Contact Native Americans: An Analysis of Mortuary Patterns, Health, and Activity in the Ohio Valley.* Ph.D. dissertation, University of Pittsburgh, Philadelphia.

Waldron, Tony 2009 *Palaeopathology.* Cambridge Manuals in Archaeology. Cambridge University Press, New York.

Walker, James W. P., and David T. G. Clinnick 2014 Ten Years of Solutreans on the Ice: A Consideration of Technological Logistics and Paleogenetics for Assessing the Colonization of the Americas. *World Archaeology* 46(2):734–751.

Walker, Phillip L. 1997 Wife Beating, Boxing, and Broken Noses: Skeletal Evidence for the Cultural Patterning of Violence. In *Troubled Times: Violence and Warfare in the Past*, edited by Debra L. Martin and David W. Frayer, pp. 145–179. Gordon and Breach Publishers, Amsterdam, Netherlands.

——— 2001 A Bioarchaeological Perspective on the History of Violence. *Annual Review of Anthropology* 30:573–596.

Walker, Phillip L., Rhonda R. Bathurst, Rebecca Richman, Thor Gjerdrum, and Valerie A. Andrushko 2009 The Causes of Porotic Hyperostosis and Cribra Orbitalia: A Reappraisal of the Iron-Deficiency-Anemia Hypothesis. *American Journal of Physical Anthropology* 139(2):109–125.

Walker, Phillip L., and Della Collins Cook 1998 Brief Communication: Gender and Sex: Vive la Difference. *American Journal of Physical Anthropology* 106(2):255–259.

Walker, Phillip L., Della Collins Cook, and Patricia M. Lambert 1997 Skeletal Evidence for Child Abuse: A Physical Anthropological Perspective. *Journal of Forensic Sciences* 42(2):196–207.

Walker, Phillip L., and Jon M. Erlandson 1986 Dental Evidence for Prehistoric Dietary Change on the Northern Channel Islands, California. *American Antiquity* 51(2):375–383.

Walker, Philip L., Patricia M. Lambert, Michael Schultz, and Jon M. Erlandson 2005 The Evolution of Treponemal Disease in the Santa Barbara Channel Area of Southern California. In *The Myth of Syphilis: The Natural History of Treponematosis in North America*, edited by Mary Lucas-Powell and Della Collins Cook, pp. 281–305. University Press of Florida, Gainesville, FL.

Walker, William H. 1998 Where Are the Witches of Prehistory? *Journal of Archaeological Method and Theory* 5(3):245–308.

Walrath, Dana 2017 Bones, Biases, and Birth: Excavating Contemporary Gender Norms from Reproductive Bodies of the Past. In *Exploring Sex and Gender in Bioarchaeology*, edited by Sabrina C. Agarwal and Julie K. Wesp, pp. 15–49. University of New Mexico Press, Albuquerque, NM.

Walsh-Henry, Heather, and Serrin Boys 2015 Creating the Biological Profile: The Question of Race and Ancestry. In *Disturbing Bodies: Perspectives on Forensic Anthropology*, edited by Zoë Crossland and Rosemary A. Joyce, pp. 121–135. School for Advanced Research Press, Santa Fe, NM.

Wann, L. Samuel, Guido Lombardi, Bernadino Ojeda, Robert A. Benfer, Ricardo Rivera, Caleb E. Finch, Gregory S. Thomas, and Randall C. Thompson 2015 The Tres Ventanas Mummies of Peru. *The Anatomical Record* 298(6):1026–1035.

Waterman, Anna J., Ana Maria Silva, and Robert H. Tykot 2014 Stable Isotopic Indicators of Diet from Two Late Prehistoric Burial Sites in Portugal: An Investigation of Dietary Evidence of Social Differentiation. *Open Journal of Archaeometry* 2:22–27.

Waters-Rista, Andrea L., and Menno L. P. Hoogland 2018 The Role of Infant Feeding and Childhood Diet in Vitamin D Deficiency in a Nineteenth-Century Rural Dutch Community. *Bioarchaeology International* 2(2):95–116.

Watkins, Joe 2013 How Ancients Become Ammunition: Politics and Ethics of the Human Skeleton. In *The Archaeology of Death and Burial*, edited by Sarah Tarlow and Liv Nilsson Stutz, pp. 695–708. Oxford University Press, Oxford, UK.

Webb, Emily C., Steven Thomson, Andrew Nelson, Christine D. White, Gideon Koren, Michael Rieder, and Stan Van Uum 2010 Assessing Individual Systemic Stress Through Cortisol Analysis of Archaeological Hair. *Journal of Archaeological Science* 37(4):807–815.

Webb, Emily C., Christine D. White, Stan Van Uum, and Fred J. Longstaffe 2015 Integrating Cortisol and Isotopic Analyses of Archaeological Hair: Elucidating Juvenile Ante-Mortem Stress and Behavior. *International Journal of Paleopathology* 9:28–37.

Wedel, Vicki L., and Alison Galloway (eds.) 2014 *Broken Bones: Anthropological Analysis of Blunt Force Trauma* (2nd ed.). Charles C Thomas Publisher Ltd., Springfield, IL.

Wegener Tams, Katrine, Martin Jensen Søe, Inga Merkyte, Frederik Valeur Seersholm, Peter Steen Henriksen, Susanne Klingenberg, Eske Willerslev, Kurt H. Kjær, Anders Johannes Hansen, and Christian Moliin Outzen Kapel 2018 Parasitic Infections and Resource Economy of Danish Iron Age Settlement Through Ancient DNA Sequencing. *PLoS One* 13(6):e0197399.

Weisdorf, Jacob L. 2005 From Foraging to Farming: Explaining the Neolithic Revolution. *Journal of Economic Surveys* 19(4):561–586.

Weiss, Elizabeth 2006 Osteoarthritis and Body Mass. *Journal of Archaeological Science* 33(5):690–695.

——— 2015a *Paleopathology in Perspective: Bone Health and Disease Through Time*. Roman & Littlefield, Lanham, MD.

——— 2015b The Surface of Bones: Methods of Recording Entheseal Changes. *Surface Topography: Metrology and Properties* 3(3):034003.

——— 2018 Biological Distance at the Ryan Mound Site. *American Journal of Physical Anthropology* 165(3):554–564.

Weiss, Kenneth M. 1973 *Demographic Models for Anthropology*. Society for American Archaeology, Memoir 27, Washington, DC.

——— 1975 The Application of Demographic Models to Anthropological Data. *Human Ecology* 3(2):87–103.

Weiss-Krejci, Estella 2005 Excarnation, Evisceration, and Exhumation in Medieval and Post-Medieval Europe. In *Interacting with the Dead: Perspectives on Mortuary Archaeology for the New Millennium*, edited by Gordon F. M. Rakita, Jane E. Buikstra, Lane A. Beck, and Sloan R. Williams, pp. 155–172. University Press of Florida, Gainesville, FL.

——— 2013 The Unburied Dead. In *The Archaeology of Death and Burial*, edited by Sarah Tarlow and Liv Nilsson Stutz, pp. 281–301. Oxford University Press, Oxford, UK.

Welch, Paul D. 1996 Control Over Goods and the Political Stability of the Moundville Chiefdom. In *Political Structure and Change in the Prehistoric Southeastern United States*, edited by John F. Scarry, pp. 69–91. University Press of Florida, Gainesville, FL.

Wells, Calvin 1960 A Study of Cremations. *Antiquity* 34(133):29–37.

——— 1964 *Bones, Bodies, and Disease: Evidence of Disease and Abnormality in Early Man*. Frederick A. Praeger, New York.

Wentz, Rachel K. 2012 *Life and Death at Windover*. Florida Historical Society Press, Cocoa, FL.

Wesp, Julie K. 2017 Embodying Sex/Gender Systems in Bioarchaeological Research. In *Exploring Sex and Gender in Bioarchaeology*, edited by Sabrina C. Agarwal and Julie K. Wesp, pp. 99–126. University of New Mexico Press, Albuquerque, NM.

Wheeler, Sandra M., Lana Williams, Patrick Beauchesne, and Tosha L. Dupras 2013 Shattered Lives and Broken Childhoods: Evidence of Physical Child Abuse in Ancient Egypt. *International Journal of Paleopathology* 3(2):71–82.

White, Tim D. 1992 *Prehistoric Cannibalism at Mancos 5MTUMR-2346*. Princeton University Press, Princeton, NJ.

White, Tim D., and Pieter A. Folkens 2005 *The Human Bone Manual*. Elsevier Academic Press, Burlington, MA.

White, Tim D., Michael T. Black, and Pieter A. Folkens 2012 *Human Osteology* (3rd ed.). Elsevier Academic Press, Burlington, MA.

Whitehouse, Nicki J., and Wiebke Kirleis 2014 The World Reshaped: Practices and Impacts of Early Agrarian Societies. *Journal of Archaeological Science* 51:1–11.

Whitney, William F. 1886 Notes on the Anomalies, Injuries, and Diseases of the Bones of the Native People of North America Contained in the Osteological Collection of the Museum. *Annual Report of the Peabody Museum* 3:433–448.

Wilbur, Alicia K. 1998 The Utility of Hand and Foot Bones for the Determination of Sex and the Estimation of Stature in a Prehistoric Population from West-Central Illinois. *International Journal of Osteoarchaeology* 8(3):180–191.

Wilhelmson, Helene, and Nicoló Dell'Unto 2015 Virtual Taphonomy: A New Method Integrating Excavation and Postprocessing in an Archaeological Context. *American Journal of Physical Anthropology* 157(2):305–321.

Willey, Gordon R., and Jeremy A. Sabloff 1993 *A History of American Archaeology* (3rd ed.). Freeman, New York.

Willey, P. 1990 *Prehistoric Warfare on the Great Plains: Skeletal Analysis of the Crow Creek Massacre Victims.* Garland Publishing, New York.

——— 2016 Stature Estimation. In *Handbook of Forensic Anthropology and Archaeology* (2nd ed.), edited by Soren Blau and Douglas H. Ubelaker, pp. 308–321. Routledge, New York.

Willey, P., and Thomas E. Emerson 1993 The Osteology and Archaeology of the Crow Creek Massacre. *Plains Anthropologist* 38:227–269.

Williams, Brenda A., and Tracy L. Rogers 2006 Evaluating the Accuracy and Precision of Cranial Morphological Traits for Sex Determination. *Journal of Forensic Sciences* 51(4):729–735.

Williams, Herbert U. 1929 Human Paleopathology, with Some Original Observations on Symmetrical Osteoporosis of the Skull. *Archives of Pathology* 7:839–902.

Williams, Howard 2015 Towards an Archaeology of Cremation. In *The Analysis of Burned Human Remains* (2nd ed.), edited by Christopher W. Schmidt and Steven A. Symes, pp. 259–293. Academic Press, Amsterdam, Netherlands.

Williams, Howard, Benedict Wills-Eve, and Jennifer Osborne (eds.) 2019 *The Public Archaeology of Death.* Equinox, Sheffield, UK.

Williams, Kimberly D., Nicholas J. Meinzer, and Clark Spencer Larsen 2019 History of Degenerative Joint Disease in People Across Europe: Bioarchaeological Inferences About Lifestyle and Activity from Osteoarthritis and Vertebral Osteophytosis. In *The Backbone of Europe: Health, Diet, Work, and Violence Over Two Millennia*, edited by Richard H. Steckel, Clark Spencer Larsen, Charlotte A. Roberts, and Joerg Baten, pp. 253–299. Cambridge University Press, Cambridge, UK.

Wilson, Andrew S., Emma L. Brown, Chiara Villa, Niels Lynnerup, Andrew Healey, Maria Constanza Ceruti, Johan Reinhard, Carlos H. Previgliano, Facundo Arias Araoz, Josefina Gonzalez Diez, and Timothy Taylor 2013 Archaeological, Radiological, and Biological Evidence Offer Insight into Inca Child Sacrifice. *Proceedings of the National Academy of Sciences* 110(33):13322–13327.

Wilson, Andrew S., Timothy Taylor, Maria Constanza Ceruti, Jose Antonio Chavez, Johan Reinhard, Vaughan Grimes, Wolfram Meier-Augenstein, Larry Cartmell, Ben Stern, Michael P. Richards, Michael Worobey, Ian Barnes, and M. Thomas P. Gilbert 2007 Stable Isotope and DNA Evidence for Ritual Sequences in Inca Child Sacrifice. *Proceedings of the National Academy of Sciences* 104(42):16456–16461.

Wilson, Gregory D. 2010 Community, Identity, and Social Memory at Moundville. *American Antiquity* 75(1):3–18.

Wilson-Taylor, Rebecca J., and Angela M. Dautartas 2017 Time Since Death Estimation and Bone Weathering: The Postmortem Interval. In *Forensic Anthropology: A Comprehensive Introduction* (2nd ed.), edited by Natalie R. Langley and MariaTeresa A. Tersigni-Tarrant, pp. 273–312. CRC Press, Boca Raton, FL.

Winkelman, Michael 1998 Aztec Human Sacrifice: Cross-Cultural Assessments of the Ecological Hypothesis. *Ethnology* 37(3):285–298.

Witt, Kelsey E., Kathleen Judd, Andrew Kitchen, Colin Grier, Timothy A. Kohler, Scott G. Ortman, Brian M. Kemp, and Ripan S. Malhi 2015 DNA Analysis of Ancient Dogs of the Americas: Identifying Possible Founding Haplotypes and Reconstructing Population Histories. *Journal of Human Evolution* 79:105–118.

Wolfe, Susan I., and Mark Q. Sutton 2006 Acorns and Dental Wear in Aboriginal California. *Society for California Archaeology Newsletter* 40(4):31–34.

Wood, James W., George R. Milner, Henry C. Harpending, and Kenneth M. Weiss 1992 The Osteological Paradox: Problems in Inferring Prehistoric Health from Skeletal Samples. *Current Anthropology* 33(4):343–358.

Wright, Lori E. 1990 Stresses of Conquest: A Study of Wilson Bands and Enamel Hypoplasias in the Maya of Lamanai, Belize. *American Journal of Human Biology* 2(1):25–35.

Wright, Lori E., and Cassaday J. Yoder 2003 Recent Progress in Bioarchaeology: Approaches to the Osteological Paradox. *Journal of Archaeological Research* 11(1):43–70.

Wright, Rita P. (ed.) 1996 *Gender and Archaeology*. University of Pennsylvania Press, Philadelphia.

Wyman, J. 1868 *Observations on Crania*. A. A. Kingman, Boston.

Xhonga, Frida A. 1977 Bruxism and Its Effect on the Teeth. *Journal of Oral Rehabilitation* 4(1):65–76.

Yaussy, Samantha L., Sharon N. DeWitte, and Rebecca C. Redfern 2016 Frailty and Famine: Patterns of Mortality and Physiological Stress Among Victims of Famine in Medieval London. *American Journal of Physical Anthropology* 160(2):272–283.

Yeh, Hui-Yuan, and Piers D. Mitchell 2016 Ancient Human Parasites in Ethnic Chinese Populations. *Korean Journal of Parasitology* 54(5):565–572.

Yerkes, Richard W. 2005 Bone Chemistry, Body Parts, and Growth Marks: Evaluating Ohio Hopewell and Cahokia Mississippian Seasonality, Subsistence, Ritual, and Feasting. *American Antiquity* 70(2):241–265.

Yeshurun, Reuven, Guy Bar-Oz, and Dani Nadel 2013 The Social Role of Food in the Natufian Cemetery of Raqefet Cave, Mount Carmel, Israel. *Journal of Anthropological Archaeology* 32(4):511–526.

Yoder, Cassady J., Douglas H. Ubelaker, and Joseph F. Powell 2001 Examination of Variation in Sternal Rib End Morphology Relevant to Age Assessment. *Journal of Forensic Sciences* 46(2):223–227.

Yoshimura, K., T. Nakahashi, and K. Saito 2006 Why Did the Ancient Inhabitants of Palmyra Suffer Fluorosis? *Journal of Archaeological Science* 33(10):1411–1418.

Young, Alexandria 2017 The Effects of Terrestrial Mammalian Scavenging and Avian Scavenging on the Body. In *Taphonomy of Human Remains: Forensic Analysis of the Dead and the Depositional Environment*, edited by Eline M. J. Schotsmans, Nicholas Márquez-Grant, and Shari L. Forbes, pp. 212–234. Wiley-Blackwell, Oxford, UK.

Yuen, Waifong 2018 *Homeless Cultural Property in the Netherlands: The Case of the "Liuquan Mummy."* Master thesis, Leiden University, Leiden, Netherlands.

Zaiac, Martin N., and Ashley Walker 2013 Nail Abnormalities Associated with Systemic Pathologies. *Clinics in Dermatology* 31(5):627–649.

Zanker, Paul 1998 *Pompeii: Public and Private Life*. Harvard University Press, Cambridge, MA.

Zegwaard, Gerald A. 1959 Headhunting Practices of the Asmat of Netherlands New Guinea. *American Anthropologist* 61(6):1020–1041.

Zejdlik, Katie J. 2014 Unmingling Commingled Museum Collections: A Photographic Method. In *Commingled and Disarticulated Human Remains: Working Toward Improved Theory, Method, and Data*, edited by Anna J. Osterholtz, Kathryn M. Baustian, and Debra L. Martin, pp. 173–192. Springer, New York.

Zephro, Lauren, and Alison Galloway 2014 Rib Fractures in the Elderly: A Case Study Using Microscopic Analysis to Determine Injury Timing. In *Broken Bones: Anthropological Analysis of Blunt Force Trauma*, edited by Vicki L. Wedel and Alison Galloway, pp. 327–335. Charles C Thomas Publisher Ltd., Springfield, IL.

Zimmerman, Michael R. 1973 Blood Cells Preserved in a Mummy 2000 Years Old. *Science* 180:303–304.

———— 1980 Aleutian and Alaskan Mummies. In *Mummies, Disease, and Ancient Cultures* (1st ed.), edited by Aidan Cockburn and Eve Cockburn, pp. 118–134. Cambridge University Press, Cambridge, UK.

———— 1998 Aleutian and Alaskan Mummies. In *Mummies, Disease, and Ancient Cultures* (2nd ed.), edited by Aidan Cockburn, Eve Cockburn, and Theodore A. Reyman, pp. 138–153. Cambridge University Press, Cambridge, UK.

Zimmerman, Michael R., Theodore A. Reyman, and William S. Laughlin 1981 The Paleopathology of an Aleutian Mummy. *Archives of Pathology and Laboratory Medicine* 105:638–641.

Zink, Albert R., Marco Samadelli, Paul Gostner, and Dario Piombino-Mascali 2019 Possible Evidence for Care and Treatment in the Tyrolean Iceman. *International Journal of Paleopathology* 25:110–117.

Zink, Albert R., C. Sola, U. Reischl, W. Grabner, N. Rastogi, H. Wolf, and A. G. Nerlich 2004 Molecular Identification and Characterization of *Mycobacterium Tuberculosis* Complex in Ancient Egyptian Mummies. *International Journal of Osteoarchaeology* 14(5):404–413.

Zinni, Debra Prince, and Kate M. Crowley 2017a Application of Dentition in Forensic Anthropology. In *Forensic Anthropology: A Comprehensive Introduction* (2nd ed.), edited by Natalie R. Langley and MariaTeresa A. Tersigni-Tarrant, Appendix A, pp. 365–380. CRC Press, Boca Raton, FL.

——— 2017b Human Odontology and Dentition in Forensic Anthropology. In *Forensic Anthropology: A Comprehensive Introduction* (2nd ed.), edited by Natalie R. Langley and MariaTeresa A. Tersigni-Tarrant, pp. 111–124. CRC Press, Boca Raton, FL.

Zuckerman, Molly K., and George J. Armelagos 2011 The Origins of Biocultural Dimensions in Bioarchaeology. In *Social Bioarchaeology*, edited by Sabrina C. Agarwal and Bonnie A. Glencross, pp. 15–43. Wiley-Blackwell, Oxford, UK.

Glossary

ablation   removal of material, such as teeth.

abrasion   wear due to abrasive material, such as tooth wear from sand in food.

acute trauma   trauma that takes place near the time of death.

adolescent   age category of a person between 11 and 21 years old.

adult   age category of a person older than 21 years.

agency   an emphasis on the power of the individual.

American Association of Physical Anthropologists   the organization of physical anthropologists founded in 1928.

anaerobic environments   environments lacking oxygen that enhance preservation.

analogy   an inference suggesting that if two things are similar in some ways, they probably will be similar in other ways.

ancient DNA (aDNA)   genetic material recovered from archaeological specimens.

antemortem   changes in organic materials that took place before death.

anthropology   the study of humans, including their biology, society, and language, both past and present.

anthropologie de terrain   a detailed analytical approach that uses the precisely recorded position of all skeletal elements and artifacts to understand the taphonomic processes.

anthropometry   the measurement of living people.

apatite   the inorganic component of bone.

appendicular skeleton   the bones of the arms, hands, legs, and feet.

archaeology   the study of the human past.

archaeological culture   archaeological entities defined by a pattern of common traits, thought to possibly represent a past society.

archaeological record   the record of past human behavior; the material remains of past human activities distributed in patterns across the landscape and in varying conditions.

archaeobiology   the study of faunal and botanical remains in an archaeological site.

articular surfaces   the surfaces of bones where they connect with other bones.

articulation   the degree that the body is in anatomical position.

artifacts   portable objects made, modified, or used by humans for a specific task; artifacts are the basic "unit" of archaeological analysis.

attrition   normal wear on the tooth enamel, associated with age.

auditory exostoses   bony protuberances found in ear canals, commonly found in individuals who have spent a great deal of time in cold water.

autopsy medical examination of a body to determine cause of death and to locate pathologies or other conditions; generally invasive.

axial skeleton the skull, the vertebral column, the ribs and sternum, the bones of the shoulder girdles, and the pelvic girdle.

ballistic force trauma trauma resulting from the impact of a projectile, such as an arrow or bullet.

Beau's lines horizontal ridges and indentations in the fingernails and toenails that can be observed visually, thought to be the result of a pause in growth of the nail reflecting some sort of metabolic or nutritional stress.

bioarchaeology the study of human remains and their cultural context to understand past cultural systems.

biocultural approach an interdisciplinary methodology that integrates the study of human remains with archaeology and anthropology; includes funerary systems, social organization, daily activities, division of labor, paleodemography, population movements and relatedness, and diet and health.

biocultural profile the biological and cultural context of an ancient individual.

biodistance the study of how closely people and populations are related based on metric and nonmetric aspects of their skeletal and dental morphology.

bioethnography the biological and cultural context of a number of ancient individuals from a single society combined to better understand that society as a whole.

biomechanics the study of the mechanical laws relating to the movement or structure of living organisms.

biomolecules organic materials such as blood, lipids, proteins, and ancient DNA (aDNA) from past people.

bioturbation any disturbance or movement of deposited materials by biological means (such as burrowing animals).

blunt force trauma trauma caused by a blunt object, such as a club or rock.

body farms locations where cadavers are placed in specific decompositional situations to study taphonomic processes.

calculus calcified plaque on teeth.

calipers a tool used to measure bones and other materials.

cannibalism the eating of individuals from one's own species.

carbon isotopes an isotope used primarily to investigate diet.

caries dental cavities.

catacomb a place where bones removed from graves are stored, most often underground.

cemetery a place where multiple bodies are interred, generally with some internal organization.

chronic trauma recurring trauma during one's lifetime.

classification the placement of materials into categories that can be used for identification and comparison.

collagen the organic component of bone.

collective cemeteries cemeteries used over time, with commingling being common.

commemorative behaviors rituals or individual behaviors showing grief, bereavement, remembrance, and commemoration.

commingled remains of multiple individuals mixed together.

comminuted fractures bone broken into multiple fragments.

compression fractures bone broken by compressions, common in vertebrae.

computerized tomography (CT) scans   a series of radiographs taken and combined to form a 3-D image.

congenital abnormalities   anatomical variations and defects that are present at or shortly after birth.

consistent with   a general, nonspecific diagnosis of a cause of a pathology.

cranial capacity   the size of the brain, generally measured in cubic centimeters.

cranial deformation   changes in the natural shape of the skull.

craniometry   the study of crania.

cremains   burned human remains.

cremation   the treatment of the dead by burning the body.

cribra orbitalia   lesions that involve the upper interior (roof) of the eye orbits, perhaps due to anemia.

criminal cannibalism   the eating of people as part of a criminal act.

cross-striations   enamel deposited daily in a series of very thin incremental layers.

crown   the upper portion of a tooth with the enamel.

culinary cannibalism   the eating of people as a normal part of the diet.

Defense POW/MIA Accounting Agency (DPAA)   the U.S. government agency responsible for the recovery, identification, and repatriation of U.S. war dead.

deformation   the change in the natural shape of bone, either incidental or purposeful.

depression fractures   bone broken into a depression, often seen in skulls that had been hit by clubs or rocks.

dentition   the teeth of an individual.

deossification   the process by which bone density is reduced.

deoxyribonucleic acid (DNA)   material that carries the genetic information of an individual and is present in virtually all organic materials.

developmental defects of enamel (DDE)   defects in tooth enamel as a result of developmental delays, such as Wilson bands and linear enamel hypoplasia (LEH).

deviant burials   any unusual burial, often for criminals or other undesirables.

diagenesis   chemical changes in a material.

diagnostic   a distinctive trait of a particular pathology.

diaphysis   the midsection of a long bone.

disease   an abnormal condition or disorder of a body structure or function.

dissection   the systematic deconstruction of a body to gain medical knowledge.

distal   the end most distant from the center of the body.

domestic violence   violence toward children, women, men, or the elderly of one's own family or group.

Down syndrome   a congenital disorder that results in intellectual impairment and telltale morphology.

eburnation   the wear on the surface of articulating bones due to bone-on-bone contact.

ecofacts   the unmodified remains of biological materials related to the activities of people, such as discarded animal bone or charcoal from hearth fires or natural pollen in an archaeological site.

ectoparasites   parasites living outside the body, such as fleas.

element   in bioarchaeology, it is a specific bone.

emergency cannibalism   the eating of people for survival in an emergency.

enamel   the hard outer layer of teeth.

endocannibalism   the eating of people from within one's own group.

endoparasites   parasites living on the inside of the body, such as intestinal worms.

entheseal change   the changes in muscle attachment sites from habitual use of those muscles.

epiphyses   the ends of long bones that fuse with the shaft of the bones, generally by the late teens or early twenties.

erosion   gradual destruction of tissue through physical or chemical means.

ethnoarchaeology   the study of how living traditional people do things and how archaeologists might apply that information to the past.

ethnocentrism   a bias toward one's own group or society.

ethnology   the comparative study of culture and society.

ethnographic analogy   the use of information about living societies to help construct models of past societies.

ethnography   the study of an extant society.

ethics   moral principles governing the behavior of a population.

etic   the view of something from an outsider's perspective, such as a member of one society studying a different society.

etiology   the cause of a disease or condition.

evolutionary theory   the study of the past from the perspective of Darwinian evolution, where the concepts of adaptation and selection are used in the analysis of biological and cultural change.

excarnation   the removal of flesh from the body.

exocannibalism   the eating of people from outside one's own group.

exostoses   bone spurs or growths.

experimental archaeology   the use of experiments with ancient materials and techniques to discover how and why things might have been done in the past.

exposed burial   a body placed in the open as part of a formal mortuary treatment.

extralegal killings   the killing of people outside the legal system, such as the intentional killing of prisoners and civilians in wartime and genocide.

features   nonportable objects used or constructed by people, such as graves.

feminist theory   a theoretical approach that emphasizes the role of females in a society.

final mortuary treatment   the final disposition of the body, such as by cremation or burial.

forensics   the analysis of human remains with a focus on medico-legal issues.

funerary system   the total system in which the dead are treated, from pretreatment of the living, to mortuary treatment of the body, to commemorative treatment of the person and/or soul.

gender   a culturally constructed category used to group people and defined by the role that a person is expected to have in a society, regardless of sex.

genocide   the mass killing of people from a particular ethnic group or religion.

geographic information system (GIS)   a system to acquire, process, and analyze geographic data

gout   a form of inflammatory arthritis characterized by periodic and painful inflammation of a joint.

grave   the place where a body is buried, typically in the ground.

green bone (or greenstick) fractures   bone that is incompletely broken; that is, broken on one side but bent on the other.

Harris lines   thin horizontal lines representing periods of arrested growth seen in the radiographs of long bones of individuals who experienced metabolic or nutritional stress during their childhood or adolescence.

helminths   worms living in the intestinal tract of a person.

histology   the microscopic study of tissues, mostly bone in bioarchaeology.

human remains   the remains of humans in a variety of forms, primarily skeletal.

human sacrifice   the killing of people as part of a ritual or ceremony.

hydrocephalus   an abnormally large head often caused by cranial expansion due to increased intercranial pressure.

hypocalcifications   discolored patches of enamel that can form during mild disruptions of the mineralization process.

infant   age category of a person up to 2 years old.

infectious diseases   those that can be transmitted from one individual to another through shared air, water, insect bites, or personal contact.

inhumation   the intentional burial of a body; the treatment of the dead by burial.

initial mortuary treatment   the preparation of the body for final mortuary treatment.

interment   the cremation or burial of a body as the final mortuary treatment.

interpersonal violence   violence within one's community or family, typically small scale, intentional, and sublethal.

intersexual   a person of neither binary sex, having variations in chromosomes, gonads, hormones, or genitals.

juvenile   age category of a person between 2 and 10 years old.

Kennewick Man (the Ancient One)   an 8,600-year-old skeleton discovered along the Columbia River in Washington State that was at the center of a court case about the study of ancient remains; the skeleton was eventually studied and repatriated in 2017.

labret   a lip plug or stud.

leprosy   a long-term infection caused by the bacterium *Mycobacterium leprae* or *M. lepromatosis* that, if left untreated, can result in disfigurement and disability.

lethal   sufficient to cause death.

life history   a term commonly used to describe the events of a life as deduced from the mortal remains and cultural context of an individual.

linear enamel hypoplasia (LEH)   arrested growth lines on teeth suggesting some metabolic or nutritional stress during childhood.

lipids   fats.

macrocephaly   an abnormally large head, due to a number of causes.

magnetic resonance imaging (MRI)   a form of medical imaging using high-frequency radio waves in a magnetic field to produce images of internal structures.

mandible   the lower jaw.

malaria   a mosquito-borne parasitic (*Plasmodium falciparum malaria*) disease that can be fatal.

Marfan syndrome   a genetic disorder that affects the connective tissues, resulting in problems with growth and development.

Marxism   the theoretical approach that explores inequality in a society.

mass grave   a single grave containing a relatively large number of individuals who died at the same time (such as war dead or victims of disease or genocide) and were afforded little funerary treatment.

mastoid process   a large muscle and tendon attachment site on the temporal bone behind the ear, generally larger in males.

materialism   the theoretical approach that emphasizes the importance of material goods, such as food and shelter.

maxilla   the upper portion of the jaw.

metabolic stress   disruption of the body systems due to some metabolic condition.

metaphysis   the junction of the epiphyses and diaphysis in a bone, where the growth plates are located.

microcephaly   an abnormally small head, due to a number of causes.

middle-range theory   a combination of logic, analogy, and theory that links the materials within the archaeological record to human behavior.

minimum number of individuals (MNI)   number used to estimate how many individuals there are in a skeletal population.

mitochondrial DNA (mtDNA)   the genetic material contained within the mitochondria, located outside the nucleus, and commonly used to track the female line.

morbidity   the rate of disease in a population.

mortality   the rate of death in a population.

mortuary analysis   the study of burial data to determine patterns of demography, status, and politics.

mortuary facilities   facilities in which bodies undergo initial treatment (such as a mortuary) and facilities for final treatment (such as a tomb).

mortuary treatment   the overall treatment of a body, from its initial preparation for final treatment to the final treatment itself (e.g., cremation or burial).

mourning ceremonies   commemorative rituals or ceremonies conducted after the final mortuary treatment is complete.

Native American Graves Protection and Repatriation Act (NAGPRA)   the federal law requiring that Native American skeletal remains and sacred objects be identified, if possible, and returned to their ancestors.

natural mummies   remains that are mummified due to natural processes, such as dry conditions.

necropolis   large cemetery associated with a city or large funerary complex, a "city of the dead."

neonatal line   a line in tooth enamel that forms as a result of the ordeal of being born.

next-generation sequencing (NGS)   a new method to produce readable copies of aDNA, faster and cheaper than PCR.

nitrogen isotopes   an isotope used primarily to investigate diet.

normative approach   the idea that a past society would have been fundamentally similar to current ones.

nuclear DNA (nDNA)   the DNA located within the nucleus of a cell.

nutritional stress   disruption of the body systems due to a lack of nutrition.

oblique fractures   bone broken at a non-90-degree angle.

orientation   the cardinal direction that an interment was facing.

os pubis   one of three major bilateral bones in the pelvis, with the two sides articulating at the pubic symphysis.

ossuary   a secondary location where the bones of multiple individuals were interred together, having been removed from temporary graves where the bodies had been put to decompose.

osteoarthritis (OA)   degenerative joint disease caused by the cumulative effects of wear and tear on the joints through activity.

osteobiography   information about an individual's appearance, health, age at death, cause of death, and other characteristics derived from an analysis of the skeleton.

osteological paradox   three major issues in forming demographic profiles: (1) demographic nonstationarity, (2) selective mortality, and (3) hidden heterogeneity.

osteology   the study of bones.

osteomalacia   a condition in adults where the bones may be bent and distorted as a result of vitamin D deficiency.

osteometric board   a tool used to measure the dimensions of bones.

osteometry   the measurement of skeletal remains.

osteomyelitis   an infection in the interior of a bone.

osteopenia   mild deossification of the bones.

osteophytes   bone lipping along the edges of a joint, commonly seen in vertebrae.

osteoporosis   severe deossification.

osteosarcoma   cancer of the bone.

oxygen isotopes   an isotope used to investigate diet and paleoenvironment.

Paget's disease   a metabolic condition that interferes with bone resorption and new bone formation.

paleodemography   the study of prehistoric populations, including their number, distribution, density, sex and age structure, mortality, and fertility.

paleoepidemiological stress model   a model that considers environment, culture, and biology as factors in stress.

paleoepidemiology   the study and analysis of the patterns, causes, and effects of health and disease conditions in defined past populations.

paleofeces   preserved ancient human fecal matter.

paleonutrition   the study of prehistoric human diet in relation to health, nutrition, morbidity, and mortality for both individuals and populations.

paleopathology   the study of pathology in past populations.

pathognomic   a definitive diagnosis of a cause of a pathology.

perimortem   changes in human remains that occurred around the time of death.

periosteal reaction   the result of an infection of the tissue on the surface of the bone, such as a lesion.

periosteum   the tissue on the surface of the bone.

periostosis   an infection of the tissue on the surface of the bone.

pH   a measure of acidity.

polio (poliomyelitis)   a disease caused by a virus that can trigger paralysis.

polymerase chain reaction (PCR)   a method to produce readable copies of aDNA, enhancing the ability to analyze it.

postprocessualism   the theoretical position that the past is largely subjective and thus unknowable; however, postprocessualism actually appears to consist of a number of new perspectives that augment processual archaeology.

porotic hyperostosis   lesions that involve the surface of the skull, perhaps due to anemia.

position   the position of a body in a burial, such as prone, supine, flexed, or semi-flexed.

postmortem   changes in human remains that occurred after death.

preservation   the state of decomposition of materials in archaeological sites; if things are well preserved, they are more likely to be recognized and recovered.

pretreatment activities undertaken on individuals prior to their death, such as care or preparations for death.

primary commemorative behaviors rituals and behavior, such a graveside ceremony, that interdigitate in time and place with pretreatment and mortuary practices.

primary inhumation a burial in its original location.

primary sexual characteristics the reproductive anatomy: penis or vagina.

primary teeth the first teeth to develop during childhood, the "baby" teeth.

processualism the theoretical approach that emphasizes the use of the scientific method in archaeological investigations.

prognathism a measure of the jaw relative to the plane of the face.

proteins complex combinations of amino acids.

protozoa one-celled organisms, such as bacteria.

proximal that end of a body part closest to the center of the body.

pubic symphysis the junction of the os pubis bones in the front of the pelvis.

purposeful mummies a preserved body that had been purposefully manipulated to enhance its preservation.

queer theory a body of theory seeking to explore diverse sexual behaviors and sexualities.

radioactive isotopes those isotopes that are unstable and will emit a particle.

radiocarbon dating a technique that measures the radioactive decay of carbon-14 atoms within an organic sample, allowing for the determination of a death date for the sample material.

radiograph (X-rays) a picture of tissue using x-rays.

remodeling the process by which old bone is replaced by new bone.

repatriation returning human remains and sacred items to their appropriate descendant communities.

research design a plan for an archaeological investigation, stating the question(s) or problem(s) to be addressed, the theoretical approach, the biases of the investigators, the kinds of data sought to address the question, and the methods to be used to recover the data.

resorption the breaking down of old bone into its chemical constituents, which are then transferred to the blood.

rheumatoid arthritis (RA) an autoimmune condition in which the body attacks the joints, causing inflammation that results in the erosion of the bone in the joints and ultimately in disfiguration.

rickets a condition in children where the bones may be bent and distorted as a result of vitamin D deficiency.

ritual (or funerary) cannibalism the eating of small portions of people as part of a ritual or ceremony.

saprophytic organisms plants and animals that subsist by consuming dead matter within archaeological contexts.

scoliosis the unnatural lateral curvature of the spine.

secondary commemorative behaviors rituals and behavior, such as mourning ceremonies, conducted at some time after the final mortuary treatment.

secondary inhumation an interment (burial or cremation) exhumed from its original location and reburied elsewhere, such as in an ossuary.

secondary sexual characteristics those sexual characteristics that develop after puberty, such as body hair, breasts, and musculature.

secondary teeth   the permanent dentition.

sexual dimorphism   the anthropometric differences between males and females, such as robustness of the bones.

sciatic notch   the notch in the ilium, wider in females.

scientific racism   the use of pseudoscience to demonstrate the inferiority of non-Caucasians.

shaft   the central portion or midsection of a linear bone.

sharp force trauma   trauma caused by a sharp object, such as a knife or sword.

shovel-shaped incisor   a depression present in the lingual aspect of the maxillary incisors, characteristic of Asian and American Indian populations.

sinusitis   infection of the sinuses.

sites   geographic locations containing evidence of past human activity.

Sky burial (Tibet)   excarnation of a body to enable it to be consumed by vultures, generally reserved for high-status people.

sociopolitical cannibalism   the eating of people for purposes of control, punishment, or intimidation.

spina bifida   a defect in which a portion of the spinal cord is exposed due to malformation of the spine.

spiral fractures   bone broken in a twisted manner.

stable isotopes   those isotopes that are stable and will not emit a particle.

stable isotopic analysis (SIA)   the measurement of stable isotopes in bone, primarily carbon, nitrogen, oxygen, and strontium, to analyze aspects of past behavior (such as diet).

strontium isotope   an isotope used primarily to investigate mobility.

subadult   a person under the age of 21.

sublethal   a physical trauma that did not result in death.

subpubic angle   the angle of the os pubis bones below the pubic symphysis, usually larger in females.

supraorbital ridge   the small ridge on the frontal bone below the orbits, generally more pronounced in males.

sutures   the junctions of the bones of the skull.

systems theory   the idea that cultural systems operate in an equilibrium and that as conditions change, cultural subsystems will also change, reaching a new equilibrium.

taphonomy   the study of what happens to biological materials after they enter the archaeological record.

Towton   a battle in England in 1461, resulting in the deaths of some 28,000 men who were buried in mass graves.

transverse fractures   bone broken at a right angle.

trauma   damage to human tissue from some outside force.

trepanation   cutting a hole into the skull of an individual while the person is still alive.

treponemal diseases   those caused by different subspecies of the bacterium *Treponema pallidum*: pinta, bejel (endemic syphilis), yaws, and syphilis (venereal syphilis).

tuberculosis   an infectious disease caused by the bacterium *Mycobacterium tuberculosis*; affects the lungs and commonly associated with crowded conditions.

Vermillion Accord   an accord on the treatment of human remains.

virtual autopsy   the use of scanning techniques to examine a body for pathologies or other conditions.

warfare   organized and sanctioned conflict between two groups.

war graves   graves of people who died in active military service but were not interred in cemeteries, such as in sunken ships.

Wilson bands   small bands of thin enamel in teeth, indicative of metabolic or nutritional stress during childhood.

wormian bones   extra small bones in the skull.

Y chromosome   the chromosome in the nucleus that tends not to recombine and is used to study the male line.

zoonosis   infectious diseases that began as crossovers from diseases in domestic animals.

Figure credits

4.17 The photograph of Alan J. Mather is courtesy of No Mans Land: The European Great War Archaeology Group and the Mather family
4.18 Alamy
4.19 Public domain. Courtesy of sylvannus, under license (en.wikipedia. org/wiki/GNU_Free_Documentation_License), no changes made
4.20 Alamy Image ID: ECYK48
4.21 Alamy Image ID: B4M13W
5.1 Photograph courtesy of Simon Mays, 2012, reproduced with permission of Historic England
5.2 Photograph courtesy of Simon Mays, 2012, reproduced with permission of Historic England
5.3 author
5.4 author
5.5 Alamy Image ID: R93JA5
5.6 Photograph courtesy of Elizabeth Weiss
5.7 Photograph courtesy of Eric Bartelink
5.8 Photograph courtesy of Marni LaFleur
5.9 author
6.1 Photograph courtesy of Eric Bartelink
6.2 Bone Clones
6.3 Courtesy of Bone Clones. This work is free and may be used by anyone for any purpose. If you wish to use this content, you do not need to request permission as long as you follow any licensing requirements mentioned on this page. Wikimedia has received an e-mail confirming that the copyright holder has approved publication under the terms mentioned on this page. This correspondence has been reviewed by an OTRS member and stored in our permission archive. The correspondence is available to trusted volunteers as ticket #2014111810020764.
6.4 Photograph courtesy of Marni LaFleur
6.5 Photograph courtesy of Marni LaFleur
6.6 Alamy
6.7 Photograph courtesy of Tony Waldron
6.8 Alamy Image ID: DGDC90
7.1 author
7.2 Bone Clones
7.3 Towton Battlefield Archaeology Project, Copyright Tim Sutherland 1999
7.4 © BARC, Archaeological Sciences, University of Bradford
7.5 author
7.6 Photograph courtesy of Simon Mays
7.7 Photograph by John Verano
7.8 Bone Clones
7.9 Courtesy of MAUNUS, under license (en.wikipedia.org/wiki/GNU_Free_Documentation_License), no changes made
7.10 author
8.1 author
8.2 Alamy image WE9N4N

8.3   Photograph courtesy of Marni LaFleur
8.4   Alamy Image ID: AMM408
8.5   Photograph courtesy of Stephanie Panzer, Trauma Center Murnau,
       Prof.-Küntscher-Str. 8, 82418 Murnau am Staffelsee
9.1   Photograph courtesy of Jim Chatters
9.2   Photograph by 120 licensed under the Creative Commons
       Attribution–Share Alike 3.0 Alamy Image ID: B2Y9P3
10.1   author
10.2   author
10.3   Alamy Image ID: T7262F
10.4   Alamy Image ID: ABJ4D6
10.5   author
10.6   author
11.1   From Wikimedia Commons, the free media repository

Index

Note: Page numbers in *italic* indicate a figure and page numbers in **bold** indicate a table on the corresponding page.

3-D imaging methods 26, 31, 156–158

Abandoned Shipwreck Act 10
ablation (removal) of teeth 142
Aborigines 9, 13, 37
abrasion 112
abscesses 111, 113, *114*, 121
accidental discoveries, of human remains 22
achieved status 177
activity/occupational stress 93–96
acute trauma 123
adolescent: bone growth of 87; estimating age at death 38
adults: disease/pathology **102**; estimating age at death 38, 39; osteomalacia in 92; paleopathologies in 83; pituitary dwarfism in 119; sex of 42, *43*; skeletal remains of 27; stature 45, 196
African Burial Ground (New York) 14–15, *14*, 22
African Burial Ground National Monument 15
afterlife 52–53, 181; for commemoration 76–77, 164; purposeful mummification for 64–65
Agarwal, Sabrina C. 3
age at death, estimating 38–42
agency 161
aggressive cannibalism 131
agriculture, hunting/gathering to 188–189
airplane crash, in Andes in 1973 131
albumin 147
Alive (1993) 131
Alva, Walter 182
American Association of Physical Anthropologists 4
American Indians 3
American Journal of Physical Anthropology 4
American/red classification 3
Ammitzbøll, T. 158
anaerobic environments, in preservation 21

analogy, use of 162
Ancestral Puebloans in American Southwest (case study) 133–135
ancestry estimation 45–46
ancient DNA (aDNA) 42, 147–152, *148*; analysis 59, 106; of burial populations 177; detection of pathogens 102; distinguishing/separating commingled remains 71; hair follicles analysis 47; to measuring biodistance 155; proteins and 91
ancient Egyptian mummification process 65, *65*, 68
Ancylostoma duodenale 116
anemia 85
Angel, J. Lawrence 5
Anglo-Saxon cemetery 155
animal burial, as part of mortuary treatment 77
antemortem/premortem 27, 83, 105, 137, 199, 202
Anthropologie de terrain approach 19
anthropology: biological 6; of the dead 1, 176–188; *see also* forensic anthropology
anthropometry 31
anticipatory grief 55
apatite 153
Apis bulls 77
appendicular skeleton 27, 49
archaeobiology 2
archaeological expectations: of cannibalism 132–133, **132**; of human sacrifice 136, **136**
archaeological records: nature of evidence 18; preservation 19–21; taphonomy 18–19
archaeological remains 17
Archaeological Resources Protection Act (ARPA) 12
archaeology 1, 21; culture 161–162; materials 147, 173, 201
Army Corps 11
arteriosclerosis 115

Gleser, Goldine C. 45
Goepfert, Nicolas 137
Goodman, Alan H. 84
Gould, Stephen Jay 4
gout 110
Grasshopper Pueblo in Arizona 126
Grauer, Anne L. 83
grave goods 49, 68; analysis of 185; for assigning
    gender 184; and associated materials 23, 49,
    56, 77; and mortuary treatments 185, 188; and
    status 164–165, 174, 176; warfare *128*
graves 68; ships as 68; war 9; *see also* mass graves
Great Basin of North America: mobility and
    pathology in 97–98; mummies in 59
Great Pyramid, at Giza 78–79, *78*
Greece 5
green bone (greenstick) fractures 124, *124*, **132**
Greenwald, Alexandra M. 154
grief 76
gross morphology 26
ground-penetrating radar 202
gut (intestinal) contents 48

Haglund, William D. 205
hair 2, 47–48, 50, 153
hammerstone/chopper marks **132**
hanging 137
Hansen's disease *see* leprosy
haplogroups (haplotypes) 149
hard tissues 26
Harris lines 87–88, *87*, 194–196
Harrod, Ryan P. 127
Hatch-Slack (C4) pathway 153
head lice 117
healed cranial depression fractures 126, *126*
health care, disability and community 198–199
health, of past populations 193
Hegmon, Michelle 161
helminths 116
hematopoietic activity 86
Hemphill, Brian E. 98
Herodotus 63
heterotopic ossification 31
hidden heterogeneity 190
histology, bone 34, 49
histomorphology 34
Holocene burials 185
Holocene hunter-gatherer inhumations 188
Holt, Brigitte 93
homicide cases 204–205
Homo erectus 3
hookworms 116
Hooton, Earnest A. 4, 86
Hopi town of Awatovi 135
horizontal social differentiation 177
Horocholyn, Kalyna 92

Hrdlička, Aleš 4
Hughes, C. 155
Huldremose Woman bog body 158
human burials, treatment of 7, 9–10
human leukocyte antigen (HLA) system 147
human races, classification of 3
human remains 1, 2; accidental discoveries
    of 22; archaeological record 18–21; bone
    development and growth 31–34; regarding
    cultural groups 13–14; dating methods 49;
    as dead body 2; definition of 15, 35–37;
    description and basic analysis of 26–50;
    discovery of 17, 21–22, 202–203; ethical issue
    in 7; excavation methods 23; in forensics 2;
    identification of 203–204; international laws
    on 8–9; laboratory treatment 26–27; left in
    places 74; measurement and description of
    skeleton 30–31; NAGPRA on 10; nature
    of archaeological evidence 18; pathogens in
    151–152; Pecos Pueblo 4; post-excavation
    handling 24; preservation 19–21; recordation
    24; recovery of 22–24, 202–203; soft tissue
    and other remains 46–48; state laws 13;
    taphonomy 18–19; U.S. laws on 9–14;
    Vermillion Accord on 8; *see also* skeletal
    remains
human sacrifice 136–137, **136**, 144
Hunt, David R. 101
Hurlbut, Sharon A. 132
hydrocephalus 118
hydroxyapatite 32, 88
hypocalcification 89
hypocone 37

Iceman (Ötzi), Italy 62, 143, 169–172, *170*, 198
Ice Princess 63
iconography **136**
imaging 40; radiography 156–157; scanning
    157–159; virtual autopsies 158–159
Inca people 48, 55, 62, *62*, 137
incidental deformation of bone 140
incorruptibles 71, *72*
"Index of Care" 198
indigenous people 7, 8, 16, 155
inequalities, exploring 187–188
infanticide 72, 190
infants: bone growth of 87; cranial sutures of
    41; determination of sex 42; estimating age at
    death 38; primary teeth 49; unwanted 72
infectious diseases **102–103**, 106–110, 120;
    crowd diseases 107–108; malaria 109–110;
    polio 109; in soft tissues 115; treponemal
    diseases 108
inhumations 57–59, 194; Holocene hunter-
    gatherer 188; positions *69*
initial mortuary treatment 55, 68